SAP PRESS e-books

Print or e-book, Kindle or iPad, workplace or airplane: Choose where and how to read your SAP PRESS books! You can now get all our titles as e-books, too:

- By download and online access
- For all popular devices
- And, of course, DRM-free

Convinced? Then go to www.sap-press.com and get your e-book today.

SAP® Predictive Analytics

SAP PRESS is a joint initiative of SAP and Rheinwerk Publishing. The know-how offered by SAP specialists combined with the expertise of Rheinwerk Publishing offers the reader expert books in the field. SAP PRESS features first-hand information and expert advice, and provides useful skills for professional decision-making.

SAP PRESS offers a variety of books on technical and business-related topics for the SAP user. For further information, please visit our website: *www.sap-press.com*.

Ah-Soon, Brogden, Marks, Orthous, Sinkwitz
SAP BusinessObjects Web Intelligence: The Comprehensive Guide (4th Edition)
2017, 814 pages, hardcover and e-book
www.sap-press.com/4412

Christensen, Darlak, Harrington, Kong, Poles, Savelli
SAP BW/4HANA: An Introduction
2017, 427 pages, hardcover and e-book
www.sap-press.com/4377

Chang, Hacking, van der A
SAP BusinessObjects Design Studio: The Comprehensive Guide (2nd Edition)
2016, 738 pages, hardcover and e-book
www.sap-press.com/3951

Ankisettipalli, Chen, Wankawala
SAP HANA Advanced Data Modeling
2016, 392 pages, hardcover and e-book
www.sap-press.com/3863

Antoine Chabert, Andreas Forster, Laurent Tessier,
Pierpaolo Vezzosi

SAP® Predictive Analytics

The Comprehensive Guide

Editor Meagan White
Acquisitions Editor Hareem Shafi
Copyeditor Yvette Chin
Cover Design Graham Geary
Photo Credit iStockphoto.com/163750943/© studiocasper
Layout Design Vera Brauner
Production Marissa Fritz
Typesetting III-satz, Husby (Germany)
Printed and bound in the United States of America, on paper from sustainable sources

ISBN 978-1-4932-1592-8
© 2018 by Rheinwerk Publishing, Inc., Boston (MA)
1st edition 2018

Library of Congress Cataloging-in-Publication Data
Names: Chabert, Antoine, author. | Forster, Andreas (Statistician), author. |
    Tessier, Laurent (Statistician), author. | Vezzosi, Pierpaolo, author.
Title: SAP predictive analytics : the comprehensive guide / Antoine Chabert,
    Andreas Forster, Laurent Tessier, Pierpaolo Vezzosi.
Description: 1st edition. | Bonn ; Boston : SAP Press, 2017. | Includes index.
Identifiers: LCCN 2017043291 (print) | LCCN 2017056346 (ebook) | ISBN
    9781493215935 (ebook) | ISBN 9781493215928 (alk. paper)
Subjects: LCSH: Data mining. | Forecasting--Data processing. |
    Forecasting--Statistical methods. | SAP ERP.
Classification: LCC QA76.9.D343 (ebook) | LCC QA76.9.D343 C445 2017 (print) |
    DDC 006.3/12--dc23
LC record available at https://lccn.loc.gov/2017043291

Contents at a Glance

Dear Reader,

Predictive analytics begins with a question. What movie are customers most likely to buy after purchasing *The Martian*? Of our readers, who is likely to sign up for our subscription service in the next six months? Are left-handed mothers of two from New York more likely to do back-to-school shopping at Target or Walmart this year? Take a dataset, create, control, and retrain a model, and you'll be well on your way to finding your answers!

Between these pages, experts Antoine Chabert, Andreas Forster, Laurent Tessier, and Pierpaolo Vezzosi give you everything you need to master predictive models and learn how to get SAP Predictive Analytics up and running. Using example datasets available on the website (*https://www.sap-press.com/4491*), they show you not just the data science of predictions, but how to create your own.

What did you think about *SAP Predictive Analytics*? Your comments and suggestions are the most useful tools to help us make our books the best they can be. Please feel free to contact me and share any praise or criticism you may have.

Thank you for purchasing a book from SAP PRESS!

Meagan White
Editor, SAP PRESS

meaganw@rheinwerk-publishing.com
www.sap-press.com
Rheinwerk Publishing · Boston, MA

Contents

3   Installing SAP Predictive Analytics   49

7   Automated Predictive Regression Models

8   Automated Predictive Time Series Forecasting Models

9   Massive Predictive Analytics

13   Automated Predictive Recommendation Models

14   Advanced Data Preparation Techniques with the Data Manager 377

PART IV   Advanced Workflows

15   Expert Analytics 415

16   Integration into SAP and Third-Party Applications   451

17   Hints, Tips, and Best Practices   467

18   Conclusion

Preface

SAP Predictive Analytics is a comprehensive solution for predictive projects. The goal of the solution is to simplify workflows for defining, executing, and maintaining projects as much as possible without compromising quality, scalability, or manageability.

The technology used in the solution merges SAP's own product, Predictive Analysis, with a solution from SAP's acquisition of KXEN, a French company that specialized (and led the market) in predictive interfaces that business analysts without deep knowledge in mathematics or statistics could use. A skilled user such as a data scientist can also benefit from SAP Predictive Analytics' simplified workflows by letting the application take care of repetitive and low value-adding tasks while concentrating on more important parts of a predictive project.

With SAP, the solution has evolved, and the latest releases feature a new server application, an API for SAP HANA, and a set of microservices available in the SAP Cloud Platform.

Objective

In this book, you'll discover the client tools and the server interface to mass produce predictive analytics projects and manage their lifecycles. The SAP HANA API and the SAP Cloud Platform microservices will be mentioned in this book but not discussed in depth.

You'll learn how to drive a successful predictive project and then see how to leverage SAP Predictive Analytics and its methodology to implement and execute projects.

With this book, you'll not only become familiar with the solution but also understand the business benefits behind its functionality: Before conducting a predictive project, you'll need to justify it with a business case, and this book will help you link your business with the technology.

The book is different from an official user guide because we'll provide step-by-step instructions for each part of the various workflows. You'll not only learn what each functionality does, but you'll see it within a global workflow that you can follow and repeat to become proficient with the tool.

SAP Predictive Analytics has many capabilities, and we won't be able to describe them all in detail in a single book, so our goal is for you to learn the most important parts of the solution and become autonomous enough to later discover its more hidden functionalities on your own.

After reading this book, you should be comfortable starting new projects with SAP Predictive Analytics, and you'll always know what to do next in your tasks.

A Note on Terminology

Throughout this book, you'll need to make a distinction between the concept of predictive analytics and the name of the product itself. Remember that each time we talk about the product, we'll use the capital letters and the full name "SAP Predictive Analytics"; when we talk about the concepts, we'll use lowercase letters as in "predictive analytics" and "predictive analysis."

Target Audience

This book should enable anyone interested in predictive projects to successfully use SAP Predictive Analytics.

You won't need deep mathematical or statistical knowledge. In some chapters, we'll explain the mathematics behind certain processes, but those parts can be skipped if you are not interested. If you are a data scientist, you'll learn how it works behind the scenes.

Typical profiles of readers would include the following:

- A project lead coordinating a team working on a predictive project: This book will describe what can be achieved, the associated costs, the possible alternatives, and best practices.

- A data analyst: Even without a strong knowledge of mathematics, analysts can use this book to see how to run end-to-end data mining, prediction, or forecasting projects.

- A data scientist: Although this book is not about mathematics and instead is a guide to using SAP Predictive Analytics, data scientists can learn what tasks can be executed with the solution and can understand in which scenarios the solution can take care of tedious or low value-adding tasks for you.

- A student: This book can be a good source of information about predictive analytics in general and about specific tools for conducting predictive projects.

Apart from these profiles, anyone interested in a job related to analytics in the SAP world can benefit of the information presented in this book.

Structure of This Book

The book is divided into seventeen chapters in four parts.

Part I: Getting Started

In this part, you'll learn fundamental information about predictive analysis and predictive projects in general as well as everything you need to get started using SAP Predictive Analytics, as follows:

- Chapter 1: You'll learn the fundamental concepts behind predictive analytics projects, how to set up a team, and what to look for to drive a successful project.
- Chapter 2: We'll provide an overview of SAP Predictive Analytics, its objectives, its benefits, and its various components.
- Chapter 3: You'll learn, step by step, how to install various parts of the solution.
- Chapter 4: You'll learn a standard methodology for running successful predictive projects, the CRISP-DM method.

Part II: The Predictive Factory

This section will guide you through the server part of SAP Predictive Analytics, as follows:

- Chapter 5: We'll provide an overview of the Predictive Factory to get you started.
- Chapter 6: You'll follow a step-by-step workflow to build an automated classification model; you'll also learn fundamental information about managing data inputs in SAP Predictive Analytics.
- Chapter 7: You'll discover how to build an automated regression model, from creating the model to applying it and improving it.
- Chapter 8: We'll show you how to predict forecasts of figures in the future, one of the most typical uses of predictive analytics.
- Chapter 9: You'll learn how to manage the lifecycle of a predictive project and how to produce and distribute the model outcomes on a large scale with just a few clicks.

Part III: Automated Analytics

This section is all about workflows that you can perform using the Automated Analytics interface in SAP Predictive Analytics, as follows:

- Chapter 10: We'll provide an overview of the interface, the tasks you can perform with it, and how you can navigate it.
- Chapter 11: You'll learn how to create a clustering model with the Automated Analytics interface.
- Chapter 12: You'll learn the concepts behind social analysis and how to create and navigate into a social network with the solution.
- Chapter 13: You'll learn how to create automated predictive recommendation models and how to use them into your own business applications.
- Chapter 14: We'll provide a detailed set of instructions on how to perform sophisticated data preparation for your projects easily, using the Data Manager interface.

Part IV: Advanced Workflows

This last part is about advanced uses of SAP Predictive Analytics, as follows:

- Chapter 15: We'll discuss the Expert Analytics interface, which can be used to create highly customized projects with your own algorithms and workflows.
- Chapter 16: We'll show you how to embed your model into any other application, one of the strengths of SAP Predictive Analytics.
- Chapter 17: We'll provide some useful hints and tips to consider to improve your projects.

Finally, the concluding section will look at future directions the solution might take, according to the product roadmap.

We hope that you will enjoy this book and become proficient with the powerful capabilities of SAP Predictive Analytics.

Happy reading!

PART I
Getting Started

Chapter 1

An Introduction to Predictive Analytics

A well-conducted predictive analytics project can make all the difference for your business. Your company can be more efficient, more competitive, and more proactive than your rivals. Starting new projects already knowing what to expect is the first step towards success.

You've probably heard a lot of talk about predictive analytics, machine learning, artificial intelligence, and so on. Reading this book shows that you want to know more about these concepts and want to use them for your needs. Great! Let's get started!

In this chapter, we'll discuss the importance of predictive analytics, how you can change your business's vision with it, how to make it work, and how other companies use it in their daily activities. Reading this chapter, you'll get an idea of how you could use predictive analytics for your needs and how to start a new project with the right mindset and organization for success. We'll focus on the concepts behind predictive analysis, setting aside SAP Predictive Analytics for the moment.

We'll also explain predictive analytics concepts using simple terms without any mathematical complexity. If you are a seasoned data scientist, you might find the descriptions a bit simple and unorthodox, but the goal is to ensure that any person reading this book understands the fundamentals and feels comfortable starting a predictive project.

Finally, we'll discuss the overall organization, mindset, and process necessary to define a predictive project. In Chapter 4, we'll go on a deep dive into the actual steps for executing a project using the CRISP-DM methodology, which is a detailed, standardized, and phased approach to predictive and data-mining activities that applies best practices to your projects.

1.1   The Importance of Predictive Analysis

For most people, when we think of predictive analysis, we first think about forecasting and about knowing in advance what is going to happen in the future. Predictive analysis, in some situations, is used exactly for that, but forecasting is not its only usage nor is it necessarily the most important one.

Predicting what might happen in the future is good, but predictions are useless if you cannot act on or react to the prediction. The goal of predictive analytics is not just to inform you of a likely future scenario but also tell you how you can influence it.

Moreover, predictive analysis solutions can give you better insight into your business, whatever it is, and help you adapt to the environment to ensure success.

A few scenarios and goals that you can achieve using predictive analysis include:

- Knowing in advance what a likely future scenario might be
- Knowing how you can influence future scenarios by acting today and also knowing the most appropriate actions to take
- Knowing in real time the best decision to make to achieve your goals
- Understanding the best response in case a specific scenario occurs in the future
- Understanding how to be proactive and ready today for a possible future scenario
- Understanding the inner functioning of your business (or of the environment you are working in)
- Seeing things that your competitors don't see and knowing how to act on these observations to your advantage
- Getting a comprehensive and deep understanding of a problem or situation and then using this knowledge to achieve your goals

You'll see in the upcoming sections how you can actively use predictive analysis to accomplish any of these goals.

Before we begin, let's clarify one thing: Predictive analysis is not useful only for making money or for businesses. A wide spectrum of usage goes beyond pure monetization. You can use predictive analysis to better understand our environment, find the internal mechanisms of how our world works, and, finally, improve our lives. Today, you'll see predictive solutions being used in healthcare, in disaster recovery management, in public security, and in many other situations where the goal is to improve or preserve people's lives.

In a purely business environment, companies that use predictive analysis have a strong competitive advantage over those that don't. The ability to understand the way the business works, and thus to adapt in real time to customer needs, make these businesses more successful and much more efficient.

Knowing the important levers to pull lets you invest your resources only on those activities. By isolating the most productive actions, you can reduce wasted money and time on less impactful activities.

As previously mentioned, predicting without acting is not of much use. In the coming sections and chapters, you'll notice that, most times, the outcome of a predictive project is not the prediction itself but rather the action recommended to achieve your goal. When we obtain real-time recommendations, the benefits are immediate and quickly pay back our investment in the project. Sometimes, this concept is referred to as *prescriptive analytics*. While not all predictive projects are prescriptive, in our experience, most are.

You may not realize that, every day, you are exposed to predictive solutions that make recommendations to you: Each time you use a GPS system, you are told where to drive; each time you enter a word in the Google search box, you'll see suggestions of other words to use; each time you look for a flight on the web, you are presented with the "best" flight for you (and for the sponsoring provider). All of these recommendations are implementations of prescriptive analytics.

One reason why we almost don't notice that we are working with predictive and prescriptive solutions anymore is because the end-user interface is simplified to the essentials. Predictive analysis projects might require sophisticated solutions and some knowledge of mathematics or programming, but the end user, the consumer of those projects, only sees a simple and natural interface.

The end user doesn't have to be bothered by the underlying complexity: The simpler and more intuitive the end-user interface is, the more likely that a predictive project will be adopted and successfully used by end users, unaware of what's going on behind the scenes.

You'll have to take many details into account when preparing a predictive analysis project. Let's start by looking at the two main kinds of outcomes from such a project, and then we can dig into the fundamental requirements for successful project execution.

1.2   Predictive Analysis: Prescriptive and Exploratory

We mentioned that prediction is useless without action, but we can be even more provocative by telling you that the prediction itself might not be the desired output of a predictive project. Real customer examples exist where the goal is not to see what is going to happen but rather to better understand what happened into the past, always keeping in mind the goal of using this information to have a better future.

Predictive analysis lets you see into the future but also gives you a deeper look into the past. Let's see how it works: In the next few sections, we'll provide a high-level description of the theory behind predictive models and then show you how these models are typically applied to make operational or strategic decisions.

1.2.1   The Fundamental Idea

The fundamental idea behind predictive analysis is quite simple: You take historical data and apply some mathematical process to learn the rules and relationships that exist within your information. These rules and relationships are what we call the *predictive model.*

For example, your past data might contain information about all the products purchased by your customers in the past three years. You have a detailed profile of each customer, and for each transaction, you know the time and the amount of purchase. Using a solution like SAP Predictive Analytics (or other tools or your own software), you can apply mathematical algorithms to the data to expose some patterns in the dataset. (We call those patterns the *behavior* of your data.)

You might find, for example, that many customers who purchase product "A" live in large cities, while customers who typically purchase product "B" live in the countryside. Apart from finding those relationships, the mathematical algorithms also measure their strength. The output of the algorithm will be rather precise, saying that, for example, 83% of customers living in large cities purchase product "A" or that 72% of customers that live in the country *and* own a car purchase product "B." These examples are rules that can be inferred from your past data.

The combination of those rules is the predictive model that you can extract from your data.

In reality, you'll have to decide what kind of analysis you want to perform on your data, meaning you'll have to decide what kind of rules you want to extract from it. Based on the kind of rules that you extract, you can gain various types of insights from your dataset.

Using this information, you might want to determine which customer characteristics are more correlated to the purchase of a specific product or, rather, which customers are similar and likely to act in a similar manner. Or, you might want to know which products are purchased together or at what time the transactions are typically performed. If you have an idea of what you would like to understand, then you can apply the most appropriate processing method to your data.

To create a good model, you'll need ensure that you have a sufficient quantity of information and that this information is of good quality. Bad information leads to incorrect results; too little information leads to poor fidelity in the model. However, you don't necessarily need a huge quantity of perfect data—what matters is the balance between the information that is available and the required minimal quality of the resulting model. Finally, you don't necessarily need all the available information you have: You can take only the data relevant to your project. Unnecessary data might raise costs and complexity and, in some situations, even decrease the quality of the results. Luckily for you, SAP Predictive Analytics has a smart approach to many situations and automatically removes unnecessary data.

The rules extracted from the data by SAP Predictive Analytics are generally more efficient than human-derived rules as the rules are really based on facts, don't suffer from stereotypes, and take into account much more detail than a human brain ever could.

Now that you have your predictive model, you can actually use it in two very different ways, as shown in Figure 1.1: You can apply the model to new data for prescriptive analytics, or you can study the insights provided by the model for exploratory analytics.

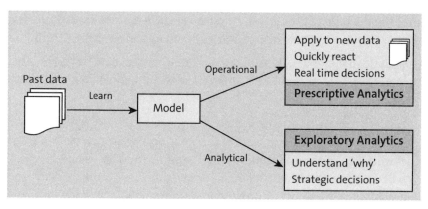

Figure 1.1 Prescriptive and Exploratory Analytics

The two uses are quite different but lead to the same goal of improving your business. Let's look at how they differ and their benefits in more detail.

1.2.2   Prescriptive Analytics

Prescriptive analytics is the most typical usage of a predictive model: You take the rules, apply them to new data (possibly in real time), and get a recommended action (again, possibly in real time).

Using the example provided in the previous section, you can build a model about a product purchased (or not) by customers and then apply this model to a list of prospects. The output will tell you the likelihood that each prospect will or will not purchase that product. You can use this model in real time if you want to propose a product to a person visiting your website or on the phone. You can also use predictive analytics to provide your salespeople with a prioritized list of prospects to visit.

When you perform prescriptive analytics, one benefit is that the recommendation is clear and simple. The user of the model is a person who doesn't have the time, the willpower, or the skills to build a complex model. The user just needs to decide whether he or she will implement the recommendation proposed by the model. Just as when the GPS tells you to turn left, you see an arrow, and you decide to follow the recommended direction or not. With this usage in mind, interfaces must present the prescription or the recommendation as simply and as effectively as possible. The less information shown, the less time will be needed to make a decision. If, for the sake of completeness, the GPS presented you with three different alternative directions at each intersection, you wouldn't be able to decide the best route, and you would miss the most important benefit of the GPS—to trust it to lead you home via the shortest path without you needing to study the road beforehand on a map.

Prescriptive analytics helps you make tactical decisions that can often be represented in a binary choice (yes/no, do/don't) or sometimes as a simple choice with a few options.

Usually, a prescriptive analytics model is directly embedded into a vertical application for the end user. To promote adoption of the solution, the prescription must be in the normal workflow of the application. You'll want to simplify the user experience as much as possible. SAP Predictive Analytics has various automation mechanisms that let you export the model directly into your application code or inside your database as an SQL view or a stored procedure.

The new data onto which you apply the model must have the same attributes (data columns) as your past data. If the recommendation for a product to purchase is based on specific customer attributes, you'll need to have the same attributes for your prospects. One benefit of SAP Predictive Analytics is that the solution automatically determines the smallest set of attributes you'll need to produce a good model, which is important if you need to make decisions in real time. If you have hundreds of attributes in your dataset, applying a model with all of those attributes might take a while to apply onto your new data. SAP Predictive Analytics selects for you only the attributes that are most important so that you can apply the model on that smaller quantity and get results more quickly. In one of our customer projects, we used SAP Predictive Analytics on past datasets with about 700 attributes to produce a model where only 30 attributes were needed. Applying an equation on 30 input values is much more efficient than applying that equation on 700 input values, and gathering 30 measures for each new entry is simpler and less expensive than gathering 700.

Extended to its limits, prescriptive analytics can offer machine-to-machine solutions. In this scenario, recommendations are no longer processed by human beings but are implemented (or not) by machines or other applications. The processing time of a human being can often be too slow unlike, for example, self-driving cars or robots that automatically shut down when their operations become dangerous.

Finally, be aware that the recommended action might not necessarily be the most probable one. Once you know the most probable action, you'll need to balance this information with your ability to execute the recommendation, its costs, and the expected revenue. You might have to conduct a subsequent evaluation that takes all this information into account to go from "most probable" to "most effective."

On the other end of the spectrum, where human reasoning is still the key factor for analysis, we find exploratory analytics. Let's look at exploratory analytics next.

1.2.3   Exploratory Analytics

In exploratory analytics, you don't apply the predictive model to new data, but you can still use it to improve your future business.

In this use case, you'll take your historical dataset and create a model that learns from that data; then you'll analyze or explore the model itself to understand how your business works.

As mentioned before, a predictive model shows the rules and patterns between the various parts of your dataset and measures the strengths of these rules and patterns.

By understanding the various correlations and how they are distributed into your data, you can deep dive into the internal functioning of the environment of your business. With this knowledge, you can make strategic decisions to change your business and increase its performance.

Using again the example given earlier involving customers and product purchases, you might see, after running a regression model, that 86% of your revenue is generated by customers living in the city and 20% by customers living in the country and owning a car but that customers living in the country without a car have a negligible influence to your business. From this information, you can make strategic decisions to change your business: You could improve your delivery services and reduce costs to customers to increase your revenue related to country customers without cars. Or, on the contrary, you could decide to stop bothering with customers in the country and just invest all your resources into better services for customers living in the city. The beauty of the predictive model is that you can measure which of the two actions would have a bigger impact on your business, and you can compare the positive effects with the costs associated with each different action.

Exploratory analytics projects always end up providing a lot of detailed information. This information must be clear and understandable even for people who are not experts in mathematics.

The deliverables of such projects could be a set of visualizations, a few presentation slides, or a text document. The goal is for the end user to understand how the business and its environment work together.

Some products, such as SAP Analytics Cloud or SAP Lumira, directly embed with the SAP Predictive Analytics technology to provide interactive outputs for exploratory analytics. In each one of those solutions, you can submit a dataset to a classification or regression method and have a visual and interactive result that shows, for example, the most influential attributes, and how much they influence, the target of your study. With SAP Analytics Cloud or SAP Lumira, you cannot perform deep predictive analyses or conduct a strongly predictive project, but you'll get good information on your data from within your usual business intelligence tool.

1.2.4   Prescriptive vs. Exploratory Analytics

You should choose between prescriptive analytics or exploratory analytics upfront when starting a project because this choice completely changes how the model is consumed: whether embedded into an application (for prescriptive analytics) or presented as a descriptive document (for exploratory analytics).

With prescriptive analytics, you'll give less (or even no) choice to the end users of the model, but you'll speed up the decision-making process. With exploratory analytics, you'll let end users decide autonomously but support the decision-making process with additional insights from the model analysis.

These two methods are equally important, and you should choose the one that best fits your requirements, your user skills, and your customer expectations.

Example

We encountered a large company that sells rather similar products (insurance policies) under different brands. Each brand has its own strategy and decides how to market and sell their products. Two brands used SAP Predictive Analytics to help their agents propose insurance policies to prospects. In our discussions with the two brands, we learned that one brand used a prescriptive methodology, while the other used an exploratory one. Both brands use SAP Predictive Analytics to group customers into a few segments automatically and then define specific insurance packages for each group. The first brand uses a prescriptive analytics approach: When a new potential customer contacts an agent, the agent enters the customer profile in an application and immediately gets the segment the prospect belongs to and the appropriate insurance package. With this approach, the potential customer can have a quantified proposal in just a few minutes.

The second brand instead uses exploratory analytics for training sessions for its agents about how the groups were formed and why groups have that shape. Agents also learned how insurance packages were built around specific segments. When a potential customer contacts an agent, they discuss the options together, and the agent tries to determine, through conversation, the appropriate segment for the prospect and the appropriate insurance package. With this approach, the brand engages in a more human and personalized relationship with its customers.

What works better? Well, both brands were satisfied of their approach and tried to convince the other that their method was the best: Both had good results, and agents (and customers) were happy in both situations.

We hope this anecdote illustrates the fundamental concepts behind predictive analysis and its practical uses. Let's turn now to the most important steps to ensure a successful predictive project.

1.3 Preparing for a Successful Predictive Analysis Project

Each predictive project is unique, but often, well-run projects share many similarities, which we'll describe in this section. In the following sections, we'll summarize some real-life project examples that the authors have studied or participated in to inspire you in your own predictive project.

Chapter 4 shows how to execute a predictive project using the CRISP-DM methodology in detail. The following sections in this chapter provide a high-level view of the process, describing more the environment, the mindset, and the organization you should have in place. We want to give you all the tools you need to achieve your goal!

1.3.1 Stakeholders

Typically, three kinds of people work together on a predictive analysis project: the business representative, the data analyst, and the information technology (IT) person.

In each profile, you may have a single person or, more often, multiple persons. In successful projects, we often see another role: the project lead.

The role of lead can be undertaken by a dedicated person or by one of the persons already working on the project with another profile. Often project leads are either a specific person or a data analyst or an IT person; more rarely, they are part of the business team.

Let's look at the different profiles involved, as follows:

- **Business representative**
  Business representatives are the key stakeholders of the project. Without a business objective, the project won't have any chance succeeding or even starting. As mentioned previously, by "business," you don't have to think only of "making money"; think of any activity that can help achieve your goals, whatever they are: providing better healthcare, optimizing costs, reducing stock, choosing the best intervention method during a natural disaster, etc.

  Business users should ideally be the origin of the project, requesting the analysis for their needs. In reality, many times, business representatives don't know what a predictive solution can achieve and don't formulate the request because they are not aware of what is possible. In this case, the data analyst or the IT team can propose a predictive project. Nevertheless, the business representatives must fully buy into the project proposal and make it their own; otherwise, the results of the predictive project won't be used.

Business users provide business insight to the rest of the team and help shape the final functionality. Be sure to keep them in the loop during the elaboration and development of a project to ensure its continued usefulness.

- **Data analyst**
  The data analyst (or the data analysis team) is responsible for actually transforming business ideas and requirements into a feasible predictive project. The data analyst must have good knowledge of the business to help shape the solution and ensure that all useful data is available and accessible. Usually data analysts have knowledge in mathematics and in development. Two useful skills of a data analyst include the ability to "see through" the data to determine if the data is appropriate for the project's needs and the ability to quickly see what can be done out of the data in its raw form or after preparing it. The ability to "see through" data is usually learned with experience on various projects, independently of any mathematical skill. Some predictive analysis tools require a deep knowledge of statistics and mathematics; SAP Predictive Analytics' automated interfaces enable users with average mathematical knowledge to work effectively on sophisticated projects.

Data Analysts or Data Scientists?

In predictive analysis, a role exists called the *data scientist*. This person is typically well versed in mathematics, specifically in statistics and in development using languages such as Python or R. The SAP Predictive Analytics solution doesn't require those specific skills, even if they could be useful assets. Because of SAP Predictive Analytics' simpler concepts and the reduced skillset needed to profitably use it, in this book, we use the term *data analyst*. Real data scientists can still use the solution and be perfectly happy with how it alleviates some tedious tasks they usually perform with less automated tools.

- **IT team**
  The IT team is responsible for implementing the project in a viable way so that the output can be repeatedly used by any business user. IT might import a predictive model into an existing application or build a new one around it. IT often deals with installing the necessary products and dealing with obstacles related to accessing the data (database setup, connectivity, security, implementation of SQL views or procedures, etc.).

- **Project lead**
  Finally, we often find a leader in a successful predictive project. This person (either with that specific role or assuming that role while also serving as a data analyst or

on the IT team) is responsible for the overall execution of the project and the exchange of information between the other three profiles. Business representatives, data analysts, and the IT team all speak different languages, have different priorities, and have different perceptions of constraints and obstacles. The project lead needs to be able to speak to all stakeholders and translate business requests into actionable methodologies and functional requirements that can be implemented. This person is not just a project manager: Project management skills might be a benefit but is not a requirement. Rather, a good project lead has the ability to be versatile and to act as a bridge and a conductor between different people. The final project output often embodies a glimpse of the project lead's personality.

In Section 1.2.4, we described two different approaches by two different brands of an insurance company. It just so happened that the project lead of the team who created an application for prescriptive analytics was also the lead of the IT team. This person was able to quickly see how to implement the model into an end-user application and shaped the solution this way. On the other hand, the project lead of the team who decided to do the training sessions was part of the data analysis team and was interested in sharing her knowledge with others.

If we look strictly at the numbers, a virtual team of three is typically the minimum size for a good project, but in general, we've see a whole range of predictive project teams involving whole IT departments, where individuals would have specific roles (database administrator, developer, tester, etc.); one or two data analysts; and one or two representatives of the business who might provide feedback from the larger business audience.

Once the project has been executed, the output might be deployed to tens, hundreds, thousands, or more business users.

1.3.2 Business Case: Objectives and Benefits

The initial phase of the project must be based on the definition of the changes that it should bring to the business. You should start with a *why* question: Why do we want to do this? Knowing the reason behind the project helps keep an eye on its objectives and evaluate if the content or the costs are going in a wrong direction. Once the reason is clear, you should ask *what*: What do we want to achieve? This analysis helps you clarify the requirements to put in place. Finally, you should ask *how* to achieve what you want so that you can shape the specific functionality you'll develop.

Taking our example of the insurance company, for the brand conducting exploratory analytics, simple responses to the above questions would have been:

- **Why do we want to do it?**
  We want to increase the revenue generated by each insurance agent and make sure that this revenue is maintained over time, thus avoiding churn of unsatisfied customers.

- **What do we want to achieve?**
  We want our customers to feel understood and cared for when contacting us. We want them to feel that we recommended the best option for them and that they won't regret it.

- **How do we want to do it?**
  We are going to train our agents so that they are comfortable in talking with customers and show customers that the agents care and have the knowledge to help them make the right choices.

An important, but often undervalued, step in planning a predictive project is to provide a way to measure success upfront. All predictive projects have associated costs, and your investments must be justified. You might want to define some reference values into account before implementing the project, and after implementation, you'll want to have a reasonable time frame within which to see the results.

In our insurance company example, one brand wanted to increase the number of safe and loyal customers who would remain with the company for at least ten years without declaring an insurance claim. While this goal is a good business objective, you would only get the first results ten years after implementing the predictive project. A better approach would be to use a success measure that could show earlier if the project was successful or not. For example, the company could have initially measured the increase in the number of contracts signed and then, running on a yearly basis, measured the decrease of insurance claims for customers who were acquired using the predictive process.

1.3.3   Requirements

Defining your requirements is a key step in the project. You must ensure that the business team can clearly express the expected outcome and how the outcome will be presented to your end users. In this phase, you should have mockups or wireframes for the solution's user interfaces (UIs) that can be tested and validated by the business team. The business should also determine the constraints on the performance of the solution, for example, where the solution will be used (a laptop, a tablet, a phone) and the level of security or confidentiality. If the output itself is to be monetized (e.g., you want to sell the resulting information to third parties), then you'll need to put in place a system to measure the consumption of the solution.

The data analyst needs to raise requirements on the quality and availability of the data from which the predictive model will learn as well as the data onto which the model will be applied.

The IT team might want to add requirements to conform to company policies related to your deployment platform, to legal policies, or to existing applications where the output model will be embedded.

One important aspect that business users and data analysts must agree on upfront is the balance between the quality of the model and its costs and development time. If no cost or time constraints exist, the data analyst might want to spend significant time and resources trying to improve the quality of the model to its maximum. Now, maximum data quality is not always necessary: Once the quality of the model is "good enough," then you don't need to improve it more. For a predictive project meant to prevent nuclear accidents, spending as much time and money as possible to have the best output makes sense; for a marketing campaign of a product, the model must just be "good enough" to be viable and guarantee a certain return on investment. The return on the investment can be calculated by looking at the lift curve of the model, which shows how accurate the model predicts compared to a random choice. We'll discuss the lift curve in more detail in Chapter 6.

Once your requirements are gathered, you can start developing the project.

1.3.4   Execution and Lifecycle Management

Once all the preparation work has been done, your goals are clear, and your requirements written down and agreed to by all parties, you can start executing the project. We'll describe in detail the process for executing a predictive project with the CRISP-DM methodology in Chapter 4. For now, we just want to recommend that you keep all stakeholders involved in each phase of the project, not only when defining the project. During the project's execution and lifecycle management, the most active profile will be the IT team, but you'll need to make sure that your data analysts control and validate each output and that your business representatives understand the results and are able to make use of them in their daily work.

Once you have successfully put the predictive model in production, you cannot sit back and relax—not for long at least. A model is based on past data, but that data may no longer represent reality. Thus, the model will need to be refreshed from time to time to ensure its accuracy. The Predictive Factory in SAP offers an automated solution to monitor the responsiveness of the model and check if the model deteriorates over time. Above a certain threshold of deterioration, you can have the model automatically retrained on newer data.

Maintaining a predictive model ends only when you decide to deprecate the model. You should remember that an outdated predictive model can return bad suggestions and can be even worse than making random choices. For this reason, make sure that your end users access only active and updated models.

We've discussed just some typical considerations to take into account when you start a new predictive project. In the next section, we'll discuss some real examples of predictive models in use in various industries and lines of business (LOBs). Use this list as an inspiration for your company and as a way to open up a discussion about your needs.

1.4   Industry Use Cases

Predictive analysis can be used in practically all industries and all LOBs. In this section, you'll find examples taken from real deployments for a number of industries:

- **Telecom**

  These companies live in a dynamic environment with customers who are acquired and churn quickly. Appropriate marketing and avoiding customer churn are their main goals when running predictive projects. In marketing, typically, companies use SAP Predictive Analytics' clustering solutions (described in Chapter 11) to create segments of their customers (and of prospects) based on their similarities and then build marketing offers specifically targeted to each segment. Looking at the segment, telecom companies can also recognize which segments are of real interest to the business and which are not worth investing in. For churn analysis, telecom companies use either a classification approach (described in Chapter 6) or run a Social Network Analysis (Chapter 12).

  With the classification methodology, these companies can see if a specific customer is likely to churn, and if so, they can propose a different offer to keep customer loyalty. With Social Network Analysis, companies can identify which groups of people are strongly interconnected and can identify the most important persons in a group. By doing appropriate marketing on the key person, they can indirectly influence the whole community.

- **Retail**

  In this industry, a major goal is to ensure that customers purchase as much as possible. Retail companies often use a recommendation methodology (Chapter 13) to analyze past purchases and the customer's profile and then suggest the most appropriate product to propose next. You might have seen this kind of recommendation when navigating in web-based marketplaces.

  On the web, it is always important that potential customers don't stop navigating through your site and go elsewhere. Tools such as Sequence Analysis in the Automated Analytics interface, briefly described in Chapter 10, Section 10.3.1, help companies understand where, when, and why users move away from their websites and enable changes to keep potential customers on your site purchase. As in most other industries, marketing campaigns are structured with segmentation solutions to ensure that the right content is sent to the right prospect.

- **Banks and financial institutions**

  These companies run marketing campaigns and customer churn analysis as well with predictive projects. Moreover, these companies use analytics for fraud detection. Today, companies managing credit card transactions and some banks use the SAP Predictive Analytics classification methodology to detect whether a transaction is fraudulent and can block the transaction before it is carried out. Risk management is another topic that can be tackled with a predictive model; using classification or regression models, a company can determine which investments or customers are safer and where a greater opportunity of revenue for minimal risk exists.

- **Consumer goods and fresh products industries**

  These companies often face challenges related to stock management. Storing products for a long time is expensive, and some products might have expiration dates, after which the product cannot be sold anymore. In this scenario, companies use time series forecasting methodologies (Chapter 8) to try to understand how much product will be consumed and when, so as to ensure that reasonable stock is available but also to avoid excessive surplus.

  Forecasting solutions apply as well in many other situations where you have to manage human resources ("How many cashiers are needed during the next promotion period?") or when planning budgets for upcoming periods.

- **Automotive companies or discrete high-tech industries**
  These industries use predictive maintenance as a key differentiator. Using time series forecasting, segmentation, and classification, these companies build models and deploy them in applications to monitor machines in real time and raise alerts when a risk of failure arises, before the failure actually occurs.

We've only described a limited set of examples of how companies today use SAP Predictive Analytics to improve their businesses. The time has come for you to ask yourself what you can do with this solution to improve your way of working and your business.

1.5   Summary

In this chapter, you learned the basic concepts behind predictive analysis. You can now choose whether exploratory analytics or prescriptive analytics is better suited for your business goals.

You've also seen the fundamental pillars, the mindset, and the organization required to run a successful predictive project. In Chapter 4, we'll go into more details about the specific methodology behind executing the predictive project.

Finally, you've seen how some companies use SAP Predictive Analytics to shape their businesses, be successful, and surpass their competitors.

In the next chapter, we'll discuss how SAP Predictive Analytics, as a solution, can help you apply what you've learned so far to improve your future business.

Chapter 2
What Is SAP Predictive Analytics?

Predictive analysis is a vast and interesting subject, and you'll need good tools to proficiently run predictive projects. SAP Predictive Analytics is a complete solution that efficiently provides you with useful and actionable results from your data. Let's explore the solution.

As presented in Chapter 1, the need for predictive analytics is widespread in business. To deliver results, with sustainable quality, is the objective of SAP Predictive Analytics. This chapter introduces you to various parts of the solution and provides an initial overview of how each component is used in the end-to-end process of building and deploying models. We'll also provide a description of other capabilities in SAP Predictive Analytics.

2.1 Building Predictive Models with SAP Predictive Analytics

A predictive model should only provide an answer to a business question or part of it. Asking the business question in a way that can be transformed into a model or a set of models is therefore always the first step of a predictive analytics project.

If the goal is to industrialize the production of its results (in the realm of prescriptive analytics), then the CRISP-DM (cross-industry standard process for data mining) methodology must be followed.

> **Note**
> We'll cover the CRISP-DM methodology in detail in Chapter 4.

For the moment, note that the deployment phase of the CRISP-DM methodology is represented in this chapter by a single step; however, the methodology actually contains three steps, all of them enabled by various parts of SAP Predictive Analytics:

- Model training and deployment
- Control of the model over time to ensure it delivers the required results
- Retraining the model when results are no longer good enough

In the first iteration, the model is trained (modeling); in the next, the model is retrained on newly available data. The same applies to the evaluation phase, performed prior to the first deployment. Over time, you'll continually control the predicted output of the model to ensure optimal quality in the results.

SAP Predictive Analytics encompasses this whole process to deliver results to many different lines of businesses (LOBs) in a controlled way.

The following sections of this chapter describe the various components used to deliver results with SAP Predictive Analytics.

2.2   Automated Analytics and Expert Analytics

In a global predictive project, the main activity is the process of model building. In SAP Predictive Analytics, two options for model building are available, as follows:

- A guided approach following a predefined flow using Automated Analytics
- A workbench approach providing the user all the freedom to build his own flow using Expert Analytics

The automated approach relies on proprietary algorithms. The aim is to remove all the technicality from building models by solving all the major hurdles that data scientists or data analysts face. The automated approach relies on the *Theory of Statistical Learning* published by Vladimir Vapnik and is an implementation of structural risk minimization (SRM) theory. Missing data, outliers (or non-statistically usable information), collinearity of the predictors, predictor distribution, and overfitting are all handled automatically for the user. As a result, the focus can be shifted from these technical constraints to scaling the number of models required to solve the business questions. Technically, the Automated Analytics tool is a client-server application implemented in C++ and Java.

Compared to the automated approach, the expert approach is much more similar to the standard tools found in the market. Expert Analytics is a visual programming interface with boxes in a drag-and-drop approach. Each box is then parameterized to perform a step in the overall flow. The flow can be simple or complex, with several branches. Expert Analytics relies on three engines: its own application engine, which provides a limited set of algorithms; the SAP HANA predictive analytics libraries (the Predictive Analysis Library (PAL) and the Automated Predictive Library (APL)); and the R engine. When connected to SAP HANA, all jobs are pushed to SAP HANA for execution.

Once your models are built, following one of these two approaches, their productization is the next step of the process.

2.3   Mass Production of Predictive Models with the Predictive Factory

Building a model can be a time-consuming task, but the lifecycle of a model or the continuous control of its quality over time are even more demanding activities. The Predictive Factory component simplifies all post-production tasks on models, from deploying the model into applications, to checking its quality, to producing variations from a single original model en masse.

2.3.1   Result Production

As described in Section 2.1, model building is only the first step of the process. A built model needs to be put in production so that results are provided to your business users. Results are produced by the execution of the equation found when applying new data to predict the future or describe the status of an object (fraud, for example). This task is handled by the Predictive Factory.

The Predictive Factory is a scheduler and a supervisor specific to SAP Predictive Analytics. The first task that can be performed and supervised is "model application" on new data. You can use the Predictive Factory on both Automated Analytics and Expert Analytics models.

By nature, scheduling means the batch production of the results. Real-time deployment will be discussed in other chapters.

2.3.2   Model Control

A model is an image of the information contained in a training dataset. The dataset uses historical data that represents a certain period of time. Over time, the data contained in actualized datasets will likely not contain the same information because of changes to behaviors, the evolving business context, etc. These changes are visible in the data as changes in the predictor distribution or as changes in the relationships between predictors and targets.

When executing the model on actual data, you'll want to be alerted if the result is not in line with the expected quality of the model, e.g., for classification, if the proportion of the detected target decreases for a given population.

The Predictive Factory allows you to schedule control tasks called *model deviations*. The goal of this task is to measure the discrepancy in the model's quality between the training phase and the last time the model's quality was assessed. Model deviations apply both for models built with Automated Analytics and for models built with Expert Analytics, if they contain the right quality key performance indicators (KPIs).

For Automated Analytics models, the Predictive Factory checks both model performance and dataset deviations. *Chi-squared* (χ^2) tests are performed on each variable of the dataset to assess if the distribution of the predictors has changed between training and now. These tests check if the variable distribution itself has changed but also verify their cross-distribution with the target. The results provide a diagnostic of the possible cause of model quality decrease.

When deviation is detected, the model should be retrained, which you can do easily with the Predictive Factory.

2.3.3   Model Retraining

The third task that can be scheduled in the Predictive Factory is *model retraining*. This activity applies to Automated Analytics models, which, as the name suggests, are by default automated. Scheduled model retraining usually cannot be applied to Expert Analytics models, which may have included manual steps in the model-building process.

Model retraining is more than model recalibration (which would mean keeping the same variables and just adjusting the coefficients to the new dataset). Instead, model retraining is really training a new model based on the provided dataset. All variables are compared against one another, and the best ones are selected using the automated approach for variable selection described in Chapter 6, Chapter 7, and Chapter 8. As a result, a retrained version of a model might need to contain different input variables than the original model.

2.3.4   Mass Production of Predictive Models

Having the ability to schedule batch production, model control, and model retraining within a dedicated interface allows you to scale the number of models that you can deploy. In fact, when the control and retraining of models is handled manually, the effort required for these steps greatly impacts the productivity of your data scientists. Without automation, each data scientist or data analyst can only handle a limited number of models.

By automating model creation and by delegating to the system the control and retraining of models, a single data analyst can handle hundreds, if not thousands, of models. The value for the company is increased, as is the productivity of the data analyst.

For individual models, the ability to control and retrain models automatically allows you to have as close to optimal models as is possible at any time.

2.4   Data Preparation

So far, we've described where and how models can be built and deployed. Between the lines, you might have noticed the importance of the dataset. Building and deploying models rely on providing the right datasets at the right time. Traditionally, datasets are produced when needed by data scientists and then used for model training and deployment.

With SAP Predictive Analytics, the end-to-end process contains dedicated interfaces for dataset production so that, when required, the right dataset is fed to model training, control, or result production. This functionality is provided by the Data Manager, within the Automated Analytics interface.

Two levels of data management are provided:

- Free data manipulation based on enriching an existing table
- A guided data manipulation process, called *analytical data management*, which relies on a strong methodology and the data manipulation capabilities of the first level

In free data manipulation, you'll take an existing dataset in a database table and enrich it via one or more of the following actions:

- Creating an outer join to another table to add new columns
- Aggregating data from transactional tables into new columns
- Computing new fields based on existing columns
- Filtering the dataset

The result is SQL code that can be executed in the underlying database. The generated SQL is adapted to the database to which SAP Predictive Analytics is connected.

To help users design their datasets, analytical data management adds a methodology to the data manipulation capabilities. This methodology is based on the decomposition of the dataset into elements, which, once combined, define the dataset:

- **Entity**
  Defines the row of the dataset.

- **Analytical record**
  Defines the columns of the dataset linked to an entity and is a reusable object for all questions related to the entity.

- **Time-stamped population**
  Defines the population of entities that should be considered for a given question and the target.

- **Reference date**
  Defines the date at which the dataset needs to be produced.

The combination of a given entity definition, the analytical record, the time-stamped population, and the reference date fully defines the required dataset. Changing the reference date means the dataset is produced as of that date.

These objects and their use will be described in more detail in Chapter 14.

The fact that dataset production is part of the predictive analytics process means that the dataset produced for each step of the process may be different. The dataset for the training phase should be as broad as possible (using as many columns as possible) and contain enough records to find a robust model. For result production, only the columns that have been selected in the model are useful and therefore are included. If model building starts from several thousand columns, but only 20 were selected by the model, then only these 20 will be included to get results.

2.5   Additional SAP Predictive Analytics Capabilities

SAP Predictive Analytics has also other modules that go beyond the classic steps of preparing data and defining classification, regression, and time series forecasting models. The following lists some additional use cases that you can implement with the solution:

- **Link analysis**
  A first set of use cases is based on graph theory and enables you to analyze graphs. The model looks at the links between entities rather than at the entities themselves. Link analysis enables two main use cases: Social Network Analysis and recommendation models.

  - **Social Network Analysis**
    Social Network Analysis is the module that allows you to define all possible link analyses. Its aim is to extract information from graphs. The first usage of Social Network Analysis is on direct graphs, i.e., for which the link between entities is direct (SIM cards, social networks, etc.). The output of the analysis includes basic network descriptions (number of neighbors, number of triangles, etc.) and more advanced descriptions based on community definitions (Louvain algorithm). The output information can be written into files or database tables, which can then be used as inputs for classification and regression models.

    The second usage for the Social Network Analysis module is on bipartite graphs, for example, linking entities of different nature like products and customers that bought the products. The new graphs can be the basis of a recommendation model because the links between products define what products are bought together. Chapter 12 is dedicated to Social Network Analysis.

    When one of the entities is a location, applying the same approach provides the ability to define colocation. A specific user interface allows you to define colocation analysis. In the same way, a frequent path analysis can be performed.

  - **Recommendation**
    Based on link analysis, a specific interface is provided for defining recommendation engines more easily. Using the same functionalities as described for Social Network Analysis, these capabilities are packaged in a simpler-to-use, recommendation-oriented interface. We'll discuss recommendation models in detail in Chapter 13.

- **Data transfer**
  The Data Manager is not an extract, transform and load (ETL) tool. Instead, the Data Manager is a semantic layer between a data schema and the required data-

sets. Consolidating data into one repository is therefore not part of the SAP Predictive Analytics solution. Data consolidation should be an IT process handled with proper ETL processes to ensure that all required data is provided in a timely way for SAP Predictive Analytics processes to proceed.

SAP Predictive Analytics still provides simple but robust data transfer capabilities. The solution allows you to transfer data from a file to a database, between files, from a database to a file, and between databases. Error handling is performed during the transfer, giving SAP Predictive Analytics a robust data transfer capability.

You can also get a list of the distinct values in a column of a table and can write these values back into a file or a database table.

- **Descriptive statistics**
  In the **Toolkit** section, where the data transfer component is available, you can perform descriptive statistics for a dataset. These statistics show the category frequency for nominal and ordinal variables, the variable distribution, and various statistics (average, median, maximum, minimum, etc.) for continuous variables.

  If a target is defined, the solution will calculate cross-statistics with the target and can also evaluate the quality of prediction of any given variable versus the target.

- **Compute optimized groups for a target**
  This functionality derives directly from the first step of classification/regression modeling. By performing the data encoding (Chapter 6 and Chapter 7) with category grouping, the output regroups variable categories in an optimal way.

- **Data visualization**
  Because Expert Analytics is based on SAP Lumira, visualization capabilities from SAP Lumira are provided as well.

2.6   Summary

In this chapter, we described the philosophy behind SAP Predictive Analytics and how these concepts were implemented in the tool. Its main focus is producing results, which implies an end-to-end process from dataset design and production, to model building, model control, result production, and model retraining. The Data Manager, Automated Analytics, and to a lesser extent Expert Analytics and the Predictive Factory provide these capabilities. Additional capabilities such as link analysis, data transfer, and descriptive statistics are also provided, while visualization is part of Expert Analytics.

Chapter 3
Installing SAP Predictive Analytics

*Installing SAP Predictive Analytics is a key step to ensuring that you
leverage the suite to the full extent of its capabilities. You'll need to
identify the proper systems, proceed with the installation, and perform a few configuration steps in your landscape. Let's get started!*

SAP Predictive Analytics contains four different components that need to be
installed to leverage the full value of the suite, as follows:

- **SAP Predictive Analytics server**
  A processing server is needed to perform predictive analytics. The SAP Predictive
  Analytics server also powers the creation of automated predictive models in the
  Predictive Factory. The server must be installed to access a fully functional Predic-
  tive Factory.

- **SAP Predictive Analytics client**
  The client connects the server in the client/server mode of SAP Predictive Analytics. Although the most often used automated model types can be created using the
  Predictive Factory, automated models based on clustering, social, and recommendation techniques can be created only using the client or the desktop.

- **Predictive Factory**
  Predictive Factory is the next-generation product in SAP Predictive Analytics with
  capabilities expected to expand over time. At the time of this writing, Predictive
  Factory allows you to create automated classification, regression, and time series
  models and relies on the SAP Predictive Analytics server to create these automated
  predictive models. You can install the server and the Predictive Factory side-by-
  side on a Windows server.

- **SAP Predictive Analytics desktop**
  The desktop offers similar capabilities for automated predictive models as a cli-
  ent/server deployment. Expert Analytics models can only be created using the

desktop. Some users also find it convenient to have a local installation of SAP Predictive Analytics on their machines.

These four main components can be downloaded from the SAP Support Portal at *https://support.sap.com/en/index.html* provided you are an SAP licensed customer.

In this chapter, we'll review the installation requirements and the installation process in detail for each of these four components. We'll also provide you with hints on how to validate the success of the installations which steps to take next. We'll conclude the chapter with several useful links and resources related to SAP HANA system installations required to fully leverage the power of SAP Predictive Analytics.

3.1   Recommended Deployments

We recommend selecting a server machine on which to install both the SAP Predictive Analytics server and Predictive Factory.

Please note these two products can be installed side-by-side on a Windows operating system. This deployment scenario minimizes the network communication latency between the Predictive Factory and the SAP Predictive Analytics server.

We also recommend installing a local client, either using the SAP Predictive Analytics server installers or the SAP Predictive Analytics client installers, in order to validate the connection from the client to the server directly on the machine where the server is installed.

Which products need to be deployed on client machines will depend on your user requirements.

If users only need to create automated classification, regression, and time series predictive models, connecting them to the Predictive Factory using their locally installed browsers is probably sufficient. If users need more automated capabilities than what the Predictive Factory currently provides, provide them with an SAP Predictive Analytics client so that they can connect to the server.

Finally, if users want to create Expert Analytics models or want to be fully autonomous, they'll need a local installation of the SAP Predictive Analytics desktop on their local machine.

3.2   Installing the SAP Predictive Analytics Server

This section covers the end-to-end process of installing the SAP Predictive Analytics server. We'll explain where to download the server. We'll cover the system requirements necessary in the machine where you want to install the server. We'll walk you through the steps for installing the server and conclude with some post-installation steps that you'll need to perform.

Related Resources

The following documentation resources can be helpful to you:

- The SAP Predictive Analytics Server Installation Guide for Windows: *http://bit.ly/2ACwoiR*
- The SAP Predictive Analytics Server Installation Guide for Linux: *http://bit.ly/2AE3NJV*
- The SAP Predictive Analytics Server Operations Guide: *http://bit.ly/2hpnUE8*

Note

The instructions in this chapter use SAP Predictive Analytics 3.2 as our example. Please download the latest version for your own installation.

3.2.1   Downloading the SAP Predictive Analytics Server

First, you'll need to have a valid S-user ID on the SAP Support site. You can find more information related to S-users at *https://support.sap.com/en/my-support/users.html*. To download the server, go to *https://launchpad.support.sap.com/#/softwarecenter*, then select the option **By Alphabetical Index (A-Z),** select the letter **P** (as in "Predictive"), select the entry **SAP PREDICTIVE ANALYTICS,** then **SAP PREDICTIVE ANALYTICS 3,** and select the entry **COMPRISED SOFTWARE COMPONENT VERSIONS**. Server versions can be found under the folder **PREDICTIVE ANALYTICS SERVER 3** (Figure 3.1). Please note that you'll need to select the proper operating system from the dropdown menu on the right.

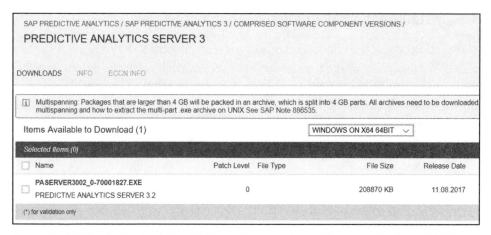

Figure 3.1 SAP Predictive Analytics 3.2 Server Executable for Microsoft Windows 64-Bit Operating System

3.2.2   System Requirements

The SAP Predictive Analytics 3.2 server can be installed on any of these operating systems:

- Microsoft Windows Server 2012 R2, 64-bit version
- Microsoft Windows Server 2016, 64-bit version
- Microsoft Windows 8 or 8.1, 64-bit version
- Microsoft Windows 10, 64-bit version
- Red Hat Enterprise Linux 7.0+ and 7.2 versions
- SUSE Linux Enterprise Server 11.3+ and 12.0+ versions

For a corporate deployment, server operating systems are preferred over desktop operating systems. The other characteristics required by the SAP Predictive Analytics 3.2 server can be found in Table 3.1.

System Characteristic	Recommendation
Free space on hard disk	1.45 gigabyte (GB)
Number of cores	8
Random-access memory (RAM)	32 GB (4 GB/core)

Table 3.1 Recommended System Characteristics

To install the server, you'll need administration rights on the target machine as well as the rights to set up various services.

3.2.3   Installing the SAP Predictive Analytics Server

The steps you'll actually take when installing the SAP Predictive Analytics server will differ depending on whether you are working with Microsoft Windows or Linux, as we'll show in the following sections.

Microsoft Windows

In Windows, the installation process is straightforward:

1. In the **License Agreement** and the **Select Destination Location** screens of the installer, validate the license agreement and the folder where the server should be installed.

2. On the **Select Components** screen of the installer, select a **Full Installation** of the server (Figure 3.2).

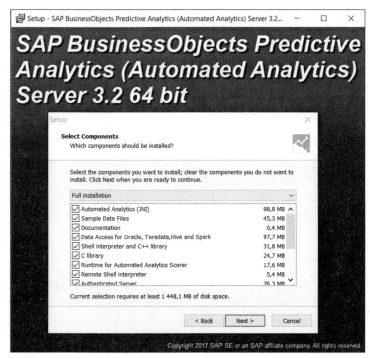

Figure 3.2 Selecting the Server Components

3. On the **Server IP Address** screen, enter the server's IP address where client machines will connect. You can leave the default value proposed by the installer, unless you have a specific configuration.

4. On the **Authentication Type** screen, select the type of authentication that should be used by the server. The recommended authentication is **System Authentication: Windows accounts (with impersonification)**. With this option, users will connect to the server using their regular Windows accounts. You'll need to declare these users in the specific Windows user group on the machine where the server is installed, named *KxenUsers*, which we'll discuss further in Section 3.2.4. The other authentication types rely on files to store user credentials, which is a less secure and less ideal method.

5. On the **Windows Domain** screen, specify the name of the Windows domain to be used for authentication.

In the final steps, you'll simply validate the location for the product's shortcuts, create desktop icons, and review the installation before launch; you can select **Next** twice then select **Install** in the **Ready to Install** screen.

Linux

If you want to deploy SAP Predictive Analytics server on a Linux machine, you'll simply decompress and extract the executable file as described below:

1. Create a group called *kxenusers* and an account called *kxenadmin*.

2. Log on as *kxenadmin*.

3. Run the command `umask 007`.

4. From the home directory of the *kxenadmin* user, run the command
   `gunzip -c </directory/distribution_file.extension> | tar -xvf -`.

   This command creates a directory named *AutomatedAnalytics_<OS_Name>* in the home directory of the *kxenadmin* user.

3.2.4   Post-Installation Steps

Once the server is installed or deployed, you'll need to retrieve your license key then put this key in the license file on the server to enable the server. You'll also need to check the client/server connection, check that the license works properly, and, if on Microsoft Windows, add the authorized users to the proper user group.

Retrieving Your SAP Predictive Analytics License

To download your license key, go to *https://support.sap.com/licensekey*, where you can request keys and monitor your key requests. You can also access a detailed how-to document that guides you through the license request process: *http://bit.ly/2nmN604*.

Installing the License: Microsoft Windows

Once you have your license, you'll need to modify the locally installed file named *License.cfg* (Figure 3.3). The *License.cfg* file is located one level above the installation folder for the SAP Predictive Analytics server.

On a default installation, you'll find the file in the *C:\Program Files\SAP BusinessObjects Predictive Analytics* folder. Add one line with the format `KeyCode<TAB><TheReceivedKeycode>` where `TheReceivedKeycode` is your license key.

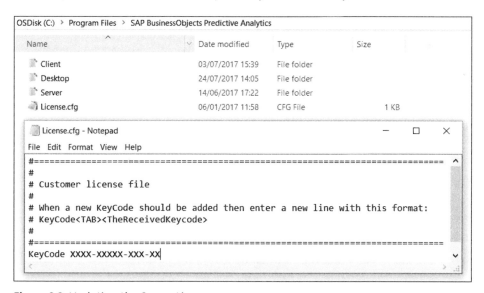

Figure 3.3 Updating the Server License

Once you've saved this change, for it to be effective, you'll need to restart the local service **SAP BusinessObjects Predictive Analytics – Automated Analytics Directory**, which will automatically restart the other linked service: **SAP BusinessObjects Predictive Analytics – Automated Analytics Server** (Figure 3.4).

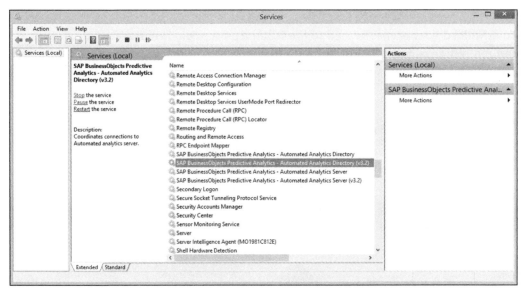

Figure 3.4 Restarting the Local Service

You can restart the server by opening the local services on the machine where SAP Predictive Analytics server is installed and restarting the service aforementioned.

Installing the License: Linux

To register the license, edit the *License.cfg* file located under the root folder where the SAP Predictive Analytics .tar archive was extracted. Enter the new key in the format described in the *License.cfg* file.

Once the license has been entered into the file and the file has been saved, restart the server using the following commands:

- Stopping the server. Enter the command:
  ```
  /softs/AutomatedAnalytics_<OsName>/kxen.server stop
  ```

- Starting the server. Enter the command:
  ```
  /softs/AutomatedAnalytics_<OsName>/kxen.server start
  ```

Connecting the Client to the Server

When you fully install a server as we've done in this section, one benefit is that the client is installed alongside the server on the server machine. Thus, you can test the client/server connection right away from this machine, which we recommend to ensure everything is running smoothly.

Checking the Server License

You should now check the validity of the server license. First, launch the SAP Predictive Analytics client and open the **Help** menu, then click on **About** to view the license expiration date for the different components.

Adding Users to the User Groups

On a Microsoft Windows operating system, you'll need to add your users to the Windows users group *KxenUsers*, which was created during the installation process to enable your users to connect to the SAP Predictive Analytics server.

The exact procedure can be found in the product documentation at *http://bit.ly/2mo2OGU*.

In a Linux operating system, to allow users to use the SAP Predictive Analytics server, you must add them to the specific user group *kxenusers*, which you created in the first step of the installation process for Linux.

Creating ODBC Connections

If you need to connect SAP Predictive Analytics to different databases, you will need install specific ODBC clients, define the ODBC connections on the machine where the server is installed, and make sure that the ODBC connections that you defined can properly connect to the databases.

This process is required when you connect to the SAP HANA database, as the ODBC client is not provided by any of the SAP Predictive Analytics installations. We do not detail the process of configuring ODBC connections for every supported database. We refer you to the following documentation resources if you need to learn more:

- Connecting to your Database Management System on Windows: *http://bit.ly/2yWS10Z*
- Connecting to your Database Management System on UNIX: *http://bit.ly/2ibJOXD*
- ODBC Fine Tuning: *http://bit.ly/2zHd8S8*

3.3   Installing the SAP Predictive Analytics Client

In this section, we'll cover all the steps required to install the SAP Predictive Analytics client. We'll cover downloading the product, system requirements, the installation process itself, and the checks you should perform once the installation is complete.

Related Resources

The following documentation resource can be helpful to you:

- The SAP Predictive Analytics Client Installation Guide: *http://bit.ly/2hyfo9E*

3.3.1   Downloading the SAP Predictive Analytics Client

Please refer back to Section 3.2.1 for the general procedure for downloading SAP Predictive Analytics products.

Client versions can be found under the folder **PREDICTIVE ANALYTICS CLIENT 3** (Figure 3.5). Please note that you'll need to select the proper operating system from the drop-down menu on the right.

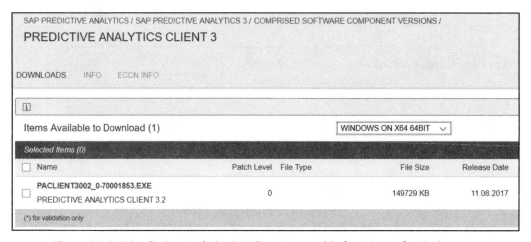

Figure 3.5 SAP Predictive Analytics 3.2 Client Executable for Microsoft Windows 64-Bit Operating System

3.3.2   System Requirements

The SAP Predictive Analytics 3.2 client can be installed on any of these systems:

- Microsoft Windows Server 2012 R2, 64-bit version
- Microsoft Windows Server 2016, 64-bit version
- Microsoft Windows 8 or 8.1, 64-bit version
- Microsoft Windows 10, 64-bit version

- Red Hat Enterprise Linux 7.0+ and 7.2 versions
- SUSE Linux Enterprise Server 11.3+ and 12.0+ versions

Some requirements for installing the SAP Predictive Analytics client include the following:

- Free space on hard disk: 475 MB recommended
- RAM: 1 GB

3.3.3 Installation Steps

For a Microsoft Windows operating system, double-click on the client executable that you downloaded to start the installation.

The installation wizard will take you through the following steps:

1. In the **Corba Name Server Information** screen, enter the TCP/IP address and port number of the SAP Predictive Analytics server.
2. It is followed by the **License Agreement** and the **Select Destination Location** screen.
3. On the **Select Components** screen, select the **Full Installation** option.
4. It is followed by the **Select Start Menu Folder** and the **Select Additional Tasks** screen. Finally, in the **Ready to Install** screen, click the **Install** button to start the installation.

For a Linux operating system, before installing the SAP Predictive Analytics client, you'll need to ensure that the correct Java Virtual Machine (JVM) or Java Runtime Environment (JRE) is set up on your computer.

Learn more about setting up the Oracle JRE at *https://docs.oracle.com/javase/8/docs/technotes/guides/install/linux_jre.html#CFHBJIIG*.

The SAP JVM can be downloaded from SAP Support Portal.

Refer to the Product Availability Matrix (PAM) to see exactly which versions are supported at *https://support.sap.com/content/dam/launchpad/en_us/pam/pam-essentials/PAM_Predictive_Analytics_31.pdf*.

The deployment procedure consists of unzipping the client .tar file in the target location, for example, in *soft/*:

```
$ gunzip -c </directory/containing/the *.TAR> | tar -xvf –
```

3.3.4   Checking the Installation

When the installation is complete, you should launch the client and connect to the SAP Predictive Analytics server to verify that the connection works. At the same time, you can check that the proper license is also in place on the server.

You can verify the version of the server in the **About** menu of the client (Figure 3.6). If the authenticated server is running correctly, the **Modeling Server Status** field will display **Modeling Server running**. This panel also allows you to see the product version of the connected server.

You can also check that the proper licenses are in place on the server by looking at the tabs **Generator Licenses**, **Component Licenses**, and **Data Access Licenses**.

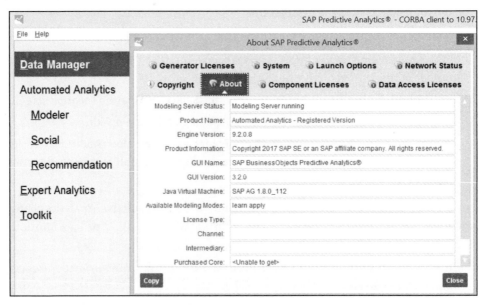

Figure 3.6 The Modeling Server Status: Running

3.3.5   Starting the Client on Linux Operating Systems

To launch the client in Linux and connect to the SAP Predictive Analytics server to create predictive models, use the following command:

```
$ AutomatedAnalyticsClient_<SYSARCH>_v<version number>/KJWizardCORBA/
KJWizardCORBA-Authenticated.sh <Name of the server>
```

3.4   Installing the Predictive Factory

In this section, we'll cover installing the Predictive Factory. As usual, we'll cover downloading the product, the system requirements, and installation and post-installation steps.

> **Related Resources**
>
> The following documentation resources can be helpful to you:
>
> - Installation & Configuration Guide: *http://bit.ly/2mpYhby*
> - Online Help: *http://bit.ly/2icKyk1*
> - Upgrading the Predictive Factory: *http://bit.ly/2zBx46h*

3.4.1   Downloading the Predictive Factory

Please refer back to Section 3.2.1 for the general procedure for downloading SAP Predictive Analytics products.

The Predictive Factory executable can be found in the folder **PREDICTIVE FACTORY 3** (Figure 3.7).

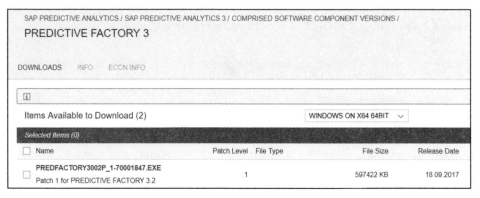

Figure 3.7 Predictive Factory 3.2 Executable for Microsoft Windows 64-Bit Operating System

3.4.2   System Requirements

The Predictive Factory 3.2 can be installed on these systems:

- Microsoft Windows Server 2012 R2, 64-bit version
- Microsoft Windows Server 2016, 64-bit version

- Microsoft Windows 8 or 8.1, 64-bit version
- Microsoft Windows 10, 64-bit version

For a corporate deployment, server operating systems are preferred. It is a best practice to install these Predictive Factory and SAP Predictive Analytics side-by side on the chosen server machine. The other characteristics required by the Predictive Factory are as follows:

- Free space on hard disk: 3 GB
- Number of cores: 8
- RAM: 32 GB (4 GB per core)

Because the Predictive Factory usually stores predictive models in local machines, you'll also need to plan for some additional free hard disk space. Table 3.2 helps you define the right amount of free space to reserve.

Free Space per Model (m) per Revision (r)	Recommendation
Small model (≤100 variables)	20 MB × m × r
Medium model (~200 variables)	200 MB × m × r
Large model (~750 variables)	1 GB × m × r

Table 3.2 Calculating the Hard Disk Space Required to Store Models

Please note that the maximum number of saved model revisions is 30 in Predictive Factory.

3.4.3   Installation Steps

Installing the Predictive Factory is straightforward. The sequence of steps is as follows:

1. In the **License Agreement** screen, accept the license agreement.
2. In the **Configure Destination Folder** screen, select the location where the product will be installed. Define and confirm the password for the Predictive Factory administrator.

The installation proceeds until complete.

3

> **Note**
>
> Please always note and remember the administrator password; otherwise, you'll be locked out of the Predictive Factory.

3.4.4 Post-Installation Steps

You'll need to complete a few more steps before you can use the Predictive Factory. These steps include retrieving and entering your license; creating servers, data connections, and users; and making sure everything is properly configured. Finally, you'll be able to create projects and predictive models.

Retrieving Your Predictive Factory License

To retrieve your Predictive Factory license, please go to *https://support.sap.com/licensekey*, where you can request keys and monitor your key requests. You can also access a detailed how-to document to guide you through the license request process at *http://bit.ly/2nmN604*.

Entering the License

One of the first post-installation steps is to enter your product license in the Predictive Factory. Right after the installation, you should launch the Predictive Factory in your browser. However, at any time, you can select **Open Predictive Factory** from the Windows **Start** menu to open the Predictive Factory in your local browser. Log on as the administrator and use the password that you entered during setup. Once logged on, open the **Settings** tab, click the pencil icon and enter the product license in **Key** field, and then click **Save**. Once the license is saved, you'll see the license's expiration date.

Adding the Automated Server

If you want to import or create automated predictive models in the Predictive Factory, you'll need to set up an automated server to process these models. Still logged on as the administrator, add a modeling server to the Predictive Factory that points to the SAP Predictive Analytics server you installed earlier by following these steps:

1. Open the **Modeling Servers** tab.

2. Click on **Add Modeling Server** and then select **Automated Server** from the list.

3. Next, give the server a **Name**. You may want to associate a **Description** to the server.

4. Then, specify the various **Connection** parameters for the server including:
   - The **Host** to connect to
   - The **Port Number** if the connection ("12345" on a default server installation)
   - The **Access Policy** (**Shared Credentials** or **Private Credentials**)
   - The credentials (**User** and **Password**) if the access policy was previously set to **Shared Credentials**

5. Once you've set the connection parameters, click the **Test connection** link to ensure that Predictive Factory properly connects to the server (Figure 3.8).

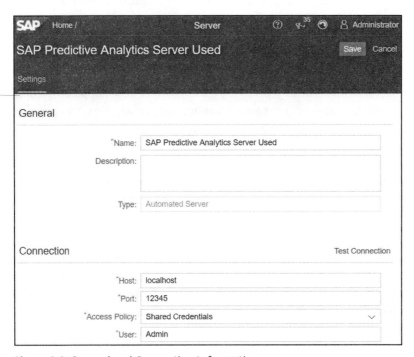

Figure 3.8 General and Connection Information

Various options can be configured on the server, including:

- The number of maximum concurrent executions
- The delegation of processing to SAP HANA
- The delegation of processing to Spark/Hadoop
- The direct in-database application

For more details on configuring these options, please refer to *http://bit.ly/2wkAyu4*.

Note

The Automated Analytics server that you want to declare as your modeling server must have the same version number as your version of Predictive Factory.

Your next step is to create the data connections associated with the server. These data connections correspond to three different purposes in the predictive projects:

- Connecting to data sources, whether text files or databases
- Connecting to repositories that store Data Manager metadata
- Connecting to repositories that store predictive models

If you are connecting to databases, you'll need to set up ODBC connections on the machine where the SAP Predictive Analytics server has been installed. If you are connecting to local files, you'll simply specify the path to these files when defining the connections.

To add a data connection:

- Click the **+** button on the **Data Connections** list.
- Give the connection a **Name** and a **Description,** then select the **Data Source Name** (if connecting to a database) or select the location of the corresponding file. If connecting to a database, you'll need to specify the access policy to the database and decide if you want to use shared or private credentials. Shared credentials need to be specified (Figure 3.9).

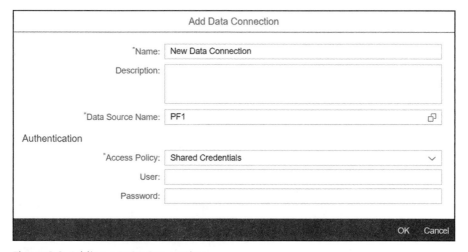

Figure 3.9 Adding a Data Connection

- Save the global server configuration once you are done defining your various data connections.

Once the server is fully configured, save the configuration. You'll be able to see the **Status** of the server (which should be **Online**) and the **Last Status Change** as well as the number of days left before the **License Expiration** date (Figure 3.10).

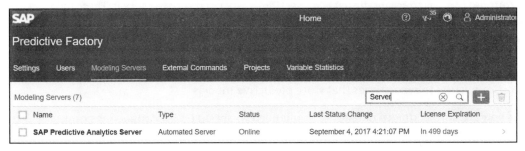

Figure 3.10 The Automated Server Is Ready!

Creating the SAP HANA Server

If you want to import your Expert Analytics models from SAP HANA to the Predictive Factory, you'll need to add an SAP HANA server and schedule regular applications of your models:

1. Open the **Modeling Servers** tab.

2. Click **Add Modeling Server** then select **SAP HANA Server** from the list.

3. As shown in Figure 3.11, you'll need to define the connection parameters to reach the SAP HANA server. Parameters to define include:
   - The **Host** (specify a name or an IP address)
   - The SAP HANA **Instance**
   - The **Mode** (**Single Container** or **Multiple Containers**)
   - Whether SSL (Secure Sockets Layer) connections are enabled
   - The credentials to connect to the SAP HANA database

4. Once you've made these settings, test the connection by clicking the **Test Connection** link.

5. The final step is to define where your models will be stored in SAP HANA. You'll need to select the relevant **Schema** from the database catalog and provide a **Name** under **Model Repository** (Figure 3.12).

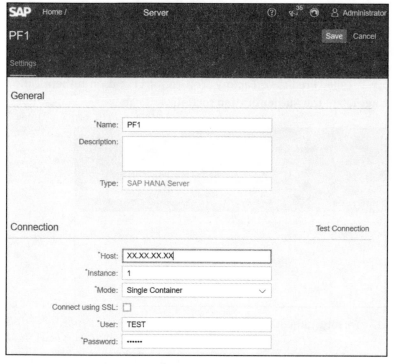

Figure 3.11 Setting Up the SAP HANA Server

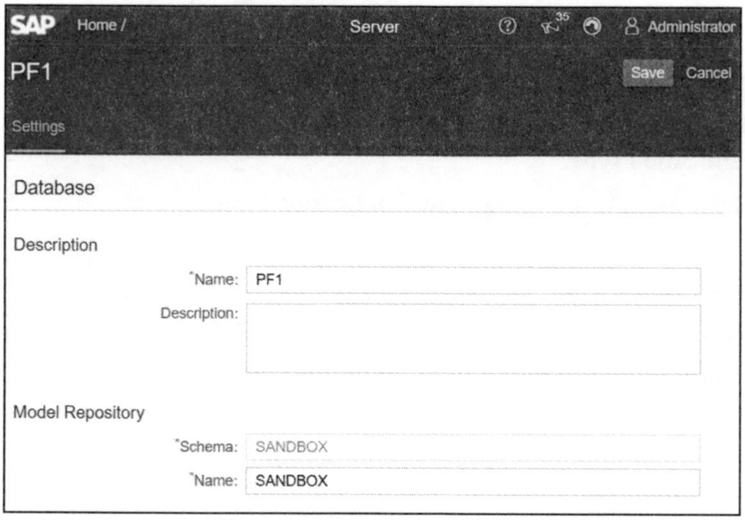

Figure 3.12 Setting Up the Model Repository

Defining the Authentication Mechanism and Setting Up Users

All users must have an account with a username and a password to access the Predictive Factory. You'll need to define the general authentication type and individually set up users and their roles in the application. The default user authentication type in Predictive Factory is called **Predictive Factory**. You can access user authentication types in the **Settings** tab in the **Authentication** section.

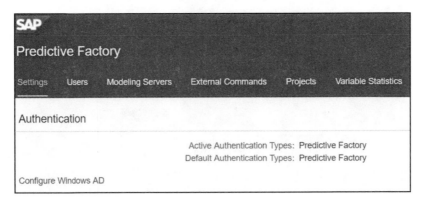

Figure 3.13 Predictive Factory Authentication

Alternatively, you can configure Windows Active Directory (Kerberos) to allow users to log in with Windows AD Authentication. For more details, please refer to *http://bit.ly/2AH0anm*.

Once you've configured the authentication, follow these steps:

1. Go to the **Settings** tab and click the edit (pencil) icon.

2. In the **Authentication** section, make sure that Windows AD has been selected as an **Active Authentication Type**.

3. Select the Windows AD option in **Default Authentication Type.**

Communication between the Predictive Factory server and its clients (browsers) uses the HTTP protocol by default. You can configure encrypted communication (HTTPS) using Secure Sockets Layer (SSL) or Transport Layer Security (TLS). For more details, please refer to *http://bit.ly/2zH7SOp*.

Next, we'll define our users by following these steps:

1. Log on to Predictive Factory with an administrator account.

2. Click on the **Users** tab.

3. Click on the **+** icon to create a new Predictive Factory user account.

4. Enter the **Name** of the person for this account.

5. If the person needs privileges in the application, select one or more **Application Roles**:

    – **Project Creator**: This user can create projects and assign projects members as analysts or project managers.

    – **Supervisor**: This user can access variable statistics for all projects.

    – **Administrator**: This user can create users and assign application roles; define access to servers, data, and repositories; and configure application settings.

6. If Predictive Factory authentication is used, enter the **Login Name** and **Password** that a user will use to log into the application.

Click **Save** and repeat the procedure for each user account you want to create (Figure 3.14).

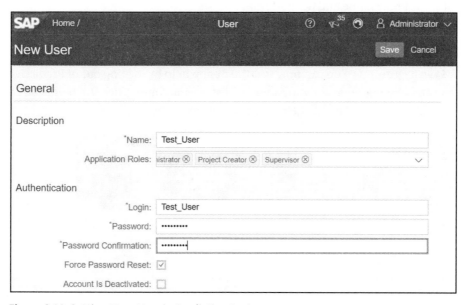

Figure 3.14 Setting Up a User in Predictive Factory

You can also create a specific password policy for the Predictive Factory, including password characters, password changes, and account lockout policy. To learn more, refer to the help page at *http://bit.ly/2hxagTk*.

Enabling In-App Help

The Predictive Factory includes in-app help content stored in the cloud that requires Internet access. If you access the Internet through a proxy, it must be enabled, and you should test in-app access before users need it.

> **Note**
>
> Help is also available in the user menu under **Documentation**. User documentation will open in a new browser window.

The procedure to activate in-app help is as follows:

1. Log on using an account with the administrator role and then click on the **Settings** tab.
2. Click the edit (pencil) icon.
3. In the **Proxy For In-App Help** section, activate the **Enabled** option.
4. Enter the **Proxy** name and the **Port** number.
5. If the proxy accesses the Internet through an identified user, enter the relevant **User** and **Password**.

Click **Save** (Figure 3.15). You can now test the in-app help by logging out of Predictive Factory and logging on again with an administrator account. Click the help icon in the main toolbar to ensure the help content appears properly.

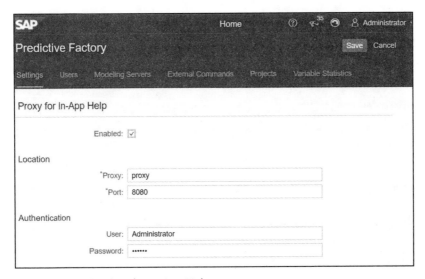

Figure 3.15 Activating the In-App Help

Enabling External Commands

An external command is a script or application that has been developed outside of SAP Predictive Analytics. You can declare the command in Predictive Factory so that analysts can schedule it as a task in their projects.

Since external commands can potentially violate security protocols, this feature is deactivated by default. Before you can declare an external command, you must enable the feature by following these steps:

1. In the Predictive Factory, select the **Settings** tab and click the edit (pencil) icon.
2. In the **External Command** section, check the **Enabled** box (Figure 3.16). Click **Save** to save the change.

Figure 3.16 Enabling External Commands

Designing external commands is covered in detail in Chapter 5.

Restarting the Predictive Factory

Predictive Factory Windows services are automatically started after installation. To stop and restart these services, when needed:

- In the Microsoft Windows **Start** menu, chose **SAP Business Intelligence • Stop Predictive Factory.**
- In the Microsoft Windows **Start** menu, chose **SAP Business Intelligence • Start Predictive Factory.**

3.5   Installing SAP Predictive Analytics Desktop

This section covers system requirements and installation and post-installation steps for the SAP Predictive Analytics desktop.

3.5.1   System Requirements

The SAP Predictive Analytics 3.2 desktop can be installed on any of these systems:

- Microsoft Windows Server 2012 R2, 64-bit version
- Microsoft Windows Server 2016, 64-bit version
- Microsoft Windows 8 or 8.1, 64-bit version
- Microsoft Windows 10, 64-bit version

The other recommended system characteristics are as follows:

- Free space on hard disk: 4 GB
- RAM: 4 GB

You must have administrator rights to install SAP Predictive Analytics desktop on the system.

3.5.2   Installation Steps

The installation process itself is rather straightforward. Double-click on the desktop executable that you downloaded.

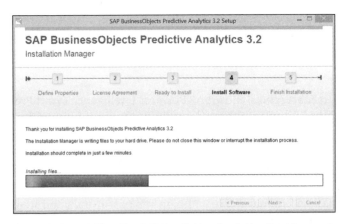

Figure 3.17 Installing the SAP Predictive Analytics Desktop

Enter the location where the software should be installed, accept the license agreement, and then start the installation (Figure 3.17).

3.5.3   Post-Installation Steps

You first post-installation step will be to enter your license. The product comes with a 30-day trial license, which is automatically activated at installation. To enter and save your license, launch the SAP Predictive Analytics desktop from the Windows **Start** menu and select **Enter keycode** located in the **Help** menu. Once you enter your license, you can see the expiration dates for the different modules of Automated Analytics and for Expert Analytics by opening **Help/About** in the menu.

Expert Analytics supports R from version 3.0 to 3.4. If you want to use R algorithms in Expert Analytics when you acquired data locally, you'll need to perform the following steps:

1. Open Expert Analytics from the main menu of SAP Predictive Analytics.

2. In the **File** menu of Expert Analytics, navigate to **Install and Configure R**.

3. In the **Installation** section, click on **Install R** (Figure 3.18).

4. Make sure you that the checkbox **Enable Open-Source R Algorithms** is selected in the **Configuration** section (Figure 3.19).

> **Tip**
>
> You can also install R locally and point Expert Analytics to the local R installation. For more information, please refer to *https://launchpad.support.sap.com/#/notes/2409635*.

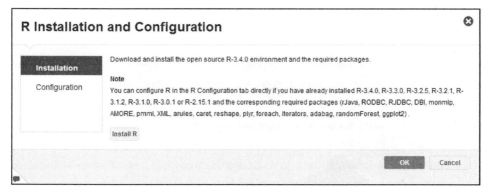

Figure 3.18 Installing R in Expert Analytics

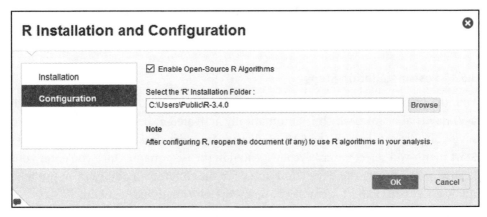

Figure 3.19 Configuring R in Expert Analytics

3.6   SAP HANA Installation Steps

SAP Predictive Analytics and SAP HANA are a powerful combo for performing predictive analytics. Before using SAP Predictive Analytics on top of SAP HANA, you need to verify the compatibility of your SAP HANA system with SAP Predictive Analytics 3.2. This compatibility is summarized in Table 3.3.

SAP HANA Support Package Stack (SPS)	SAP HANA Supported Revisions
SAP HANA 1.0 SPS 12	Revisions 122.04 and higher on the SPS 12 branch
SAP HANA 2.0 SPS 0	All revisions
SAP HANA 2.0 SPS 1	All revisions

Table 3.3 Supported SAP HANA Revisions

There are a couple of installation steps that can be taken on an SAP HANA system so that SAP HANA can be leveraged by SAP Predictive Analytics. These steps may include the following:

- **Installing the Automated Predictive Library (APL)**
  APL offers multiple benefits, as follows:
  - APL makes it possible for you to delegate the processing of some Automated Analytics and Predictive Factory models to SAP HANA. The data is processed in

SAP HANA and is not moved between the SAP HANA and the SAP Predictive Analytics systems. You can refer to this link to learn more: *http://bit.ly/2hBeKVQ*.

- Once APL is installed, some of the Automated Analytics algorithms can be used in Expert Analytics. You can refer to this link to learn more: *http://bit.ly/2hrwgv6*.

- You can use the scripting capabilities of SAP HANA and directly invoke the automated capabilities of APL in SAP HANA.

The installation of the APL is detailed in the following document: *http://bit.ly/2h1dZ7I*.

- **Installing the Predictive Analysis Library (PAL)**
  Once PAL is installed on the SAP HANA system, some of the PAL algorithms can be leveraged by Expert Analytics. You can refer to the following link to learn more on PAL (make sure to select the appropriate SAP HANA version once in the help portal): *http://bit.ly/2hzEwts*.

- **Installing an R server alongside SAP HANA**
  The benefit of setting up a R server alongside SAP HANA is to be able to leverage the extended palette of possibilities offered by the R statistical language in Expert Analytics, using SAP HANA as the data source. For more information, refer to the SAP HANA R Integration at *http://bit.ly/2A3PpdX*.

Please note that beyond the installation steps, you will need to make sure that the appropriate rights are given to the SAP HANA users that will be using SAP Predictive Analytics.

3.7 Summary

In this chapter, we covered how to install the four components that make up the SAP Predictive Analytics suite: the server, the client, the desktop, and the Predictive Factory. Now, you have a complete understanding of the possible installation options. In the next chapter, we'll take you through the important steps of any predictive analytics project.

Chapter 4
Planning a Predictive Analytics Project

This chapter describes the fundamental steps involved in a predictive analytics project. A number of methodologies are available to data analysts for planning their analytics project. This book uses the well-known CRISP-DM approach, which we'll describe in detail in this chapter.

When creating your first predictive analytics project, hopefully you'll be excited and keen to create predictive models immediately. Maybe you already have some data in mind and wonder if it contains anything interesting. After all, getting a new look at data you might already know well and extracting more value is fun and exciting.

When implementing a predictive analytics project, you must follow a quite stringent approach. After all, you need to predict something that adds value to your business. Without following a methodology, chances are you will not achieve your full potential. This is where the CRISP-DM (cross-industry standard process for data mining) methodology comes in. The methodology itself is independent of any specific tool.

In this chapter, we'll focus on the most fundamental aspects of the CRISP-DM approach. We'll introduce key steps and show you how they are supported with SAP Predictive Analytics.

To help link this theoretical methodology to a project, we'll show you how these steps can be implemented in a common marketing case. We'll pretend we're a bank that wants to know which customers are likely to sign up for a credit card. The same methodology also applies for any other predictive project; you've already seen many examples in Chapter 1, Section 1.4, and may well already have further use cases in mind.

We'll also touch on different user roles and tasks involved in a project. Whilst one person alone could implement a comprehensive project, in practice, usually a group effort is required.

Further Reading

A number of resources are available on the web if you would like to look more deeply into the CRISP-DM approach. We recommend entering "CRISP-DM" into your search engine of choice.

4.1   Introduction to the CRISP-DM Methodology

A predictive analytics project is a continuous cycle. Whilst its starting point may be clear, most projects run as long as business requirements are supported through the predictive insight. This ongoing cycle is shown in Figure 4.1.

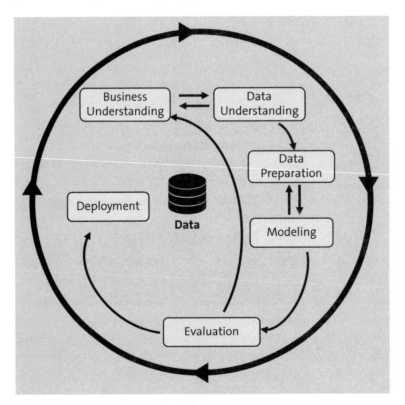

Figure 4.1 The CRISP-DM Methodology

During such a project, often, three different kinds of stakeholders collaborate, as introduced in Chapter 1. To focus on the methodology, in this chapter, we won't mention the project lead but instead focus on these roles:

- Business representatives provide insight and knowledge about the business challenges to be addressed and the benefits of the predictive models put into production.

- Data analysts understand the data and create and maintain predictive models; they can also act as a bridge between business users and IT experts, if needed.

- IT experts install and maintain the software, take care of technical data availability, and deploy the results into the relevant business processes.

The six phases of the CRISP-DM methodology involve the following considerations:

- **Business understanding**
  The project starts with a business understanding. What is the business challenge you are trying to address? You must have a clear understanding of the challenge because the following steps all work towards achieving a solution for that challenge. If the task and desired business benefit are not clearly defined, you might end up creating a predictive model that fails to add value to the business. As such, involving the relevant business departments is crucial. Chapter 1 provided details about developing a specific business case. Typically, the business understanding step is a collaboration between the data analyst and the business user.

- **Data understanding**
  Tightly linked to a business understanding is an understanding of the data; you must investigate to determine what data is available that might be related to the business requirement. Creating a predictive model requires some relevant historical data to train predictive models. If no relevant data is available or if the data is insufficient, the business case needs to be adjusted or discarded completely. The IT department will be able to advise on the data availability for this project. Most likely, during this project phase, you'll go back and forth between a business understanding to a data understanding many times. Typically, the data understanding step is a collaboration between the data analyst, the business user, and the IT administrator.

- **Data preparation**
  Once a business case has been found for which data is available, the process moves to data preparation. The relevant data might be spread over multiple systems and

needs to be linked, either physically through data movements or logically through joins.

However, joining the data is not sufficient. The data needs to be brought into the structure required by the predictive model. Often, new columns need to be created through aggregation. Even if your original data might seem rather simple, through aggregation, you could end up with hundreds, if not thousands, of columns.

Data preparation in a predictive project is similar to a data warehouse project. Many skills used in business intelligence projects will be required. In many projects, these data modeling steps will consume most of your time. Do not underestimate the effort that may be required to access the data. Whilst relevant data might exist in the corporation, you may still need to gain access to that data. The owner of the data might need convincing to grant you access. Depending on the type of data, legal aspects might present a challenge to the access to and use of the information.

Typically, the data preparation step is a collaboration between data analysts and the IT administrator, with constant feedback from business users for verification and further input on the business case.

- **Modeling**
  The data preparation phase is followed by the modeling phase. In this step, predictive models are created. Typically, many different models will be considered to achieve the best results. You will cycle back many times to the data preparation phase, working on improving the quality of your predictive models. The models are often created by the data analyst.

- **Evaluation**
  The best model found then needs to be evaluated against the earlier business understanding. The data analyst discusses the value of the model with the business users. If the model does not provide the expected business value, you would go back to the business understanding phase to start another iteration of the CRISP-DM cycle.

- **Deployment**
  If the model, however, provides the expected value, the model can move into the deployment phase. The model's insight is brought into the business process it supports. In this phase, the data analysts hand the model over to the IT department.

As long as the model is in production and providing the value to the business, the predictive project is still ongoing. A model needs to be regularly assessed to determine if it still provides the business value or if the model's quality has deteriorated over time. Any predictive model will lose some quality if not retrained regularly, as the data on which the model is based changes over time. An old model would then be describing an outdated situation, and therefore, the predictive quality of the model would suffer. Also, you'll need to assess whether your business requirements have changed, which can require the creation of a completely different predictive model. Typically, the deployment step is done either by the data analyst or, for more complex requirements, by the IT expert.

4.2   Running a Project

In this section, we'll explain the individual steps of a project both conceptually and practically, using a common example. Imagine we are a bank and want to improve the effectiveness of our marketing campaigns. No matter which industry you work in, or which process you would like to optimize, the steps of your own project will be similar.

Please note that this chapter focuses only on the most important aspects of the CRISP-DM methodology. We hope this overview will help you better understand the overall idea behind SAP Predictive Analytics and how to utilize it. Additional details about the CRISP-DM methodology are valuable but beyond the scope of this book, and we recommend further reading on the methodology.

In this section, we assume that the system infrastructure is already in place and that any relevant software has already been installed. (See Chapter 3 for guidance on installation.) This section will be organized according to the phases in the CRISP-DM methodology: business understanding, data understanding, data preparation, modeling, evaluation, and deployment.

4.2.1   Business Understanding

Let's get started with the business understanding. To help create meaningful business cases that can be supported with a predictive model, we suggest starting a discussion about your company's or department's strategy and challenges. The data analyst should try to understand the business and its challenges in detail. Do not jump to early conclusions and be sure to listen and question the business user. What does your company want to achieve, or on a more detailed level, what are the expectations of the different departments? Your company might be focusing on winning new customers, cross-selling additional products to existing customers, or preventing existing customers from leaving. Find out about the strategy and tactics and be specific. Then, prioritize your various goals and start with the most important ones. For our bank, one focus area was strengthening relationships with existing customers that only currently have a single account.

Now, look for activities that help achieve your chosen goal. In our bank, we can strengthen relationships by contacting existing customers to cross-sell complementary products. Adding a credit card to the account, for example, would be a desirable goal.

> **Use Case**
> In order to give you a hands-on learning experience, we decided to pick a use case for which we have real and relevant data available. We'll also discuss the credit card use case in more detail in Chapter 14.

Next, try to identify scarce resources or bottlenecks that are preventing the success of your chosen activity. This bottleneck could be a million different things but often is something common, such as limited financial resources or manpower. For our bank, a limitation was how often we have the opportunity to communicate with our customers. Banks cannot contact customers as often as they would like. Too many emails, letters, or phone calls would overwhelm and annoy customers. So, the number of interactions is limited. At the same time, each interaction comes at a price, so costs are another bottleneck. Therefore, when we have the opportunity to get in touch with the customer, we want to maximize the value of this interaction. We only want to contact customers for whom the offer is relevant.

These steps have shown to be effective in developing a scenario and business case:

1. First, know the strategic direction the company or department wants to move towards.

2. Then, identify activities that support the strategy.

3. Finally, find a resource that is limited and therefore restricts the success of that activity.

A predictive model can maximize the value this limited resource can deliver. As simple as this concept is, you may want to get back to it often to challenge and shape a predictive scenario.

For our bank, we have now identified the facts we need for our use case, as shown in Table 4.1.

Topic	Answer
Aim	Strengthen relationships with existing customers, who currently have only a single account.
Activities	Contact existing customers who only have a single account to cross-sell complementary products. Adding a credit card would be a desirable goal.
Scarce resources	Number of interactions with customers.
Predictive	Maximize the value of a communication by recommending only the most relevant products, personalizing communication beyond conventional customer segments.

Table 4.1 Developing a Banking Use Case

Going through these topics forms a good basis for defining our business case. We're almost done; we just need to add some more context. In our case, we should specify exactly which customers to include and which to exclude. Also, we need to specify a time frame in the future when we hope the customer will sign up for the credit card. The following question can help finalize a business case, though many others are possible:

Which of our customers that currently own only a single account and have never had a credit card with us are likely to sign up for a credit card in the next 3 months?

Notice how the group of customers is clearly defined. For instance, customers who used to have a credit card are excluded, as they have already rejected the product for some reason. Also, notice the time frame. We specifically identify customers likely to sign up in the next 3 months. The next time we contact our customers, the ones with the highest affinity for a credit card can receive a suitable suggestion. Instead of working with gut feel, we can optimize the process with predictive insight. If the marketing department agrees that such a prediction would add value, we have a relevant use case, and we can create a predictive model for it.

Don't hold back—create multiple such use cases. You can then prioritize them and implement the best candidate. Work from one model can often be reused for another, and creating subsequent models might be even faster (see Section 4.2.3).

To help the project along, try to find management sponsors who are willing to throw their weight behind this project. Such support can often do wonders.

If you skipped the previous steps, you may well be able to create a strong predictive model, but would it really predict anything that brings value to the business? Your model might find some patterns that are irrelevant to the business. For example, let's say we have a prediction that, if a customer bought product A, there is an extremely high chance he will also purchase product B. That model was created by an analyst who had skipped the business understanding. It turned out that the two products were part of a bundle. Whoever purchased product A also had to purchase product B. Needless to say, this model did not add any new insight, a good part of the analyst's efforts was done in vain, and time was lost.

Similarly, if you are asked to work with a certain database and "see what you can find" with a predictive model, you should be cautious. If what to look for is not clear, you might find interesting things, but none of them will bring any business value. For a better chance of success, define the business case first.

Use Case: Demand Forecast for a Manufacturing Business

An improved demand forecast can help a manufacturer in many different ways. Appropriate quantities can be produced to deliver goods when ordered, without having to stockpile large quantities, tying up space in the warehouse and financial capital. To provide business value, the demand forecast needs to be more accurate than the current process. Let's fill in our template for developing use cases, see Table 4.2.

With this template, we can explore the following question: What are the expected sales quantities for the 100 most important products in 3 months' time?

Topic	Answer
Aim	Increase customer satisfaction
Activities	Deliver ordered quantities on time in the correct quantity
Scarce resources	Warehouse space and capital tied up in material stored in the warehouse
Predictive	Make best use of warehouse space and capital by producing appropriate quantities, enough but not too much.

Table 4.2 Developing a Manufacturing Use Case

Use Case: Identify Insurance Fraud

Insurance companies need to verify that an insurance claim is legitimate and not fraudulent. Due to the large number of claims, not every case can be investigated as thoroughly as might be desired. The compliance team needs to focus on the most suspicious cases. SAP Predictive Analytics can help prioritize claims where the team should be spending their time to achieve best results. Let's fill in our template, as shown in Table 4.3. Using this template, we can explore the following question: What is the probability that a liability insurance claim is fraudulent?

Topic	Answer
Aim	Reduce insurance fraud
Activities	Verify insurance claims are justified
Scarce resources	Manpower available to investigate individual claims
Predictive	Make best use of the employee's time by identifying the most suspicious claims

Table 4.3 Developing an Insurance Use Case

4.2.2   Data Understanding

Based on the selected use case, you now need to find out what data is available to support that use case. All the relevant data might already be held in a single place, or the data may be spread out over multiple systems. Find out what data exists and how to access that data. Who can grant access to the data, and how can the data be accessed technically? You'll also want to look at the data to get an initial understanding of what is there.

Our bank may want to use personal information about customers, such as gender or address. Another interesting data source can be the activity in the customer's account. What was the average balance in the account last year; what was the maximum or the minimum balance? How many days was the account overdrawn last year? A further example of a valuable data source could be the customer relationship management (CRM) system. How many days ago was the last interaction with the customer? To which previous marketing campaigns has the customer responded? This data will be available somewhere. In this phase, you'll find out what exactly is available. Especially in larger organizations, this fact finding can take time. And, once a relevant source of data has been found, you may not have access to it. The owner of the data might not be willing to grant you access right away. Having the backing of the business department, ideally with a management sponsor, can help your case.

When you have access to the data, you'll want to look inside and find out what exactly is held in that database. What tables exist, which columns, how many rows? And within the rows, what information is held? How many values are missing? Are there any database views you can leverage that already join some tables? Looking at a first set of data might lead to ideas for further data sources that you have not yet considered.

SAP Predictive Analytics contains some functionality to gain an understanding of the data. In the Automated Analytics Windows client, you can select a data source and then click on the magnifying glass button to open a screen showing summaries of the data, as shown in Figure 4.2.

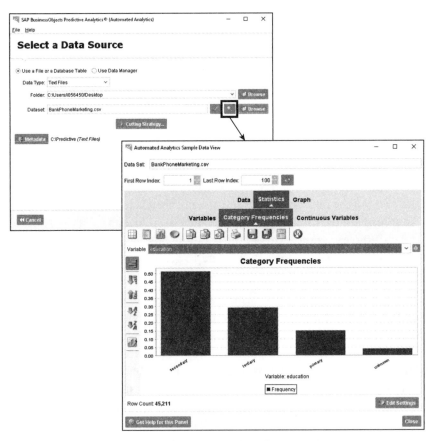

Figure 4.2 Data Understanding in Automated Analytics

The number of missing values is shown for each column. For text columns, you can see which values appear and how often the same values appear. For continuous variables (numerical), you can see minimums, maximums, means, and standard deviations. In addition, the **Category Frequency** tab shows the overall distribution of numerical values.

Within Expert Analytics, you can find additional functionality to understand the data. Right-click on the first node on the left-hand side in Expert Analytics and select **Run up to Here**. Then, click through the **Data Insight** icons on the right-hand side, as shown in Figure 4.3.

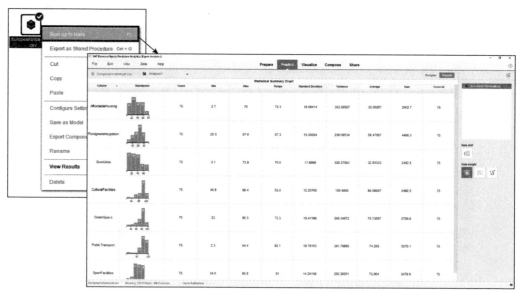

Figure 4.3 Data Understanding in Expert Analytics

However, leveraging a dedicated business intelligence tool for the data understanding phase can also be useful. SAP Lumira or SAP Analytics Cloud are two options from the SAP portfolio.

4.2.3   Data Preparation

By now, you have a clearly defined business case and a good understanding of the available data. Now, the data needs to be joined and structured for the purpose of predictive analytics. Most likely, this phase will require the most time in your SAP Predictive Analytics project. Note that SAP Predictive Analytics connects to a single data source. Therefore, if your data is spread over multiple sources, the first step is to bring together the data before using SAP Predictive Analytics. You can move data physically into a single place, for instance, with an extract, transform and load (ETL) tool.

Alternatively, you can logically join the data without permanent duplication. If SAP HANA is the data source, you can use SAP HANA smart data access if your SAP HANA license allows this. The smart data concept connects SAP HANA to an external source and makes the external data appear as a table in SAP HANA. Now, SAP Predictive Analytics can connect with SAP HANA as a single system, although the data is really spread over multiple places. Data retrieval will take longer, of course, because the data must be retrieved each time it is accessed.

With the data now available in a single place, the individual tables can be joined within the database, for example, by using database views or calculation views in SAP HANA. These views allow IT experts to provide business domain-specific content.

However, creating database views is optional; the data can also be joined in the Data Manager of SAP Predictive Analytics, which provides a powerful semantic layer. Data analysts can also leverage the Data Manager to model the data beyond the structure provided by IT. Please note that Expert Analytics cannot directly access the Data Manager layer. As a workaround, you can save the structure created by Data Manager as a database view, which Expert Analytics can then connect to.

Let's look closer at some common options for preparing your data for a predictive use case.

Aggregating Transactional Data

Most likely, your data is stored in a transactional format. For our bank example, transactions that have occurred in an account are available row by row, with one transaction per row. After all, the data is coming from transactional systems where the data is stored in that format; a typical example is shown in Figure 4.4. For use in most predictive models, the data must be in a different format, however. All items whose future behavior you would like to predict need to be described in a single row of data. If our bank wants to predict the behavior of a customer, each customer must be described in a single row. The transactional data (salary transfers, withdrawals, direct debits, etc.) needs to be restructured, and further data manipulation might also be required.

Account ID	Date	Transaction Type	Amount	New balance
8105	04. Jan	Withdrawal	-300	2400
8105	25. Jan	Salary	4000	6400
8105	30. Jan	Transfer	-2000	4400
8105	07. Feb	Withdrawal	-200	4200
8105	15. Feb	Withdrawal	-100	4100
8105	24. Feb	Salary	4000	8100
8105	27. Feb	Withdrawal	-50	8050
8105	28. Feb	Transfer	-2000	6050
8105	9. Mar	Withdrawal	-100	5950
8105	24. Mar	Salary	4000	9950
8105	28. Mar	Withdrawal	-250	9700
8105	30. Mar	Transfer	-2000	7700
8105	25. Apr	Salary	4000	11700
8105	27. Apr	Withdrawal	-250	11450
8105	28. Apr	Transfer	-2000	9450
8105	3. May	Withdrawal	-500	8950
8105	19. May	Transfer	-700	8250
8105	25. May	Salary	4000	12250
8105	26. May	Withdrawal	-300	11950
8105	29. May	Withdrawal	-100	11850
8105	30. May	Transfer	-2000	9850
8105	23. Jun	Salary	4000	13850
8105	30. Jun	Transfer	-2000	11850
8105	30. Jun	Withdrawal	-300	11550

Figure 4.4 Raw Transactional Data

These data manipulations can be defined in the graphical interface of Data Manager. With a few clicks, you can create hundreds or even thousands of aggregates (i.e., average, sum, min), turning rows of data into columns. Dynamically creating these aggregations can save time by avoiding the manual hardcoding of dozens, hundreds, or even thousands of variables in SQL. Note that the Data Manager transforms the data through SQL on the fly; the results do not have to be persisted in a new table. Therefore, the Data Manager can be easily added to a project, is rather lightweight, and does not complicate the architecture.

Remember to Leverage the Data Manager

The Data Manager graphically structures the data for use in predictive models, for instance, by joining tables and views and turning transactional data through aggregations into the appropriate format.

Our bank can use the Data Manager to transform the transaction data within an account into information such as the following:

- Minimum balance last quarter
- Minimum balance two quarters ago
- Difference between minimum balances of the last two quarters

Let's look at an example. Figure 4.4 shows the transactions of an individual account. Whilst a lot of information is available for a predictive model, due to its structure, we cannot use the data in the predictive model.

By using the Data Manager, we can restructure the data, a process done logically; that is, you do not need to physically duplicate the data into a new table. Since we want to predict a customer's behavior, we'll aggregate the data on the granularity of the customer. The results are shown in Figure 4.5, which clearly shows that the account of this person had a minimum amount of 2,400 Euros two quarters ago and 8,250 Euros last quarter. The amount has increased by 5,850 Euros. Similarly, we could calculate the increase in percent, and many further aggregations are possible.

Account ID	Min Balance Last Quarter	Min Balance Two Quarters Ago	Difference in Minimum Amounts
8105	2400	8250	5850

Figure 4.5 Raw Data Aggregated into Columns

At this point, we can understand the history of the item or the person we want to predict. In Data Manager terminology, the subject we are modeling is called an *entity*. We will use this term even though using the Data Manager is not compulsory; the term is useful even if you choose to connect directly to the database without the Data Manager.

Target Variable and Dynamic Time Concept

To carry out a prediction, we're still missing the most important column, our target variable. The target variable takes two roles. When training a model, the target variable is a flag indicating whether the entity has performed the behavior we are looking for in the past. When predicting the future, this information will tell us the probability of another entity performing the same behavior in the specified time frame.

This example shows clearly that we are looking at the same situation from different moments in time. Our use case defined in Section 4.2.1 specifies that we want to predict the probability of a customer signing up for a credit card within the next 3 months. We are looking into the future and call this 3-month period the *future target period*. To predict who will sign up in the next 3 months, we need to know who signed up in the previous 3 months. We call this time frame the *past target period*. This information allows us to train the model. The two target periods are shown in Figure 4.6.

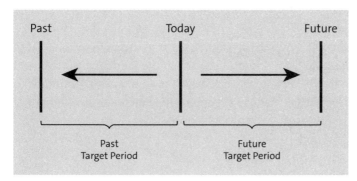

Figure 4.6 Target Periods

The past target period allows us to calculate the target variable on which to train the model. Did a person sign up for the credit card or not? To find a rule to predict the behavior, we need to collect information about how that person behaved before the target period. In other words, when training a model, we'll pretend we are at the beginning of the past target period and try to describe the person as we know them at that moment. Let's say the person is exactly 30 years old at that point. An age variable would hold that value. To predict the future, we are now back at today. The length of the future target period is clear (3 months), but as we are working with the actual future, we don't know what will happen. However, now we can look at our customers from today's point of view and describe these people accordingly. The customer we looked at earlier is slightly older, for instance; now the age variable for him would show 30.25.

You may notice how the time plays into these variables. The term *last quarter* in Figure 4.5 is dynamic on purpose. Every time the data is accessed a date parameter called a *time-stamp* can be passed, and such time-related variables find the appropriate context. So instead of hardcoding a variable for the "1st Quarter 2018," the logic remains dynamic, and the exact time frame of "Last Quarter" depends on the date parameter that was passed. Similarly, the time-context is also taken into account for the target variable. The target variable describes the behavior you want to forecast. To predict who will sign up for a credit card next quarter, you can look at who signed up for a credit card in the previous quarter and how the customers behaved before the quarter in which the card was adopted. Again, the data logic can be reused constantly for both training and applying the model whenever needed.

This dynamic time concept is crucial for having scalable predictive machinery in place. Time-related columns must adjust themselves as described without requiring constant manual interventions. The Data Manager takes care of these adjustments automatically.

From the transactional raw data, you can derive thousands of variables to consider in the modeling phase. Don't hold back—models created in the Predictive Factory and Automated Analytics can handle extremely wide datasets with tens of thousands of variables. Bring in any information that could possibly help increase the strength of the predictive model. Later on, during the modeling phase, variables that don't provide value to the predictive model will be excluded from models created in the Predictive Factory and Automated Analytics.

Dealing with Dates

In the data preparation phase, you can also turn calendar dates into time durations. We generally do not recommend using date columns in the data for training a model. The exact date when a customer was born, for instance, is almost always irrelevant. Relatively few customers will be born on the same date. And if the exact date is used, the tool will not know how different dates are related to each other. Instead turn a birth date into the person's age, and now, you have a column that might be meaningful for your model.

Please do not think that dates were unimportant—they are! Just try to turn dates into durations, which are often more meaningful for predictive analytics.

Data Quality and Missing Values

Of course, predictive models benefit from good data quality. The better the data quality, the better your chances for a good predictive model. However, models created in the Predictive Factory and Automated Analytics can handle missing values in the data. Missing values in a column (whether text or numerical) are treated as a unique group. Often rows with missing data in a column have something in common. This commonality might help improve the predictive model. Only when using Expert Analytics would you need to conventionally handle missing values, typically during the modeling phase.

Reusing Content

The data logic you create can be reused for many other predictive models. A customer's history is a customer's history and remains valid for different use cases, no matter whether you create a purchasing affinity model or a churn analysis model or something else.

Not only can you reuse the same data content, you can also reuse the data logic that has been implemented!

4.2.4 Modeling

By now, we have our business case and supporting data structured for use in our predictive models. We can start the predictive modeling process. A decisive phase, the modeling step is the most exciting for many users. You'll try to find the most suitable predictive model to help the business case that was chosen initially. You probably know by now that, in SAP Predictive Analytics, you can choose from two different approaches: You can take an automated or a more conventional expert approach. Our suggested approach is shown in Figure 4.7.

> **Reminder**
>
> You must have your business case clearly defined during the business understanding phase. You want to create a predictive model that forecasts information that is valuable to a business dimension. If the business case is not clearly defined, you might create a mathematically strong and beautiful model, but you'll regret not spending more time on the business case if your business does not derive any value from the model.

Figure 4.7 Choice of Modeling Environments

Predictive Factory and Automated Analytics

We recommend you leverage the automated approach of developing models in the browser-based Predictive Factory whenever possible. Its framework allows you to create and maintain hundreds or thousands of predictive models with relative ease. If you do not have a data science background, the automated approach allows you to create predictive models without the need for a degree in statistics. If you are a data scientist, the approach will help to improve your productivity by freeing up your time.

The toolset is currently in a transitional phase, and some activities require you to use the desktop installation of Automated Analytics.

The automated approaches use a sophisticated framework to create predictive models independently, adjusting themselves to the datasets you provide without requiring manual intervention. These automated approaches always follow best practices and can handle the challenges an expert user would normally deal with manually, including the following:

- Handling missing values
- Handling outliers
- Increasing robustness by binning text variables and banding numerical values (grouping the values of a variable to support the quality of the predictive model)
- Selecting which variables to use in the predictive model
- Creating and testing many different models
- Selecting the best model

The efficiency and scalability of these automated approaches free up the data analyst's time, which can be better spent on high-value activities, such as:

- Supporting and experimenting with additional business challenges through predictive models
- Deepening your understanding of business challenges to address more specifically
- Enriching the underlying datasets to capture additional trends
- Increasing the involvement in how the predictive models are being used in the business department, strengthening the positioning of trusted advisors to improve business processes

A number of core machine learning functionalities are provided in the automated approach. The business questions you are trying to solve determine which one of the following functionalities you'll choose:

- Classification models predict a yes/no probability, answering, for example, "Will a prospect buy a product or not in the next six months?" or "Will an employee quit his job in the next year?"

- Regression models estimate a numerical value that is not a probability, answering, for example, "What is the estimated value of a used car?" or "By how many minutes is a flight likely to arrive late?"

- Time series forecasting models are regularly occurring measures that answer, for example, "What is a company's cash flow per day for the next two weeks?" or "How many quantities of each product will the company sell every month for the next year?"

- Clustering models find groups of items that appear to be similar, answering, for example, "Which of my retail stores have similar sales patterns?" or "Which groups of customers behave similarly, and what makes them similar?"

- Recommendation models find events that often occur together. A retailer can use this functionality to recommend complementary products. This model is particularly suitable for companies with hundreds or thousands of products. If your company is selling only a few products, you should create classification models to estimate a person's purchasing affinity for each individual product.

- Social Network Analysis is similar to, but goes far beyond, the recommendation model and can be used for rather different use cases. By creating a network of information, Social Network Analysis can determine complex relationships through link analysis. A telecommunications company could use it to create a communication network of its customers to identify key customers to pay special attention to. The company can therefore be proactive and try to prevent such customers from switching to the competition and possibly taking other customers with them.

The classification, regression, and time series models are available in the browser-based Predictive Factory. Clustering models, recommendation models, and Social Network Analysis require the Windows interface of SAP Predictive Analytics.

Expert Analytics

Even if you consider yourself an expert, we believe Automated Analytics could be a great tool in your portfolio. It is efficient, can create and maintain a large number of strong models, and can really be your workhorse. Whenever you would like to take a more conventional approach with individual algorithms, then go into Expert Analytics.

Using a graphical interface, you can create analytical workflows to model complex requirements. Whilst Expert Analytics can be used on a wide range of data sources, when connecting to SAP HANA, additional algorithms become available. Should these additional algorithms not suffice, the functionality can be extended through R syntax. R is an open source language with a vast amount of functionality for predictive purposes.

Please note that Expert Analytics is meant for users comfortable with conventional algorithms. All the steps handled automatically by models created in the Predictive Factory or Automated Analytics will have to be manually performed. You'll need to handle missing values (delete rows, delete columns, estimate missing values); deal with outliers (ensure they don't distort the model); select different predictive algorithms; configure and fine-tune them; select the best model; etc.

4.2.5   Evaluation

By now, we've put in our best effort to get the best predictive model for our business case. However, we'll still need to thoroughly verify whether the model really does meet expectations.

Does the model provide the value we expect based on the business case? To answer this question, you should verify how the model compares to the status quo. Imagine, in our bank, that we call 1,000 customers every month to promote our credit card. How many people usually sign up each time?

Hopefully, our call center is not randomly calling customers from our CRM database. This behavior would easily be beaten by a predictive model. Maybe the call center is selecting their target audience today by applying some selection criteria, like people over 40 who withdraw money abroad. If they like to travel, they might appreciate another credit card. This selection might result in a larger number of signed credit card contracts. Our predictive model only provides a value to the business if it is better than the existing process.

To evaluate the model, the analyst needs to meet with the business stakeholder to discuss the model's performance to ensure the desired goals are being met. Also, you should discuss the individual steps of the model creation process to see if any concerns about the predictive model or its use have arisen. For example, you might notice that a data source is used that was once available but that cannot be relied upon in the future. Therefore, you'll need to ensure that data's availability or remove it from the project.

If a predictive model appears to be too good to be true, maybe it is too good to be true. This problem can easily occur if "forbidden data" was used when training the model.

In classification, only the target variable is allowed to refer to the future. Imagine our bank wants to predict who will sign up for a credit card in the next 3 months. When you train that model, you'll look who signed up for a card in the last 3 months—the past target period. No other information may come from this period, or the model will be incorrect. Imagine you use a predictor variable that counts the number of credit card transactions during the past target period. The model will be extremely strong; if a customer has charged at least one credit card transaction, he/she must have a credit card. However, this incorrect model would not be able to predict the truly unknown future, and you do not know how many card transactions the person will have. Carefully judge your predictor variables.

A model's quality is measured differently depending on the type of analysis, which we'll discuss in detail in later chapters of this book. If your model is found to be good for productive use, you can move to the deployment phase.

However, if the model does not meet the criteria, you'll have to go back to the business understanding. You might try restating the business case differently. Maybe the model was not strong enough to predict activity next quarter. If you make the time frame longer, the model might improve because it will have more data available and therefore can possibly find a better pattern. Or, maybe you need to find a completely different business case to optimize with a predictive model.

4.2.6 Deployment

If your project has made it to the deployment phase, congratulations! You've created a predictive model that delivers the desired business value. But, your project is not quite finished. After all, you need to bring the model's insight into your business processes to make different, better decisions. Also, the quality of any predictive model deteriorates over time. When a model is created, it describes the situation as well as it can at that moment. The situation will change over time, though; your customer's behavior might be slightly different next month compared to today. So, the model will not fit as well as it did, as it had been created for a different situation. As a result, your models need to be retrained every so often to ensure they are providing the best possible value.

SAP Predictive Analytics provides a number of options to bring your predictions into the business processes. The options give you flexibility for your different use cases. In the following sections, we will look at recurring/batch scoring and real-time scoring and then move on to the topic of model maintenance.

Recurring/Batch Scoring

Your model can be applied to new data to produce predictions, which can be written into a database or into a file, where business applications can access the predictions. You can manually create these forecasts (which can be probabilities or scores) in the Predictive Factory user interface in SAP Predictive Analytics and write them into a database. We recommend using this option when prototyping a model.

For ongoing use, which should not require manual intervention, you can use the Predictive Factory. The model you created can be imported into the Predictive Factory, which can apply the model and output forecasts on a schedule of your choosing. Whenever predictions are saved, you can either overwrite the previous forecast, or you can add the prediction into a specified table to build up a history, which is useful for seeing how predictions change over time. For our bank, this information could tell us whether the purchasing affinity of an individual customer is rising or falling.

If you have specific requirements for applying the model in batches, which might not be possible with the current version of the Predictive Factory, then you can leverage a scripting language from Automated Analytics called *KxShell Script*. Everything that Automated Analytics does can be scripted, and this script can be modified to cater to specific requirements. You do not need to create scripts from scratch. You can carry out a task in Automated Analytics to obtain a script file that contains all the logic of your steps, making custom scripting more efficient. Access your script files in the **Save/Export** menu in Automated Analytics; look for the **Expert Shell Script** option.

Using the recurring/batch scoring option is suitable if your predictions are expected to be rather static, without constant fluctuations. If predictions are calculated based on your data warehouse, which is filled with data daily, you can create and persist the scores after the data load.

Real-Time Scoring

If, however, your use case requires real-time calculations of predictions, the previous recurring/batch scoring will not suffice because new data is constantly received. The predictions might be too old because the latest information was not available. In this case, you can recalculate the predictions on the fly using Automated Analytics to output the trained model as calculation logic, using the option **Generate Source Code**. This option is available for classification, regression, and clustering models.

The logic can be saved in various programming languages, such as SQL syntax for various databases, Java code, or even SAS code. The SQL syntax can be embedded directly as an additional column into a view or stored procedure. The programming code can be embedded directly into your application. You can also produce SQL syntax to create a user-defined function in SAP HANA, which could produce predictions based on parameter values from your applications.

You can also apply the model while data is being streamed into SAP HANA. Just generate the source code for type **CCL code for SAP HANA Smart Data Streaming**, and the logic can be embedded into your streaming process. The scores can be calculated and acted upon even before the data is written into SAP HANA.

Model Maintenance

Your model is now deployed in production, delivering value to your business. The model still needs to be maintained to keep its best possible predictive strength, or it will deteriorate over time, as explained at the beginning of this section. As all data changes over time, all models deteriorate automatically.

Of course, you could manually open the trained and saved model in SAP Predictive Analytics, manually retrain it, and create predictions for your business process. Whilst this process may be sufficient for prototyping, in productive use, the process needs to be automated to efficiently maintain all models. Automation is possible either through the Predictive Factory or through scripting.

The Predictive Factory is the server component that maintains the models automatically. You can define a recurring schedule that determines how often the Predictive Factory should look at a specific model, as shown in Figure 4.8. For automated models, the Predictive Factory assesses whether the input data has changed significantly since the model was trained, by comparing a summary of the current data with summary statistics of the data that was collected when the model was trained. Only if the data is significantly different will the Predictive Factory either notify you or automatically retrain the model, according to your preference. A model created in Expert Analytics connected to SAP HANA can be imported into the Predictive Factory and can be retrained and applied every time at the scheduled interval.

If you've chosen an automated model for real-time scoring deployment, you have one further step: You'll need to update the scoring equation in your application.

Alternatively, if you have requirements that the Predictive Factory can't meet, you can leverage the KxShell Script option. Similar to the model creation phase, you can use the scripting language to implement more complex requirements.

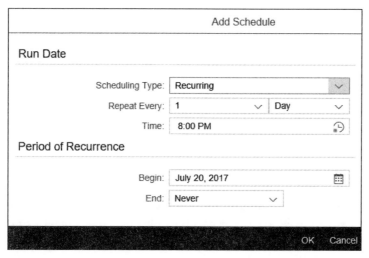

Figure 4.8 Scheduling Model Retraining in the Predictive Factory

4.3   Summary

Now, you're familiar with how to use the CRISP-DM methodology to implement a predictive analytics project. In this chapter, we introduced the individual steps of the methodology and explained how these steps can be implemented with SAP Predictive Analytics. Hopefully, our example bank targeting customers for a credit card made the discussion a bit easier and less abstract.

Apologies for mentioning quite a few times that you must have a clear business case identified in the first step. We are quite obsessed with this requirement because having a clear use case is fundamental for any successful predictive project. However, don't make finding a business use a huge scientific project either. Obtain a promising use case and start your predictive journey.

So, after the theory, let's have a look at the actual software. In the next chapter, you'll become familiar with the Predictive Factory interface, where you'll create and maintain your predictive models.

PART II
The Predictive Factory

Chapter 5
Predictive Factory

The Predictive Factory is where models are deployed (for result production, model control, and model retraining) and, increasingly, created. In this chapter, we'll provide a high-level view of the Predictive Factory's philosophy and how it works.

This chapter will introduce you to the Predictive Factory by describing the philosophy behind the Predictive Factory and how to use it to fulfill the promises of massive predictive analytics. How to use the Predictive Factory is described in detail in Chapter 6, Chapter 7, and Chapter 8 (model creation using the Predictive Factory) and in Chapter 9 (deployment in Predictive Factory). Setting up servers and users is described in Chapter 3.

In this chapter, we'll discuss the core of the philosophy behind the Predictive Factory and its project-oriented approach. Additionally, we'll describe how to set up *external executables*, which allow you to schedule the execution of third-party software from the Predictive Factory, and we'll take a quick look at variable statistics.

5.1 Predictive Factory: End-to-End Modeling

The Predictive Factory schedules tasks, defined at the model level, to handle the overall lifecycle of SAP Predictive Analytics models. SAP Predictive Analytics' main purpose is to industrialize the production of predictive results for companies and enable businesses to scale up to cover the needs of various lines of business (LOBs). Within a unified Predictive Factory interface, you can perform the following tasks:

- Creating models
- Deploying models in batches
- Controlling models
- Retraining models

Putting models in production requires batch or real-time deployment, controlling models, and retraining models, as follows:

- **Result production**
  When looking at the predictive process, after dataset design and model creation, the next step is to produce results: probabilities for classification models, values for regression and time series forecasting models, and groups for clustering models. The Predictive Factory provides scheduling capabilities for batch producing results but does not provide real-time deployment capabilities, which are described in Chapter 16.

- **Control**
  Result production, however, is not the end of the process, because model quality eventually degrades, making models not suitable for production. As a result, the model's ability to accurately make predictions decreases as the data changes. Data change is linked to the evolution of the environment and of the behavior of the object under study. Controlling model quality is the second capability provided by the Predictive Factory.

- **Retraining**
  When model quality degrades, a model will need to be retrained. We cannot expect that the same model quality will be achieved after retraining, but retrained models have the best possible quality at a given time. Model retraining is the third feature of the Predictive Factory.

For time series forecasting, described in detail in Chapter 8, the control capability is not used because models are systematically rebuilt before being used. For classification, regression, and clustering, the three steps are provided.

Clustering is rather specific as training clustering models is rarely fully automated unless the model serves as a technical step of a broader predictive analytics project using segmented modeling. Only variable distribution deviation can be used for non-supervised clustering models. These tasks may also be used for Expert Analytics flows imported into the Predictive Factory.

The Predictive Factory uses a project-oriented approach. A project contains a set of models used to address a business question. However, flexibility is provided to users to organize projects as they see fit. Projects are assigned to users, called *members* within the project, with different levels of interaction.

5.2   Creating a Project

When connecting to Predictive Factory, the landing page contains tabs for **Settings**, **Users**, **Modeling Servers**, **External Commands**, **Projects**, and **Variable Statistics** (Figure 5.1).

Figure 5.1 Available Tabs in the Predictive Factory

Note

Chapter 3 describes settings, users, and modeling servers in more detail. Data connectivity provided through the server connection must be defined as discussed in Chapter 3, Section 3.4.4.

When you have project creation rights as described in Chapter 3, you can create a project. In the **Projects** tab, create a new model by clicking on the plus **+** button.

The project creation process includes providing the project a name and description, specifying the **Members** who can access the project and their **Project Roles**, and specifying the **Modeling Server** to be used, as shown in Figure 5.2.

You can add as many users as required, and two **Project Roles** are available: **Project Manager** and **Analyst**. Project managers have control over the project and can create models, define tasks, etc. Analysts are only given reporting capabilities on the status of the project.

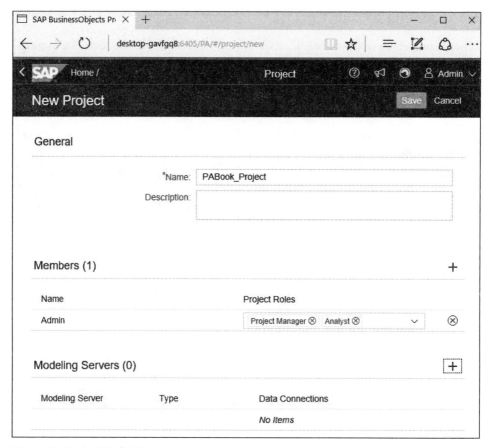

Figure 5.2 Project Definition

Add a **Modeling Server** by using the dropdown menu (shown in Figure 5.3). You'll choose which data sources will be exposed in the project and with what roles. Data sources must, however, be defined in the modeling server first. At least one model repository must be defined in **Model Repositories** because models are the compulsory object on which the project relies. For **Data Manipulation Repository**, locate where metadata from the Data Manager is stored. Only one **Data Manipulation Repository** can be defined. **Exposed Data Connections** defines where data is available either as datasets (defined without the Data Manager) or as files used by the Data Manager. A project can contain several of each type of data connection, but only one modeling server is assigned per project.

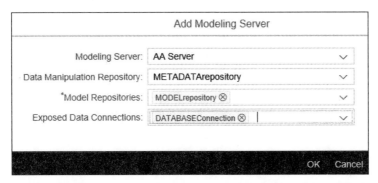

Figure 5.3 Defining the Modeling Server and the Roles of the Different Data Sources

Once defined, the new project will appear in the list of available projects. By clicking on the project, you can define or import a model. See Chapter 6, Chapter 7, or Chapter 8 for more information on creating models in the Predictive Factory and Chapter 9 for information on importing models. Tasks can also be defined on each model, as described in Chapter 9.

5.3   External Executables

The Predictive Factory can schedule tasks to be executed outside of SAP Predictive Analytics by defining external executables.

To create a new external executable, click on the **External Command** tab and then on the plus (**+**) button. Figure 5.4 shows the parameters you need to set up an **External Command**.

Enter a **Name** and then the location of the program to be executed in the **Command** field. If you are creating an external command using KxShell Script, you'll use *kxshell.exe* with a specific script that was stored in *C:\PA_book\scripts\regression.kxs*. The "-DTRAINING_STORE_PROMPT" in this field value defines a prompt value to be used when executing this task. Some important fields and options are as follows:

- The **Working Directory** corresponds to where the program to be executed is located.
- **Authentication** gives access to the external executable. If you were creating a command that requires database access, you would enter your database login and password in these fields.

- **Command Parameters** may be added. In our example shown in Figure 5.4, we are defining the value of the prompt defined in the script.
- When an external executable is defined, a new task type will be available for new tasks: **External Command Task** (Figure 5.5).

Defining an external task (Figure 5.6) requires a **Parameter Value** (in our example, for segments) if parameters are defined and a **Schedule**. We'll describe defining schedules in Chapter 9.

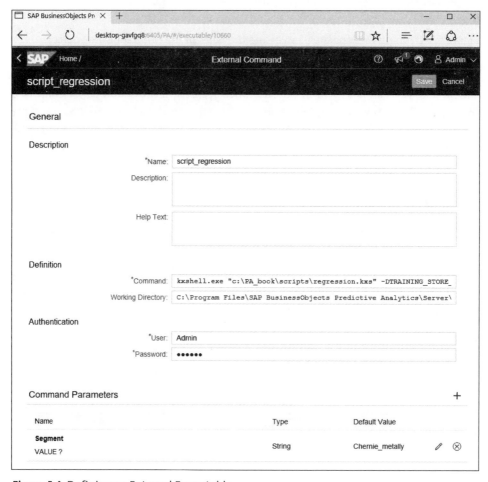

Figure 5.4 Defining an External Executable

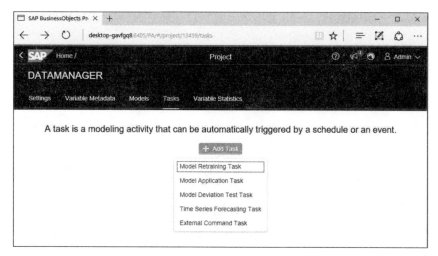

Figure 5.5 Using External Executables

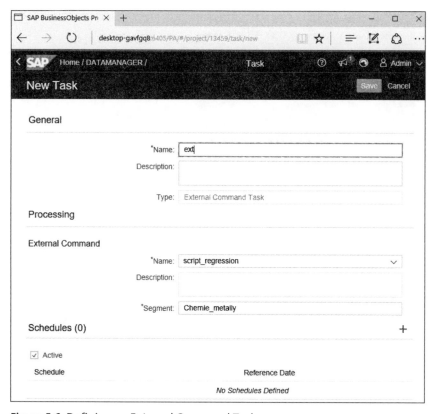

Figure 5.6 Defining an External Command Task

5.4   Variable Statistics

The last tab of the landing page is the **Variable Statistics** tab. Figure 5.7 shows the output, which corresponds to statistics on the usage of variables, i.e., the number of
models a variable is used in, the number of times a variable is among the top 5 variables in a model, etc.

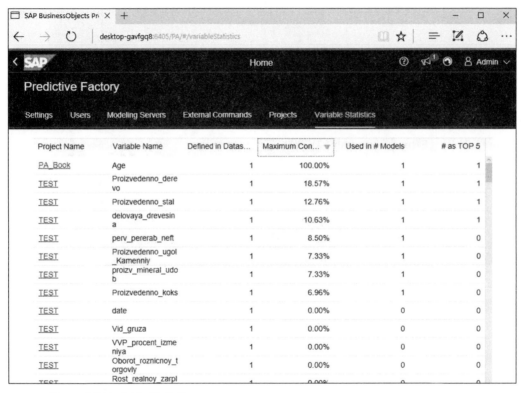

Figure 5.7 Variable Statistics

5.5   Summary

In this chapter, we've only described the first part of the process of using the Predictive Factory, from creating a project to using external executables and looking at
variable statistics. In Chapter 9, we'll provide a more detailed description of produc-
tionization.

Chapter 6

Automated Predictive Classification Models

A wide variety of business problems can be addressed using classification models, a key technique of SAP Predictive Analytics. This chapter describes everything you need to know about classification models, from their creation to their application to provide predictions for your business users.

Many business questions can be tackled using classification models. These questions can be found across many different industries such as retail, telecommunications, banking, insurance, manufacturing, and finance, to name a few lines of business (LOBs), ranging from sales and marketing, to operations, human resources, and compliance.

Examples of such questions include:

- Is this prospect or customer likely to buy my product?
- Should I immediately block this credit card transaction?
- Should I grant or deny this credit to my customer?
- Will this product meet my quality expectations at the end of the manufacturing chain?
- Is this trusted employee likely to leave my company?

This chapter provides a comprehensive view of automated classification models. First, we'll introduce you to classification models and describe how they can be used in practice. Once you are more familiar with the concept, we'll guide you through creating a classification model in Predictive Factory. You'll understand what makes a good classification model and how to understand and interpret these models.

You'll also learn how to further improve a classification model if necessary. You'll apply the classification model to a new dataset and see how you can leverage the model's predictions to answer your business questions.

We'll conclude this chapter with a detailed explanation of the powerful combination of automated data preparation and automated model creation which make it possible to provide the power of predictive analytics to everyone in your company.

6.1   Introducing Classification Models

In this first section, we'll explain the technique behind classification models and introduce the example that we'll use throughout this chapter.

6.1.1   The Classification Technique

In machine learning and predictive analytics, classification consists of identifying to which class a new observation belongs, on the basis of a training set of data containing observations whose class is known.

Typically, you'll have two classes, and you'll generate a mathematical equation (also known as a *predictive model*) that discriminates between the two classes as well as possible (Figure 6.1).

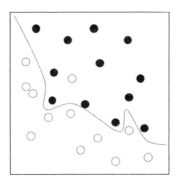

Figure 6.1 A Classification Model Separating Two Classes

Creating a classification model is typically performed with a training dataset that contains observations whose output class is already known. In the terminology of machine learning, classification is considered a supervised learning technique. We'll cover the specific data science techniques used behind the scenes in detail in the last section of this chapter.

For example, let's say that you want to increase sales of an existing product and need to decide if a prospect is "likely to buy" or "not likely to buy" this product.

First of all, you'll collect historical information about past purchases to create a training dataset (Table 6.1).

Customer Identifier	Customer Name	Age	Gender	Location	Bought
1	John Doe	25	Male	Los Angeles	Yes
2	Alberto Zapata	36	Male	Mexico	No
3	Marie Curie	66	Female	Paris	Yes
4	Anton Checkkov	44	Male	Moscow	No
...	...	...	...	...	

Table 6.1 A Simplified Training Dataset

You'll train the predictive model on this historical data, which has known links between explanatory variables (e.g., age, location) and outcomes (purchase or non-purchase). This phase is the *learning phase*.

During the learning phase, SAP Predictive Analytics uses the available data to define a model (an equation) to predict whether, based on the explanatory variables, a customer will purchase the product or not.

The classification model can be applied to new customers to determine possible outcomes. When you apply the classification model, you don't know the outcome but want to determine:

- if the customer is likely to buy our product
- the probability the customer will buy the product

In our example output shown in Table 6.2, Homer Simpson has a 70% probability to purchase the product, but Beck Hansen only has a 10% probability.

Customer Identifier	Customer Name	Age	Gender	Location	Likely to Buy? (Prediction)	Likely to Buy? (Probability)
101	Homer Simpson	35	Male	Springfield	Yes	70%
102	Beck Hansen	47	Male	Los Angeles	No	10%
...	...	...	...	...	....	....

Table 6.2 A Simplified Application Dataset

6.1.2 Step-by-Step Classification Example

Let's now introduce the example that we'll use throughout this chapter.

Imagine you are working for an insurance company as a data analyst. Your company wants to sell an insurance policy designed for recreational trailers, which are called "caravans" in our example in this chapter. The company resources that can be leveraged include telemarketers and email campaigns. You can use these resources to reach out to your customers and prospects and propose they subscribe to the policy.

However, you cannot afford to contact every customer and every prospect in your company's databases nor would this be a smart use of your resources—you could bore your contacts with recurring phone calls and emails with limited chance of success.

So, the business questions to resolve are who to contact first and how to ensure the people you contact will subscribe to the policy. To these ends, you'll perform the following steps:

1. First, you'll learn from past experiences across different channels to determine which customers have subscribed (and which have not) to the policy after they were contacted.

2. Then, you'll use SAP Predictive Analytics to find a rule that separates the two groups: those that subscribed and those that did not. In this step, you'll train a classification model to separate the classes. We'll cover this step in more detail in Section 6.2. Generally, you'll provide as much information as possible on the contacts you've had, such as all customer-related information and the entire history of interactions with each customer, as well as their socio-demographic characteristics.

3. Next, you'll need to understand the classification model and whether the quality of the model matches your needs. This step is typically interactive, and you'll have to play with the data you already have, the data that you can add to the picture, and the quality of the resulting predictive model. We'll cover this step in more detail in Section 6.3.

4. When you're satisfied with the quality of your classification model, you'll apply the model to your data. "Applying" in this sense means taking the knowledge that's now built into the classification model and using it to understand whether the next person on your telemarketer's call list has a high chance of subscribing to the insurance policy or not. The applied model will let you know if the chance is high or low, the reasons a potential subscriber might subscribe, and other useful information. You can even maximize your campaign's return on investment and decide the ideal number of customers to contact. We'll cover applying the predictive model in more detail in Section 6.4.

We've provided two datasets as part of this book's data samples:

- A training dataset: *Caravan - Dataset for Training.csv*
- An application dataset: *Caravan - Dataset for Application.csv*

Both datasets are available for download at *www.sap-press.com/4491*. Copy them to a local folder on the machine where the SAP Predictive Analytics server is installed.

You can also refer to *http://liacs.leidenuniv.nl/~puttenpwhvander/library/cc2000/data.html* for a detailed explanation of the various data fields in the datasets.

> **Note**
>
> We are grateful to Peter van der Putten, who gave us permission to reuse these datasets. Please refer to this link if you want to learn more: *http://liacs.leidenuniv.nl/~puttenpwhvander/tic.html*.
>
> P. van der Putten and M. van Someren (eds). *CoIL Challenge 2000: The Insurance Company Case*. Published by Sentient Machine Research, Amsterdam. Also a Leiden Institute of Advanced Computer Science Technical Report 2000-09. June 22, 2000.

6.2   Creating an Automated Classification Model

In the previous chapter, we explained the user interface and the concepts behind Predictive Factory. In this section, we'll walk you through the steps required to create a classification model in Predictive Factory, using our trailer insurance example.

6.2.1   Prerequisites

The following prerequisites must be met before you can create a classification model in Predictive Factory:

- Predictive Factory has been installed, and you've provided a valid license, created users with appropriate security rights (see Chapter 3, Section 3.4).
- The SAP Predictive Analytics server has been installed, and you've provided a valid license (see Chapter 3, Section 3.2).
- The SAP Predictive Analytics server has been added to the Predictive Factory as a modeling server (see Chapter 3, Section 3.4).

6.2.2   Creating the Data Connections and the Project

You'll need to add two data connections to the modeling server (see Chapter 3, Section 3.4):

- First, you'll create a data connection to store models locally. Enter "Caravan Models" as the connection name. This connection should point to the local folder of the machine where SAP Predictive Analytics server is installed.
- Then, you'll create a data connection pointing to the datasets that you'll use, which you can name "Caravan Datasets." This connection also points to the local folder where you copied the different datasets.

You must also create a Predictive Factory project:

- You can name the project "Automated Classification Models" (Figure 6.2).
- You should give the **Project Manager** and **Analyst** roles to your user.
- Your model repository connection is called **Caravan Models**.
- Your data connection is called **Caravan Datasets**.

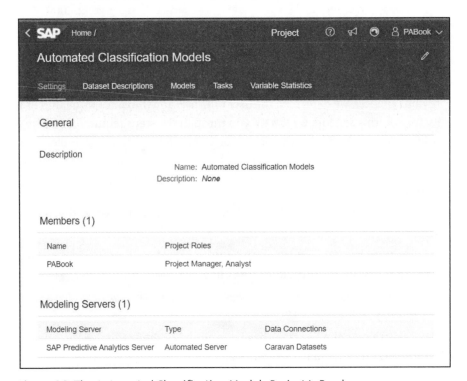

Figure 6.2 The Automated Classification Models Project Is Ready

6.2.3   Creating the Model

To begin creating an automated classification model, click on the **Models** tab of your project. Next, click on the **Add Model** button and select **Classification** (Figure 6.3). The **New Model** page will open (Figure 6.4).

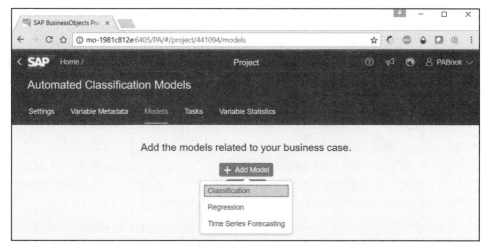

Figure 6.3 Creating a Classification Model

Figure 6.4 The New Classification Model Screen

The process of creating a classification model has been simplified to its most essential steps; you'll answer some simple questions and fill out the form as you would on any website.

The questions you'll need to ask yourself include the following:

- **What is this classification model for?**
  A meaningful **Name** helps you retrieve your model later on, so take some time to think about the most appropriate name for your model. The **Business Question** field helps you document the business purpose of the model. As Predictive Factory is a collaborative multi-user environment, we recommend documenting the reason for creating this model.

  In our example, you'll name the model "My First Classification Model."

- **What is the data source for the model?**
  You'll need to specify the **Input Dataset.** Your dataset can come from one of several different possible data sources: A text file, database table, or database view. In the case of SAP HANA, this de facto includes the following:

  - A time-stamped population or temporal analytical dataset created using the Data Manager (see Chapter 16). You'll be prompted to provide a reference date so that the analytical dataset can be created.

  - A data manipulation created using the Data Manager

  For our example, select the *Caravan - Dataset for Training.csv* as the input dataset.

> **Note**
> SAP HANA's analytic and calculation views can be used as data sources. If an SAP HANA view has been associated with your input parameters, you'll need to answer some prompts before the corresponding input dataset can be created and used as your data source.

- **What is my target variable?**
  As we discussed in Chapter 4, Section 4.2.3, a target variable is a field in the dataset containing the classes that you want to predict with your classification model. The target variable accepted for a classification model should be defined as a nominal variable and can take only two different values. Often, the most fruitful class to explain is the one that appears least frequently in the dataset. This class will be

used by default in both Automated Analytics and the Predictive Factory. In Automated Analytics, you can change the default setting.

For our example, select the target variable CARAVAN.

- **Should I exclude any variables from my dataset?**
  You might want to exclude some variables from consideration in the classification model. These reasons are listed in Table 6.3.

Variable Type	Reason for Exclusion
Database identifier	All values are different and therefore add no value.
Input variable fully correlated with the target variable	The model generated is perfect but useless.
Another target variable	You typically cannot action a target variable, and you do not want to use it as an input variable.
Constant variable	Does not add any value to the model.
Fully empty variable	Does not add any value to the model.

Table 6.3 Reasons for Excluding Variables from the List of Input Variables

Note

Please note that all the variables not explicitly excluded from the input dataset will be considered as potential input variables for the classification model.

In general, if you are not sure if any variables should be removed, you can trigger the model creation and keep all input variables as part of the model. The model creation process will highlight for you any suspicious variables. You can then create the model again after removing those suspicious variables.

In our example, you don't need to exclude any variables.

- **Should I change the metadata of the variables?**
  A best practice is to look at the types of your different variables by clicking on the link **Edit Variable Metadata**.

Make sure that the **Type** given to a variable is the appropriate one.

You may also need to update the **Missing Value** field to the appropriate value if missing values should be recognized in a certain way for this particular variable.

Frequent examples of missing value encoding could be for instance, "N/A," "?," "empty," "9999," and so on.

Different types of variables exist: nominal, ordinal, continuous, textual. A *nominal* variable is a discrete and unordered set of values like postal codes or hair colors, for instance. An *ordinal* variable is defined as a discrete and ordered set of values like customer satisfaction rating (from 1 to 10); a medal's metal (gold, silver, bronze); a net promoter score (from 1 to 10); or the number of children in a family (from 1 to *x*). A *continuous* variable is a real number that can take any value, for instance, a bank account balance or any ratio or calculated value. A *textual* variable is a variable that contains text. Table 6.4 lists more examples.

> **Note**
>
> If a quantitative variable can take any value, it's *continuous*. If a quantitative variable can only have discrete values, then it's *ordinal*. In some cases, the decision to make a variable continuous or ordinal can be subjective, as a variable that takes on enough discrete values can be considered continuous for practical purposes.

Variable Type	Examples
Nominal	Marital status, occupation, gender
Ordinal	Flips of a coin, number of products purchased, people in a car
Continuous	Customer spend, customer value, total time for voice calls, ratios, calculated values
Textual	Tweets, customer product appreciation

Table 6.4 Examples of Various Types of Variables

In our example, you should set the types of all variables to *ordinal*, except for the variables MOSTYPE, MOSHOOFD, and CARAVAN, should be set to the *nominal* type.

- **Should I let the tool select the best variables for me?**
  You should! By default, the **Leverage most contributive input data set variables** option is set in the **Variable Selection** field of the Predictive Factory. The automated creation of classification models relies on strong data science mathematical principles. These built-in, automated techniques find the best possible variable subset in order to create a classification model that is as compact as possible. However, if

you want to customize the variable selection or keep all the dataset variables as part of your classification model, you still have those options. We won't directly cover these options until Chapter 17.

In our example, you should not change the default **Variable Selection** options.

> **Note**
>
> A best practice is to make sure you include as many variables as possible as part of the input dataset. The automated variable selection process makes it possible to take into account in the model only the variables that contribute enough to the model.

Once you've properly filled out the various fields (Figure 6.5), you can either click **Save** to save the parameters of your model or click **Save and Train** to save and train the classification model. For our example, click **Save and Train**.

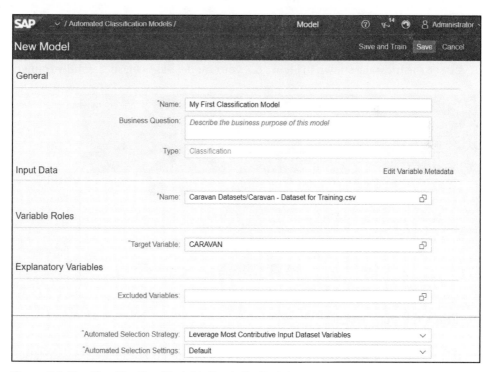

Figure 6.5 The Classification Model Is Ready for Training

A new running task will be triggered and will appear in the corresponding **Task Runs** list. Once the task is completed, a notification will appear in the **Notifications** list (see Figure 6.6). This notification indicates whether model creation was successful or if warnings or errors arose. To address warnings or errors, click on the corresponding notification, which will take you directly to the warning or to error message in the **Messages** section of the **Status** tab.

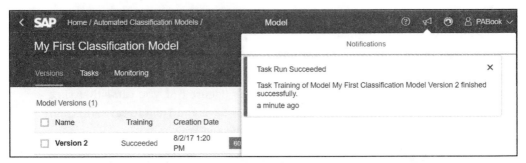

Figure 6.6 A Successful Model Training Notification

If you see the message shown in Figure 6.7, your model has been successfully trained.

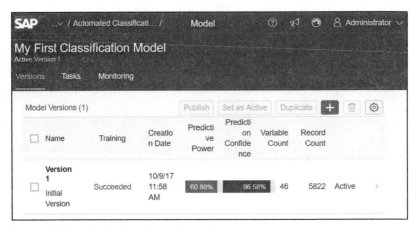

Figure 6.7 The Model Has Been Trained!

In this section, we walked you through how to create an automated classification model. In the next section, we'll describe how to understand and improve an automated classification model.

6.3   Understanding and Improving an Automated Classification Model

In this section, we'll first explain how you can understand an automated classification model. Then, we'll explain how to improve an automated classification model if necessary.

6.3.1   Understanding an Automated Classification Model

Once the classification model has been created, you'll need to interpret it.

Key elements to take into consideration include:

- The **Predictive Power** and the **Prediction Confidence** indicators
- The **Variable Contributions** report
- The status of the model and the errors or warnings that arose during model creation

Advanced debriefing capabilities include:

- **Detected Curve**
- **Error Matrix**
- **Profit Simulation**
- **Performance Curves**
- Dataset and model statistics

We'll cover these capabilities in detail in the upcoming sections.

Predictive Power and Prediction Confidence

Predictive Factory creates a classification model based on the best possible compromise between the model's accuracy (measured by its **Predictive Power**) and the model's robustness (measured by its **Predictive Confidence**). Therefore, first looking at these indicators when interpreting the model is crucial. These indicators will be displayed in the **Overview** report after the model is trained. Click on the model that you generated (Figure 6.7), then click on the **Reports** tab and select the **Overview** report (Figure 6.8).

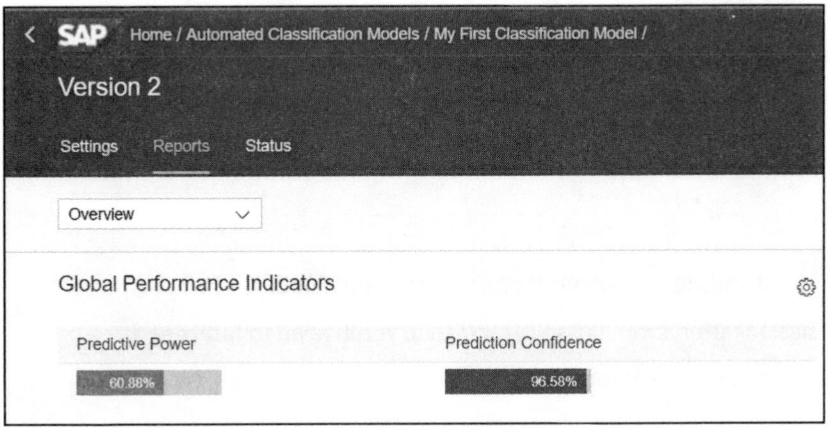

Figure 6.8 Global Performance Indicators

Predictive power is the quality of the model, measuring our ability to predict the values of the target variable using input variables that are present in the input dataset.

The **Predictive Power** indicator takes a value between 0% and 100%. This value should be as close as possible to 100%, without being equal to 100% (100% would be a hypothetically perfect model; 0% would be a random model with no predictive power).

However, no exact threshold exists to separate a "good" model from a "bad" "good" in terms of predictive power. As a result, the **Predictive Power** indicator is color-coded with a neutral color (blue) in the Predictive Factory. You'll make the judgment call whether to include more significant variables as part of the base dataset to improve the accuracy of the model.

Prediction confidence is the robustness of the model, measuring the capacity of the model to achieve the same performance when applied to a new dataset with similar characteristics as the training dataset.

The **Prediction Confidence** indicator takes a value between 0% and 100%. This value should be greater than or equal to 95%; anything less, and you should consider the model as not robust enough and therefore not reliable if applied.

The **Prediction Confidence** indicator is color-coded in a more suggestive manner in the Predictive Factory: A value greater than or equal to 95% appears in green, while a value less than 95% appears in red.

These indicators are normalized (between 0 and 1), easy to understand and interpret, and reliable.

Variable Contributions

The **Variable Contributions** report presents by default the top 5 variables contributing to the model. The contribution of a variable to the model can be defined as its relative importance to the model. The sum of all variable contributions equals 100%. For instance, the variable PPERSAUT contributes 11.07% to the overall model (see Figure 6.9).

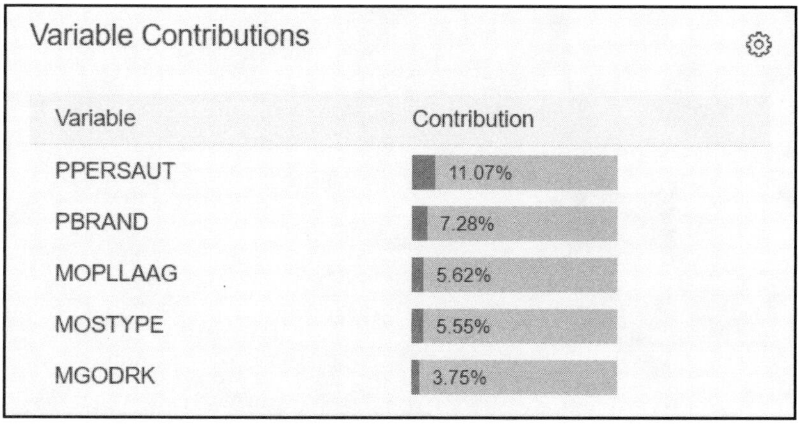

Figure 6.9 Top 5 Variables Contributions

You should now open the **Variable Contribution** report.

This report displays three elements:

- **Variable Contributions** shows the contributions of all variables to the model.
- The **Grouped Category Influence**
- The **Grouped Category Statistics**

The **Grouped Category Influence** report shows the contribution of each variable's grouped category and whether the influence of the category is positive (corresponding to a higher frequency of the targeted class), neutral, or negative (corresponding to a lower frequency of the targeted class).

Please note that the graph defaults to the first alphabetical variable and not to the most contributing one, this has to be updated in the variable selector. For our example, change the variable selector to PBRAND (Figure 6.10).

Notice that the categories **[4;5]** and **[3]** positively influence the target variable, while the other categories negatively influence the target variable.

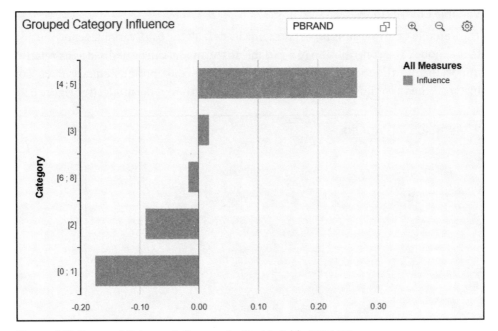

Figure 6.10 Grouped Category Influence for the Variable PBRAND

Finally, the insightful **Grouped Category Statistics** report displays, for each category of the contributing variable, the following information on a scatterplot:

- The x-axis represents the % of positive cases for the target variable.
- The y-axis represents the frequency of the category for the input variable.

In our example shown in Figure 6.11, we set variable selector to Mostype.

When analyzing this graph, you'll be more interested in the categories on the right-hand side because these categories have a higher frequency of positive cases.

Consider two interesting scenarios:

- A category with a high value on the x-axis and a low value on the y-axis is not frequent on the input variable but corresponds to a higher frequency of the targeted class. This is the case of the grouped category {3;8;13;36} in the example shown in the Figure 6.11.
- A category with a high value on both the x-axis and the y-axis is frequent as part of the input variable and also corresponds to a higher frequency of the targeted class.

Both cases are interesting to examine in detail (Figure 6.12).

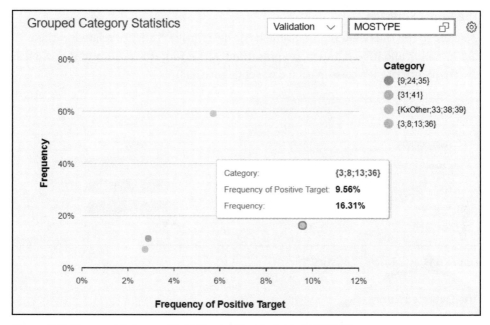

Figure 6.11 Grouped Category Statistics for the Variable MOSTYPE

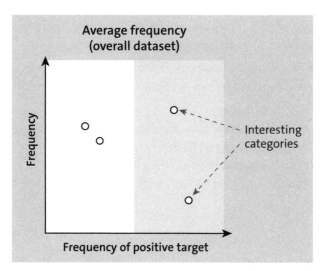

Figure 6.12 Interesting Categories in the Grouped Category Statistics Graph

The Target Statistics

Go back to the **Overview** report. Some basic descriptive statistics related to the estimation and validation datasets are presented in the **Target Statistics** report, such as the frequency of each class in each dataset (Figure 6.13).

Target Statistics		
Data Partition	Target Category	Frequency
Estimation	1	6.16%
Estimation	0	93.84%
Validation	0	94.54%
Validation	1	5.46%

Figure 6.13 The Target Statistics

The Detected Curve

The **Detected Curve** (called **% Detected Target** in the user interface) is a good representation of the detection accuracy of your classification model, represented over two axes. The x-axis shows the overall dataset population in percentages, and the y-axis represents the percentage of positive cases detected. The population is ordered on the x-axis from the most likely to the least likely positive observations.

The performance of the classification model (blue curve) is compared to the performance of a random model (red curve) and to the performance of an ideal model, called the **Wizard** (green curve).

The detected curve allows you to understand what percentage of the overall population you should contact if you want to detect a given percentage of the positive cases. In the example shown in Figure 6.14, notice that you'll only need to contact the top 20% of the overall population in order to detect 60% of those that are likely to buy a trailer insurance policy.

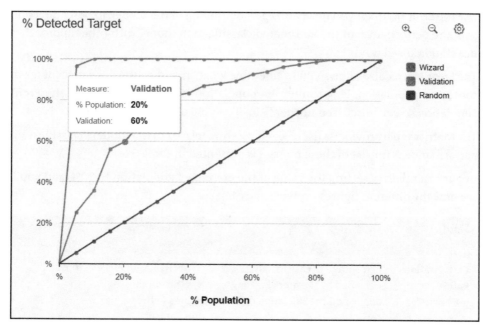

Figure 6.14 The Detected Curve

The Error Matrix

Now, select the **Error Matrix** report in the **Reports** tab. This report contains an error matrix and a list of metrics.

The **Error Matrix** is a table that represents the performance of the classification model, comparing the predicted values to the actual values, both for positive cases (corresponding to the desired behavior) and negative cases (Table 6.5).

Total	Predicted Positive Cases	Predicted Negative Cases
Actual Positive Cases	True positive (TP): Number of correctly predicted positive cases	False negative (FN): Number of actual positive cases that have been predicted negative
Actual Negative Cases	False negative (FP): Number of actual negative cases that have been predicted positive	True negative (TN): Number of correctly predicted negative cases

Table 6.5 Calculations of the Error Matrix

Use the **Error Matrix** if you need an expert debriefing of the model. Experts can compare the performance of the automated classification model with other approaches in a standardized way.

The **Error Matrix** also allows you to fine-tune what should be the ideal percentage of **contacted population**. Fine-tuning the population is also possible using the **Profit Simulation** screen (discussed further below), relying on a notion of profit and cost.

The **Metrics** table provides a list of key indicators related to the model's classification performance. A full list of these metrics is presented in Table 6.6.

In our example, try setting the value of the **Contacted Population** to 20%, and you'll see how the different figures evolve (Figure 6.15).

Metric	Definition	Formula	Best Possible Value
Classification Rate	Percentage of cases accurately classified by the model when applied on the validation dataset.	$(TP + TN) \div N$ where N is the number of records in the validation dataset	100%
Sensitivity	Percentage of actual positive cases that have been correctly predicted.	$TP \div (TP + FN)$	100%
Specificity	Percentage of actual negative cases that have been correctly predicted.	$TN \div (FP + TN)$	100%
Precision	Percentage of predicted positive cases that are actually positive cases.	$TP \div (TP + FP)$	100%
F1 score	Harmonic mean of Precision and Sensitivity (Sensitivity and Precision are evenly weighted).	$2 \div ((1 \div Precision) + (1 \div Sensitivity))$	1
Fall-out	Percentage of actual negative cases that have been incorrectly predicted as positive.	$FP \div (FP + TN)$ or $(100\% - Specificity)$	0%

Table 6.6 Metrics: Definitions and Formulas

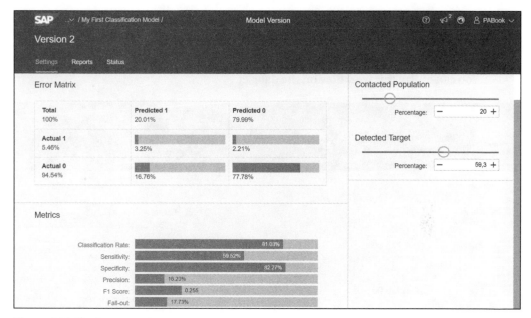

Figure 6.15 The Error Matrix

The Profit Simulation

Now, let's explore the **Profit Simulation** report, which makes it possible to maximize the profit to be made when contacting prospects by setting the ideal contact threshold. You can associate a notion of *profit* to all the predicted positive cases that revealed correct (true positive (TP) in the **Error Matrix**), and you can associate a notion of *cost* to all the predicted positive cases (**Predicted 1** in the **Error Matrix**).

Once you are done, click on the **Maximize Profit** button to determine the optimal percentage of the overall population that should be contacted to maximize total profit.

For example, let's say contacting a prospect costs you $5 dollars to contact a prospect and that your company gains $100 only if a prospect subscribes to the policy. First, set the **Cost Per Predicted Positive** to "5" and the **Profit Per Actual Positive** to "100." Then, click on **Maximize Profit,** which determines that:

- The optimal percentage of the overall population to contact is 34.8%, or 536 prospects.

- This makes it possible to detect 81.6% of the potential policy subscribers, 69 of them exactly.

- The **Total Profit Using Predicted Contacts** is $4,220, computed as (69 × 100) − (536 × 5). The **Total Profit Using Random Contacts** is $220. The difference between the two corresponds to **Total Gain** of $4,000 dollars or +1818.18% (Figure 6.16).

You can replay this workflow on the dataset.

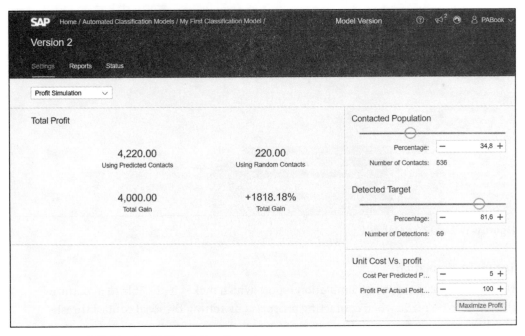

Figure 6.16 The Profit Simulation Report

The Performance Curves

In addition to the **Detected Curve**, three other model debriefing curves are presented in the **Performance Curves** report:

- **Lift Curve**
  Compares the classification model to the random model and to the wizard model then expresses how many times the model is capable of detecting positive cases compared to a random model. For instance, if my model is capable of detecting 23.75% of the positive cases, when targeting 5% of the population, then the lift is equal to 23.75 ÷ 5 = 4.75.

- **Sensitivity Curve**
  Detects the ability of your classification model to discriminate positive cases in terms of a compromise between sensitivity and specificity.

- **Lorenz Curve**
  Checks values for [1 – Sensitivity] or for specificity against the overall population, comparing the classification model to the random model and to the ideal model.

The Model Statistics

Some model statistics are presented in the **Status** tab (Figure 6.17):

- The name of the training dataset used, the number of variables, and the number of records it contains
- The number of variables that were kept as part of the model
- The time that was required to train the classification model
- The type of model (i.e., **Classification**)
- The modeling server user that was used to train the model

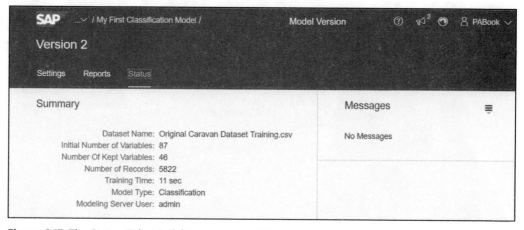

Figure 6.17 The Status Tab: Model Summary and Messages

The Model Status

Most of the time, the **Training** status of the model will be **Succeeded**, meaning that the training ran smoothly. However, sometimes model training fails or warnings are raised to your attention.

If an error arises during the training phase (Figure 6.18), the model will not be created. Refer to the **Messages** section in the **Status** tab to see what exactly caused the problem (in the example shown in Figure 6.19, no input variables were used).

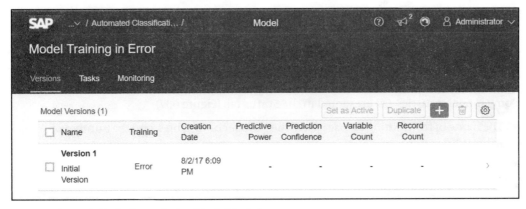

Figure 6.18 An Error during Model Training

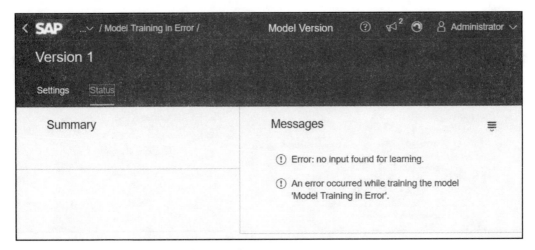

Figure 6.19 No Input Variables Used

If warnings rise during the training, the model will be created (Figure 6.20). However, you should look into the warnings that were raised and see if anything should be fixed (in the example shown in Figure 6.21, a warning has been raised due to an incorrect variable type).

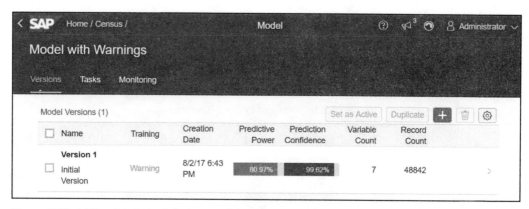

Figure 6.20 A Warning Raised during Model Training

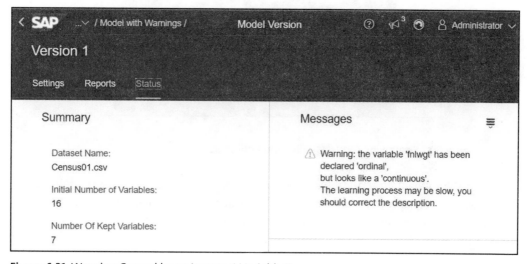

Figure 6.21 Warning Caused by an Incorrect Variable Type

In the next section, we'll see how to improve the performance of our classification model.

6.3.2 Improving an Automated Classification Model

You might face different situations where you need to improve the performance of an existing classification model:

- If the model has low predictive power, the quality of your model is low.
- If the model has low prediction confidence, the robustness of your model is low.

Figure 6.22 summarizes the possible situations and actions that can be taken.

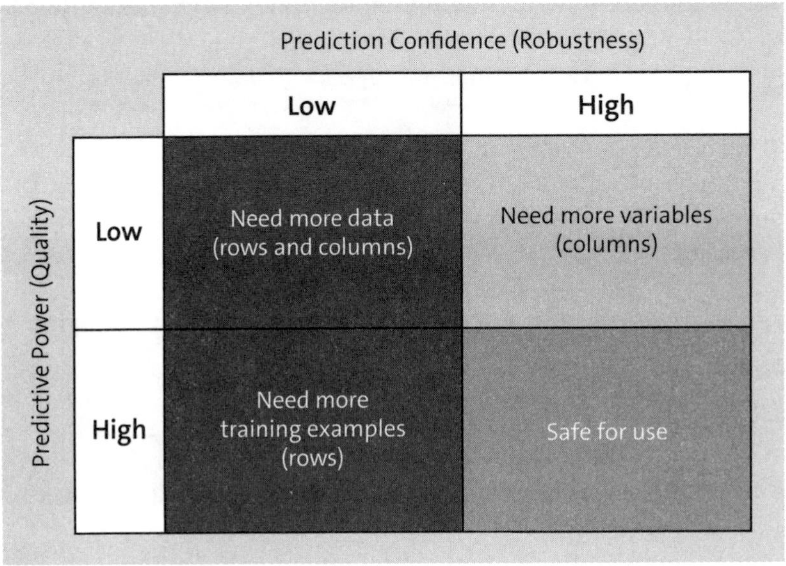

Figure 6.22 Improving Model Quality and Robustness

In the following sections, we'll look at how you can improve your model, starting with the steps you can take to maximize its quality. We'll then cover how to improve its prediction confidence and predictive power.

Process Steps

In this section, we'll talk about a sequence of steps that you should follow when creating a model to make sure you maximize the quality of the model.

First note that poor model quality could be caused by the underlying data; you might have to go back to the definition of the dataset.

The following are a few guidelines when building the datasets that you will use as the foundations for the predictive models:

- You can build an accurate model with 1% positive cases (target) or even less, provided you have a sufficient number of positive records. The Predictive Factory can evaluate the model's performance by detecting the least frequent category in the target.

- You should gather at least 1,000 records with positive records (empirical rule). This is fully derived from the way the automated algorithm is being implemented. A model is considered robust only if a sufficient number of records has been used as part of the training dataset.

- Do not limit yourself in terms of input variables; we have seen customers using datasets with as many as 15.000 variables. Including all relevant variables usually increases the quality of the predictive model.

Some steps to maximize the quality of the classification model (and improve it iteratively) include the following:

- Make sure to set the types of your variables properly, as discussed in Section 6.2.3. Setting an incorrect variable type or staying on the default types guessed by the software might downgrade the quality of the model.

- Variables directly linked to the target variable should be excluded (e.g., the Card Provider if target is "Own a Card Yes/No" or the birth date if the target is Age). If your model's predictive power is close to or equal to 1, you probably have such variables in your dataset.

- To improve the model's predictive power, you'll need to increase the number of useful variables using the Data Manager or add columns used by another algorithm (social, text mining) for instance.

- To improve the model's prediction confidence, you'll need to increase the number of records, specifically positive ones.

Improving the Prediction Confidence

Strictly speaking, any predictive model with a prediction confidence less than 0.95 should be discarded as unreliable. The red color-coding helps you identify right away whether your classification model is not robust.

Model robustness depends on the number of records in the dataset. So, to improve the prediction confidence of a model, additional observation rows should be added to the training dataset.

As a general rule of thumb, you ideally should have more than 1,000 cases corresponding to the least represented class in your dataset (which is also usually the class that you want to study).

If you are below this number, you may still be able to achieve sufficient prediction confidence, but not comfortably so.

If the number of rows is fixed and you cannot do anything about this fixed number, you can still maximize the robustness of your model with some specific techniques, which we'll discuss further in Chapter 17.

Improving the Predictive Power

As we mentioned earlier, determining what constitutes low predictive power can be difficult.

Some SAP customers may still achieve tangible returns on investment when using models with "low" predictive power on a 0 to 1 scale. So, the ideal value for predictive power really depends on the industry and use case.

A low predictive power value typically reflects the difficulty of explaining the target variable based on the input variables. If you want to significantly improve predictive power, consider adding or creating more variables in the training dataset.

You can create more relevant, domain-specific variables using the Data Manager, SQL scripts, or an ETL (extract, transform, load) tool like SAP Data Services, for instance.

To add columns to an existing dataset, you might need to compute derived variables from raw data, obtain more data from corporate systems, or even get external data to combine with the corporate data.

In general, we recommend you use the Data Manager, which supports you during the variable creation process thanks to a powerful user interface. The resulting datasets can be reused both in Automated Analytics and the Predictive Factory. Refer to Chapter 14 to learn more information about the Data Manager.

Preparing the ideal dataset is an iterative process: You will first check the model's performance on a base dataset and then progressively enrich the dataset if you need to increase the model performance.

Two additional ways to improve predictive power include the following:

- **Adding columns produced by another algorithm**
  You can analyze the links using the Social Network Analysis module in Automated Analytics and then use the results (like information on communities) as input variables to enhance the classification model. We'll cover this option in Chapter 12.

  You can run text mining algorithms then use the results (e.g., entities, sentiments) as input variables for the classification model. Similar techniques can be used for regression models.

- **Segmented modeling**

  Instead of using a single model for the entire dataset, you can define several models, one for each segment of the dataset. The model can then capture behaviors that are specific to a given segment and produce more accurate predictions.

  The segment can be a dimension in the data like country, physical store, plant, or product reference, or a segment can be a cluster identifier resulting from a clustering algorithm run against the overall dataset.

  Please note that segmented classifications are not available in the Predictive Factory user interface; you'll need to use specific scripting techniques to perform segmented modeling.

Advanced techniques, only available in Automated Analytics and not directly in Predictive Factory, include using composite variables or increasing the base polynomial degree of the classification model. The use of these techniques is covered in Chapter 17.

Note

A few dos and don'ts:

- Do not rely on manual variable selection. Always rely on automated variable selection.

- Do not add manual structures into the variables, unless you have specific business constraints imposed by the business. Always rely on automated category grouping and variable binning.

6.4 Applying an Automated Classification Model

We've now reached a key step where we'll apply the classification model and generate predictions. First, you should check for any model deviations. A model can be safely applied only if no significant deviations can be found on the application dataset. Deviations are covered in detail in Section 6.4.1. Once you are sure that you can safely apply the classification model, you can use either manual or automated application options. We'll cover these options in Section 6.4.2.

6.4.1 Prerequisites

However, before you can apply your classification model, you'll have to ensure that no issues prevent the application:

- Your classification model must be robust, defined as a prediction confidence greater than or equal to 0.95.
- The calculation of predictive confidence assumes that the application dataset is significantly similar to the training data. You must check whether any data differences (called *deviations*) exist between the training dataset and the application dataset.

In the following subsections, you'll create and run a model deviation test task to check for possible deviations before applying the model.

Creating a Model Deviation Test Task

To create a model deviation test task, follow these steps:

1. First, set your model as active. Go to the **Versions** tab, check the version 1 of your model, and then click the button **Set as Active**.

2. Click on the **Tasks** tab and create a new **Model Deviation Test** task (see Figure 6.23).

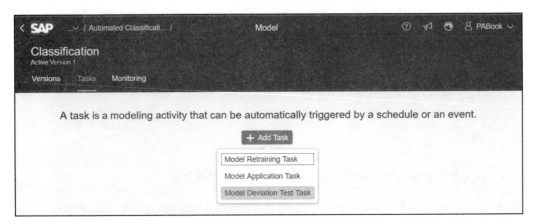

Figure 6.23 Creating a Model Deviation Test Task

3. Give the task a name (for example "Model Deviation Test Task") and select the **Model** that you want to use for the application. The model version that is used is the active one.

4. For **Input Dataset**, use the application dataset *Caravan - Dataset for Application.csv*. The application dataset may or may not contain the target variable. The values of the target variable may or may not be filled out.

5. The model deviation test task will compare the dataset used to train the classification model with the application dataset you select and evaluate the potential data deviations (**Deviant variables, Categories with problem**). Optionally, if the application dataset contains a filled target variable, the **Predictive Power** and the **Prediction Confidence** indicators, as well as the **Categories with problem towards target**, are also computed.

> **Note**
>
> Running a model deviation test task on an application dataset where the target variable is filled is an example of *back-testing*.

6. You can schedule the task regularly, so that model deviations are checked each time each time, before you proceed with the model application.

Set the various fields as shown in Figure 6.24 and click **Save** to save the task.

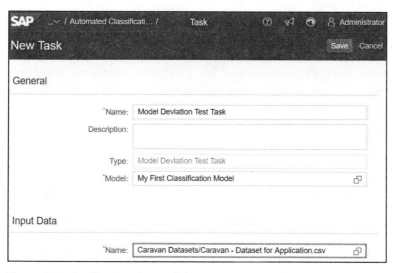

Figure 6.24 Configuring the Model Deviation Test Task

Running the Model Deviation Task

When you run the model deviation test task (Figure 6.25), if no deviations have been detected on variables or categories in the **Deviations** report of the **Reports** tab, you can safely apply the model.

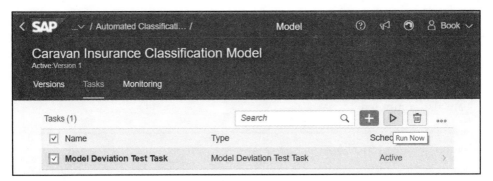

Figure 6.25 Running the Model Deviation Test Task

Understanding the Results

The **Model Deviation Test Task** calculates the deviation probability for three different groups:

- The variables used in the training dataset
- The variable categories used in the training dataset
- The target mean of the variable categories used in the training dataset

The deviation probability is a value between 0 and 1, indicating the deviation of each group by comparing these groups in the training and application datasets. Each value indicates the following:

- 0: No deviation found.
- 1: No corresponding value (for the variable or the variable category) was found in the application dataset.
- 0.95 or more: A strong probability of deviation that should be investigated.

You can see the deviations in the report **Deviations** of task run results.

> **Note**
>
> The probability of deviation is actually a standardized χ^2 (chi-squared) test and is significant above 0.95.

Understanding Deviations

If you encounter a deviation, you'll need to determine its cause. Some reasons why a deviation may occur include the following:

- **A data quality issue**
  For instance, a variable could suddenly become empty or contain a single value. Using the results of the data deviation analysis, you can determine what is going on. Then, depending on the outcome, you can check with the person in charge of the data quality in your organization to fix this issue.

- **Customers are changing**
  Customer behavior frequently changes, which impacts your data and your models. In this case, you'll need to compute a fresher model on more recent data. Typically in Predictive Factory, you'll use the event-based scheduling feature to trigger model retraining tasks when deviations are detected.

- **The original model wasn't robust enough**
  In this case, you should improve the original model, making sure to reach a prediction confidence greater than or equal to 0.95.

> **Note**
>
> A compact model, using fewer variables has less chance of showing data deviations.

In any case, you need to understand any data deviations before you can apply a model. You should never apply a non-robust model as is. If your application dataset contains a filled target variable, the prediction confidence will be calculated and should be superior or equal to 0.95. You'll need to take prediction confidence into account in addition to data deviations and not apply the predictive model in that case.

> **Note**
>
> If the variables or variable categories with deviations are not among the top contributors in the model, their impact on performance may be limited.

6.4.2   Applying a Classification Model

Once data deviations have been checked, you can apply the model on the application dataset *Caravan - Dataset for Application.csv*. You want to predict the target variable, which is not known, for new observations.

This model application can be scheduled on a regular basis, and tasks can be chained so that the model application is triggered right after a model retraining task or right after a model deviation test task.

In the upcoming sections, we'll explain how to define a model application task in Predictive Factory and the outcomes of such an application task.

Defining an Application Task

Go to the **Tasks** tab of the project, click **Add Task**, and select the **Model Application Task** (see Figure 6.26).

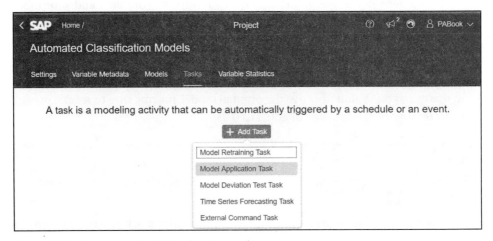

Figure 6.26 Creating a Model Application Task

Complete the following steps to create the application task:

- Give an explicit **Name** and **Description** to the task. For our example, enter "Model Application Task" for the name.

- Select the **Model** that should be applied to the input dataset. At least one version of the model should be set as active; otherwise, you will not see any models in the selection popup window.

- Select the **Input Dataset.** The input dataset is the application dataset *Caravan - Dataset for Application.csv*.

Next, you'll specify the parameters of the table that will contain the results of the application in the **Output Table** section. The application task stores, for each dataset record, the result of the application. You need to specify:

- The **Table Destination** is the location of the table that will be used. You can use Caravan Datasets as the table destination.

- The **Name** of this table. You can enter "Application Results" as the table name.

- The **Table Generation Policy** dropdown list specifies how to manage output tables when models are applied in succession. You can either:
  - Overwrite the table each time you apply a model by selecting the **Single Table (Overwrite)** option
  - Write the results of the application of the new records in the existing table by selecting the **Single Table (Update)** option
  - Write each application in a new table by using a specific suffix

  For our example, choose the **Single Table (Overwrite)** option from the dropdown list (Figure 6.27).

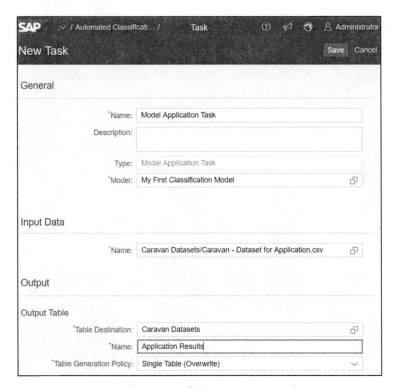

Figure 6.27 Basic Configuration of the Application Task

Outcomes of the Application Task

After completing the basic configuration steps, you'll add predictions (known as the **Output Columns**) to the application task, which is where you'll get your business value.

Table 6.7 describes the different output columns and guides you to the ones you should prioritize.

Section	Output Column	Description	Column Name (in File or Database)	Guidance
Model Variables	All variables	All the variables of the input dataset.	Original variable name in the dataset	Useful if you want to avoid joining your results to the base table. Be cautious, however, about the amount of data that may be generated!
Contextual Information	Apply Date	The date of the model application.	*Apply Date*	Useful if you require full traceability about the model used for the application.
	Training Date	The last retraining date for the model.	*Build Date*	
	Model Name	The model name.	*Model Name*	
	Model Version	The model version number.	*Model Version*	
Statistics	Approximate Quantile	For each row in the application dataset, the number of the quantile that this row belongs to. Predictive Factory considers 10 quantiles only; quantile 1 has the highest scores.	*quantile_rr_ <target>__ <nb_quantiles>*	Useful if you require specific prospect targeting based on the quantiles. Please note these quantiles are approximate because they are determined based on the validation dataset then used as such on the application dataset.

Table 6.7 Different Output Columns When Applying Classification Models

Section	Output Column	Description	Column Name (in File or Database)	Guidance
Statistics (Cont.)	Outlier Indicator	1 if the row in the application dataset is considered an outlier, 0 if it's not.	*outlier_rr_ <target>*	Reserved for detailed analysis.
	Variable Contributions	Contribution of each variable to the result. The sum of variables contributions equals the predictive score. Contributions can be positive or negative.	*contrib_ <var>_ rr_<class>*	Useful to highlight the top contributing variables for a given data point and which kind of variables contributed the most. Variables can be ranked by score.
Predictions	Predicted Category	Predicted class, based on the best score.	*decision_rr_ <target>*	The decision is based on a default threshold in the product that cannot be changed and is, therefore, not useful.
	Prediction Score	Score for the positive predicted class.	*rr_<target>*	Scores are harder to use than probabilities, as scores cannot be interpreted easily by end users.
	Prediction Probability	Probability that the record corresponds to positive case.	*proba_rr_ <class>*	This field is the most important because it provides us with the probability of getting a positive case, which is easy for end users to interpret.

Table 6.7 Different Output Columns When Applying Classification Models (Cont.)

Section	Output Column	Description	Column Name (in File or Database)	Guidance
Predictions (Cont.)	Prediction Confidence	The confidence level for the predicted value.	*bar_rr_ <target>*	Should be used if you need to consider confidence in addition to the probability.

Table 6.7 Different Output Columns When Applying Classification Models (Cont.)

You can apply the classification model by using the **Prediction Probability** and **Prediction Confidence** in the **Predictions** field. Click **Save** to save your application task. Then, check the application task and click the **Run** button in the toolbar to run the task right away.

Applying a Model in Automated Analytics

Thus far, we've described the various application options available in Predictive Factory. Now, we'll present the additional options available in Automated Analytics, which is a separate component of the suite:

- The classification model can be exported as code in SQL, UDF, CCL, C, C++, Java, JavaScript, etc., thus enabling you to integrate the processing of the model directly into the database logic for SAP HANA, SAP Vora, SAP HANA smart data streaming, and major third-party databases as well as in applications. The model can be used to generate scores, probabilities, or error bars. In Automated Analytics, once you've generated the model, go to **Save/Export**, then **Generate Source Code** (Figure 6.28).

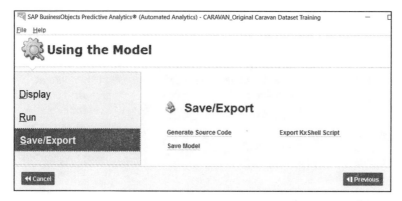

Figure 6.28 Generate Source Code and Export KxShell Script Options

- The classification model can be exported as a script, using the **Export KxShell Script** option, enabling you, for instance, to prototype a classification model and to extend the model to perform a segmented classification.

- The classification model can be used to run a simulation on a data record and evaluate the corresponding score and probability values. This option is found in the **Simulation** option of the **Run** screen.

- In the model application screen (**Run/Apply model**), you can select advanced options, specifically gain charts and reason code options, using the **Advanced Apply Settings...** button as follows:

  - A gain chart allows you to divide a core list into equal-width n-bins (10, 20, 100, etc.). A gain chart provides insight for each bin, such as the estimated number of responders versus the actual number of responders (when actual value is known). Please noµte three different types of gain charts can be created: training, transversal, and apply (see Table 6.8). To see the training and transversal gain charts, the appropriate option has to be selected when creating the classification model.

Type	Score Boundaries Defined on	Scores Calculated on
Training	Validation	Validation
Transversal	Validation	Application
Apply	Application	Application

Table 6.8 Different Types of Gain Charts

  - The reason code enables you to see the reason for a decision and is widely used in credit scoring where it's mandatory for legal reasons to provide an answer why a credit cannot be granted. A reason code is the combination of {variable, value} that most influenced the decision. You can set up reasons codes in different ways, for instance, to understand which variables most positively influence or most negatively influence the overall score.

6.5   The Data Science behind Automated Predictive Classification Models

The goal of the automated techniques embedded in SAP Predictive Analytics is to quickly create predictive models that are as good as the models fine-tuned by data scientists.

Automating predictive analytics greatly increases the productivity of the predictive process (Figure 6.29). Users can concentrate on the many business questions they have to solve and can focus on translating these business questions into meaningful datasets, which will serve as the data foundation for the models.

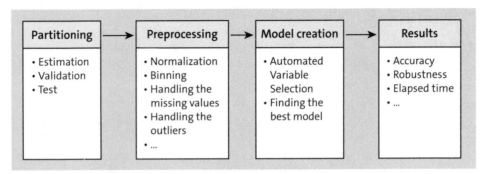

Figure 6.29 Automation of Predictive Analytics Made Possible

Currently, we are at a tipping point when it comes to data science automation. According to Gartner, more than 40% of data science tasks will be automated by 2020.

In the next section, we'll first go into detail on the foundations of automated analytics techniques. We'll also explain how automated data preparation and automated data encoding are performed behind the scenes.

6.5.1   Foundations of Automated Analytics

Automated analytics techniques were initially brought to life by the French company KXEN. From day 1, the focus at KXEN was to provide a high degree of automation in the predictive process to free users from the repetitive tasks associated with data preparation, data encoding, and algorithm selection.

Automation is key for users without a strong data science background to create and operate predictive models. Data scientists can benefit as well from these automated solutions that make analytics processes more productive and operationalizes findings faster. The following section explains the core techniques combined to create automated classification models.

The Core Techniques

The mathematical problem that needs to be resolved is the following:

Given a set of observations X, each of this observation measured using several input variables V and a target Y, find a function that combines the different values of the input variables V to approximate the target Y (Figure 6.30).

What does a regression or classification model look like?

A model is a degree 1 polynomial equation. For example:

$Y = aV1 + bV2 + cV3 + ...$

Where:

- Y is the target variable
- Vs are the input variable categories.
- a, b, c, etc. are the weights assigned by the predictive process corresponding to the model coefficients. These weights can be either constant or calculated.

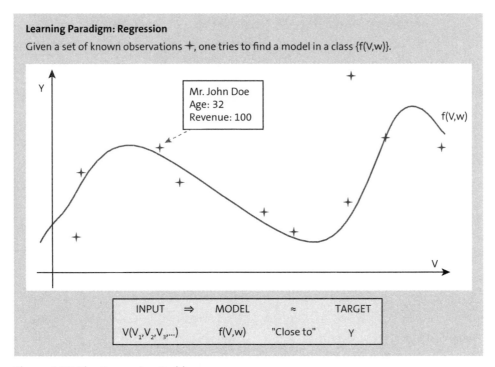

Figure 6.30 The Regression Problem

The goal of the automated engine is to obtain the "best possible" model, combining accuracy (the ability to distinguish both classes) and robustness (the reproducibility of results on a new set of data). Thus, the model is learned on a training dataset and tested on a test dataset through an iterative process.

When we define the notion of "best possible" model, we should try to avoid two traps:

- The first trap is called *overfitting*. Overfitting happens when the algorithm learning the model tries too hard to fit to the data that is contained in the training dataset. Overfitting generally leads to few errors in the predictive model on the training dataset. However, it also leads to a high-test error on data where the output is not known, which makes the model useless, at it cannot be applied to new data.

- The second trap is called *underfitting*. Underfitting occurs when the algorithm is not able to fit the data that is contained in the training dataset well enough. An underfitted model would have a high error on the training dataset and a high error on the test dataset.

A good model avoids, as much as possible, these two traps and minimizes errors globally by considering both the training dataset and the test data. Such a model can be considered robust and applied to new datasets (Figure 6.31).

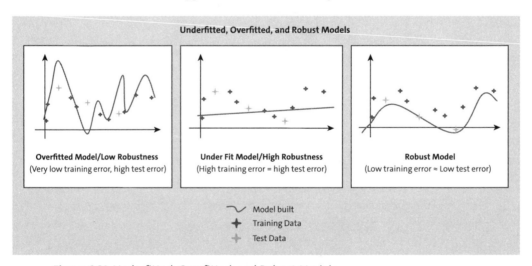

Figure 6.31 Underfitted, Overfitted, and Robust Models

SAP Predictive Analytics relies on structural risk minimization (SRM) to address the tricky problem of fit. SRM balances a model's complexity against its success at fitting the training data. SRM was theorized by Vladimir Vapnik, the father of statistical learning theory and the co-inventor of the Support Vector Machine (SVM) algorithms. SRM is based on the Vapnik-Chervonenkis theory, itself related to statistical learning theory.

A summarized interpretation of SRM can be found in Figure 6.32. With SRM, a good model is the best possible compromise between minimizing error and minimizing unreliability. In other words, SRM reconciles the quality of the model (the accurate description of training data) with its robustness (the accuracy of the predictions when applying the model to new data).

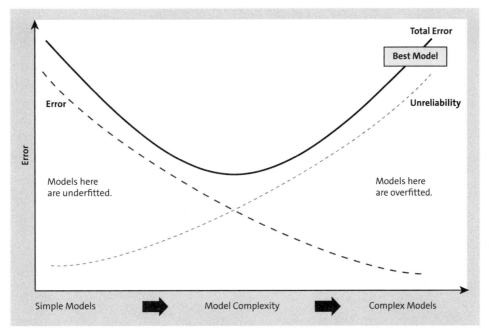

Figure 6.32 The Different Types of Models

In the following section, we go into detail about the relevant principles and techniques used to perform the model selection.

Model Selection

Let us now explore in more detail the techniques enabling the model selection. First, we need to define the concept of Vapnik-Chervonenkis (VC) dimension. For the remainder of this section, the VC dimension is presented as the variable h.

> **Note**
>
> The *VC dimension* is a measure of the complexity of a class of functions and is defined by the maximum number of observations that it can separate.

Statistical learning theory is based upon four principles:

1. **Consistency**

    If the number of observations (n) is large enough, then the prediction error on new data is similar to the learning error—the model is robust and can be trusted when applied to new data. This scenario may occur if your model is part of a class of functions with finite VC dimensions, like a polynomial, for instance.

2. **Convergence speed**

    The ability to generalize (safely apply the model to new data) increases when the number of observations (n) in the training dataset increases (Figure 6.33). Models are robust if the number of observations is high enough.

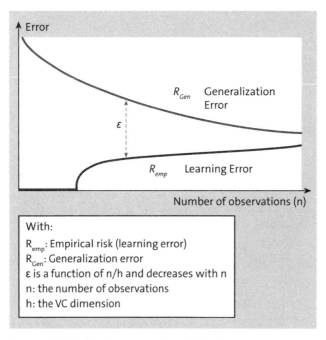

Figure 6.33 The Convergence Speed Principle

3. **Generalization capacity control**
   If the ratio n/h is large, the model generalizes well. Conversely, if n/h is small, the model overfits. For a given n, h must be large enough, but not too large! An optimal balance must be found between training and generalization errors (Figure 6.34).

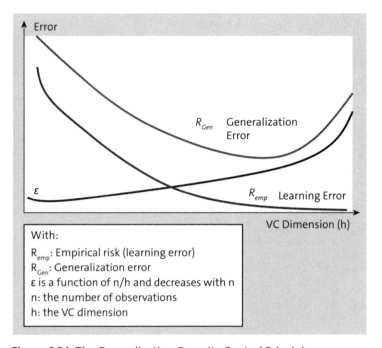

Figure 6.34 The Generalization Capacity Control Principle

4. **Strategy to obtain good algorithms: structural risk minimization** The best compromise between accuracy ($Remp$ small) and robustness ($RGen$ small) corresponds to the complexity of h where $Rgen$ is the minimum. Structural risk minimization (SRM) recommends progressively increasing h and building a succession of models until the minimum of $Rgen$ is found (Figure 6.35). In SRM, Vapnik suggests working on embedded classes of functions of increasing VC dimension, e.g., polynomials of increasing degrees.

Figure 6.36 shows an overview of Vapnik's principles applied to estimation and validation datasets. Basically, the VC dimension is increased iteratively until the error on the validation dataset starts increasing. This point is the stop point for the algorithm, where the best possible model is generated.

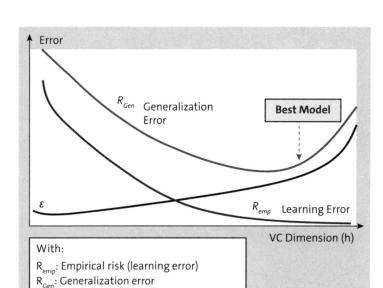

Figure 6.35 Finding the Best Model

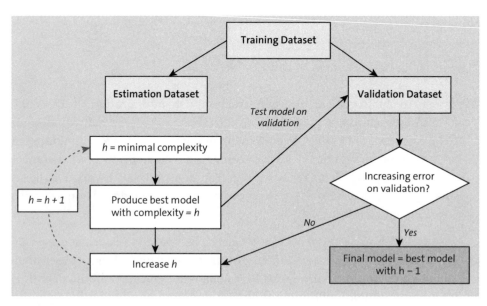

Figure 6.36 Vapnik's Principles: Process Overview

In product implementation, the degree of the polynomial is set to 1 by default. The lambda (λ) parameter of the ridge regression is the one used in order to increase the VC dimension. For more details on ridge regressions, please refer to *https://en.wikipedia.org/wiki/Tikhonov_regularization*.

The implementation is described at a high level in Figure 6.37.

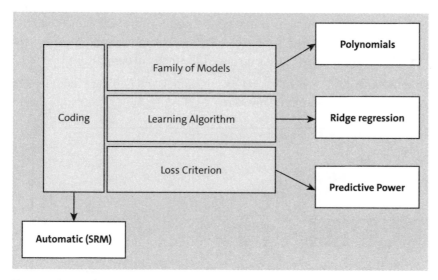

Figure 6.37 Implementation in Automated Analytics and Predictive Factory

Multiple ridge regressions are created on the whole dataset. Ridge regressions are configured with a lambda parameter, and many models are created with different lambda values. Out of those models, the one with the largest sum of predictive power and prediction confidence is selected. Now, an iterative process starts to find an even better model, as follows:

1. The variables with the smallest impact on the model are eliminated.
2. A new set of ridge regressions with different values for lambda are produced on the smaller dataset.
3. The best model is chosen again. If this model is better than the selected one from before, this model becomes the model that has to be beaten.
4. The process continues with step 1 until the sum of predictive power and prediction confidence of the best model in step 3 is smaller than before.

Eventually, the model with the highest sum of predictive power and prediction confidence becomes the chosen model, delivering the best compromise between accuracy, robustness, and simplicity.

Computing Simple Model Indicators

End users need to gauge the accuracy and reliability of predictive models using debriefing indicators that are easy to understand, thus, the purpose of the **Predictive Power** and **Prediction Confidence** indicators. These two indicators are also used during the model creation process. Let's now see how they are computed.

Open Automated Analytics, create a classification model, and generate the **Detected Curve** using **Display/Model Graphs** (Figure 6.38).

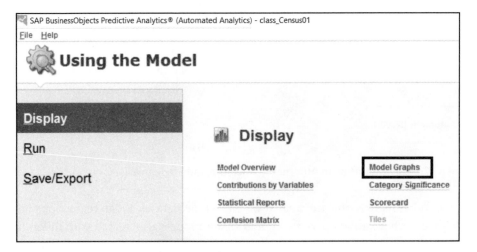

Figure 6.38 How to Access the Detected Curve

Select the option **All Datasets** in the **Datasets** selector of the toolbar, so that both **Validation** and **Estimation** dataset curves are displayed.

An explanation of the relationships among the indicators is shown in Figure 6.39.

The predictive power is equal to the ratio $C \div (A + B + C)$.

When the classification model is closer to the random model, the value of C approaches 0, and the predictive power approaches 0.

When the classification model is closer to the wizard model, the value of C comes closer to the term $(A + B + C)$, and the predictive power approaches 1.

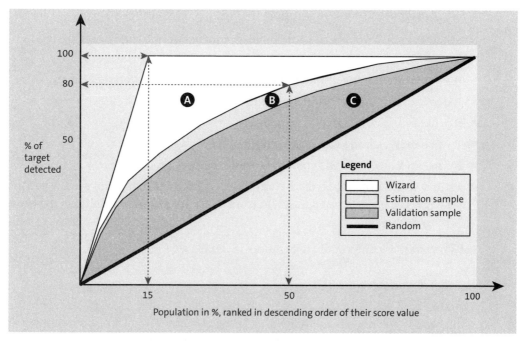

Figure 6.39 Areas Used to Calculate Indicators

> **Note**
>
> The **Predictive Power** indicator can be related with standard model quality indicators:
>
> Predictive power = 2 AUC – 1 (AUC: Area under ROC Curve)
>
> GINI coefficient = $(1 - \tilde{O}1) \times$ Predictive Power

The prediction confidence is equal to $1 - B \div (A+B+C)$.

When the term B is small (which means the incremental error on the validation dataset is small), then the prediction confidence is closer to 1.

When the term B is high (which means the incremental error on the validation dataset is high), then the prediction confidence is lower, and the model should be discarded for not being robust enough.

6.5.2   Automated Data Preparation

The SRM approach used in the Predictive Factory and Automated Analytics has multiple benefits:

- It's not limited by the number of variables included in the dataset.
- It does not assume specific data distributions.
- It is not sensitive to variable correlations.
- It can handle missing values and outliers.
- It can handle datasets with many records.
- Estimation and validation datasets are created automatically thanks to the cutting strategy. The use of a test dataset (beyond the estimation and validation datasets) is purely optional.

Let's review these different benefits more in detail.

Number of Variables

The statistical learning theory does not relate the number of variables with the robustness of the model. In other words, using as many variables as you want won't have a negative impact on robustness. In fact, the more variables you include for consideration, the more likely you'll obtain a well-performing model.

Tools like the Data Manager will support you in this feature engineering or in the variable creation process.

Conclusion

Use as many variables as you can in your datasets. If a variable is suspected to decrease the quality of the model, you'll be alerted so that you can decide whether to remove it.

Data Distributions

The structural risk minimization (SRM) theory does not require a data distribution, either for the input variables or for the target variable. The entire approach implemented in Automated Analytics and the Predictive Factory is a nonparametric approach.

Conclusion

You don't need to check the data distributions of the different variables beforehand.

Variables Correlations and Variable Multicollinearity

Multicollinearity can be a concern when training and applying predictive models. Multicollinearity occurs when two or more input variables are highly correlated. Certain algorithms require you remove the correlated variables from the base dataset, or the model quality could be significantly impacted.

The automated approach does not require specific preparation on variable correlation as the ridge regression algorithm in the implementation is not sensitive to multicollinearity. However, a specific operation is conducted on the correlated variables during the automated data preparation. Refer to Section 6.5.3 to learn more.

Suitable contributions are assigned to the variables, so that each variable contributes to the model according to the actual additional information gained. Out of two correlated variables, the most important variable will have a larger impact. The second variable's impact is reduced accordingly and might not even be included in the final model at all.

Conclusion
You can keep correlated variables in the dataset.

Missing Values

A missing value is an empty cell in your dataset. Some algorithms are sensitive to missing values. Some algorithms cannot even handle missing values. When you use some of these algorithms, you may need to:

- Fill in the missing value manually
- Ignore the complete variable or record corresponding to the missing cell
- Fill the value automatically with an educated guess based on the mean, median, the most frequent value, or the most probable value

None of these techniques is ideal, as they artificially create information that is not present in the original dataset and thus bias the learning process.

In the automated approach, missing values are not excluded but instead are replaced with a constant called *KxMissing*, which the model will treat as any other category. However, missing values come rarely by chance and may, for instance, reflect a person's unwillingness to answer embarrassing questions. Thus, the fact that values may be missing may also convey significant information.

> **Conclusion**
>
> You can keep missing values in your dataset.

Outliers

Outliers are typically abnormal values and can be very low or very high values for continuous variables or rare values for categorical variables (ordinal and nominal variables). Outliers can significantly influence a predictive model when standard techniques are being used, which could lead to incorrect predictions.

Using the automated approach, outliers are automatically treated during the data encoding phase:

- For nominal/ordinal variables, outliers are grouped into a dedicated category (*KxOther*) containing categories with other infrequent values.
- For continuous variables, their impact is reduced; they are grouped into the bin for the smallest or largest values of the encoded variable.

> **Conclusion**
>
> You can keep outliers in your dataset.

Number of Records

The statistical learning theory induces that the model robustness (measured by prediction confidence) will be higher when the number of records is higher.

> **Conclusion**
>
> Use as many records as you can in your dataset.

Datasets and Cutting Strategy

At least two datasets will be needed in order to create and cross-validate a classification model. The first dataset is the estimation dataset, and the second dataset is the validation dataset.

These two datasets are automatically created for you behind the scenes by a cutting strategy. The cutting strategy divides the original dataset in two smaller datasets (or three if you include a test dataset).

This cutting strategy allows for cross-validating models (Figure 6.40).

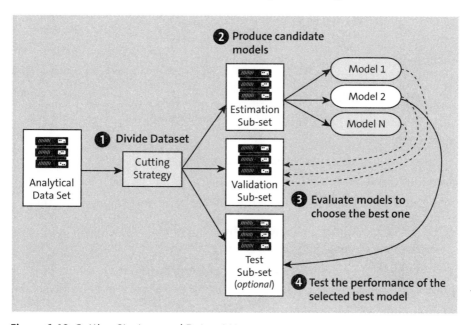

Figure 6.40 Cutting Strategy and Dataset Use

The default cutting strategy used in the Predictive Factory is the *Random without test* strategy, which divides the initial dataset in a random manner into the an estimation set and a validation set:

- Generally, 75% of records overall will be distributed to the estimation set.
- The remaining 25% of records overall will be distributed to the validation set.

With the default cutting strategy, no test set is used to create and validate the classification model. Therefore, all the data from your training dataset can be used for estimation and validation sets, which can potentially lead to a more robust model!

Conclusion

Keep the default cutting strategy.

6.5.3   Automated Data Encoding

The automated data encoding component automatically transforms raw data into a "mineable" source of information by grouping (binning) together values of the input variables. This process occurs behind the scenes and does not require any user intervention.

The objectives of binning the variables are multiple:

- Performance
    - The nonlinear behavior of continuous variables is captured.
    - The impact of outliers is minimized.
    - "Noise" from large numbers of distinct values is removed.
- Understandability
    - Grouped values are easier to display and understand.
- Speed
    - Predictive algorithms are faster as the number of distinct values decreases.

Using the SRM cross-validation approach, the data encoding component automates the essential preprocessing required for modeling.

The results provided by the automated data encoding are the most robust possible with respect to the business question (target) and, therefore, are the most reliable from a data perspective.

The data encoding component deals with the following steps:

- Encoding the different variables to prepare them adequately in order to create the best possible models
- Transforming the continuous variables so that the nonlinear relationships that may exist are included in the data
- Compressing the different variables by grouping categories together (using SRM principles)
- Automatically handling missing values and outliers
- Optimizing the input variable encoding based on the target variable, so the encoding is different and tailored for each specific dataset

Let's look at how the encoding is done for the nominal, ordinal, and continuous variables. At the end of this section, we'll also look at how advanced options can be used to influence variable and data encoding. In addition to the automated approach, manual encoding is also available.

Variable Encoding: Nominal Variables

As a reminder, a nominal variable is a discrete and unordered set of values or categories, for instance, a postal code.

The basic principle for the encoding of a nominal variable is to calculate the target mean (percentage of target class) for each category of the nominal variable and to group the categories having similar target means.

The detailed process is as follows:

- All the missing values are assigned to a dedicated category named *KxMissing*.
- Nonrobust (infrequent or unstable) categories are assigned to a dedicated category named *KxOther*. A χ^2 (chi-squared) test is performed to compare the target mean for every category in the estimation dataset to the target mean in the validation dataset. The dataset is randomly divided by the strategy, so we expect the target mean to be equivalent between the estimation and validation subsets. If the target mean is not equivalent, an issue exists in the robustness of this category. The category should be considered an outlier.
- Similar categories are then compressed together when they have similar target means. As part of this process, *KxMissing* and *KxOther* categories can be grouped with other categories.

Let's take an example based on customer occupation. For the sake of our example, we'll assume that the following information is part of the dataset:

- We have only three occupations in our database: *Doctor, Astronaut*, and *High Mountain Guide*.
- Our target variable is "working above a 3000m altitude."

In our dataset, we do not know the occupations of some of our customers. This missing information corresponds with missing values in the dataset.

Occupation	Target Mean Estimation	Target Mean Validation
Doctor	0.01	0.01
Astronaut	0.6	0.4
High Mountain Guide	0.4	0.6
Missing Values	0.01	0.01
Dataset Average	0.2	0.2

Table 6.9 Uncompressed Categories

We can see that the target mean for the estimation dataset and the target mean for the validation dataset are quite different for customers with the occupation of *Astronaut* and *High Mountain Guide* (Table 6.9). We will consider these categories as non-robust and group them together as *KxOther*.

We also see that the target mean is rather similar for the customers working as *Doctors* and for the customers whose occupation is unknown. We will group these two categories together.

Once we are done with these two steps, we have two remaining grouped categories, the first one is [Doctor; KxMissing] and the second one is KxOther (which groups the *Astronaut* and *High Mountain Guide* customers). The variable is now fully encoded (Table 6.10).

Occupation	Target Mean Estimation	Target Mean Validation
[Doctor; KxMissing]	0.01	0.01
[KxOther]	0.5	0.5
Dataset Average	0.2	0.2

Table 6.10 Compressed Categories

Variable Encoding: Ordinal Variables

As a reminder, an ordinal variable is defined as a discrete and ordered set of values like a customer satisfaction rating for instance (on a 1 to 5 scale).

Two encodings are performed for each ordinal variable that is part of the dataset:

- A standard encoding is performed. This encoding uses a regular encoding of the ordinal values (starting from 0 to n-1 where n is the number of ordinal categories). The resulting variable is named *<variable name>*.

- A target mean encoding is performed for each category resulting from the first encoding. The resulting variable is named *c_<variable name>*. Some examples of such variables are shown in Figure 6.41.

The target mean encoding used for ordinal variables is similar to the encoding used for nominal variables, except that only similar and adjacent categories can be compressed together.

As an example, if we have a variable that measures a rating on a 1 to 10 scale, the variable categories could be grouped from the original values [1;2;3;4;5;6;7;8;9;10] to the grouped categories [1;2;3;4], [5;6;7], and [8;9;10]. These categories could not be grouped as [1;2;3;4], [5;6;8], and [7;9;10] because the order of the categories must be preserved with the compression.

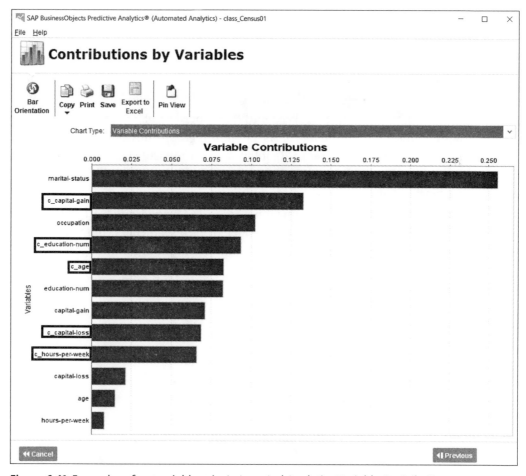

Figure 6.41 Examples of c_<variables> in Automated Analytics Variable Contributions

Missing values are assigned to the category *KxMissing*. Nonrobust categories are assigned to the category *KxOther*.

Variable Encoding: Continuous Variables

As a reminder, a *continuous* variable is a real number that can take any value, like a bank account balance, for instance.

Two encodings are performed for each continuous variable that is part of the dataset:

- The first encoding is a standardization encoding.
- The second encoding is a piecewise continuous encoding.

The standardization encoding transforms the variable so to have a mean of 1 and a standard deviation of 1. The variable resulting from standardization encoding is called *<variable_name>*.

Piecewise continuous encoding makes it possible to catch nonlinear relationships between the input variable and the target variable and consists of the following steps:

1. The standardized variable is sliced into *N* groups of similar frequency comparing both estimation and validation subsets. These *N* groups are called *bins*. The default number of these bins is set to 20. If bins are not robust (when comparing target mean on estimation and validation datasets), then they are grouped with the closest neighbor bin.

2. A piecewise continuous encoding is built from the binned variable. Linear models are calculated for each segment. The slope of each segment is compared to their neighbors in order to check if segments can be grouped together (Figure 6.42).

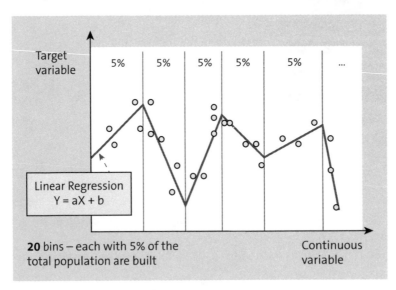

Figure 6.42 Piecewise Continuous Variable Creation

3. Similar and adjacent bins are compressed together (e.g., 1.5, 2.6, 5.2, 11.8, 12.0, 13.1 → [1.5 – 12.0], [12.0 – 13.1]) (Figure 6.43).

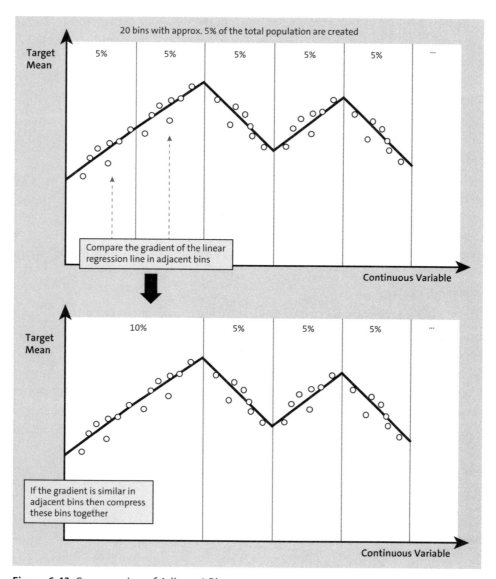

Figure 6.43 Compression of Adjacent Bins

4. Then, the encoding is normalized.

5. Missing values are assigned to a dedicated category named *KxMissing*.

6. Outliers are included in the smallest or largest bin, so their effect on the model in mitigated.

A new encoded variable is created as a result of the piecewise continuous encoding process called $c\_<variable\ name>$, where $<variable\ name>$ is the name of the original continuous variable.

Dual Encoding

You may have noticed that each ordinal and continuous variable of the dataset is encoded in two ways. One type of encoding is not always the clear winner over the other, across all models and datasets.

Because SRM frees us from having to limit the number of variables, we can use two encodings of the ordinal and continuous variables to see which one works best. This technique is called *dual encoding*. In most cases, the two encodings will be highly correlated. Remember, however, that we are using a ridge regression as the basis of the implementation, so multicollinearity is not a problem in the resulting model.

Advanced Options

The grouping of categories can be influenced using two advanced options.

The first option is to change the default number of bins (as shown in Figure 6.44). This number can be changed either from the Automated Analytics user interface or using scripting capabilities. You cannot change the default number of bins in the Predictive Factory when creating the classification models. In general, we do not recommend changing the default number of bins.

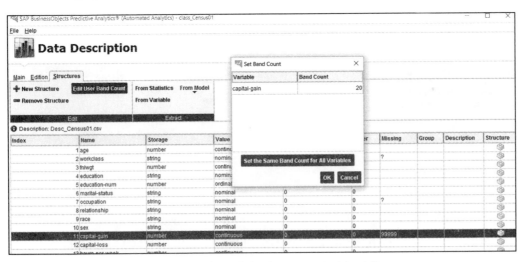

Figure 6.44 Changing the Number of Bins in Automated Analytics

The second option is to use variable structures, which can reflect business segments or business rules that are typically derived from the business standpoint. For example, the marketing department may require that customers be grouped according to certain age ranges (Figure 6.45). Variable structures can be created for continuous variables or ordinal variables.

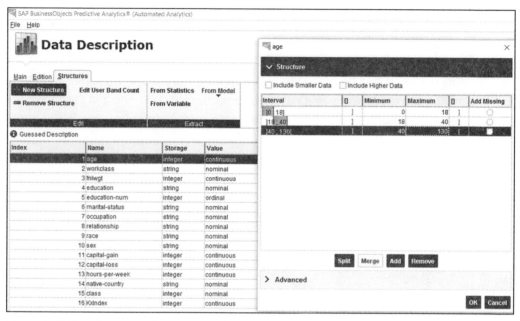

Figure 6.45 Creating a New Structure on the Variable Age

In general, we recommend prioritizing the performance of the model by letting the automated variable encoding proceed. Variable structures should be used only when the business requires. Degradation of the model's performance should be measured by creating a baseline automated model to compare against the performance of a model using variable structures.

Useful Reads

- Andreas Forster, "How does Automated Analytics do it? The magic behind creating predictive models automatically," SAP Community: *http://bit.ly/2wuMldi*
- Erik Marcade, "Machine Learning Automation: Beyond Algorithms," SAP document: *http://bit.ly/2wEZgEF*

6.6   Summary

We've now reached the end of this chapter, and we hope that classification models are no longer a mystery to you! Let's summarize what we covered in this chapter.

Automated classification models are a great way to describe the behaviors of two distinct classes by creating a sophisticated mathematical equation also known as a *predictive model*. Once you've created your classification models, you'll easily gauge their quality using two strong standardized indicators: the **Predictive Power** indicator and the **Prediction Confidence** indicator.

Using the deviation task in the Predictive Factory, you can check whether applying a classification model to a new dataset where the output classes are not yet known is a good idea. Using the application task, you can trigger the creation of model outcomes directly into the database.

The next chapter discusses automated regression models in detail. Regression models have many similarities (and a few differences) with classification models, as classification models are a special kind of regression model.

Chapter 7

Automated Predictive Regression Models

One of the most powerful automated techniques provided by SAP Predictive Analytics is regression. Automated regression models help you create predictive models that will predict numerical values and can be used in many different types of business scenarios.

Automated regression models can be easily created and managed using the Predictive Factory or Automated Analytics. This chapter starts with a general introduction to regression models in Section 7.1. Then, we'll guide you through the process of creating an automated regression model in Section 7.2. In Section 7.3, we'll explain how this model works and how to improve this type of model. Finally, in Section 7.4, we'll show you how you can apply an automated regression model to your data to create predictions.

However, because we don't want to repeat the information shared in Chapter 6, this chapter will focus on the most important major differences between classification and regression models.

7.1 Introducing Regression Models

Regression is a technique to estimate the value of an output variable y, based on the values of several input variables x. The simplest form of regression, linear regression, uses the formula of a straight line ($y = mx + b$) to determine the appropriate values for m (the slope of the line) and b (where the line crosses the y-axis) to predict the value of y based upon a given value of x (Figure 7.1).

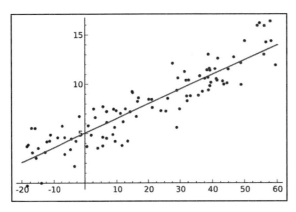

Figure 7.1 Linear Regression

When you create regression models using SAP Predictive Analytics, you'll handle one output variable *y* and many input variables *x*, leading to a more complex mathematical equation.

Example of business questions that correspond to regression models could be:

- What is the total possible revenue that could be generated from a customer?
- What is the predicted quality index for this production piece?
- What is the expected number of customer incidents or calls in the coming month?

The major difference between automated classification and regression models in SAP Predictive Analytics is the nature of the output variable *y*, as follows:

- For classification models, the output variable is *nominal* and can take only two different values.
- For regression models, the output variable is *continuous*.

7.2   Creating an Automated Regression Model

In this section, we'll walk you through the steps to create an automated regression model. We'll use two datasets (one for training, one for application) related to predicting the energy use of household appliances (*https://archive.ics.uci.edu/ml/datasets/Appliances+energy+prediction*), provided by the UCI Machine Learning Repository. The goal of this regression problem is to predict the energy use of appliances in a low-energy building. The following is the corresponding list of variables:

- `date` year-month-day hour:minute:second
- `Appliances` (the output variable): Energy use in Wh
- `Lights`: Energy use of light fixtures in the house in Wh
- `T1`: Temperature in kitchen area, in Celsius
- `RH_1`: Humidity in kitchen area, in %
- `T2`: Temperature in living room area, in Celsius
- `RH_2`: Humidity in living room area, in %
- `T3`: Temperature in laundry room area
- `RH_3`: Humidity in laundry room area, in %
- `T4`: Temperature in office room, in Celsius
- `RH_4`: Humidity in office room, in %
- `T5`: Temperature in bathroom, in Celsius
- `RH_5`: Humidity in bathroom, in %
- `T6`: Temperature outside the building (north side), in Celsius
- `RH_6`: Humidity outside the building (north side), in %
- `T7`: Temperature in ironing room, in Celsius
- `RH_7`: Humidity in ironing room, in %
- `T8`: Temperature in teenager room 2, in Celsius
- `RH_8`: Humidity in teenager room 2, in %
- `T9`: Temperature in parents' room, in Celsius
- `RH_9`: Humidity in parents' room, in %
- `T_out`: Temperature outside (from Chièvres weather station), in Celsius
- `Press_mm_hg`: Pressure (from Chièvres weather station), in mm Hg
- `RH_out`: Humidity outside (from Chièvres weather station), in %
- `Windspeed` (from Chièvres weather station): In m/s
- `Visibility` (from Chièvres weather station): In km
- `Tdewpoint` (from Chièvres weather station): °C
- `WeekStatus`: Whether the day is a weekday or is a weekend day
- `Day_of_week`: The day in the week from Monday to Sunday

More details on the dataset's structure and its variables can be found directly at the UCI dataset website.

Note

The full citation for this dataset is as follows:

Luis M. Candanedo, Veronique Feldheim, and Dominique Deramaix, "Data driven prediction models of energy use of appliances in a low-energy house," *Energy and Buildings*, Volume 140, 1 April 2017, Pages 81–97, ISSN 0378-7788, *https://archive.ics. uci.edu/ml/datasets/Appliances+energy+prediction*.

Before creating your automated regression model, you must have performed the basic steps of creating a Predictive Factory project that points to a dataset folder and to a model folder, as shown in Figure 7.2. These steps were described in detail in Chapter 5.

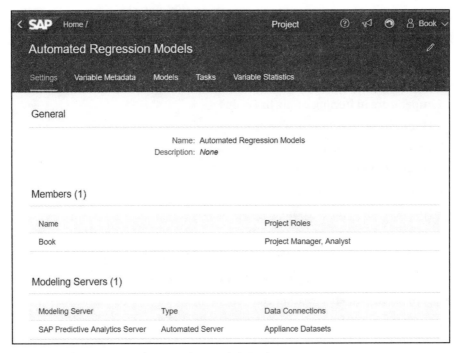

Figure 7.2 The Automated Regression Models Project

Next, open the **Models** tab of your project. Click on the **Add Model** button and select the entry **Regression**, as shown in Figure 7.3. The **New Model** page will open.

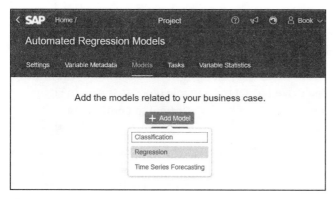

Figure 7.3 Creating a Regression Model

The process for creating a regression model is not significantly different from creating a classification model. To summarize, you'll set the following parameters (see Figure 7.4):

- The **Name** of the model and the **Business Question** that the model will help resolve: For example, you could enter "Appliance Energy Prediction" and "Predict the energy use of the appliances in a low-energy building" in the respective fields.

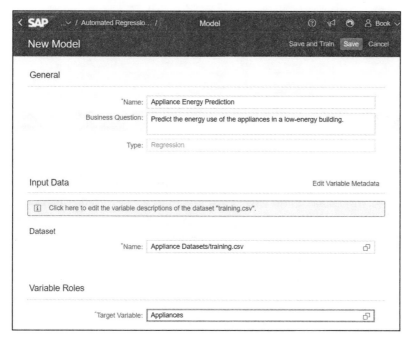

Figure 7.4 Setting the Parameters of the Regression Model

- The **Input Data** set: You should use the dataset *training.csv*.
- The **Target Variable** under **Variable Roles**: You should choose a continuous variable as your target; for our example, select the variable **Appliances** from the list of values.
- **Edit Variable Metadata**: You'll need to set the variable types as shown in Figure 7.5; set the variable type for the variable lights from **Ordinal** to **Continuous**.

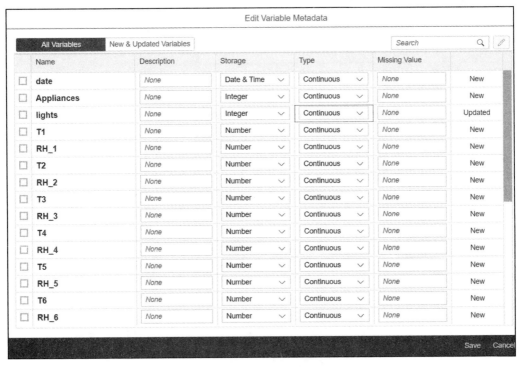

Figure 7.5 Variable Metadata: Lights Variable Updated

Click **Save** and then **Train** once you've configured your various parameters. The resulting regression model has a **Predictive Power** of 66.39% and a **Prediction Confidence** of 97.95%, as shown in Figure 7.6. Thus, the model is of good quality even if not all the variability of the target variable is explained, and the model is robust as the **Prediction Confidence** is greater than 95%.

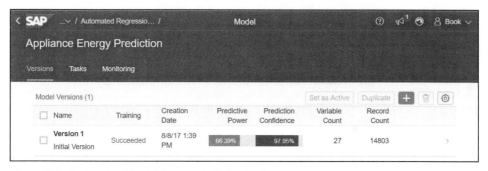

Figure 7.6 Regression Model Successfully Trained

In this section, we walked you through creating an automated regression model. We chose to create this model using the Predictive Factory, but the same model could also be created in Automated Analytics. In the next section, we'll discuss how you can interpret, understand, and improve your automated regression models.

7.3   Understanding and Improving an Automated Regression Model

Once you've created an automated regression model, you'll need to understand it, and various debriefing capabilities are available to help you understand the model. You might also need to improve the model further to reach a satisfactory quality level. We'll cover both these activities.

7.3.1   Understanding an Automated Regression Model

Key elements to take into consideration to debrief an automated regression model include:

- The **Predictive Power** and the **Prediction Confidence** indicators
- The **Predicted vs. Actual** curve
- The **Variable Contributions**
- The status of the model and the errors or warnings that arose when the model was created

Advanced information is also available to help you understand the results:

- Dataset statistics
- Model statistics
- Other performance indicators (available only in Automated Analytics)

We'll discuss each of these elements in turn in the following sections.

Predictive Power and Prediction Confidence

The interpretation is similar to what we detailed in Chapter 6. In a nutshell, the **Predictive Power** ranges from 0 (a random model) to 1 (a perfect model). **Predictive Power** should be as close to 1 as possible (but not equal to 1; if this happens, you have an input variable that fully explains the result).

The **Prediction Confidence** must be greater than or equal to 0.95; otherwise, the model is not robust enough and should be discarded. In our example, we obtained a model of average quality and high robustness.

The Predicted vs. Actual Curve

This curve displays the prediction accuracy of your regression model by presenting the actual target value as a function of predicted target values. The following curves are displayed:

- The **Validation** curve represents the actual target value as a function of predicted target values.
- The **Wizard** curve represents the hypothetically perfect model, where all predicted values are equal to actual values.
- The **Error Min.** and **Error Max.** curves display the range for the actual target values. The area between the error min and the error max is equal to the model prediction ± 1 standard deviation and is called a *confidence interval* around the prediction.

A major difference between the **Validation** and the **Wizard** curves indicates that the predicted values are not reliable. You may need to improve your model.

In Figure 7.7, notice that the model tends to be less reliable on the extreme values of the appliance energy consumption and that the confidence interval tends to be wider.

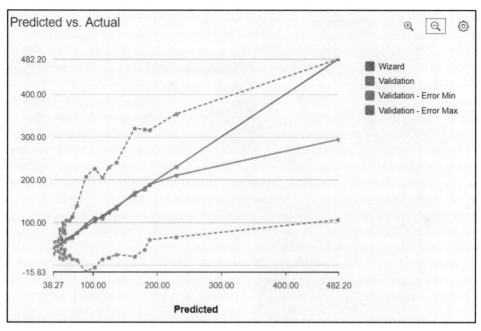

Figure 7.7 Predicted vs. Actual Curve

The following is a short description on how this graph shown in Figure 7.7 was built:

- About 20 segments or bins of predicted values were built. Each of these segments represents around 5% of the population.
- Some basic statistics were computed on the actual values, such as the segment mean, the target mean, and the variance of the target inside the segment.
- A dot on the graph corresponds to the segment mean on the x-axis and the target mean on the y-axis.

Variable Contributions

The variable contributions report is the same one presented for classification models, and its interpretation is similar. In our example, notice our top variable contributions are date_h (14.72%), T_out (8.72%), T8 (8.72%), lights (5.1%), and RH_6 (4.62%). We can also see which particular hour ranges in the day have an influence on appliance energy consumption, as shown in Figure 7.8.

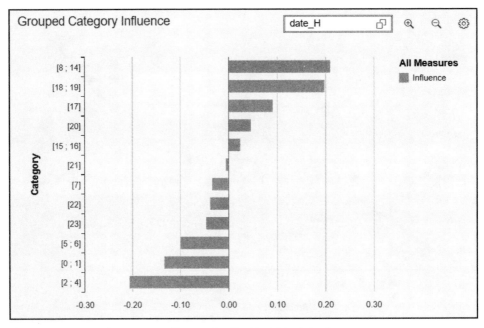

Figure 7.8 Grouped Category Influence for the Variable date_h

Status of the Model

Identical to statuses in classification models, model training can succeed, lead to an error, or trigger a warning. Warnings must be understood and taken into account. Errors need to be resolved to correctly train the model.

Dataset Statistics

Some basic descriptive statistics related to the **Estimation** and **Validation** datasets are presented in the **Overview** tab, which displays the **Mean** for the target variable as well as the **Standard Deviation** (Figure 7.9).

Target Statistics				
Data Partition	Minimum	Maximum	Mean	Standard Deviation
Estimation	10	1,080	97.19	102.21
Validation	10	910	100.36	104.54

Figure 7.9 Target Statistics

Model Statistics

Some model statistics are presented in the **Status** tab:

- The name of the original dataset used, the number of variables, and the number of records the dataset contains
- The number of variables that were kept as part of the regression model
- The time that was required to train the regression model
- The type of model (in our case, regression)
- The modeling server user that was used to train the model

Other Performance Indicators

Other model performance indicators are available in the **Statistical Reports** of Automated Analytics:

- **L1** (mean absolute error): the mean of the absolute values of the differences between the predicted and the actual values (city block distance or Manhattan distance)
- **L2** (mean square error): the square root of the mean of the quadratic errors (Euclidian distance or root mean squared error (RMSE))
- **Linf** (maximum error): the maximum absolute difference between the predicted and the actual values (upper bound) (Chebyshev distance)
- **Error Mean**: the mean of the difference between the predicted and actual values
- **Error Standard Deviation**: the dispersion of errors around the actual result
- **R²** (coefficient of determination): the ratio between the variability (sum of squares) of the prediction and the variability (sum of squares) of the data

These indicators should be low as possible, except for the **R²**, which should be high (its maximum is 1). These indicators can be calculated for both the **Estimation** and **Validation** datasets. The detailed formulas for each of these indicators is available in the product documentation at *http://bit.ly/2eKkf2I*.

7.3.2   Improving an Automated Regression Model

To enhance the quality of a regression model, you should use the same strategies that we described for classification models.

First, you'll need to ensure that your model is not too perfect, which would be caused by a leaker variable. You'll also need to make sure your variable types are correctly set at this might influence the performance of the model.

Then, if the prediction confidence and/or the predictive power of your model is too low, you'll need to improve them, which usually implies adding more variables to improve the predictive power and adding more rows to improve the prediction confidence. The table shown in Figure 7.10 summarizes your options.

Predictive Power (Quality)	Prediction Confidence (Robustness): Low	Prediction Confidence (Robustness): High
Low	Need more data (rows and columns)	Need more variables (columns)
High	Need more training examples (rows)	Safe for use

Figure 7.10 Improving the Model Quality and Robustness

In Automated Analytics, you can also change advanced options to improve regression models. This specific option is explained more in detail in Chapter 17.

7.4 Applying an Automated Regression Model

Regression models can be applied in many different ways including the use of Predictive Factory and Automated Analytics, scoring code, and KxShell Script. Before applying a model, you should check its quality. Let's cover how you can determine if a model can be safely applied, and then we'll explain how you to apply the model.

7.4.1 Safely Applying an Automated Regression Model

You'll have to make sure that no issues prevent the application of the regression model. You should not apply a model whose prediction confidence is less than 0.95. You'll also need to check if any significant data differences exist between the training dataset and the application dataset. To check for those differences, you can create a model deviation test task and run that task against the application dataset. To create a model deviation test task, follow these steps:

1. In your Predictive Factory project, click on the **Tasks** tab and create a new **Model Deviation Test** task (Figure 7.11).

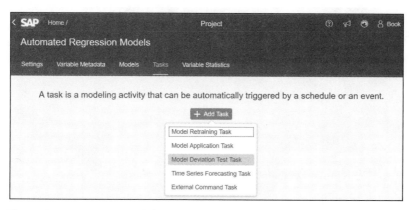

Figure 7.11 Creating a Model Deviation Test Task

2. Select the **Model** that you just created and set it as active.

3. Select the application dataset as your **Dataset** under **Input Data** (Figure 7.12).

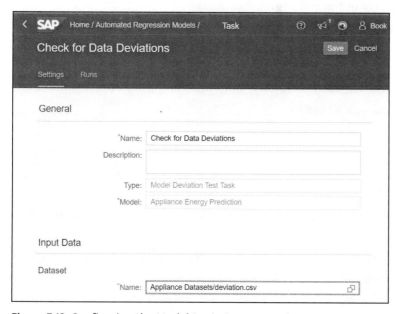

Figure 7.12 Configuring the Model Deviation Test Task

As shown in Figure 7.13, when running the model deviation task on the application dataset, no deviations were detected on variables or categories. You can safely apply the model. If deviations were detected on the data, you might need to retrain your model to integrate these significant data changes.

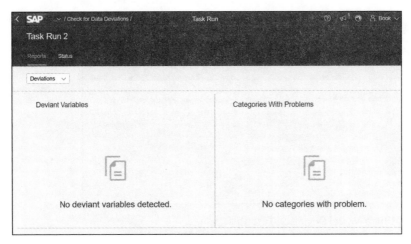

Figure 7.13 No Deviations Detected on the Application Dataset

7.4.2   Applying an Automated Regression Model

In this section, we'll present two different ways to apply regression models: using the Predictive Factory and using Automated Analytics.

Applying the Model in Predictive Factory

To apply the model, you'll need to:

- Open your Predictive Factory project.
- Select the **Tasks** tab.
- Add a new task by clicking the **+** button and then selecting **Model Application Task** from the dropdown list, as shown in Figure 7.14.

The screen that allows you to configure the application task will open, and you'll configure the task in the following way:

- **General/Name**: Enter "Applying the Model." You can also provide a description.
- **General/Model**: Enter "Appliance energy prediction."
- **Input Data/Dataset/Name**: Browse for the *application.csv* file and select the folder where it's located.

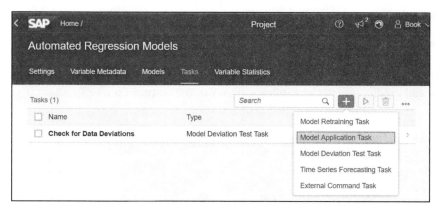

Figure 7.14 Creating a Model Application Task

- **Output/Output Table/Table Destination.** Select the location where your datasets are stored.

- **Output/Output Table/Name:** Enter "Application Results."

- **Output/Output Table/Table Generation Policy:** Select **Single Table (Overwrite)** from the dropdown list.

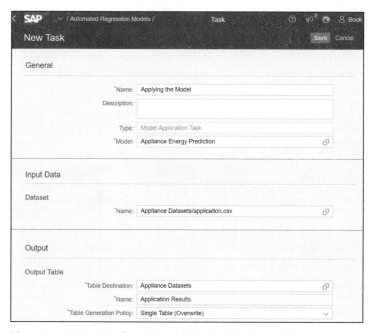

Figure 7.15 Basic Configuration of the Application Task

Outcomes of the Application Task

We won't go into detail for all the possible fields that you can create when the regression model is applied. We'll focus on the columns that are different from than when applying a classification model. Beyond the basic configuration, the value comes when we add predictions to the application task in the **Output Columns** section (Figure 7.16).

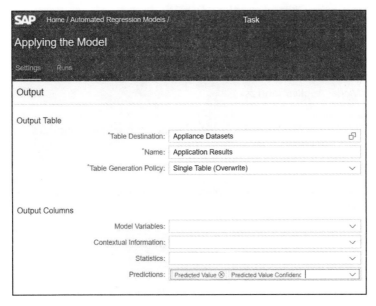

Figure 7.16 Output Columns

Table 7.1 explains the different output columns and the columns they correspond to and guides you on which ones to prioritize.

Section	Output Column	Description	Column Name (in File or Database)	Guidance
Statistics	**Approximate Quantile**	Use this option to split the output file into approximate quantiles and to assign to each dataset line the number of the quantile containing the line.	`quantile_ rr_<target>_ <nb_quantiles>`	Useful if you require specific prospect targeting based on quantiles.

Table 7.1 Different Output Columns When Applying a Classification Model

Section	Output Column	Description	Column Name (in File or Database)	Guidance
Statistics (Cont.)	**Approximate Quantile** (Cont.)	Predictive Factory considers 10 quantiles only. Approximate quantiles are constructed based on the sorted distribution and the boundaries of predicted scores from the validation sample. Score boundaries are used to determine approximate quantiles on the application dataset.		Please note that these quantiles are only approximate because they are based on the validation dataset then used as such on the application dataset.
	Outlier Indicator	A row is considered an outlier if the difference between the predicted value and the actual value exceeds the confidence level for the predicted value (the error bar).	`outlier_rr_ <target>`	Useful when a detailed analysis is needed.
	Variable Contributions	Contribution of each variable to the result. The sum of the variables' contributions equals the predictive score. Contributions can be positive or negative.	`contrib_<var>_ rr_<class>`	Highlights the top contributing variables for a given row. With some postprocessing, it's easy to determine the reasons leading to a specific prediction.
Predictions	**Predicted Value**	Predicted value, an estimation of the actual value.	`rr_<target>`	An important field, we usually want to get this value first.
	Predicted Value Confidence	The confidence level for the predicted value, also known as the error bar.	`bar_rr_ <target>`	In addition to the predicted values themselves, we need the confidence around the values.

Table 7.1 Different Output Columns When Applying a Classification Model (Cont.)

The other columns in the **Model Variables** and **Contextual Information** sections have similar outcomes as when we created classification models, as discussed in Chapter 6.

You can output the following information as predictions: the predicted value and the predicted value confidence (see Figure 7.17).

	A	B	C	D
1	KxIndex	Appliances	rr_Appliances	bar_rr_Appliances
14	13	50	45	35.81540511
15	14	50	43	33.25141676
16	15	40	42	37.95655697
17	16	20	42	37.95655697
18	17	50	43	33.25141676
19	18	40	45	35.81540511
20	19	50	45	35.81540511
21	20	40	44	34.53341094
22	21	50	49	100.6474495
23	22	70	53	127.568469

Figure 7.17 Actual Value, Predicted Value, and Predicted Value Confidence

Applying a Model in Automated Analytics

Beyond what we just described for the Predictive Factory (simple model application directly in file or database), additional options for applying a model can be also found in Automated Analytics, such as:

- Exporting regression models as source code
- Exporting the model as KxShell Script
- Running a simulation

You can also generate gain charts at training time (Figure 7.18) as well as at application time (Figure 7.19). The gain charts sum up the actual values and the predicted values per quantile as well as presents the min and max scores per quantile.

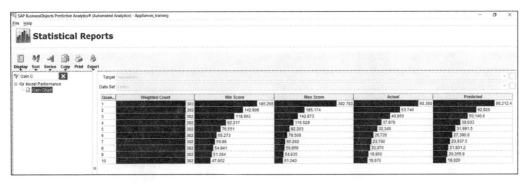

Figure 7.18 Training Gain Charts in Automated Analytics

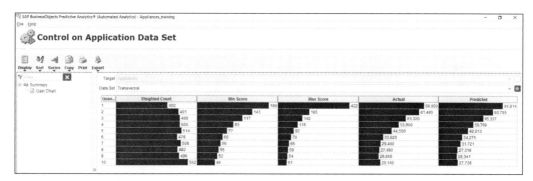

Figure 7.19 Transversal Gain Charts in Automated Analytics

Finally, reason codes can also be exported, similar to what can be done with classification models; reason codes highlight the variables making the most significant contributions to the final score.

7.5 Summary

In this chapter, we presented automated regression models—what they are, how to create them either using Predictive Factory or Automated Analytics, how to understand and improve them if necessary, and how to apply them in our business context. Regression models share multiple similarities with classification models as well as a few key differences.

Chapter 8
Automated Predictive Time Series Forecasting Models

This chapter introduces the concept of forecasting a time series, which represents a measure that reoccurs at constant time intervals. We'll show you how to forecast a single time series and we'll show you how to increase the forecast's accuracy by providing additional context.

While the term might sound complex, *time series* describes a simple concept and is a measure of events that occur at regular time intervals. Think, for example, of a manufacturer's monthly sales quantities, any company's daily cash flow, or the hourly demand for fresh bread in a supermarket.

Knowing which quantities to expect in the future allows a business to plan and act accordingly, as follows:

- Knowing more accurately the sales quantities to expect helps the manufacturer produce the appropriate quantities, ensuring the ability to deliver on receipt of an order without having to maintain excessive stock levels.

- Knowing more accurately the cash flow to expect in the following days allows the finance department to optimize their financial planning, benefitting from their supplier's payment terms whilst reducing costs for short-term liquidity.

- Knowing more accurately the hourly demand for fresh bread allows the retailer to decide how much bread to bake during the day, allowing the baker to offer fresh quality whilst reducing food wastage.

Thousands of different examples exist illustrating how time series forecasting can help a business operate more efficiently. And the beauty is that time series forecasting is quite easy, as we hope to show in this chapter.

In our example, we'll start by forecasting the number of bicycles rented in London every day. This initial forecast can be improved by adding context to the data, such as the weather. The ability to forecast many similar time series at once can be shown, for example, by forecasting how many passenger vehicles are registered each month in a number of European countries. Individual time series are created for each country to capture their unique trends. We'll also look into the concept of how to produce these time series automatically.

8.1   Creating and Understanding Time Series Forecast Models

Let's begin by looking at a common use case for time series forecasting: estimating the future demand for a product. In our specific example, we want to predict how many bicycles will be rented in the coming days in London. Many cities have rental schemes where a person can easily rent a bicycle for a short ride. The basis for our forecast is a daily summary of how many bicycles were rented in the past as shared by Transport for London at the London Datastore (*https://data.london.gov.uk/dataset/number-bicycle-hires*).

The historical daily rental numbers from January 1, 2013, to April 15, 2017, are shown in Figure 8.1.

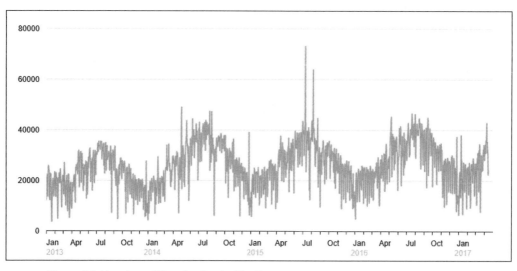

Figure 8.1 Number of Bicycles Rented by Day

While at first the numbers might seem rather erratic, over time, we can look for different patterns that are often hidden in such data. A time series forecasting model tries to capture the following effects:

- Trends over time: A trend describes whether the data is increasing or decreasing over time and, if so, how. For our example, we might hope to see a small trend of increasing rentals over the years.

- Recurring cycles: Does any cyclical pattern keep occurring? Such a pattern will be clearly visible. Rental numbers peak in the summertime and decrease in the winter. Other similar patterns might exist, i.e., on a weekly or monthly level.

- Fluctuations: Certain movements in the data cannot be explained by trends over time or recurring cycles. We'll see how to capture as many of these fluctuations as possible.

- Residuals: Any unexplained fluctuations are called *residuals*. The fewer residuals, and the smaller they are, the better the model.

Now that you know the basic terms, let's create a time series forecast! We'll start with a dataset consisting of just a single date and a single measure. We'll conduct some analysis on that time series and see how adding additional variables can increase the forecast's accuracy.

8.1.1   Creating and Training Models

To forecast our first time series, copy the file *LondonBikesDaily.csv* (available for download at *www.sap-press.com/4491*) into *C:\Predictive\FlatFiles* on the computer you have installed the SAP Predictive Analytics server. While we are here, also copy the files *LondonBikesDaily_Extended.csv* and *VehicleRegistrations.csv* into the same folder; we'll use them later on in this chapter.

The *LondonBikesDaily.csv* file contains the rental history discussed earlier in Section 8.1, upon which our forecast will be made. The last few rows are shown in Table 8.1.

Date	Count
2017-04-12	32570
2017-04-13	30343
2017-04-14	22357
2017-04-15	24627

Table 8.1 Rental History in April

Date Format in Flat Files

When working with a flat file, the date must be formatted according to ISO 8601, which is YYYY-MM-DD.

Sequence of Dates in Flat Files

When working with a flat file, rows must be sorted by date, with the oldest on top and the most recent measurement at the bottom.

Missing Values

If an historical value of the measure that you want to forecast is unknown, then do not include that date in the historical dataset. SAP Predictive Analytics will assume that the missing date is the beginning of the time period to forecast. Just delete the date/row for which the historical measure is not known. The tool can handle such incomplete time series.

To use this data, you must make these datasets known to the Predictive Factory by following these steps:

1. Log on to the Predictive Factory and go into the **Modeling Servers** section, as shown in Figure 8.2.

Figure 8.2 Modeling Servers

2. Click on the modeling server that you created in Chapter 3 and switch to the **Edit** mode by clicking on the pencil icon in the top-right corner.

3. Scroll to the bottom of the screen and create a new **Data Connection**. Name this connection "Flat Files." Click on the icon next to **Data Source Name**, and the available **Data Providers** will be listed.

4. Click on **Text Files** and specify the folder *C:\Predictive\FlatFiles*. The data connection description screen should look like what's shown in Figure 8.3.

Edit Data Connection	
Description	
*Name:	Flat Files
Description:	
*Data Source Name:	C:\Predictive\FlatFiles
	OK Cancel

Figure 8.3 Data Connection Description Screen

5. Confirm these settings by clicking **OK**, then click **Save** on top of the screen to create the new data connection.

6. To store the model's metadata, create a folder called *C:\Predictive\ModelRepo* and create another data connection to that folder. Name that connection "ModelRepo".

We are now ready to create a new project, in which we'll carry out the time series forecast. To begin, follow these steps:

1. On the Predictive Factory website, create a new project as introduced in Chapter 5, Section 5.2.

2. On the **Projects** tab, click **Add Project**, as shown in Figure 8.4.

Figure 8.4 Adding a Project

3. Name the project "Bicycle Rental Forecast" and assign both the **Project Manager** and **Analyst** roles to the **Administrator** as shown in Figure 8.5.

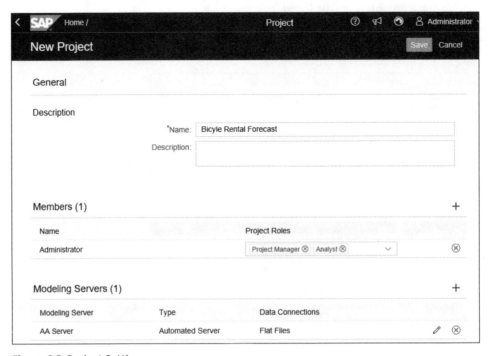

Figure 8.5 Project Settings

4. Specify your **Modeling Server** and the **Data Connections** as shown in Figure 8.6.

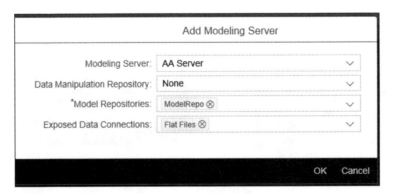

Figure 8.6 Modeling Server and Data Connections

5. Click **OK** and save the new project with the icon on the top right. The new project will be displayed, as shown in Figure 8.7.

Figure 8.7 The Newly Created Project

6. Click on the project, and you'll be given the option to create a new model, as shown in Figure 8.8. Click on **Add Model**. You would use **Import** if the model was created in the Windows-based version of SAP Predictive Analytics and needs to be maintained by the Predictive Factory.

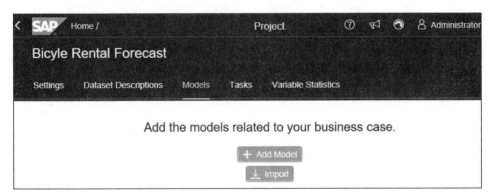

Figure 8.8 Adding a Model

7. Next, select the **Time Series Forecasting** option. The **New Model** screen will open. Enter the name "Daily Demand" in the **Name** field. Select the source file *London-BikesDaily.csv*, which contains the historical records of daily rental numbers.

8. Click **OK**, and the top of your screen should look like what's shown in Figure 8.9.

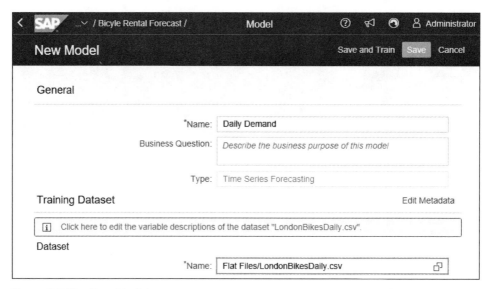

Figure 8.9 The New Model

9. In time series forecasting, it's important that information about the date is recognized in true "Date" or "Date & Time" format. Click on **Edit Metadata**, and for each column, the variable storage and type will be displayed. For the **Date** variable, **Storage** type **Date** should have been recognized, as shown in Figure 8.10. Remember that earlier we mentioned the date specified in a file has to have the format YYYY-MM-DD. If dates are not in this format, they might not be recognized. If a date is not recognized, you cannot simply change the dropdown in the **Storage** column. You'll have to change how the data is stored in the file.

Figure 8.10 Variable Types

10. Close the **Edit Metadata** window, scroll down, and set the **Signal Variable**, which represents the measure we want to forecast, to **Hires** and set the **Date Variable** to

Date, as shown in Figure 8.11. Ignore the **Segmented by** option for now. We'll use it later when forecasting multiple time series in Section 8.2.

Figure 8.11 New Model

11. Scroll down further and enter "15" in the **Number of Forecasts** field: A forecast will be created for 15 days following the end of the historical data. Since the historical data ends on April 15, 2017, the forecast will examine the period from April 16, 2017, to April 30, 2017.

12. Select the **Generate Positive Forecasts Only** checkbox to ensure that no negative values are predicted, which is suitable for the context of our forecast (the number of bicycle rentals cannot be negative). Your settings should look like what's shown in Figure 8.12.

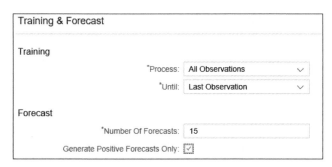

Figure 8.12 Number of Periods to Forecast

13. Do not change the other settings on the page, which allow you to use only a subset of the historical training data, which can be helpful for example if you have a rather long history. Restricting the data thus ensures that patterns from long ago, which might not be relevant anymore, do not distort the model. No hard rule on how much history is ideal exists, but having a pattern appear 4 or 5 times in the history is useful. So, if the data has a yearly pattern, 4 or 5 years of history might be a good starting point. However, longer or shorter stretches of history can also work well.

14. Click **Save and Train** on the top right. The model settings are saved, and immediately a forecasting model will be trained. After a few seconds, you should see that the model was trained successfully, as shown in Figure 8.13.

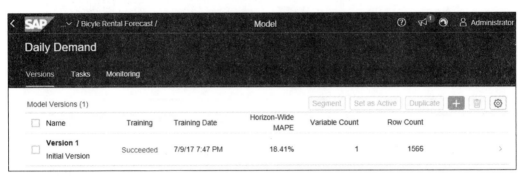

Figure 8.13 A Successfully Trained Model

8.1.2   Understanding Models

Using the model we just created and trained, we can now walk through the model to understand its most important attributes. The quality of the model is described with the horizon-wide mean absolute percentage error (MAPE) value of 18.41%. While quite a mouthful, MAPE simply represents by how many percentage point on average the daily forecasts are wrong in comparison to the actual values. So, for our data, on average, the model estimated that our records were too high or too low by 18.41%. The lower the MAPE, the better the model. In Section 8.4, we'll discuss how model quality is calculated in more detail if you want to learn more.

A MAPE score alone does not say a lot about how much value that model can bring to your business and use case. As long as the model is more accurate than your current process, or is more efficient to create, then the model is adding some value to the business. In Section 8.1.4, we'll improve the model further.

The Predictive Factory also displays the **Variable Count** is 1, because our forecast was trained only with the date variable. The **Row Count** of 1566 represents how many days of history were found. So, we know the bicycle rental history for 1,566 days, from January 1, 2013, to April 15, 2017.

For now, click anywhere on the horizontal panel representing the model, and its summary will be shown. Click on the **Reports** tab, and more details about the trained model will be displayed, as shown in Figure 8.14.

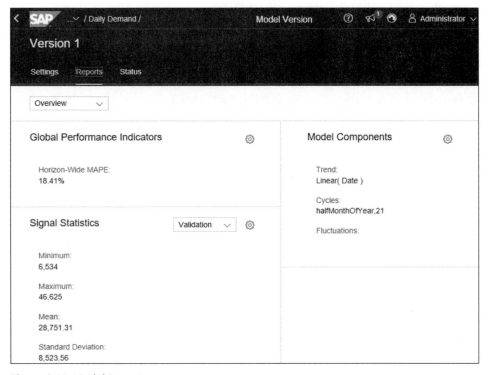

Figure 8.14 Model Report

The left-hand side shows some summary statistics about the measure we forecasted. The maximum number of rentals on a single day was 46,625; the mean value was 28,751.31. The standard deviation is a measure of how the numbers of hires are spread across days.

The right-hand side displays the model's main logic. The terms *trend*, *cycles*, and *fluctuations* might be familiar to you from Section 8.1. A trend describes whether/how the data increases or decreases over time. Cycles describe recurring patterns, and fluctuations can describe some of the remaining unexplained variance.

Our model consists of the following components:

- A linear trend over time was found, so the number of rentals tends to increase or decrease. We'll see more information about this trend in just a few pages.

- Two cycles were found. One half-monthly cycle exists over the year, a pattern that breaks the year down into 24 windows. The number of rentals in the first half of July, for instance, might be very different to the second half of December. Given the weather, this pattern seems natural. The time series forecasting model identified this cycle without knowing the rental context, like the weather. In addition, a second cycle with a length of 21 days was identified. So, this pattern keeps repeating every 3 weeks. In Section 8.4.3, you'll see which other types of cycles are considered.

- No fluctuations are listed. In other words, no autoregressive component was found to explain some of the remaining fluctuations.

Don't worry if you don't know what an autoregressive component is. If you would like to know, however, we'll touch upon this topic in Section 8.4.4.

To see the forecasted value, select **Forecast** from the upper dropdown menu. You'll see the model's predictions as forecasted values in blue on top of the historical actuals in green, as shown in Figure 8.15. The model has forecasted the unknown future for the next 15 days but also estimates the known past. Seeing which values the model would have predicted in the past compared to the actual values helps see and understand how the model works and its quality.

Use the magnifying glass icon to zoom into the chart and scroll to the right. You can now see the forecast of the future 15 days much clearer. The forecast is complemented by a prediction range whose bounds are shown as **Error Min** and **Error Max**. The narrower this range, the more accurately the model describes the data.

The distance of the prediction range's bounds (**Error Min** and **Error Max**) to the forecasted value is equal to two standard deviations of the residuals on the validation data. In Section 8.4.1, we'll explain what data is included as part of the validation set.

Some data points in the chart are marked with a red circle as outliers. On these historical dates, the forecast was rather far from the actuals. For example, on December 25, 2016, the number of rentals was unexpectedly high. On January 1, 2017, the number was unexpectedly low. The settings icon allows you to make changes to the chart, i.e., you can hide outliers if desired. Just click on the settings icon and remove the term **Outliers** from the selection for the **Y-Axis**.

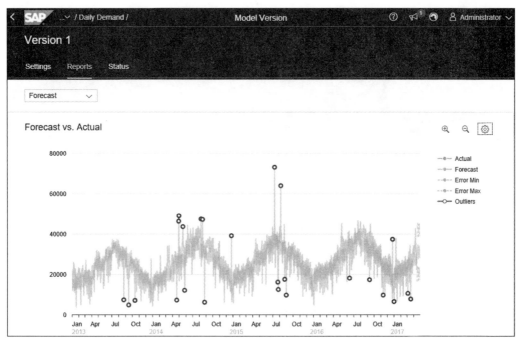

Figure 8.15 Forecast Chart

Outliers are identified in the following way: On these dates, the absolute difference between the actual and the forecasted value was larger than three times the standard deviation of the residuals of the estimation data. In Section 8.4.1, we'll explain what data is included as part of the estimation set.

If you scroll down, you'll see a table with the forecasted values and the bounds of the prediction range. Any outliers are listed in a separate table.

At the bottom of the page, the **Signal Anomalies** section is not relevant for now. An anomaly occurs if a forecast for future dates was performed, and the eventual true value falls outside the prediction range. We'll say more about this scenario in Section 8.3.

To analyze the pattern found by the time series, select **Signal Analysis** from the drop-down list on top. The signal is still shown, as before, as a green line. However, now, the individual forecast components of the model are also shown, as can be seen in Figure 8.16.

The linear trend is shown with a red line, which is clearly increasing. The overall number of rented bicycles has been on the rise over the years. Zoom into the chart, and what appears to be a thick yellow line at the bottom becomes a line chart showing the cycles that were detected. The cycle of 21 days, for example, contains a pattern that shows clear peaks during the middle of each week and lower demand on the weekend.

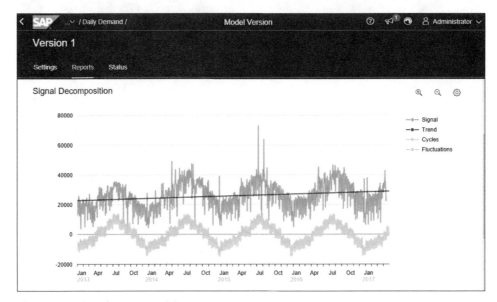

Figure 8.16 Signal Decomposition

So, thus far, we've trained a forecasting model, analyzed its workings, and seen the forecasted values in the Predictive Factory. Now, let's save those forecasts to a database or to file.

8.1.3   Saving Time Series Forecasts

In our example, we'll save our forecasts to a file. Go back to the **Settings** tab and click on **Apply** at the top right, as shown in Figure 8.17.

Figure 8.17 Saving Forecast Values

You'll need to specify the location of the historical data, but the screen might already show the file used when training the model, *LondonBikesDaily.csv*. If the file is not shown, just select the file as before. Specify how many days you would like to forecast; for our example, let's stick with 15 days.

The **Table Destination** specifies where the forecasts should be saved. Remember, you will only see the data connections that have been added when you first set up the modeling server and in the project's settings. Select the **Flat Files** option. When you select the folder, the files in that folder will be grayed out, which is as expected, as the Predictive Factory will create the destination file for us. After selecting the folder and clicking **OK**, enter the destination file name manually: "LondonBikesDemandForecast.csv."

Different levels of detail can be written into that file. Just set **Forecast Information** to **Forecasts, Lower Bound, Upper Bound**, which might have already been selected by default. We'll explain below what the different options do. Your screen should look similar to what's shown in Figure 8.18 and Figure 8.19.

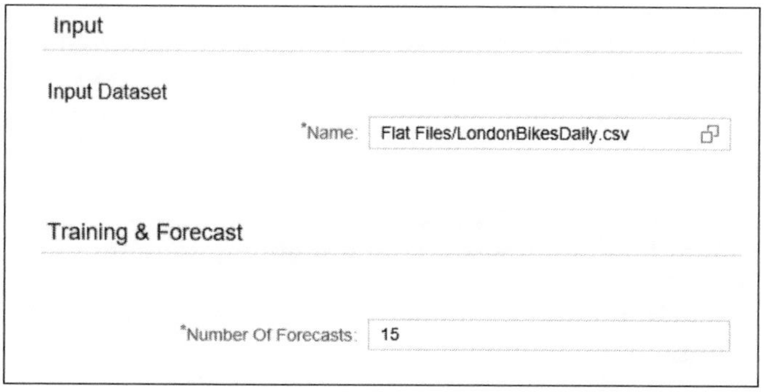

Figure 8.18 Applying the Model, Upper Screen

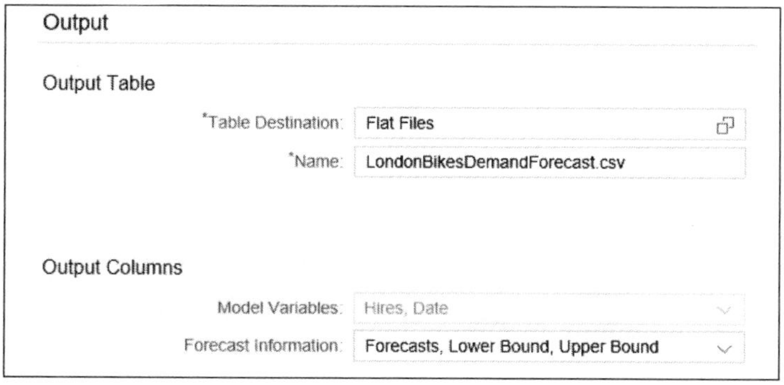

Figure 8.19 Applying the Model, Lower Screen

To save your forecasts to a database, the Predictive Factory can either create the target table for you in the correct structure, or you can just write the forecast into an existing table. The settings for creating and writing into an SAP HANA table are shown in Figure 8.20. Remember that, if you would like to write to a database, then the data connection must have been added when you first set up the modeling server and in the project's settings.

Figure 8.20 Writing Forecasts into an SAP HANA Table

Click **OK** to return to the model's settings. The rotating icon on the top right indicates that the process of producing the forecasts and saving them to file has started. Click on the icon, and you'll eventually see confirmation that the process has successfully completed, as shown in Figure 8.21.

Figure 8.21 Confirmation Message

Now, open the file that was created. You'll see these columns:

- The date.

- An index column called `KxIndex`.

- The actual recorded value for historical dates in the column `Hires`.

- The forecasted value beginning from the earliest possible date than can be forecasted in the column `kts_1`. For example, if the model's components use an autoregressive component, then the first forecast can only be done after the length of the correlation.

- The forecasts for the 15 future dates are complemented with the lower and upper bounds of the prediction range. The bounds, which are called **Error Min** and **Error Max** in the Predictive Factory are labeled `kts_1_lowerlimit_95%` and `kts_1_upperlimit_95%` in the output. Defining these bounds was discussed earlier in Section 8.1.2.

These forecasted values in the file can now be picked up for their intended purpose. With our forecast of the future demand for the next 15 days, the bicycle rental scheme could, for example, ensure that sufficient bicycles are available on each day. Days with low demand could be used to maintain some of the bikes that are not needed; the expected demand could be used to plan how many employees should be on duty in the customer service center.

A more granular forecast would also be helpful. Predicting how many bicycles will be rented per individual location per hour, for example, could be valuable for ensuring bicycles are available. We don't have that level of detail in our sample dataset, but we'll show you in Section 8.2 how to scale the creation of time series forecasting models to cater to such a requirement.

Most likely, the output columns created with the **Forecast Information** option set to **Forecasts, Lower Bound, Upper Bound** as discussed in our example will be the most useful columns for most of your own projects. However, the Predictive Factory can also produce further columns with additional information. You can control this by changing the **Forecast Information** option. For every choice, the date, the index, the actual historical value, and the forecast are included.

Some of the available options include the following:

- **Forecasts, Lower Bound, Upper Bound**
  Also includes the upper and lower bounds, representing the prediction range introduced earlier.

- **Forecasts**
  Also includes the 15-day forecast as determined from historical actual values. In

our example, you will also get 15 individual forecasts for every day beginning from January 2, 2013, to April 15, 2017, which could be helpful if you'd like to further analyze the model's forecasting performance over a known history.

- **Forecasts, Trend, Fluctuation, Periodic**
  Includes the content of the above **Forecasts** option plus, for each forecasted value, a decomposition of the trend, fluctuation, and periodic component. Let's look at the kts1_Trend column, for example. Comparing the value in this column between two dates/rows shows an overall trend that was found. Since the trend that was identified on the bicycle data is linear on the date, the increase per day is constant in the model. In our case, the number of rentals goes up on average by 3.95 per day. You can find this value by taking the difference of two subsequent values in the kts_1Trend (or kts2_2Trend) column and any other of the trend columns. If a non-linear trend had been identified, then the changes in the different trend columns might differ.

- **Forecasts, Trend, Fluctuation, Periodic, Noise**
  Includes the content of the above option plus additional columns that show how the residuals (the difference between the actual and forecasted value) are reduced by adding components to the model, beginning with the trend, the recurring cycles, and finally an autoregressive component that might help explain some of the remaining fluctuations.

In the next section, we'll try to improve the model's forecasting accuracy by adding additional context/columns to explain some of the remaining fluctuations, thereby reducing the MAPE.

8.1.4   Increasing Model Accuracy

In the previous sections, the model we created had a MAPE of 18.41%. On average, the model estimated 18.41% too high or too low. This forecast was easy to create as we only had to provide the history of dates and rental numbers.

If you would like to improve the accuracy of the forecast, you can provide additional context to the dates and measures. For example, a person might or might not want to rent a bicycle for many reasons. Just think of the weather; if it is raining heavily, the number of rentals might go down. By extending the data with columns that add such context (e.g., the average temperature of the day), we can give the Predictive Factory a way to improve the model. These columns with additional information are called *extra predictables*. The file *LondonBikesDaily_Extended.csv* includes the date and the number of rentals as before, plus some additional columns including information on temperature, visibility, wind speed, whether or not it's a holiday, etc.

Some of these variables will hopefully help explain how many bicycles were rented. You can be creative at this point and bring in your understanding of the business context. What additional information could help describe the time series? In financial forecasting, for example, a column that counts the number of days to the next closing deadline might help.

To allow the model to produce a forecast, these additional variables should also be provided for the dates you want to forecast. Therefore, our file *LondonBikesDaily_Extended.csv* also now contains the 15 dates to forecast, from April 16, 2017, to April 30, 2017. The **Hires** column is still empty for the 15 future dates as we don't know their true values yet. The remaining columns, however, hold the corresponding information for these 15 days.

Some information is easy to specify for these future dates, e.g., whether a day is a working day or not. Other information, such as the weather forecast, may have to be acquired. If you were unable to acquire such a weather forecast, then that information cannot be used in the model. This concept of extra predictables also allows you to play with scenarios; you can carry out one forecast to know the predicted number for a maximum temperature of 10°C and then carry out another forecast for the maximum temperature of 25°C. Calculating such dimensions can give you a best case or worst case scenario, for instance.

Missing Values in Extra Predictables

The tool can handle missing values in the extra predictable columns, for both historical and future dates. So even a predictable variable that is only partially known can still be included in the model. Obviously, the more available data, the better the chance of finding a pattern that will increase the model's accuracy.

To create a new forecasting model, we can remain in the project we created in the previous section and continue as follows:

1. Go into the **Models** tab, click the **+** button and create a new **Time Series Forecasting** model (Figure 8.22).

2. Create a model similar to what we created in the previous section. Name the new model "Daily Demand Extended" and select the file *LondonBikesDaily_Extended.csv* as its source. You can change the metadata, such as the variable type, but you don't have to here.

Figure 8.22 Creating a New Time Series Forecasting Model with Extra Predictables

3. Set the **Signal Variable** to **Hires** and the **Date Variable** to **Date** as before. We do not need to exclude any of the extra variables; they are all columns we hope will improve the model.

4. At the bottom of the page, enter "15" as the **Number of Forecasts** and select the **Generate Positive Forecasts Only** option.

5. Leave all other options unchanged. Click **Save and Train** on the top right. The model will be created and may a little longer than before because the additional columns increase the computation time.

When the model has been finalized, we'll see an improved MAPE of 12.28%, as shown in Figure 8.23. The extra predictables have clearly improved the model, which had a MAPE of 18.41% without these variables.

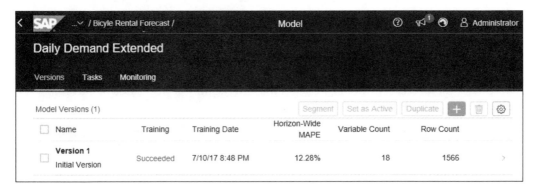

Figure 8.23 The Improved Model

Click into the new model, and you will see, on the **Reports** tab, that **ExtrasPredictables** appear as linear **Trend** component, as shown in Figure 8.24. This term refers to the additional variables. Also, a cycle was found for the column Precipitationmm, which reports the rain per day in millimeters.

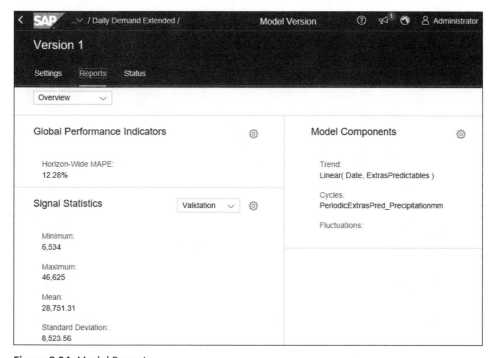

Figure 8.24 Model Report

To see the new forecasts, change the dropdown list to **Forecast**; the improved model will appear, as shown in Figure 8.25. Compare this chart to the forecast without the extra variables, shown in Figure 8.15. Notice how the improved forecast manages to follow the actual values much more closely.

Of course, you can now save the forecasted values to a file or to a database using the **Apply** option as shown earlier, in Figure 8.17.

By now, we've learned a lot about forecasting a single time series automatically. Whilst we hope you found this process easy enough, often hundreds or even thousands of similar time series need to be forecasted. The next section explains how to create such a large number of time series forecasts.

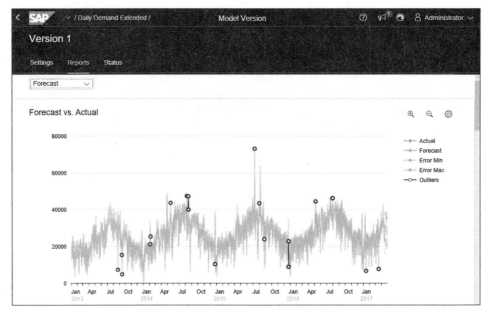

Figure 8.25 Forecast Chart

8.2   Mass Producing Time Series Forecasts

You may often find yourself in a situation where similar time series need to be forecasted. A manufacturer, for instance, might want to know the future monthly sales quantities of the most important 100 products, which alone would require 100 time series. Now, imagine doing this for the top 100 products for 10 different regions. That makes 1,000 models alone that need to be created every month.

Predictive Factory allows you to segment time series in order to handle such requirements efficiently. So far we have only forecasted a single time series; therefore, the history of the data we worked with only contained that single time series. To forecast multiple time series at once, just provide the different historical time series as a single source, but identified with an additional column so that the individual time series can still be identified. If you'd like to see an example, take a look at the *VehicleRegistrations.csv* file.

Let's try this concept out by forecasting how many cars (or passenger vehicles to be precise) will be registered in the next 12 months in a number of different European countries. Our history contains the monthly car registrations for 29 different countries, from Austria to the United Kingdom. This data was obtained from the European

Automobile Manufacturers Association website (*http://www.acea.be/statistics/tag/category/by-country-registrations*). The historical data is held in the file *VehicleRegistrations.csv*. If you have not yet copied the file, as discussed in Section 8.1.1, into the *C:\Predictive\FlatFiles* folder, then please do so now.

Notice that, in the file, the data is aggregated on a monthly level. However, the time series forecasting needs specific dates. Hence, each month is identified by the first day of the calendar month. December 2015, for instance, is represented by 2015-12-01. Similarly, if your data was aggregated by the week, you could select the week's Monday to specify the week (or you can use any other weekday, just be consistent).

The file contains these three columns:

- Country (i.e., Austria, Belgium, Bulgaria, etc.)
- Month (in the format YYYY-MM-DD)
- Registrations

Further predictable columns could help improve the forecast. For simplicity, we won't use any extra predictable columns in our example. To begin:

1. Create a new project called "Vehicle Registrations." Use the same settings as our first project, which we created in Section 8.1.1. Remember to add both project role types to the user. Your settings should be similar to what's shown in Figure 8.26.

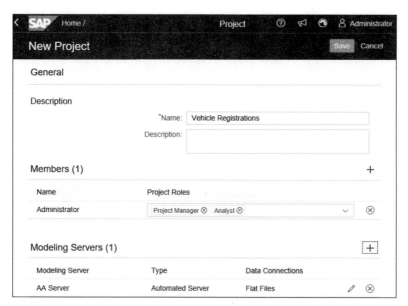

Figure 8.26 New Project to Forecast Multiple Time Series

2. Save the project and then open it. Click on **Add Model** and choose **Time Series Fore-casting**. Name the model "Vehicle Registrations by Country" and select the file *VehicleRegistrations.csv* as its training dataset.

3. Click on **Edit Metadata** to see that the month column storage is recognized as "Date" (Figure 8.27).

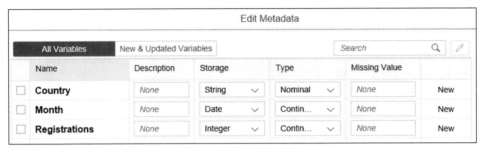

Figure 8.27 Metadata Settings

Close that window and scroll down. Then, set **Signal Variable** to **Registrations**, set **Date Variable** to **Month**, and set **Segmented by** to **Country**. These settings allow the Predictive Factory to create an individual time series forecast for each country found in the dataset. The settings should be similar to what's shown in Figure 8.28.

Figure 8.28 Project Settings

4. Scroll down further and ask for 12 forecasts, in order to predict a full year. Also, you can select the **Generate Positive Forecasts Only** checkbox, as a negative number of registrations is impossible. Leave the other settings unchanged, as shown in Figure 8.29.

Figure 8.29 Project Settings

5. Click **Save and Train** for the Predictive Factory to produce individual forecasts for each country. As we have 29 different countries in the data, we will receive 29 individual forecasts. As such, this request may take a few minutes to complete. However, you can keep working on other tasks in the Predictive Factory. The notification icon on the top right will indicate when the forecasts have been completed.

When done, the first summary shows a MAPE of 10.10%, as shown in Figure 8.30, which means that the average of the MAPEs of all time series is 10.10%.

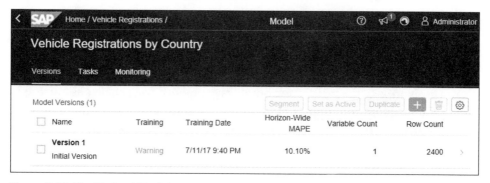

Figure 8.30 The Trained Model

Click into the version and go to the **Reports** tab. The ten time series with the best and worst MAPEs are shown (Figure 8.31).

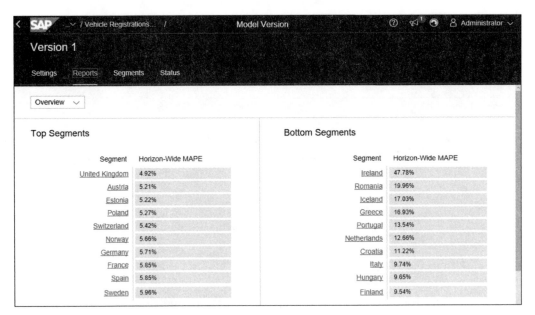

Figure 8.31 Top and Bottom Segments

Click on any country. To see the actual and predicted values, change the dropdown to **Forecast**. The actuals and the forecast for the United Kingdom, for example, show big spikes in vehicle registrations in March and September, as shown in Figure 8.32. These spikes exist because, in the United Kingdom, the digits on the number plate of a car indicate during which half-year period the car was registered. Every March and September these digits change, so it seems many people are waiting to register a car until the new digits are used.

If you want to view another forecast, click the small white arrow pointing left, right next to the SAP logo. If you click on Switzerland, for example, you'll see different patterns in monthly registration numbers, which the model tried to accommodate. As shown in Figure 8.33, the registration numbers per month don't change as much as in the United Kingdom, for instance. However, two peaks occurred throughout the year, now in March and June. June 2012 is flagged as an outlier because significantly more vehicles were registered than the model predicted. This spike was probably because a more stringent law on emissions came into force in July 2012.

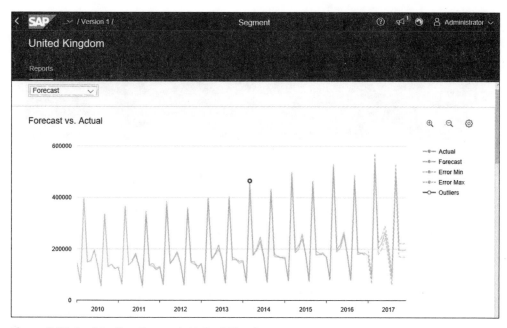

Figure 8.32 Registration Forecast: United Kingdom

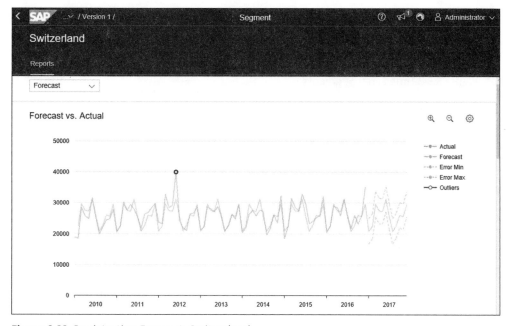

Figure 8.33 Registration Forecast: Switzerland

If you go into the **Segments** tab, you'll see all the countries in the dataset. For each country, a unique forecast was created, as shown in Figure 8.34.

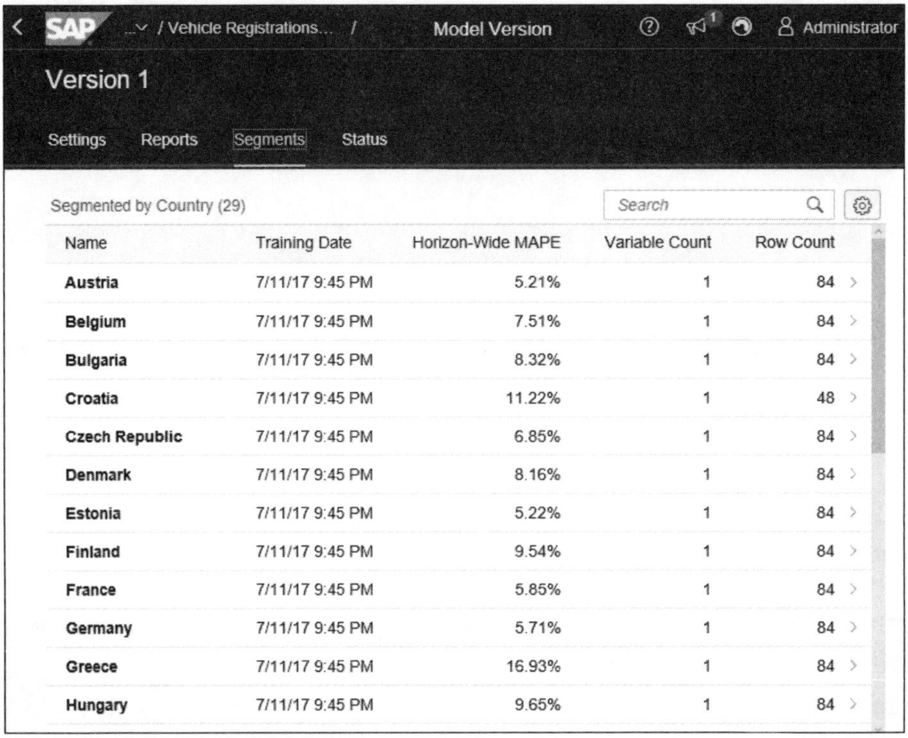

Figure 8.34 Time Series Segments

Any warnings that might have occurred are shown on the right on the **Status** tab. For each warning, two different entries appear on this page. First, the warning itself is mentioned, followed by another entry specifying which time series the warning refers to.

In our case, we received a warning that the model chosen for 3 of the time series is only confident in the forecast for a shorter horizon than the requested 12 months.

Now we would like to save the forecasts to a file. Go into the **Settings** tab and click **Apply**. As **Input File** select *VehicleRegistrations.csv*. Set the **Number of Forecasts** to 12. For **Table Destination**, select **Flat Files** and type "VehicleRegistrationsForecast.csv" as the name for the output. The screen should look like what's shown in Figure 8.35.

Figure 8.35 Applying the Models

For any other options, keep the default settings and click **OK**. When the task completes, you'll find the *VehicleRegistrationsForecast.csv* file in the folder *C:\Predictive\ FlatFiles*.

Segmenting a Time Series on Multiple Levels

More complex scenarios can also be accommodated. If you want to produce forecasts specific to a region as well as a product, for example, you'll need to segment on a column that concatenates the region's name with the product name.

8.3   Productizing the Forecast Model

By now, we know how to create one or many different time series using the latest available data. If you are doing a monthly demand forecast, most likely you'll want to create a new demand forecast every month. In this chapter, we'll see how to use the Predictive Factory to automate such a requirement, where a time series forecast needs to be created at a fixed schedule.

For a hands-on example, let's go back to the daily rental numbers of our London rental bike scheme. Imagine that, day after day, we want to forecast the rental numbers for the next 15 days. For simplicity, we'll use the data without extra predictables, as earlier in Section 8.1.1. Just note that exactly the same process to a forecast time series on a recurring basis as shown in this chapter applies to time series that have additional predictables or that use segmentation or both.

The basis for such a recurring forecast is a normal time series forecasting model. Therefore, we can make use of the model we created in Section 8.1.1. To begin:

1. Open the **Bicycle Rental Forecast** project and click on the **Daily Demand** model. You should see the model that was trained successfully earlier on, as shown in Figure 8.36.

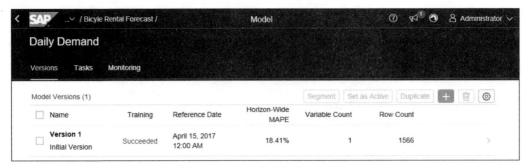

Figure 8.36 A Trained Time Series Forecasting Model

2. A recurring schedule is specified by attaching a task to this model, which can only be done for models in an active state. Therefore, activate this model by selecting the model and then selecting the **Set as Active** checkbox. On the right-hand side, you should now see the model is flagged as **Active**, as shown in Figure 8.37.

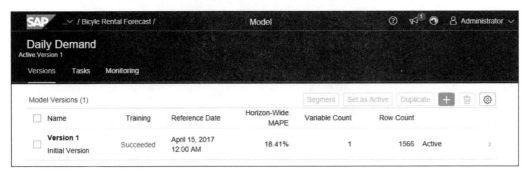

Figure 8.37 Active Model

3. Now, go into the **Tasks** tab, click **Add Task**, and select **Time Series Forecasting Task**. Name the task "Schedule Daily Retrain and Forecast." As **Input Dataset** select *LondonBikesDaily.csv*. Scroll down and set **Number of Forecasts** to "15." Next, select the **Generate Positive Forecasts** checkbox only. Your settings should be similar to what's shown in Figure 8.38.

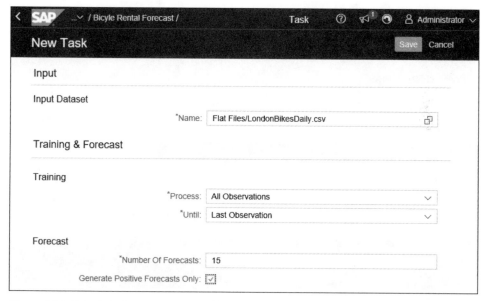

Figure 8.38 Schedule Screen, Upper Half

4. Let's say that, every time a new forecast is created, we want the new forecast written to a file. To do so, select the **Generate Output Table** checkbox and set **Table Destination** to **Flat Files** (remember, this data connection we have already used many times). Enter the name of the file that will be created, e.g., "*LondonBikesDemandForecast_DailySchedule.csv*." Keep the setting for **Table Generation Policy**, which will overwrite the same file with every schedule.

Alternatively, with the policy **One Table Per Run**, each forecast could be written to a new, unique file, with the date-time stamp added to the end of the file name. This feature allows us to keep the forecasting history because the old forecasts won't be overwritten by new forecasts. In our tests of writing to files, the timestamp was added to the file extension, thereby changing the file type. So, this setting might be best suited for database tables as destinations. The policy **Single Table (Update)** maintains a history of forecasts, adding new rows or updating existing rows if needed.

5. Finally, define the schedule interval. Click on the **+** button next to **Schedule** and set to repeat every 1 day, as shown in Figure 8.39.

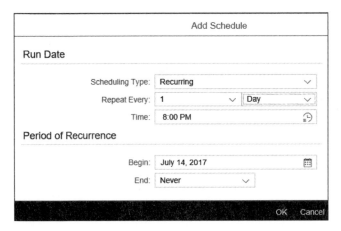

Figure 8.39 Schedule Interval

6. Click **OK,** and your settings should look like what's shown in Figure 8.40.

Figure 8.40 Schedule Screen, Lower Half

7. Click **Save** and we see the active schedule, as in Figure 8.41.

Figure 8.41 Active Schedule

Now, every day at the specified time, a new time series forecasting model will be trained on the latest available data, and a new forecast will be written to the specified file. Similarly, of course, the forecast could have been written to a database. Our example assumes that the history will be updated daily, after which the time series finds an additional day in the history.

Every time a forecast is carried out through this task, which can be triggered either through a scheduled time interval or manually by clicking the **Run Now** button, the most important model statistics are added to the display on the **Monitoring** tab, as shown in Figure 8.42. By default, the models' MAPE and number of variables are displayed, providing insights into how the model's quality changed over time.

Despite all your best efforts, however, sometimes actual values fall outside the prediction range. Unique effects in the past may be invisible and thus cannot be considered in the forecasting model; in extreme cases, the actual value falls outside the prediction range. Such strong differences between prediction and reality are flagged by the Predictive Factory as **Signal Anomalies**, which are listed in the model's **Report** tab when looking at the **Forecast**. You'll find signal anomalies listed at the bottom of the screen. Should an anomaly occur, you can notify the business users working with these numbers. At the same time, you can try to describe the special circumstances with an extra predictable column to increase future forecasting accuracy.

To leverage the identification of anomalies, you'll need to train a model whilst ignoring the most recent signal values. Therefore, the model itself does not know the future it is predicting, but the Predictive Factory is aware of these values. Should any of true values fall outside the prediction range, an anomaly is found.

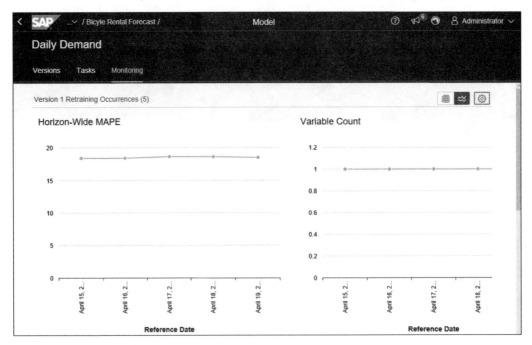

Figure 8.42 Monitoring

Let's look at a brief example. Say you have a model that forecasts monthly values for the next 3 months. You have already scheduled a task that runs every month to forecast the following 3 months. To use the anomalies, you can add another monthly task, dictating that the model training data should finish 3 months earlier. This rule is specified in the **Training & Forecast** option by setting the **Until** option for the training to **Reference Date**, as shown in Figure 8.43.

Training & Forecast		
Training		
	*Process:	All Observations ∨
	*Until:	Reference Date ∨

Figure 8.43 Restricting Training Data

Because of this setting, when specifying the schedule, the **Reference Date** option appears. You'll need to set the **Definition** to **Run Date Shift**. Specify the appropriate shift as shown in Figure 8.44.

Figure 8.44 Reference Date

Please note that this anomaly feature can also be used without a schedule. In this case, you'll set the **Until** option to **User-Defined Date** and then manually specify the appropriate date. Anomalies can also be detected in a segmented time series.

Now, we have an automatic forecasting factory that can produce thousands of forecasts with ease.

8.4   The Data Science behind Automated Time Series Forecasting Models

While the person using the automated approach to forecast time series may not need to know in detail how the forecasting model is created, some users will appreciate having a deeper understanding of how the models are determined.

The overall approach of how time series forecasting models are created by identifying different patterns in the data is explained in the following sections. At first, a time series is split into different parts, so that patterns can be identified and verified. Different patterns are considered. Early on, the time series is stabilized by removing any overall trends. Recurring cycles are deduced, and the tool tries to explain remaining fluctuations. We'll look at the concept of smoothing the data and consider how a model's overall quality is calculated.

8.4.1   Data Split

Initially, historical data is split in two parts to allow the model to identify and verify patterns in the data. The default **Sequential without test** cutting strategy places the first 75% of the data into the estimation set, and the remaining 25% is used for validation. Alternatively, using the **Sequential** cutting strategy, the first 60% of the data is placed into the estimation set, the next 20% goes into the validation set, and the remaining 20% is placed in a test set.

227

8.4.2 De-trending

Many, if not most, time series forecasts will show an overall trend over time, either increasing or decreasing somehow. In the first step, Automated Analytics will try to identify such trends. The following approaches are considered:

- Lag 1: Compares the value of two subsequent dates to assess whether there is a trend in the data. Imagine you have subsequent values of 100, 103, and 106. The lag 1 values for this short example are 103 – 100 = 3 and 106 – 103 = 3. This artificial case indicates a linear trend of an increase of 3 per time period. In reality, the difference between the 2 days will vary, but a common value can be approximated.

- Lag 2: Similar to lag 1, but the value of a date is compared with the value of two time units before. So for the above example this would be 106 – 100 = 6.

- Second order differencing: Uses data where the lag has already been deduced to carry out another lag analysis on top. This approach can determine how a trend changes over time.

- Linear in time: Internally, an additional variable is added to the dataset invisible to the user, representing an index of the time intervals. The first time interval is represented with a 1; the 20th time interval is represented with 20. This option looks for a linear relationship between the *time* and *target* variables.

- Polynomial in time: Similar to above, but a polynomial relationship between the Time and Target variable is considered.

If extra predictable columns are used, these are also taken into account attempting to identify a trend:

- Linear in extra predictables
- Linear in time and linear in extra predictables
- Polynomial in time and linear in extra predictables

The term *linear in extra predictables* might need some explaining. Trends that are being looked for are not necessarily directly related to time. These trends refer to how the value of one extra predictable column impacts the target variable, answering, for example, whether a linear relationship exists between the maximum temperature and how many bicycles are rented.

When training a model, any trend identified will be deduced from the original measurement in order to obtain a stable series. This stability helps identify further patterns in the data that might have been obscured by the above trends.

8.4.3   De-cycling

Having obtained a stable time series, in the next step, recurring time patterns are looked for. Various cycles are considered that fall into these three categories:

- **Seasonal**

  The following *seasons* are considered (we are using the terminology that is also used in the official documentation): dayOfYear, dayOfMonth, dayOfWeek, monthOf-Year, halfMonthOfYear, weekOfYear, weekOfMonth, hourOfDay, minuteOfHour, secondOfMinute. Most of these are self-explanatory. The cycle dayOfWeek, for instance, describes a weekly pattern. But some terms, like halfMonthOfYear, might need explanation. halfMonthOfYear looks for a yearly pattern, breaking each month in half, thereby looking at 24 intervals. Usually, the split within the month is done between the 15th and 16th days of the month. For February however, as a shorter month, this split is between the 14th and 15th day.

- **Periodic**

  Further cyclical patterns with lengths not covered by the above calendar-related periods can be considered. If a cycle had a length of 3 days, for example, the above seasons could miss the cyclical pattern, although the pattern could be caught with the periodic approach.

- **Cycles on extra predictables**

  Depending on the measure to be forecasted, you may want to use extra predictables that act as a counting flag, which might be useful, for example, for daily cash flow forecasts. Imagine you receive payments every working day, and your finance department ensures that, each Friday, the week's finances have been cleared as much as possible. The model might benefit from having a predictable column to indicate whether each Friday is the 1st, 2nd, 3rd, 4th, or 5th Friday of the month. For any other day, the variable would remain empty, but Fridays would be flagged "1," "2," "3," "4," or "5," and a cycle related to cash flow might be identified. Fridays themselves could have an impact, but also whether a Friday falls early, late, or at the end of the month (often financial closing dates fall at the end) can further impact the cash flow.

Due to the nature of a cyclical component, only continuous and ordinal variables can be considered.

8.4.4 Fluctuations

Once any potential trends and cycles have been deduced from the historical signal, some unexplained fluctuations in the signal may still exist. This step in the time series analysis attempts to explain some of these remaining fluctuations using an autoregressive approach.

This autoregressive approach attempts to estimate a date's unexplained fluctuation through a regression using the fluctuations of previous dates as an extra predictable. The order of an autoregressive model indicates how many previous dates are being used. An autoregressive model with order 3 for instance is represented by "AR(3)." In this case, the fluctuations of the previous 3 dates are part of the model.

8.4.5 Smoothing

In addition to the above concept, conventional models of type *triple exponential smoothing* are also considered. This smoothing approach is similar to a weighted average with more recent observations weighted stronger. The triple exponential smoothing is also trying to identify a trend and seasonality and seems to be chosen primarily for shorter time series.

8.4.6 Model Quality

A model's quality is assessed with the horizon-wide MAPE, which is found by testing the model on the validation part of the historical dataset, the last 25% of the historical records. If the model is fitted to forecast 15 days, for instance, then for each date of the historical dataset a 15-day forecast is done. To be precise, the forecast is conducted from the first possible date onwards. If the model contains an autoregression of order 3, for example, then the first forecast is done for the 5th date and thereafter. The known value of the 4th date is used in combination with the previous three values for the autoregression, thus producing the first forecast for the 5th day. Therefore, no earlier forecasts can be produced.

Let's follow our example of a 15-day forecast to explain how a model's quality is determined. When the 15-day forecast is conducted, remember that the model is not just forecasting a single value that would occur in 15 days' time. The model is forecasting the next day, the day after, and so on, up to 15 days into the future.

Using the validation dataset, individual MAPEs are then calculated for each of these 15 different distances. For instance, for the horizon of 1 (just 1 day into the future), all forecasts made for the next day are compared with the actual historical value, and a MAPE for the distance 1 is calculated. The formula for calculating individual MAPEs is as follows, with n representing the number of records in the validation dataset:

$$Individual\ MAPE = \frac{1}{n}\sum_{i=1}^{n}\left[\frac{(Actual_i - Predicted_i)}{Actual_i}\right]$$

The average of the individual MAPEs of each forecast distance is the horizon-wide MAPE. So, if the forecast horizon is 15 days, then the average of the 15 individual MAPEs is reported as the quality indicator for the overall forecast.

8.5   Summary

In this chapter, we've shown you how easy it is to get started with time series forecasting. A history of only two columns (time and measurement) is sufficient for an automated forecast. Adding extra predictables to describe the time interval further can significantly improve the forecast. We recommend using such extra predictables whenever possible. With a segmented time series, hundreds or thousands of similar time series can be forecasted with a few clicks.

The most important points to remember when preparing your own data for forecasting include the following:

- Ensure that the data is aggregated on the time unit you want to forecast. For instance, if you like to forecast monthly values for the next quarter, then aggregate your data by month.

- Provide a column of type **Date** to identify the time units. Working with monthly intervals for instance, you can choose the 1st day of each month. Should the data be stored as string or in a text file, use the format YYYY-MM-DD. Time units smaller than date can also be used.

- If the data is stored in a flat file, the data will need to be data sorted by date, with the most recent date information at the bottom of the file.

- Add further variables (extra predictables) to the dataset if you would like to improve the forecast's accuracy. These variables also should be provided for the future dates you want to forecast.

Time Series Forecasting in Automated Analytics

In this chapter, we focused on time series forecasting using the web interface in Predictive Factory. We prefer using the Predictive Factory, which allows you to create single time series as well as mass produce time series forecasts. However, time series can be forecasted also in the Windows-based user interface of Automated Analytics. Using that graphical interface, only a single time series can be forecasted, but more configuration options are available.

One special aspect of using time series in Automated Analytics: In the **Data Description** window, you'll have to manually enter "1" into the **Order** column for your date variable. Only when that value is set will your time series forecasting model will be created. This rule applies to both using flat files and databases as sources.

Chapter 9
Massive Predictive Analytics

In this chapter, we'll show you how to use the Predictive Factory to deploy models, specifically producing results in batches, control model quality and dataset deviations, and retrain models. A key advantage to using SAP Predictive Analytics is that all these steps are automated.

As mentioned in Chapter 1, SAP Predictive Analytics is designed to productize predictive models. In other words, once a model has been created, its deployment (the production of its results), control over the model, and possibly its retraining are handled, for the user, through a specific interface called the Predictive Factory.

This interface has a strong impact on the scalability of what you can do, because most manual tasks that data scientists usually handle will be taken care of. The first part of this chapter will help you understand the massive predictive approach. We'll then go through the various parts of industrializing the whole process, i.e., batch deployment, model quality control, automatically retraining models, scheduling, and combining these tasks.

Let's start with a use case to illustrate what we mean by a massive approach: sales forecasting.

When considering an organization that sells products in stores, forecasting the sales per shop, per product category, for example, could be of great interest. But this forecasting may require you to create and deploy hundreds, even thousands, of time series models to provide the forecasts that can be subsequently used by your business.

A corollary to this example is the need to provide deployment capabilities but also control and maintenance capabilities. SAP Predictive Analytics' Predictive Factory is where you will set up productization in three steps that can be combined: batch deployment, model control, and model retraining, which we'll describe in the following sections.

9.1   Deploying Predictive Models in Batch Mode

Two parallel processes can be taken depending on the type of model. For time series forecasting models, deployment and recalibration are done in one step. For classification, regression, and clustering models, deployment and recalibration are different steps; each will be described in a different section.

9.1.1   Deploying Times Series Forecasting Models

Once you've created a time series forecasting model, as described in Chapter 8, the next step is to put the model into production in the Predictive Factory. Two different paths are offered for this step: importing a time series forecasting model created in Automated Analytics or creating a model in the Predictive Factory itself. Since the process of creating a time series forecasting model in the Predictive Factory was covered in Chapter 8, we won't discuss it in this chapter.

Importing a Time Series Forecasting Model

After a model is created in the Automated Analytics user interface (Part III of this book), you'll need to import it into a project in the Predictive Factory.

Go to the project to which you want to import the model. Then, click on the **MODELS** tab and then on the **Import** button. You'll be given a choice of server you want to use: an **Automated Modeling Server** or an SAP HANA server (Figure 9.1).

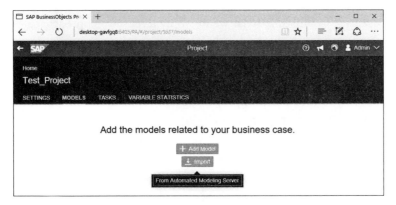

Figure 9.1 Adding a Model

You'll be provided a list of models available in the model repository defined in your project (Figure 9.2). Only one model repository is available per project.

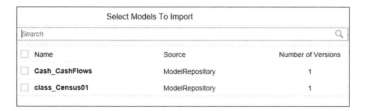

Figure 9.2 Selecting the Model to be Imported

Once a model is selected, click on **OK** to launch the import process (Figure 9.3). The model then needs to be set to **Active** before any tasks can be defined in it. If not already active, select the checkbox next to the model and then click on the **Set as Active** button.

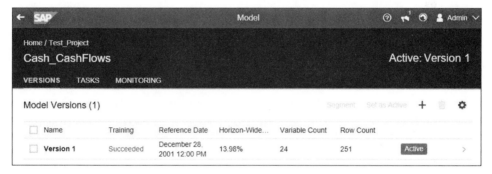

Figure 9.3 View of the Imported Model

Defining a Time Series Forecasting Deployment Task

Regardless of how you created the model, the next step is to define a time series forecasting task. Click on the **TASKS** tab and then the **Add Task** button (Figure 9.4).

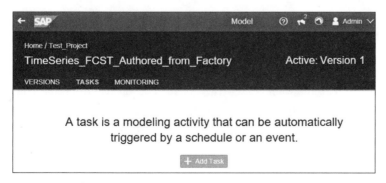

Figure 9.4 Adding a Task

Enter the task parameters, i.e., **Input**, **Forecast**, **Output**, and **Schedules** (Figure 9.5).

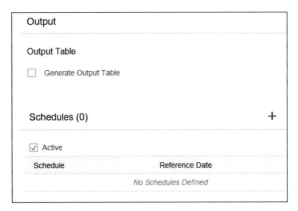

Figure 9.5 Defining a Task on a Time Series Forecasting Model

The **Input** defines the dataset to be used to retrain and execute the model. In the **Forecast** field, enter the **Number Of Forecasts** (generally the same number as in the training to be consistent) and the **Training Period**. The training period corresponds to the time period of the dataset to be used. You may want to define a consistent time interval, which can be moved, to retrain your models. In our example shown in Figure 9.6, last 3 years will be considered.

Figure 9.6 Setting the Retrain Depth

To finish setting up the task, you'll need to add a schedule. In our simple example shown in Figure 9.7, we created a weekly recurring, never-ending schedule that triggers the task every Sunday at 2 pm starting on May 7th, 2017. We defined reference dates as with time-stamped run dates. In-depth description on scheduling and combining tasks en masse is provided in Chapter 9, Section 9.5.

When your task is fully defined, click on the **Save** button. Now, go back to the **TASKS** tab, where the task should show as **Active**.

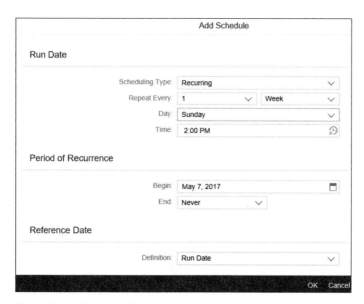

Figure 9.7 Schedule of the Task

9.1.2 Deploying Classification/Regression Models

As with time series forecasting models, classification, regression, and clustering models must first be imported or created in a project in the Predictive Factory (Chapter 6). Once the model is available in the Predictive Factory and set as **Active**, you can create a **Model Application Task** (Figure 9.8), which is usually first defined as a control task.

The **Input**, **Output**, and **Schedules** section must be defined.

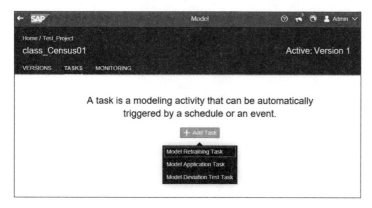

Figure 9.8 Choosing the Task

Under **Input**, note that how datasets are managed changes the parameters you'll set. When creating the model, you either used SAP Predictive Analytics' Data Manager (see Chapter 14) or a .csv or .txt file, a table, or a database view. These options involve different flows in the Predictive Factory user interface when deploying your models. One advantage of using the Data Manager is that the dataset is created on demand when the task is executed, without any work outside of SAP Predictive Analytics. When using SAP HANA views, if prompts are exposed, the dataset is also produced on demand according to prompt values. When using other data sources, the process of making the right dataset available must be managed outside of SAP Predictive Analytics (i.e., using an extract, transform and load (ETL) tool, SQL scripts, or Python scripts). The synchronization between the SAP Predictive Analytics process and the dataset production process must also be managed.

How you maintain the **Input** section of a task depends on whether the model was created in the Data Manager or via other sources. Depending on the data sources defined in the project, you may just have to browse and choose the right dataset (Figure 9.9).

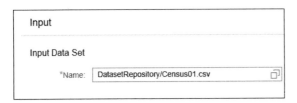

Figure 9.9 Choosing the Input Dataset

The Data Manager uses a metadata repository that you must define when setting up an Automated Analytics server (Chapter 5). The model contains an explicit link to analytical records in the Data Manager to avoid problems with what variables should be used. The only part of the dataset that you need to define here is the time-stamped population (Figure 9.10). The time-stamped population contains a time-stamp prompt that defines when the dataset will be produced (Figure 9.11).

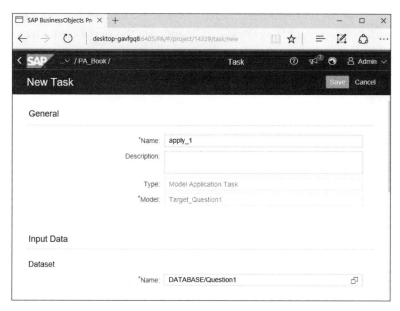

Figure 9.10 Selecting a Time-Stamped Population

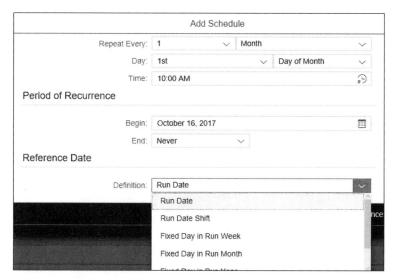

Figure 9.11 Defining When the Dataset Needs to be Produced

In the **Output** section, you'll set the **Output Table** as well as the **Output Columns**. For **Output Table**, you'll define where the results will be written, the name of the table, and how they will be written (Figure 9.12). For this last step, **Table Generation Policy**, you have three options:

- **Single Table (Overwrite)**
- **Single Table (Update)**, which applies only for databases
- **One Table Per Run**

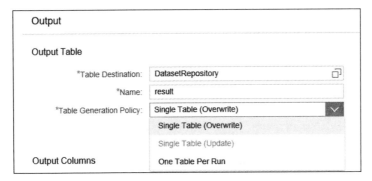

Figure 9.12 Defining the Output Table

If you choose **One Table Per Run**, you can also define a **Table Cleanup Policy**, which determines whether all tables are kept or only the most recent ones (Figure 9.13).

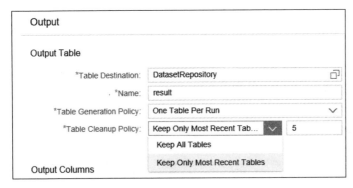

Figure 9.13 Cleaning Policy

Under **Output Columns**, only the **Predictions** field is compulsory. You have four options: **Predicted Category**, **Prediction Probability** (the most used), **Prediction Confidence**, and **Prediction Score** (Figure 9.14). Chapter 6 provides more details about each of these options.

Output Columns	
	☐ Predicted Category
Model Variables:	☑ Prediction Probability
Contextual Information:	☐ Prediction Confidence
Statistics:	☐ Prediction Score
Predictions:	Prediction Probability ⊗

Figure 9.14 Predictions Output

Three other possible parameters for **Output Columns** are **Model Variables** (to get dataset variables in the output), **Contextual Information** (**Apply Date, Training Date, Model Name, Model Version**), and **Statistics** (**Approximate Quantile, Outlier Indicator, and Variable Contributions**).

The **Schedules** section is common to all tasks. The example we described in Section 9.1.1 for a time series forecasting task applies in this section as well, but we'll describe the **Schedules** section in more detail in Section 9.4. For now, click on the **Save** button to activate the task, which will be triggered according to the schedule you defined.

9.2   Model Quality and Deviation

After a model is deployed for batch execution, you won't be able to use it forever because its quality will eventually drop. This drop occurs because the data about the "environment" of what is predicted changes. For example, if we consider customers, both the market and their own behavior changes constantly. The dataset used to produce the results will most likely show changes, when compared to the training dataset, in data distribution over time. These changes will in turn affect the results when executing the model. In classification models, the detection capacity, i.e., the quality of a model, will eventually degrade. In regression models, the values provided will increasingly diverge from reality. In clustering, the group definition will need to change.

For these reasons, controlling models over time is of utmost importance for results to add value to your business processes.

SAP Predictive Analytics' Predictive Factory addresses these issues, with a specific task for classification, regression, and clustering models available to run such controls.

9.2.1   Model Deviation Test Task Parameters

As soon as you've deployed a model for batch execution or defined a real-time execution process, you should define a model deviation test task (Figure 9.15).

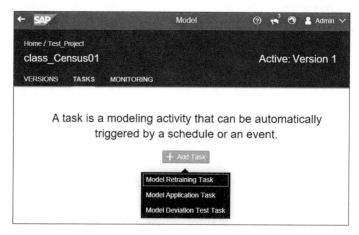

Figure 9.15 Defining a Model Deviation Test Task

Only two things are required to define a model deviation test task: an **Input Dataset** and a **Schedule**. For a model application task, whether you use Data Manager or not depends on what input is being used.

9.2.2   Model Deviation Test Task Outputs

The **RUNS** tab at the **TASKS** level shows all the times the task has run (Figure 9.16).

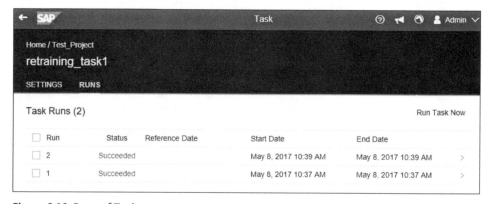

Figure 9.16 Runs of Tasks

Click on a run to open its reporting window (Figure 9.17).

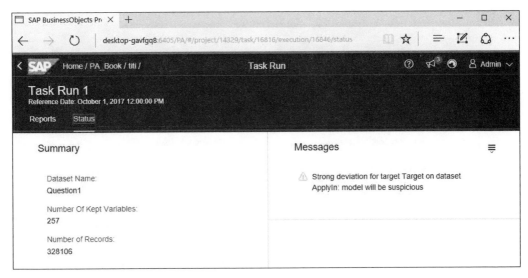

Figure 9.17 Report on a Model Deviation Task

The report contains the performance of the model on the control dataset (Figure 9.18). Performance is expressed as predictive power (KI) and prediction confidence (KR). The prediction confidence measured in this case corresponds to the one measured between the training and control datasets and expresses the robustness of the model over time.

The report also contains dataset deviation information. When you save a model created with Automated Analytics, not only is the equation of the model saved but also statistics about the training dataset. As a result, you'll be able to perform a χ^2 (chi-squared) test between the training dataset and the control dataset to measure differences in the distribution of the variables. These tests are performed on each variable, on the categories of variables, and on the cross-statistics of the variables with the target. The cross-statistics of a variable with the target do not consider the variable's distribution but instead considers the proportion of positive cases per category (for binary targets) and the average of the target (for continuous targets).

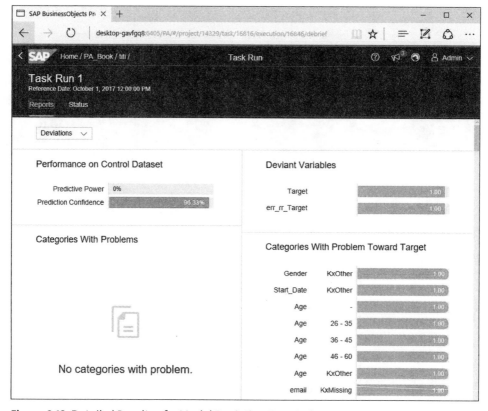

Figure 9.18 Detailed Results of a Model Deviation Test Task

9.3   Automatically Retraining Models

Once a model is in production and being controlled regularly, the logical next step is to retrain the model automatically when needed.

9.3.1   Defining a Model Retraining Task

In the **TASKS** tab, click on the plus **+** button and then select **Model Retraining Task** (Figure 9.19).

Defining a model retraining task requires you define the **Input Dataset**, **Training Parameters**, and **Schedules**. For other tasks, using the Data Manager can make all the difference in how you set up an input dataset.

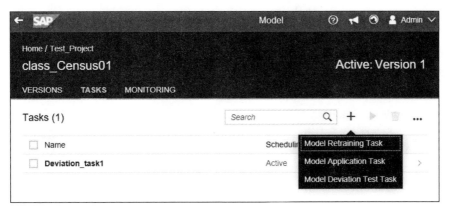

Figure 9.19 Defining a Model Retraining Task

Training Parameters define which variables in a dataset should be used for model retraining and how data encoding should be handed in regression models. For the variables to be used to retrain the model, you can select one of the following approaches (Figure 9.20):

- Using the **Variables of the Initial Model**, which simply means recalibrating the coefficients of the initial model
- Using the **Most Contributive Training Data Set Variables**, where a variable reduction process is launched, potentially leading to a completely different set of variables in a new model
- Using **All Training Data Set Variables**

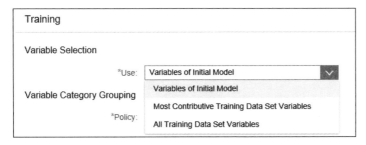

Figure 9.20 How to Handle Variables

In principle, we recommend the second option (using the **Most Contributive Training Data Set Variables**), because your objective is to retrain the model in a way that considers any variable, including those not selected in the initial model, that could be of interest to retraining while, at the same time, producing a usable model (one with enough but not too many variables) if the dataset is very large.

We recommend the second option even more if you are using the Data Manager because changes in the analytical record (i.e, the addition of new columns) will automatically be taken into account.

Further parameters can be set with this option. We recommend selecting **Default** in the **Automatic Selection Settings** dropdown list, which corresponds to an iterative process where the less well-ranked variables are removed, and the model is recalibrated. The process is repeated in the next iteration, which occurs if less than 5% of the sum of KI + KR is lost when compared to the best iteration, which sets the maximum KI + KR value. Among all iterations, the model that is kept is the one with the least number of variables and with a maximum deviation of 1% of the sum of KI + KR loss when compared to the best model.

Selecting **Custom** in **Automatic Selection Settings** dropdown list allows you to define your own parameters for the variable reduction process under **Variable Selection**. Choose either the **Best Model** or the **Last Model**, the maximum and minimum number of variables to keep, the way iteration proceeds (either by entering the number of variables to be removed at each iteration or the **Percentage of Information To Keep**), and finally the **Maximum Global Performance Loss** (Figure 9.21).

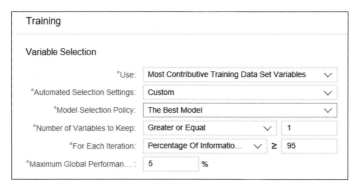

Figure 9.21 Variable Selection Definition

The **Percentage of Information To Keep** at each iteration means that the best ranked variables in terms of contribution to the model are kept at each iteration.

Maximum Global Performance Loss is the selection criterion that defines, among all models computed in the process, which variables should be chosen. If 5% is the value entered into the **Maximum Global Performance Loss** field, then the chosen model will have the least number of variables with a minimum value of predictive quality + prediction confidence (KI + KR). In other words, if a model's performance is at least 95% of the maximum KI + KR of all the variables under study.

Next, set how to handle **Variable Category Grouping** (Figure 9.22) during the data encoding phase of model training. You can either **Keep Initial Category Grouping**, which means that, for the set of variables used in the initial model, the system will not change how variables were encoded or grouped into categories. This option simply recalibrates the coefficients of the model.

Alternatively, if you choose **Recalculate Category Grouping**, how variables are encoded and categorized will be fully recomputed.

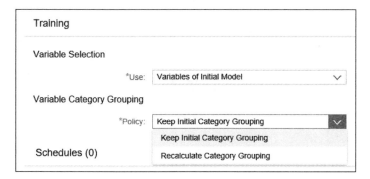

Figure 9.22 Variable Encoding Definition

Under **Policy**, we recommend combining **Most Contributive Training Data Set Variables** and **Recalculate Category Grouping** for full model retraining without accounting for other changes.

Scheduling of this task is the same as the other tasks and is detailed in Section 9.4.

9.3.2   Model Retraining Task Outputs

A first view of the model retraining task can be seen in the **RUNS** tab (Figure 9.23).

Click on a task run, which opens the **REPORTS** tab and displays a high-level debriefing report about the retrained model (Figure 9.24).

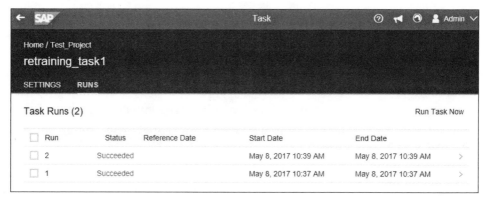

Figure 9.23 Model Retraining Runs

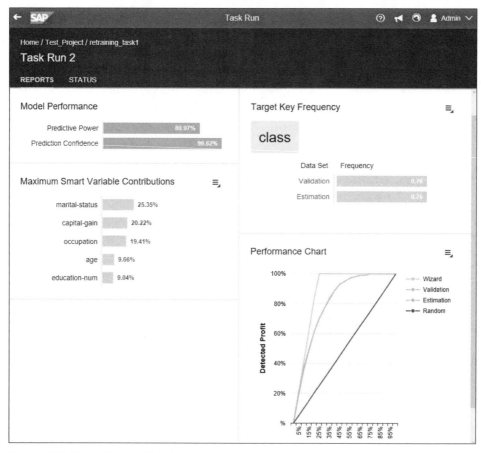

Figure 9.24 Model Retrain Debrief

In the **STATUS** tab, you'll find basic information about the model. You can toggle between two views by clicking on the icon to the right of **Messages** (Figure 9.25). If you choose **Detailed Logs**, the report will show logs that describe the training process. Select **Log Highlights** to only show warnings and errors.

Figure 9.25 Model Logs

A higher-level report is available in the **MONITORING** tab at the model level. This report shows the evolution of four indicators for each retraining: predictive power (KI), prediction confidence (KR), variable count, and row count.

You can toggle between tabular and graphical formats for this report by clicking the icons to the left of the gear icon (Figure 9.26).

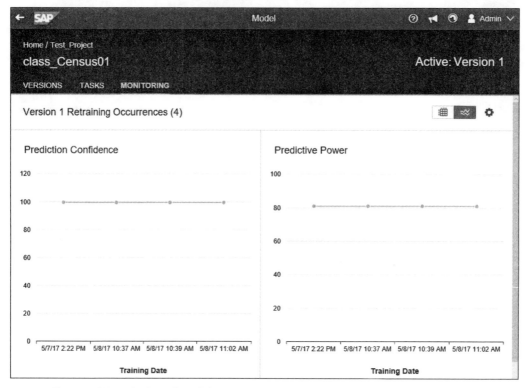

Figure 9.26 Evolution of Model KPIs over Time

9.4   Scheduling and Combining Massive Tasks

Scheduling tasks is the core of the Predictive Factory. Different options are available for you to use in your projects: scheduling each task independently, triggering a task based on results from another task, or running a task immediately. Triggering tasks using other tasks is how you combine tasks to create a fully automated process with control. When the chain of tasks is executed, results will be produced if no deviation is detected, or models will be retrained if deviation is detected.

9.4.1   Scheduling Tasks Independently

For every task, you can set a schedule in the **Schedules** section (Figure 9.27).

Figure 9.27 Scheduling Parameters

For **Scheduling Type**, you have three different options: **Recurring**, **Once**, and **Event-based**. For now, we'll focus on the first two options. Event-based scheduling will be described in Section 9.4.2.

If you select **Once**, you'll only have to enter the **Day** and **Time,** and the task will be scheduled (Figure 9.28).

Edit Schedule

Run Date

Scheduling Type:	Once
Day:	May 8, 2017
Time:	5:00 PM

Figure 9.28 Scheduling a Task at a Given Date

Select **Recurring Schedules** to schedule a task several times following a specified pattern (Figure 9.29). How frequently a task is executed is defined by the **Repeat Every** section. The shortest period is a minute, but we do not recommend this interval if many models are involved. Indeed, when a task is executed, the model is loaded into the automated server before being deployed, before undertaking a deviation test, or before retraining, all of which take time and may lead to performance issues.

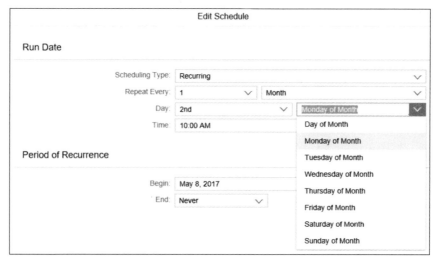

Figure 9.29 Scheduling a Recurring Task

When the schedule will take place is defined in the next section and depends on the frequency of model application. A complex example, for a monthly schedule, is shown in (Figure 9.30).

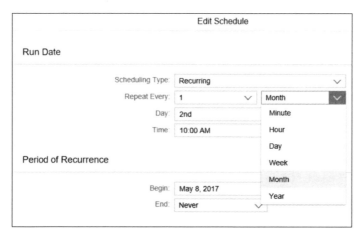

Figure 9.30 Defining Schedule Frequency

You can choose a specific day of the month (e.g., the 5th of each month) or even a specific day of a specific week in the month to comply with IT constraints (e.g., the first Saturday of the month).

The **Period of Recurrence** field defines when the schedule of the task begins and when it ends (possibly never).

9.4.2   Event-Based Scheduling

Event-based scheduling uses the results of another task to trigger other tasks. You can trigger a task (for model application or model retraining) in one of three ways linked to the execution status of another task, i.e., if the latter task **Succeeded**, **Finished with Warnings**, or **Failed** (Figure 9.31).

Figure 9.31 Events to Trigger Execution

To trigger another task from a model deviation test task, two additional items are available: **Anomaly Detected** and **No Anomalies Detected**. In a model deviation test task, if either the model or the dataset deviates, an anomaly is logged, which can then trigger a model retraining task, for example.

9.5   Deploying Expert Analytics Models

When working with Expert Analytics, you may also want to schedule the execution of a stream from the Predictive Factory, which is only possible for streams that use SAP HANA. The first step is to add and define an **SAP HANA Server** as the **Modeling Server**, as discussed in Chapter 3, Section 3.4.4.

Next, you can import your file into Predictive Factory from within a project by clicking on **Import • Predictive Pipeline from File** on the **Models** tab (see Figure 9.32).

> **Tip**
> The stream must first be saved as a .zip file export.

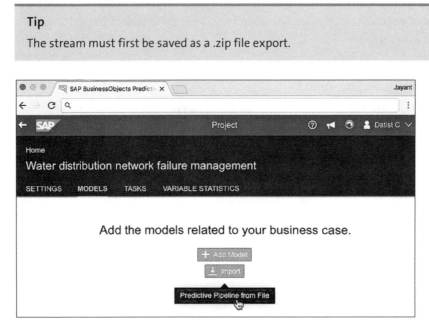

Figure 9.32 Importing a Predictive Pipeline from a File

Select the .zip file containing the predictive pipeline saved from Expert Analytics. Once it has been imported, it will show in the list of available models (see Figure 9.33).

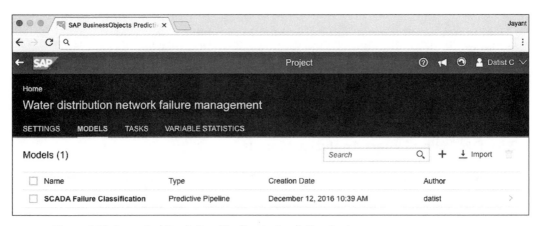

Figure 9.33 Imported Predictive Pipeline in Predictive Factory

As for any other model, **Tasks** can be defined for this model. In Figure 9.34, you can see the definition of a **Model Application Task**.

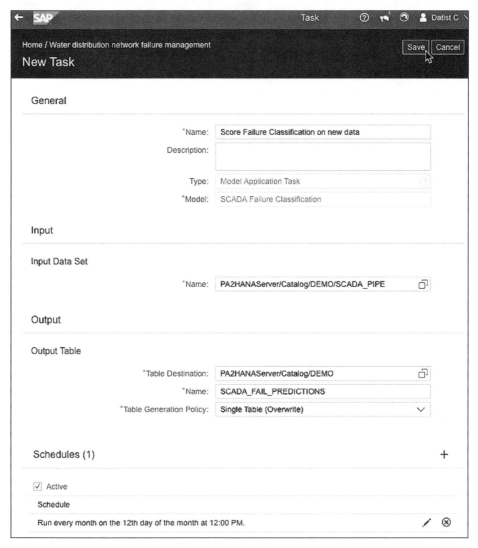

Figure 9.34 Definition of a Model Application Task for a Predictive Pipeline

Reports are the same for tasks scheduled for models that come from Automated Analytics as for those that come from Experts Analytics.

9.6   Summary

In this chapter, you've seen how to productize models using the Predictive Factory: deploying in batches, controlling model quality, and retraining the models. Doing these tasks ensures that you'll always get the best possible results from each model.

PART III

Automated Analytics

Chapter 10

Automated Analytics User Interface

Automated Analytics is the historical user interface of SAP Predictive Analytics. Originally created to provide a visual way to manage the sophisticated APIs of the product, Automated Analytics has become the main entry point to help nontechnical users perform complex predictive projects.

Today, the Automated Analytics interface in SAP Predictive Analytics is the main entry point for various kinds of predictive projects. You have access to Automated Analytics when you install the SAP Predictive Analytics desktop or the SAP Predictive Analytics client, as we described in Chapter 3.

Since SAP Predictive Analytics 3.0, some workflows previously only available in Automated Analytics have been added to other interfaces, such as the Predictive Factory. Nonetheless, at the moment, Automated Analytics remains an important piece of the solution, and investing some time to better understand how it works will help you make the most out of it.

In this chapter, we'll provide an overview of this interface and provide some information on features that don't have a dedicated chapter in this book so that you can understand the potential benefits of those features. (Take the information in this chapter as a teaser to inspire your further exploration of the product.)

To begin, let's answer the following question: Since Automated Analytics is but one of the possible interfaces you can use, when should you use it?

10.1 When to Use Automated Analytics

The Automated Analytics interface is handy if you want to work without connecting to a server or for tasks that cannot yet be done solely on a server-based solution.

As of SAP Predictive Analytics 3.2, the typical uses available only in Automated Analytics are automated clustering (Chapter 11), Social Network Analysis (Chapter 12), predictive recommendation models (Chapter 13), and data preparation (Chapter 14). Moreover, Automated Analytics provides some useful tools to quickly move datasets or to quickly analyze their content. The powerful data preparation functionality of Automated Analytics makes it a good candidate to prepare the information you want to use in the Predictive Factory. You can also use the data prepared by Automated Analytics in Expert Analytics by exporting and reimporting it.

We recommend you use the automated or guided interfaces (Automated Analytics and Predictive Factory). You should use Expert Analytics only when the automated modules are not sufficient for your needs. With automated interfaces, the time and cost of building a predictive project is lower, and the final model is of a good quality and can be put into production quickly. Automated Analytics offers the best balance between time, cost, and quality.

When using Automated Analytics, you can save your models and then open them in the Predictive Factory for mass usage, such as automatically generating hundreds of time series analysis models from a single model. Since some automated workflows are now available directly in the Predictive Factory (classification, regression, time series analysis), you should just use the Predictive Factory interface. If you use the server for those workflows, you'll avoid having to change environments, and thus, you can train yourself and your team on a single interface.

Let's now look at the Automated Analytics interface itself in more detail and explore what you can do with it.

10.2   Navigating the User Interface

After installation, from the Windows **Start** menu, find and launch the application from **All Apps • S • SAP Business Intelligence • SAP BusinessObjects Predictive Analytics.** The initial page shown in Figure 10.1 will open.

Be aware that, based on the version you installed and on some rebranding made by SAP, the *BusinessObjects* label might have disappeared, as the product, at the time of this writing, is currently called SAP Predictive Analytics.

The initial page opens by default on the **Data Manager** panel, but before we discuss this panel, notice the following three zones at the bottom of the page (two of them are quite handy; one is being deprecated):

- The **Subscribe to the newsletter** link lets you sign up and receive a newsletter with information on new releases, best practices, and upcoming events related to SAP predictive analytics solutions.

- The **Ask a question in the Predictive Analytics community** is a helpful link that opens the web page of the community on the SAP Community website. The community is a lively space where customers and SAP employees exchange information, share best practices, and help each other solve common problems. The community is your first go-to place whenever you have doubts or want to know more about SAP Predictive Analytics.

- The **Send us feedback through SAP Idea Place** used to send you to a site where you could submit ideas for improvements. This site is being removed because SAP is using the new Customer Influence program, and this link might become inactive.

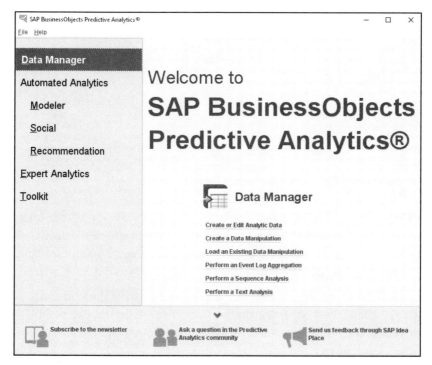

Figure 10.1 Automated Analytics: Initial Page

At the top of the page, you can set your product preferences via the menu path **File • Preferences**. You can set multiple parameters to influence, not just the look of the interface, but also the functioning of the product and the way the predictive models are trained and executed.

Of the various settings, let's begin with the **Model Training Delegation** settings, as shown in Figure 10.2.

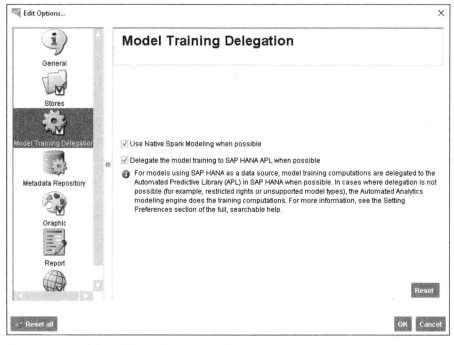

Figure 10.2 Model Training Delegation Preference Settings

By selecting these checkboxes, you can force Automated Analytics to push the learning phase of a predictive model to Spark or SAP HANA sources whenever the data is found there. You can find the exact supported versions at *https://support.sap.com/content/dam/launchpad/en_us/pam/pam-essentials/PAM_Predictive_Analytics_31.pdf*.

These settings avoid moving the data out of the sources and make the sources do all the calculations, when possible. Thus, the performance of the model definition should improve, and the resources needed on the SAP Predictive Analytics desktop or server machine should be reduced.

Going back to the initial page, the **Help** menu lets you find more information on the product. Contextual in-application help is also available by pressing the [F1] key; wherever you are in the interface, the contextual help opens the most appropriate page to guide you in the task you are performing. Two options of note include the following:

- **Help • Contact Support…** automatically creates a .zip file containing detailed information about your installation. When you contact support, you can provide the file to them to expedite the investigation.

- **Help • Enter Keycode** lets you add a new keycode to enable the application if your original one has expired. Be aware that the keycode used here also applies to Expert Analytics. If Expert Analytics asks you for a keycode, you'll have to add it via this Automated Analytics help command.

Going back to the initial page, you can select any module by clicking on its name in the list at the center.

If you click, for example, on **Create or Edit Analytic Data**, a new page will open. We'll discuss this page in depth in Chapter 14, but for now, we do want to point out the three buttons that appear at the bottom of the screen, as shown in Figure 10.3. You'll see and use these three buttons in every step of all Automated Analytics workflows:

- The **Next** button lets you move to the next step in the workflow. This button is enabled only if the minimum necessary information has been entered already. If this button is disabled, you are missing something on the displayed page.

- The **Previous** button brings you back one step in the workflow.

- The **Cancel** button brings you back to the initial page of the module you are in. (In our example here, you would return to the page shown in Figure 10.1.)

Figure 10.3 Automated Analytics: Typical Bottom Buttons

Notice that usually the information that you've input into the various prompts (text fields, checkboxes) is kept when you click the **Previous** button. Some information (for example, file names and directories used) are kept even when you press the **Cancel** button. This memorization saves time if you just want to modify something in a previous page and then move ahead, but you need to pay attention if you go back and forth. You'll need to ensure that the latest settings are exactly what you wanted and not something that was carried over from a previous execution.

Now, let's move on and see what the different modules do. Click on the **Cancel** button to return to the initial page.

10.3   Exploring the Automated Analytics Modules

The initial page shown in Figure 10.1 is for the Data Manager module. To change to another page, simply click on one of the module links on the left side of the screen. In the following sections, we'll explain what each page is for and what actions you can perform with each available option.

10.3.1   Data Manager

The Data Manager is a powerful environment that you can use to prepare your data for the predictive project. Given the importance of this module and of this subject, Chapter 14 is completely dedicated to the Data Manager and covers the first three options on the page in detail.

For now, let's focus on the three other remaining options shown in Figure 10.1, which are quite useful:

- **Perform an Event Log Aggregation** automatically enriches an existing dataset with measures aggregating over time. For example, if your data includes information about customer purchases over time, you can use the tool to calculate, for each customer, the number of purchases, the total, the average, etc. in different periods and also add information about variations of those measures across different periods. The enriched dataset is then typically used for classification, regression, or clustering models.

- The **Perform a Sequence Analysis** module lets you take a log of events and analyze their sequence. You can use this analysis, for example, on the path a customer takes to visit your web site. The tool automatically detects paths (e.g., going from a **Welcome** page to the **Search** page, or vice versa) and events (e.g., the customer buys a product). All this information is then aggregated and added to the dataset and now can be used to predict the most probable next page for a new visitor or the probability of a purchase based on the pages visited.

- The **Perform a Text Analysis** module helps you analyze datasets that contain text. This module automatically extracts words and their roots (stems) from a dataset and enriches it with other information. For example, you can take a file with customer comments on a product and associate the comments with whether or not the customer has purchased the product. The text analysis module, associated with a classification, can tell you which words that appear in the comments are closely correlated to the purchase (or not) of a product.

As mentioned, we won't be able to describe all these modules in depth. But, we hope the information we provided can help you decide whether these modules could be useful for your project.

10.3.2 Data Modeler

Back on the initial page, click on the **Modeler** tab on the left part of the screen; the page shown in Figure 10.4 will appear.

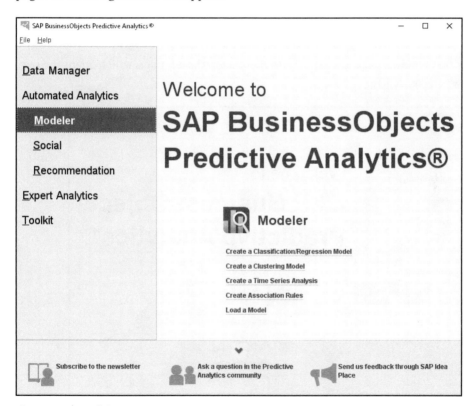

Figure 10.4 Modeler Main Page

On this main page, you'll start all your Automated Analytics projects. In this book, we cover classification, regression, and time series models in the Predictive Factory interface in Chapter 6, Chapter 7, and Chapter 8, respectively. If you want, you can start the equivalent workflows in the Automated Analytics interface.

The only remaining item of importance on this page (and it is important!) is the **Create Association Rules** module. With this module, you can see if, in a series of events, some rules may exist that associate two events together. For example, in the browsing history on a website, the module can tell you how often people go from a specific page to another. Given an ordered series of events, you can understand the predecessor event and the successor event and thus infer some causal and consequential relationships between these events. Finally, selecting other items on the left, you can go to the **Social**, **Recommendation**, and **Expert Analytics** modules, which will be detailed in Chapter 12, Chapter 13, and Chapter 15, respectively.

10.3.3   Toolkit

Back on the initial page, click on the **Toolkit** tab on the left page, which opens the page shown in Figure 10.5.

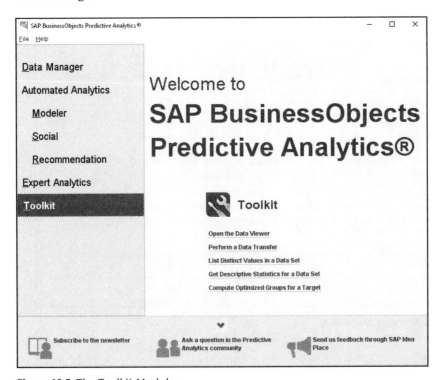

Figure 10.5 The Toolkit Module

This module can be handy, before starting a predictive project, to better understand the data you have and ensure your data is available for analysis and well-formed. Your options on this page are as follows:

- **Open the Data Viewer**

  This module opens a tool that lets you discover and analyze the data you want to work with. The Data Viewer tool is also automatically used when you start a new model from the Automated Analytics interface. Thus, we'll present this module in detail when we discuss the workflow of creating a clustering model in Chapter 11. For now, the Data Viewer is available to allow you to analyze your data before deciding how to use it and to determine its usefulness (or not) for your project.

- **Perform a Data Transfer**

  This module enables you to move data from one place to another in a few clicks—in its simplicity, a powerful transfer tool. You'll select the source data (from a file or a database) and the target location (another file or database). Optionally, you can decide which source fields are transferred to the target location, and you can also filter the source before the transfer. If you become familiar with this module, you might start using it often, even outside of predictive projects, because it is a quick alternative to more complex and heavy extract, transform and load (ETL) solutions when moving small datasets.

- **List Distinct Values in a Data Set**

  With this module, you can analyze your data and find all distinct available tuples. This information gives you more visibility on the content in your source. After selecting the dataset, you'll choose which fields you want to consider, and the tool will find all the different tuples of those fields.

- **Get Descriptive Statistics for a Data Set**

  This module tells you how the available data would be used by a classification, regression, or clustering algorithm. This module also contains a hidden gem (**Generate Association Rules**), which is quite useful.

  After selecting your dataset, you can choose a target variable and the information to be analyzed as if you were creating a model to predict that variable. In the results, you'll see typical statistics information showing the influence of each category on the target. With this analysis, you'll be able to understand if the dataset contains appropriate information for your task.

  The hidden gem is enabled by selecting a simple checkbox in the page just before the calculation of the statistics: the **Generate Association Rules** checkbox shown in Figure 10.6.

10

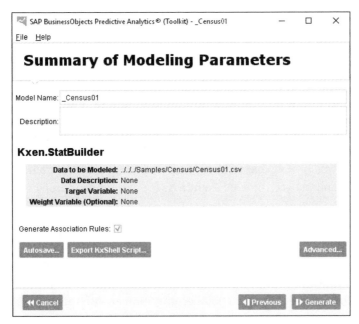

Figure 10.6 The Generate Association Rules Checkbox in the Descriptive Statistics Tool

When you select the functionality, the tool analyzes the data and shows all the correlations between the fields. For example, you might discover that when field **Age** contains **18**, then the most correlated **Product Value** is **T-Shirt**, but when **Age** contains **35**, then the most correlated **Product Value** is **Shorts**. Notice that this analysis does not indicate a cause-and-effect relationship, just one of simple correlation. The association rules found in this module are different from the association rules in the Automated Analytics Modeler (discussed in Section 10.3.2). In the Automated Analytics Modeler, you evaluated the correlation between different events (where all event types were in the same column of the dataset); in the Toolkit, you are evaluating the correlation between values in different fields of the same dataset.

- **Compute Optimized Groups for a Target**
  This final module runs the first steps of a classification, regression, or supervised clustering model to define how variable categories should be organized to better explain the target variable. This tool doesn't generate the model (the scoring equation) but shows the influences of the variables on the target. This shortcut is especially useful if you want to conduct some exploratory analytics to better understand your business.

10.4   Summary

In this chapter, you learned how to navigate around the Automated Analytics interface, and we described the different modules available and their use. We presented some information superficially to provide a quick overview of the functionality to help you decide if Automated Analytics is worth exploring for your business.

In the next chapter, you'll use Automated Analytics to build a clustering model. Chapter 11 is a hands-on chapter where you'll play with the navigation knowledge you acquired in this chapter.

10

Chapter 11
Automated Predictive Clustering Models

Clustering automatically creates segments of your customers, products, or other business entities. Helping you better understand your environment, clustering allows you to concentrate and target actions to a few groups of entities rather than working individually with each entity.

Clustering is a predictive analytics approach that creates groups of records from your dataset (called *clusters* or *segments*) based on their mathematical closeness. Two records in the same cluster are more "mathematically similar" than two records in different clusters, and this similarity is measured by the values of their attributes.

SAP Predictive Analytics provides an automated module for clustering in the Automated Analytics interface. The module takes care of various tasks for defining and generating a clustering model and lets you concentrate on higher-value tasks, such as finding other data to improve the model or brainstorming ideas on how the model can benefit your business.

The use of clustering can be of a great help when you want to better understand your business or take appropriate actions to improve the business. The fundamental idea is that any of your business subjects (your products, customers, employees, departments, etc.) can be submitted to a clustering analysis, which creates groups that can then be analyzed as a whole. Practically, you'll reduce the scope of your analysis from a lot of individual data points to a just few groups of data points showing similar characteristics.

Ideally, data points in the same cluster behave similarly and thus should have the same reaction when you interact with them.

The most typical use for clustering is to create customer groups for marketing campaigns or to enrich a dataset, which is then fed into a classification or regression algorithm. You can take all of your customers and have them grouped into a few clusters.

After analyzing the typical profile of customers in a cluster, you can create a targeted marketing campaign for that profile.

This approach lets you balance the benefit from creating a personalized campaign against the cost of conducting a specific campaign for each of your customers.

Other typical uses relate to identifying groups of customers who might churn or employees who want to leave the company. Internet of Things (IoT) scenarios may involve identifying which among thousands of input sources, like sensors, have similar behaviors.

In this chapter, you'll learn how to create a clustering model, how to understand its output, and how to apply it to new data. We'll also provide some information on the concepts behind supervised and unsupervised clustering and provide a short description of the mathematical process used to create clusters.

11.1   The Clustering Approach of Automated Analytics

Automated Analytics has a specific module dedicated to clustering under the Modeler component. The module simplifies the workflow as much as possible; time-consuming activities that don't necessarily improve the model's quality are automatically taken into account by the tool. Thus, you can concentrate on higher-value activities. As with the other components in Automated Analytics, a secondary goal is to speed up the process of defining and creating clustering models to decrease the cost of predictive modeling and to enable the mass creation of more models. However, the Automated Analytics approach doesn't compromise on the final accuracy of the generated model.

You'll be able to set various properties of the algorithm that creates the model using a wizard-like interface, but the bulk of the work will be done for you automatically without compromising on model quality.

The mathematical approach is described in Section 11.4, but for data scientists, we'll just mention that, behind the scenes, the clustering module manages a centroid method based on the K-Means algorithm.

In Automated Analytics, clustering can be either supervised or unsupervised. When unsupervised, the clustering analysis puts together data points that are considered similar with regard to all of their attributes. When supervised, the clusters are adjusted to provide a distribution that explains their influence on the target variable. This information is obtained by organizing the input values in groups with a similar influence on the target variable. The target can be either a continuous or a nominal variable, with only two values. As a result, you can interpret the results as though a regression or classification model. In general, we recommend using supervised clustering because the output better answers your business question and also because you can reuse the output as an input for a classification model.

Finally, Automated Analytics provides an option defining clusters using SQL statements. This option reduces the mathematical exactitude of the output but allows for exporting the model into your database for easy processing.

11.2   Creating a Clustering Model

In this section, we'll explain how to create a clustering model using a sample dataset. The detailed step-by-step process will help you understand how to use the tool, how to interpret the output of the model, and how to export your model into an application or into a database to be executed on new data.

To illustrate, we'll use a simple public dataset that can be found at *https://archive.ics. uci.edu/ml/datasets/Wholesale+customers* and which is extracted from Abreu, N. (2011). *Analise do perfil do cliente Recheio e desenvolvimento de um sistema promocional.* Mestrado em Marketing, ISCTE-IUL, Lisbon.

The dataset file can also be downloaded from SAP PRESS at *www.sap-press.com/4491.*

In our example, we'll suppose that the dataset file, called *Wholesale customers data.csv,* is saved in the *C:\Predictive* directory of the computer running Automated Analytics on SAP Predictive Analytics desktop.

The Wholesale Customers Dataset

The sample file comes from a study for clustering from the Instituto Universitário de Lisboa, Portugal, and consists of data about the expenses of customers of a wholesale distributor.

The dataset contains 6 continuous integer fields showing the annual expenses of a customer in different areas (fresh produce, milk, groceries, frozen products, detergents and paper, and, finally, delicatessen).

The Channel nominal field shows if the purchase took place via a retail channel (value 1) or from a hotel or restaurant (value 2).

The Region nominal field shows if the sale took place in Lisbon (value 1), in Oporto (value 2), or somewhere else (value 3).

To create a clustering model, you'll perform the following actions:

1. Launch the clustering module and import the data.
2. Analyze the dataset content.
3. Choose the variables to use when defining the model and determine the number of clusters to generate.
4. Generate the model and analyze the cluster profiles.
5. Apply the model to a dataset.
6. Export the model to an external application for productization.

Our example is an unsupervised clustering model, but in subsequent sections, we'll explain the differences between supervised and unsupervised clustering.

In each step, we'll also provide a description of optional or advanced functionalities that you can take into account but that won't be used in our example.

It's time for you to play with the tool—let's get started!

11.2.1   Starting the Clustering Module and Importing the Data

After launching Automated Analytics, start the clustering module by clicking on the **Create a Clustering Model** entry on the main Modeler page.

On the **Select a Data Source** page, shown in Figure 11.1, you can use the **Browse** buttons to find the dataset file saved in the *C:\Predictive* directory.

Figure 11.1 Selecting a Data Source

After selecting the directory and the file, you can leave the default settings to start creating your clustering model; however, before going ahead, we'd like to first explore the various settings available on this page. By changing these settings, you can import various kinds of datasets and use them in different ways.

The **Use File or a Database Table** radio button lets you select files from your local machine or tables from a database. You can control the type of source from the **Data Type** dropdown list (where you can select text files, Excel files, SAS or SPSS files, or database table types). When selecting the **Data Base** data type, the **Browse** buttons will display a list of available ODBC database connections, ask for a username and password, and let you select a database table.

The **Use Data Manager** option lets you select an analytical record and a time-stamped population defined in a database source. How to define these artifacts in the Data Manager is discussed in Chapter 14.

The wrench icon 🔧 lets you change the default settings when reading the file. Click on the icon to open the **Settings** page, as shown in Figure 11.2.

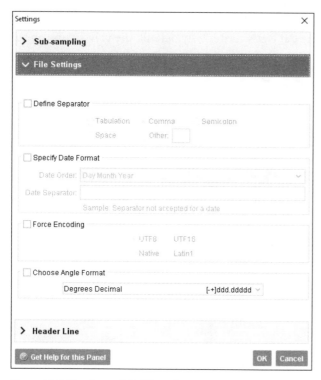

Figure 11.2 The Import Settings Page

You can find detailed information on this page by clicking on the **Get Help for this Panel** button or pressing F1, but the most typical changes that you'll do here include the following:

- In the **File Settings** section:
    - Defining a field separator rather than use the default
    - Changing the date input format to adapt to the dataset file
- In the **Header Line** section:
    - Setting how many rows at the beginning of a dataset must be skipped so that the data is read only from the first useful row

Be aware that this page is the first place to try and change settings if you encounter problems when importing files. For example, when you have date fields listed as text, separate fields may appear merged, incorrect entries may appear at the beginning of a dataset, or field names and content may be detected incorrectly.

When you have made the appropriate changes, click the **OK** button to return to the **Select a Data Source** page.

On this page (Figure 11.1), press the loop button 🔍 to open the **Sample Data View** page where you can explore the dataset's content. By default, the view opens on the **Data** tab and presents the first 100 records, as shown in Figure 11.3.

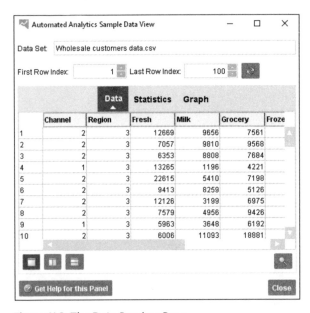

Figure 11.3 The Data Preview Page

You can show more (or fewer) records by changing the **First Row Index** and **Last Row Index** values in the interface and hitting the refresh button ↻. You can also easily order by column values by clicking on the column title.

The **Statistics** tab is useful for more insights into the dataset's content and to understand if the dataset contains useful data or problematic values.

After selecting the **Statistics** tab and clicking on the **Compute Statistics** button, you'll have a choice between computing statistics over the entire dataset or only partially. Then, you'll see the **Variables** page, which shows a list of detected fields, their types, and the number of missing values for each field. More interestingly, in the **Category Frequency** tab, shown in Figure 11.4, you can see how variables are distributed across values.

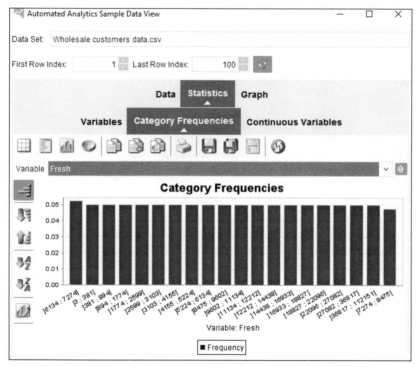

Figure 11.4 The Category Frequency Tab Showing the Distribution of a Continuous Variable

Nominal variables are displayed with the frequency of each value; continuous variables are grouped in 20 bins of equal frequency: the larger the bin interval, the lower frequency for each element inside the bin.

Finally, the **Continuous Variables** tab (Figure 11.5) shows some useful information on variables with continuous values.

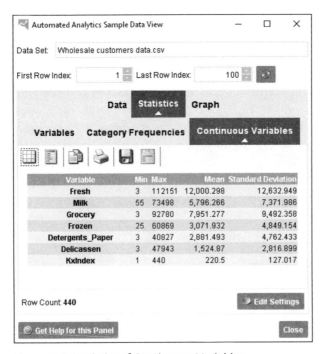

Figure 11.5 Statistics of Continuous Variables

You can see the maximum, minimum, and mean values of and the standard deviation for each variable. All the information in the **Statistics** tab helps you understand the quality of the dataset and to check that the data is suitable for the analysis you want to run.

Click on the **Close** button to go back to the **Select Data Source** window (Figure 11.1).

Now, click on the **Cutting Strategy…** button to select a different cutting strategy than the default **Random Without Test**. Information about choosing a cutting strategy can be found in Chapter 6.

For our example, you don't have to change any options; you'll just keep the defaults. Click on the **Next** button of the **Select a Data Source** screen shown in Figure 11.1. You have now successfully imported the dataset. In the next step, you'll analyze the data analyzed by the tool.

11.2.2   Analyzing the Dataset's Content

After you have selected a data source, the **Data Description** page, shown in Figure 11.6, opens. Click on the **Analyze** button at the top, and the tool will detect the necessary information about the dataset fields.

Figure 11.6 The Data Description Page (after Clicking the Analyze Button)

This page shows you the information detected by the tool within the dataset and lets you modify this information if the automated detection is incorrect or if you want to personalize how data will be interpreted. This page is important because this information controls how variables will be encoded for the model. Good encoding is necessary for the quality and correctness of the resulting model.

In the main table displayed on this page, you can check the information assigned to each variable and change it when necessary by double-clicking on the cell you want to modify. The definition of each column is described in Table 11.1.

Column	Description
Index	This column is just a numerical index to give an ID number to each variable.
Name	This column displays the name of the variable as found in the dataset.
Storage	This column displays the type of the variable (Number, Integer, String, Date, Datetime, or Angle). You can change this value by double-clicking on the table cell.
Value	This column displays the content type of the variable (Continuous, Nominal, Ordinal, or Textual). The value type defines the way that the variable is encoded for the model. For more information, see Chapter 6. You can change this value by double-clicking on the table cell.
Key	This column shows whether the variable is a primary key of the dataset (value 1) or a secondary key (value 2). Variables that are not keys have a value of 0. You can change this value by double-clicking on the table cell.
Order	This column shows whether the variable has an order (value 1) and can be used in an Order By clause. You can change this value by double-clicking on the table cell.
Missing	Provides the value to be used when the variable is null. By default, the tool will use the KxMissing label, but you can enter a text to override the default.
Group	This column displays the group to which a variable belongs, if any. You can put multiple variables in the same group if, together, they provide a single piece of information. Variables in the same group are not crossed when working with models of order 2 or bigger. You can manually set the group information by double-clicking in the cell and providing a group name.
Description	This column provides a text description of the variable.
Structure	This button opens the **Structure** definition page where you can override the automated encoding of the variables.

Table 11.1 Description Columns in the Dataset

At the top of the page, three tabs give you a better control on how the dataset is described, as follows:

- The **Main** tab (Figure 11.6) lets you automatically analyze the dataset by clicking on the **Analyze** button. The most important elements on this tab are as follows:
  - The **Save Description** button lets you save the actual description of the dataset in a file or in a database table. The opposite, the **Load Description** button, opens

a description that was previously saved and applies the description to the dataset. Usually, a description is made for a dataset and applied to the same dataset when loaded again.

- The **Save in Variable Pool** button lets you save the description of a single variable or of all the variables. The information in the variable pool is then automatically applied across different datasets each time a variable with the name found in the variable pool is encountered. This technique can be used to share definitions across datasets. The **Remove from Variable Pool** button takes away the description of the selected variable from the pool.

- Finally, the **View Data** button opens the **Sample Data View** page, which we discussed in Section 11.2.1. Clicking on the **Properties** button simply resumes the variable description already displayed in the table but in a nicer format.

- The **Edition** tab, shown in Figure 11.7, gives you control over the **Storage**, **Value**, **Missing**, and **Group** columns of the description by clicking the respective buttons. Three important buttons on this tab are as follows:

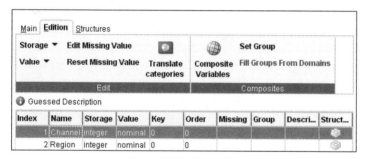

Figure 11.7 The Edition Tab of the Data Description Page

- The **Translate categories** button lets you provide a translation of the values of a variable. You can associate to each value a text in different languages. This information is useful when doing a textual analysis of the information where you want to make sure that different words are associated to the same concept in different languages.

- The **Composite Variables** button lets you associate two values as the latitude and longitude of a single position variable. The two source variables must be of storage **Angle**. When associated, the two variables will always be used together. With the same button, you can also force some variables to be crossed together when creating a predictive model.

- The **Set Group** button lets you add multiple variables to the same group.

- The last tab, the **Structures** tab, is shown in Figure 11.8. This tab gives the same control that you have when double-clicking on the **Structure** column in the main table. A structure can be used to override the automated encoding of the variable provided by the tool.

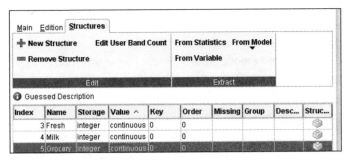

Figure 11.8 The Structures Tab of the Data Description Page

You can define a new structure for a variable clicking on the **New Structure** button. For nominal variables, you can define how the various values of the variable (named **Categories** in the interface) must be grouped together. For ordinal and continuous variables, you can define the number of intervals (the **Band Count**) and the content of each interval to be used for the encoding. When editing a structure, you can also open the **Advanced** tab, as shown in Figure 11.9. Here, you have the following two options:

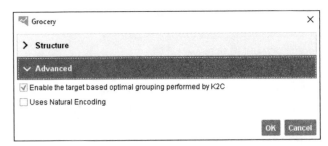

Figure 11.9 The Advanced Tab in the Structure Definition Interface

- Selecting the **Enable the target based optimal grouping performed by K2C** checkbox tells the tool take into account both the structure you defined and the structure automatically generated. The tool will determine the best structure for the model.

- Selecting the **Uses Natural Encoding** checkbox tells the tool to also use variables directly without any encoding based on the target.

As shown in Figure 11.8, the **From Statistics**, **From Variable**, and **From Model** buttons automatically fill in the structure using information already available in the statistical distribution, in the variable pool, or in another model. You can override the content after loading it.

Going back in the main **Data Description** page (Figure 11.6), notice the button and the **Add Filter in Dataset** checkbox. If you select the checkbox, you'll be asked on the next page to define a filter on the dataset itself. You could, as for our example, limit the analysis to a single value of the Channel field or for a single Region. The filter here is useful when using Predictive Factory because you can tell the application to automatically change the value of this filter and hence automatically produce multiple models, one for each value chosen. This workflow is described in more detail in Chapter 9. For the time being, do not set any filter. For our example, you don't have to modify any default values after clicking the **Analyze** button. Click **Next** to go to the page for selecting the variables to be used to build the model.

11.2.3   Choosing the Variables and Setting the Model Properties

In this step, you'll provide a list of variables to consider and, optionally, change the main parameters for how the model is defined. On the **Selecting Variables** page shown in Figure 11.10, you'll set which variables the model should use.

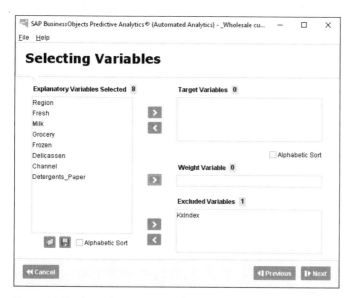

Figure 11.10 The Selecting Variables Page

To move a variable from one group to another, click on its name and use the right or left arrow buttons. Variables can be placed into one of four groups, as described in Table 11.2.

Group	Description
Explanatory Variables Selected	The variables you place in this group describe and explain your model. For clustering, place all variables that you want to consider as dimensions for your analysis of this group.
Target Variables	The variables you place in this group will be used as targets for supervised clustering. Each variable creates a different model. No variables in this panel means that the tool will use unsupervised clustering.
Weight Variables	The variables you place in this group provide different weights to the record where they belong. For example, a value of "3" for a weight variable of a record means the tool will count the record three times when generating the model. You can use this variable to skew the model definition using the records you consider more important.
Excluded Variables	The variables you place in this group will not be considered for the model. These variables are usually indexes or IDs or variables that are highly correlated to other variables in the explanatory group. Two highly correlated variables don't carry additional information and can even decrease the quality of the model.

Table 11.2 The Roles of Variables in the Model

For our example, you'll use the default content of the page when you open it. In other words, the **Target Variables** group will remain empty and an unsupervised clustering will be performed.

Click **Next** at the bottom of the page, and the **Summary of Modeling Parameters** page will open (Figure 11.11). On this page, you'll find the following options:

- At the top of the page, the **Model Name** and **Description** fields let you enter a name and information you want to share about the model. The read-only section with the blue background quickly summarizes some of the previous choices you made.

- The **Find the best number of clusters in this range** fields lets you choose the minimum and maximum number of clusters to be considered by the tool. Putting the same number in both boxes actually provides a fixed value. The values set in these fields are only requests because the final result may contain fewer clusters than you requested (more clusters might be unstable). Also, an additional cluster than what you requested may appear: This cluster contains all items that could not be logically placed in the other clusters.

- The **Calculate SQL Expressions** checkbox is very important: When not selected, the tool defines the best possible clusters using the mathematical approach described in Section 11.4. When the checkbox is selected, the tool adjusts the clusters so that they can be expressed using SQL sentences. The mathematical accuracy of the cluster might be reduced, but you'll be able to export the model into a database to apply the model to new data.

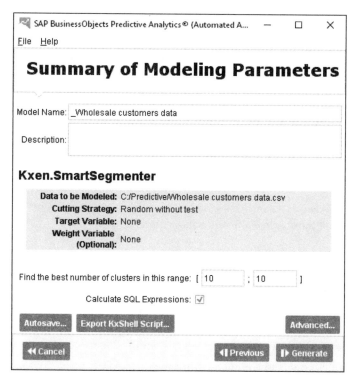

Figure 11.11 The Summary of Model Parameters Page

- The **Autosave** button lets you define the location where the model will be saved automatically (usually the model is saved after it is generated, but the autosave option can be useful if the model is taking a long time to generate). Once generated, the model will be automatically saved at the location you specify.

- Clicking on the **Advanced** button opens the **Specific Parameters of the Model** page where you can override some important parameters. You must be careful on this page because changing parameters might not enhance the quality of the model and might increase its generation time. You can decide whether you want to obtain a detailed description of the influence of the variables on the model by selecting the **Calculate Cross Statistics** box. If you are conducting a supervised clustering, you can define the desired value of the target variable by setting it in the **Target Key** column. By default, this value is the least frequent value in the dataset. The **Distance** dropdown menu lets you override the definition of distance between two records in the cluster definition according to the settings described in Table 11.3.

Setting	Description
System Determined	This setting keeps allows uses the best distance methodology automatically determined by the tool after the dataset is read.
City Block	This setting defines distance as the sum of the absolute differences of the coordinates of the points.
Euclidean	This setting returns the square root of the sum of the square differences of the coordinates.
Chessboard	Also known as "Manhattan style," this setting uses the maximum value of the absolute difference of the coordinates.

Table 11.3 Various Distance Definitions Available for Clustering

Finally, the **Encoding Strategy** lets you choose whether you'll use the default encoding of variables; if you want to force an **Unsupervised** encoding, even during supervised clustering; or if you want to force a **Uniform** encoding where all variables are distributed at regular interval (i.e., between −1 and +1).

For our example, do not change any advanced settings.

Set the number of clusters between 3 and 5 on the main page (Figure 11.11) and keep the **Calculate SQL Expressions** checkbox selected, then click on the **Generate** button to start the model definition process.

11.2.4   Generating the Model and Analyzing the Cluster Profiles

After clicking the **Generate** button, a new page will open showing some logs of the ongoing calculations. The information is displayed and refreshed quickly, and you probably won't be able to read it. Don't worry, if something goes wrong, you'll be notified. If all goes well, a detailed log of the performed actions will open in the subsequent page, the **Training the Model** page, which shows by default the **Model Overview** (shown in Figure 11.12).

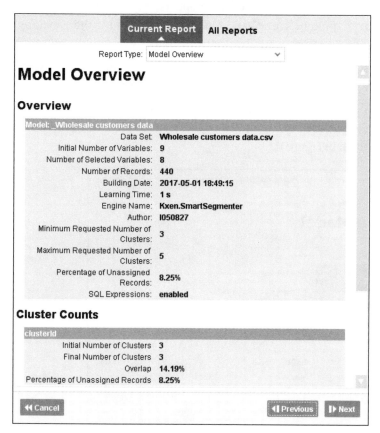

Figure 11.12 The Model Overview after Generation

You can choose the style of report to display with the **Report Type** dropdown menu at the top of the page. The **Model Overview** style is shown by default, and we recommend using it. The **Executive Report** style is useful for a detailed summary of the model, but you'll find the same information and more in a better interface afterwards.

From this overview, notice that you have 440 records in the dataset and that 8.25% of them have not been assigned to any cluster. (This value is quite high but should be expected if you had selected the **Calculate SQL Expressions** checkbox, which tends to build clusters that are less able to include all available records while keeping the SQL sentence readable.)

Also notice that 14.19% of records were overlapping, meaning they appear in more than one cluster. The generation of the SQL takes this overlap into account, and the final version of the model will ensure that a record appears only in one cluster. Knowing the number of overlapping records can help you understand if the generated clusters are different (no overlaps) or similar (many overlaps).

Finally, notice that, in the end, only 3 clusters were generated. At similar quality, the tool generates the minimum number of clusters requested so as to simplify the debriefing and usage of the model.

Click **Next** to enter in the debriefing and model application interface called the **Using the Model** page, as shown in Figure 11.13.

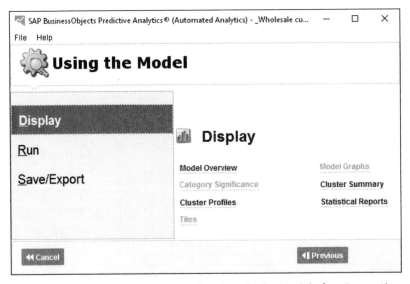

Figure 11.13 Main Interface to Debrief and Apply the Model after Generation

From this page, you can display the model information to better understand how the model was built, apply the model on new data, and save and export the model into a database so that the model can be executed in an external application.

Your first task is to understand what kind of content has been put in each cluster. Click on the **Cluster Profiles** link, and the relevant debriefing page will open, as shown in Figure 11.14.

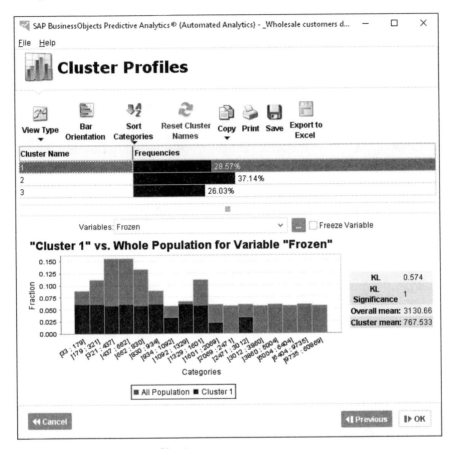

Figure 11.14 The Cluster Profiles Page

The top table shows a list of all clusters and the percentages they represent. In our example, Cluster 1 contains 28.57% of the records of the dataset.

When you click on a cluster line on the table, you'll see at the bottom a bar chart representing how that cluster population is distributed by variable. By default, the display shows the variables with the highest variation for each cluster (in this case, the Frozen variable for Cluster 1).

In the graph, the red bars represent how the total population of the dataset is distributed over the various values or intervals of the variable. The blue bars show how the population of the selected cluster is distributed on the same variables. If a blue bar is higher than the red bar, the cluster population has, in terms of percentage, more records for that value than the total population. If the red bar is higher than the blue bar, then the cluster population is underrepresented for that value.

In Figure 11.14, notice that Cluster 1 contains many records with low Frozen values and no records with high values, while the global population overall is equally distributed over the same variable. In other words, customers in Cluster 1 spend less on frozen food than the global average population.

Clicking on another cluster on the table changes the display on the bottom, always showing the variable that changes the most for that cluster.

You can see how the same variable is distributed across various clusters by checking the **Freeze Variable** checkbox and then changing the cluster selection.

Looking at this representation, you can easily see the different profiles of each cluster. One useful approach is to build a qualitative matrix to help you visualize all the cluster profiles in a single place, which is possible when you have a limited number of clusters and a limited number of variables.

Using our sample, you can build a matrix, as in Table 11.4, where *low* and *high* mean that the cluster presents a low or high level of expenses in the specific area, while *homogeneous* means that a strong bias does not exist.

	Cluster 1	Cluster 2	Cluster 3
Frozen	Low	High	Mid-Low
Delicatessen	Low	Homogeneous	Mid-High
Fresh	Mid-Low	Mid-High	Homogeneous
Grocery	Mid-Low	Mid-Low	High
Milk	Homogeneous	Mid-Low	High
Detergent/Paper	Homogeneous	Mid-Low	High
Channel	Homogeneous	Retail	Hotel/Restaurant
Region	Homogeneous	Homogeneous	Homogeneous

Table 11.4 A Qualitative Matrix Showing the Profile of Each Cluster

From this table, you could decide to run a marketing campaign that divides your customers in two groups. For Cluster 2, you can run a campaign to propose more fresh and frozen food to retail customers; for Cluster 3, a campaign for groceries, milk, and detergents to hotels and restaurants. The profile of Cluster 1 is a lot less diversified and seems to have, in general, a low impact on purchases. Thus, you might want not to spend money on specific marketing campaigns for that group, or you might run a generic campaign. You can also see that Region is not a discriminatory variable: Homogeneous across all clusters, this variable is not really important for your segmentation.

You can also have a graphical representation of the cluster profiles by selecting the **Cluster Summary** link on the **Using the Model** page (Figure 11.13).

The **Cluster Summary** page (Figure 11.15) compares all the clusters over 3 measures that you can select using the **X axis** $\boxed{x}$, **Y axis** $\boxed{y}$, and **Size** buttons at the top.

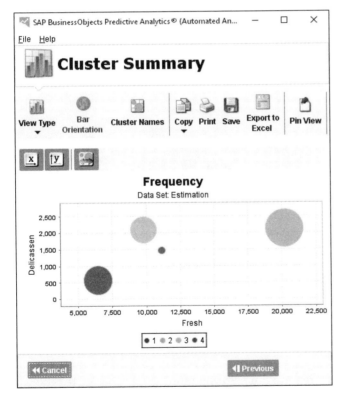

Figure 11.15 The Cluster Summary Page

In the example shown in Figure 11.15, the size of the bubble represents the frequency of the cluster. Expenses appear on Delicatessen on the vertical axis and on Fresh food on the horizontal axis. From the display, you can see that Cluster 2 and Cluster 3 have higher purchases on Delicatessen than Cluster 1.

Notice also that a small Cluster 4 displayed. This cluster is an additional group containing unassigned records (remember that 8.25% of the total population are unassigned, according to the model overview). This additional cluster can be useful to display if you notice that the model has a strong bias on some variable of analysis. For example, you could find that the customers in Cluster 4 are outliers who consume a lot of groceries, and you might want to run a campaign specifically for them.

As a final analysis, you might want to check the SQL generated by the model. Either select navigate to **View Type • SQL** in the **Cluster Profiles** page (Figure 11.14) or select the **Statistical Reports** link (Figure 11.13) and then navigate to **Cluster Details • Cluster SQL Expressions**, as shown in Figure 11.16.

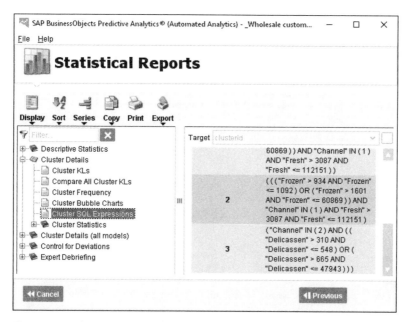

Figure 11.16 The SQL Where Clause Defining Each Cluster (Showing Clusters 2 and 3)

Reading the various statistical reports can help you more deeply analyze the model, but for now, we'll stop here and move to the next step: applying the model to a dataset.

11.2.5   Applying the Model to a Dataset

The goal of creating a clustering model is to group your existing records into clusters. You also use the model to predict in which cluster a new record will fall. With Automated Analytics, you can easily apply the model to either a new set of records or to the dataset you used to define the model so that you can enrich it with cluster information. In both cases, you'll perform the following steps:

1. From the main window shown in Figure 11.13, select the **Run** module and then the **Apply Model** link.

2. The **Applying the Model** page will open where you can define how and on what data the clustering model you just created should run (shown in Figure 11.17).

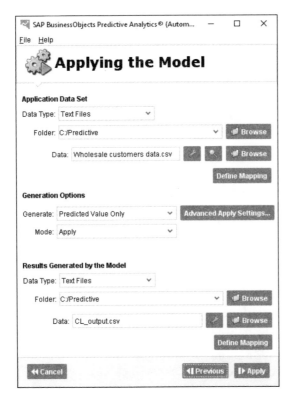

Figure 11.17 Page for Applying the Model to a Dataset

The objective on this page is to perform the following actions:

- Select the dataset onto which you want to apply the model (the list of records you want to divide in each cluster based on the model you created)

- Define the format of the output you want to obtain
- Choose where to save the output information

3. Select your dataset in the top section called **Application Data Set**. The same functionality for selecting a data source was discussed earlier in Section 11.2.1. An additional button, **Define Mappings**, lets you specify the corresponding fields between the application dataset and the fields you used to create the model if the field names differ.

4. In the **Generation Options** section, choose the format of the output. In the **Generate** dropdown menu, choose from four output templates or to define a custom formatting. The possible options are listed in Table 11.5.

Option	Description
Predicted Value Only	The output contains two columns only: the ID of the record in the dataset and the name of the cluster where it has been assigned.
Cluster ID Disjunctive coding	The output contains a column with the ID of the record and a column for each cluster. In each cluster column, the value is 1 if the record is in the cluster and 0 if not.
Cluster ID Disjunctive Coding (+ Copy Data Set)	This option results in the same output as above but additionally includes the complete record information (the ID, the cluster disjunctive columns, and a column for each variable of the dataset). This output is well formed and can be used as an input for a classification or regression analysis.
Cluster ID Target Mean	This option is available only for supervised clustering. This option includes an additional output column that shows the target mean of the cluster on the target variable (thus measuring how "close" the cluster is to the target variable). This information can be useful on its own as well as an input for further classification analysis.
Advanced Apply Setting	Clicking the **Advanced Apply Settings...** button lets you control the output in detail. For example, you can add, for each cluster and record, statistical information on the probability of belonging to the cluster, the distance from the centroid, and other information.

Table 11.5 Clustering Output Options

The disjunctive options, specifically with the copied dataset, can be quite useful to feed the clustering output into a classification model: By running a classification, you'll gain a better understanding of the content of each cluster.

5. From the **Mode** dropdown menu, decide if you really want to generate an output (select **Apply**) or if you just want to update the statistics information visible in the model statistics set of documents (select **Update Only Statistics**).

6. Finally, in the **Results Generated by Model** section of Figure 11.17, you can define where to save the generated output. This section has the same functionality of the top section where you select the input dataset.

For our example, select the *Wholesale customers data.csv* as the application dataset, leave the **Predicted Value** only output option, and add the name of a new file to create in the resulting output (you can use any name, but we called ours *CL_output.csv* in Figure 11.17).

Click on the **Next** button to create the output file, which you can read by clicking on the **View Output** button on the following page.

Now, you've seen how to apply the model onto a dataset using the Automated Analytics interface, but most of the time, you'll need to apply the model directly onto data in a database or within a workflow of an external application. For these cases, you'll export the model as we discuss in the next section.

11.2.6   Saving and Exporting the Model

To reuse the model after generation, you'll need to save the model by going to the **Save/Export** module on the main **Using the Model** page (Figure 11.13) and clicking the **Save Model** link. A new page will open, giving you the choice of saving the model as a file or in a database. The model can now be reopened in Automated Analytics and also in Predictive Factory. You can use Predictive Factory to automatically schedule the refreshing or the application of the model. If you added a filter, as we did in Section 11.2.2, you can then tell Predictive Factory how to replace the filter to generate multiple models.

If you want to export the model into an external application, select the **Generate Source Code** link in the **Save/Export** module. The **Generating Code** page will appear (as shown in Figure 11.18).

Figure 11.18 The Generating Code Page to Export the Model to Other Applications

Using this screen, you can generate code or a function that requires as input the variables used for the model generation and that returns as output the cluster into which the input fits. You can use this code, for example, in an application that takes values for a customer to obtain the group into which a customer is categorized. Using this interface, you'll select the type of code you need for your application (typically the development language of your application) and the name of the text file where you want the code to be generated, as follows:

- The **Target to be used** dropdown list is enabled only when you run a supervised clustering model. This list lets you choose the target variable for generating scores and estimates.

- The **Code type** dropdown list lets you choose the language of the code to be generated. Many different languages are available, from generic SQL, to database-specific SQL, to JAVA, C, and C++, and even code for SAS applications.

- In the **Output** section, you'll name the text file where you want the code to be generated. You also have the option of displaying the code when finished.

After your choices have been made, click on the **Generate** button, and the code will be written. Depending on the code option chosen, you might be prompted to provide the $Dataset and $Key values (respectively, the dataset table that contains the data onto which you want to apply the clustering model and the column in the table that represents the IDs of the records).

After the file is generated, you can open it, copy the code, and paste it into your application. Minimal adjustments might be required to integrate the generated code correctly with your previously existing code.

Play with the various code types to see some examples of outputs. In Figure 11.18, we used settings to generate a file containing SQL code optimized for SAP HANA.

You've now created the model, applied it to new data, and even exported it into another application. In the remaining sections of this chapter, you'll learn more about supervised clustering and the clustering module's mathematical approach.

11.3 Supervised and Unsupervised Clustering

The example shown so far demonstrated unsupervised clustering: In the **Selecting the Variables** page (Figure 11.10), you didn't enter a target variable. If you had selected a target variable (or more than one), then a supervised clustering would have been performed.

With supervised clustering, all the explanatory variables are encoded to provide better explanations of the target variable, using the same target mean-based encoding found in classification and regression models. Moreover, the target variable was not used to define the cluster when you generate the SQL code. As a result, you obtain a model that tries not only to define groups of records but also tries to create groups that explain the value of the target variable or have a distribution that provides a better view on how a cluster relates to the target. This technique can be tailored to answer specific business questions and is a clustering methodology well suited for operational use.

In our example, you might want to do a supervised clustering using Channel as the target variable. Perhaps you want to create better marketing campaigns for retail customers or hotel and restaurant customers. To run the test, just go back to the page shown in Figure 11.10, add the Channel variable as a target key, and then rebuild the model using the same settings (e.g., same number of clusters between 3 and 5).

Now, when you look at the model overview, notice the sections related to the target key, as shown in Figure 11.19.

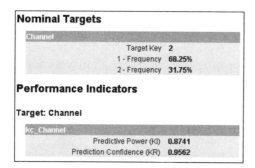

Nominal Targets

Channel

Target Key	2
1 - Frequency	68.25%
2 - Frequency	31.75%

Performance Indicators

Target: Channel

kc_Channel

Predictive Power (KI)	0.8741
Prediction Confidence (KR)	0.9562

Figure 11.19 Model Overview with Additional Information for Supervised Clustering

The good predictive power of 0.87 (87%) shows that the chosen clusters are actually providing a quite accurate prediction of the target channel.

Looking at the cluster profiles (an example is shown in Figure 11.20), notice that Cluster 4 and 5 are quite interesting for your task.

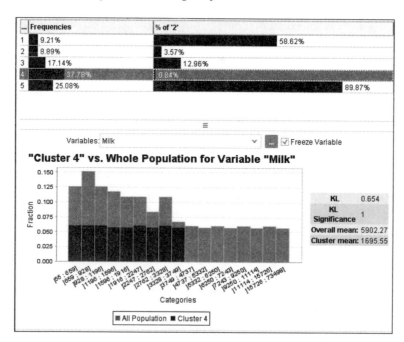

Figure 11.20 Cluster Profiles in Supervised Clustering

Cluster 4 and 5 have the most records. The population of Cluster 4 consists mainly of retail customers (channel is 1), while the population of Cluster 5 consists of hotels and restaurants (channel is 2). Looking at the other variables, notice that Cluster 4 members have low expenses on Milk, Paper, and Groceries—exactly the opposite of members of Cluster 5. This kind of information might lead you to build specific, customized marketing campaigns just for the members of those two clusters. With supervised clustering, the tool generates all the statistical information related to the category's significance.

11.4   The Data Science behind Automated Clustering Models

Automated Analytics uses a K-Means algorithm based on centroids to calculate the clusters.

The process is iterative:

1. At the beginning, a number of random points are generated (one point for each cluster you want); these points are called *centroids*.

2. Then, clusters are created by the points in the dataset that are closer to each centroid, based on the definition of distance you chose (as discussed in Section 11.2.3).

3. Then, for each cluster, the algorithm calculates the center as the point that minimizes the sum of distances from each point.

4. The centroid is then assigned to the newly calculated center. If the old centroid and the new center coincide, you have a stable solution and the process ends. If instead the centroid and the new center don't match, the iteration starts again from step 2.

In Automated Analytics, you have the option of asking for the generated SQL code to define the clusters. If this option is enabled, an additional step occurs after the clusters are defined where the clusters are adjusted slightly so that they can be expressed with an SQL where clause, which is usually less expressive than a mathematical function. These adjustments might cause some points to go outside a cluster (and these points are considered unassigned records), and some points might fall into two different clusters. In this case, the algorithm automatically modifies the SQL where clause to avoid having points in multiple clusters.

11

11.5   Summary

In this chapter, we discussed what is clustering and how to successfully define a clustering model with Automated Analytics in SAP Predictive Analytics. You learned about most of the options for customizing the model to best fit your needs, and you've seen the difference between unsupervised and supervised clustering (the recommended option).

In the next chapter, we'll keep working with Automated Analytics and learn how to build a Social Network Analysis model.

Chapter 12
Social Network Analysis

Social Network Analysis lets you analyze the relationships between people, products, locations, and events—not just analyzing social networks as its name might suggest. You can work with a large number of small interactions and infer the "big picture" to help better understand your business.

Social Network Analysis is one of the latest modules added to SAP Predictive Analytics. Initially, the functionality was included to help phone companies predict customer churn and run better marketing campaigns, but the solution has been generalized to benefit other industries as well. For example, a quality engineer could receive alerts generated by devices and analyze which errors are linked. You can also use Social Network Analysis to enrich a dataset with information that can then be fed into a classification, clustering, or regression model to increase its quality.

In Social Network Analysis, you'll analyze sets of data about entities as in other predictive analytics workflows; the main difference is that the most important information in Social Network Analysis is the relationship between entities. Other attributes are useful but not the core of the analysis.

For example, when looking at three customers, in most analysis workflows, you would look for their ages, their genders, and their incomes. In Social Network Analysis, you instead look at how they interact with each other—how each potential customer has contacted one another. From that analysis, perhaps you would find stronger relationships between certain persons and that some individuals could, for example, influence other people in the social network.

SAP Predictive Analytics also lets you analyze indirect relationships, such as when people often purchase similar products, called a *transactional relationship*. With transactional relationships, even if no direct link exists between customer X and customer Y, you could use customer X's information to recommend to customer Y a new product that had just been purchased by customer X, if the two customers have similar purchase patterns. This kind of analysis is described in Chapter 13, which is dedicated to recommendations.

The goal of the Social Network Analysis module is to simplify and automate as much as possible the task of finding all the possible information within a graph of relationships, direct or transactional. With a few clicks in Automated Analytics' typical wizard-like interface, you can quickly get deep and visual insights on complex data.

In this chapter, after looking at the terminology and some functionalities of Social Network Analysis, we'll show you how to run an end-to-end social analysis project with the module.

12.1   Terminology of Social Network Analysis

In SAP Predictive Analytics, the network or relationships you want to analyze is called a *social graph*. The subjects of the graph are the *nodes* (people, products), which are connected by *links*. The links represent the event that created the relationship between two nodes and can be *directed* (Mary calls Tim) or *undirected* (Mary and Tim meet). If the link is directed, then the first node, called the *source* node, is considered the one that performs the action while the second, known as the *target*, is considered the object onto which the action is performed. The link can also have a *weight*, which is a measure of its strength. As an example, the duration of a phone call can be considered its weight.

Each node has a *degree*, which is the number of connections it has with other nodes. All nodes directly connected to another node are its *neighbors*. A node with many neighbors might experience strong *social pressure* if many of its contacts act similarly, meaning neighbors can influence a node directly with their actions or behaviors. If you are the only one wearing green shoes and all of your 50 friends wear yellow shoes, you might be tempted to buy yellow shoes over the weekend.

Groups of nodes that interact a lot together are called *communities*. SAP Predictive Analytics automatically detects communities in a graph and can also group communities together to find communities of communities and build hierarchies of communities.

Some nodes can be anomalously connected to other nodes. For example, a call center could be considered a node with an enormous quantity of outgoing links and no incoming links. These hyper-connected nodes are called *mega-hubs*. Mega-hubs can be detected by the tool and are usually removed from the analysis because they don't carry useful information and are considered noise in the network.

In the SAP Predictive Analytics methodology, a node can belong to a single community. Within the community, the Social Network Analysis module understands what the *role* of the node is, as shown in Table 12.1.

Role	Description
Local	A node that has interactions only within the community
Passive	A node that has usually a low degree and is mainly the target of the interactions within the community
Social	A node that has a lot of connections within the community and outside of it.
Bridge	A node that has a few connections within its own community but who is connected with other communities

Table 12.1 Roles of Nodes in Communities

If you want to run a viral marketing campaign, then you should target nodes that act in a social or bridge role as they will spread the information more than those in passive or local roles. In a network of products, a bridge could be a product suggested to customers with a local purchase pattern to try to change their habits and encourage them to start looking at other kind of purchases.

Finally, each node or link can have specific *attributes* (for a person, the age, the gender, etc.), and you can view this information when navigating the network.

12.2   Automated Functionalities of Social Network Analysis

SAP Predictive Analytics provides some out-of-the-box features to automate the analysis of a network. In the following sections, we'll look at some of these features to help you get the most business value out of the basic information that subjects are linked together.

12.2.1   Node Pairing

The same physical entity might appear under different nodes in two versions of a social graph. As mentioned earlier, a person may have changed phone operators and phone companies between two analyses of the same network.

The Social Network Analysis solution has a functionality that enables you to find network elements that, even if different points, are likely the same physical entity. This functionality is called *node pairing*.

With node pairing, for example, you can find customers who continuously switch phone companies to benefit from new customer offers. Node pairing can also identify cases of identity theft or cases when the single person appears under different identities.

Node pairing analyzes the connections of nodes in social graphs taken at different times and isolates nodes that have many neighbors in common (you can set a specific threshold) and that could hence be the same node. Once those nodes are identified, the pairing can be confirmed (or inferred) by analyzing the attributes of the two proposed nodes. (If the algorithm proposes two nodes as the same but one is called Jane and the other Tim, then the similarity might just be a coincidence.)

12.2.2   Communities and Roles Detection

The Social Network Analysis module identifies group of nodes that interact together as communities. Communities can consist of people that often talk on the phone, exchange mails, or meet in the same places or can consist of products typically purchased together or events triggered together in many scenarios. Social Network Analysis detects communities and, at a coarser granularity, communities of communities.

If you build the same social graph over many time spans, you can also analyze how the relationships within the communities have evolved over time and how community attributes have changed in the same period. You can use this information to validate if an action you've made in a community (e.g., a marketing campaign) has had the desired outcome or not.

Within each community, Social Network Analysis can also automatically detect the role of each node (as per Table 12.1). You can output this information for each node (the community and "community of community" it belongs to, its role in the community) and use it to improve another analysis, such as a classification, a regression, or a clustering model.

12.2.3   Social Graph Comparison

The social graph comparison functionality lets you compare two different graphs and shows what nodes and links appear in both graphs or only in one graph.

Using this feature, you can see the similarities between different scenarios. For example, you can create two graphs showing communications between people: one filtered to show only SMS messages and the other to show only phone calls. By comparing the two graphs, you'll see which users use both SMS and voice or use only one method.

Filtering by date, you can also see the newest contacts of a specific node or see the contacts that have disconnected from a node.

12.2.4   Bipartite Graphs Derivation and Recommendations

When you create a transactional social graph, you can link two different groups of nodes, called *populations*, and find out the relationships inside each population and between populations.

The bipartite graph derivation finds these relationships by automatically finding the indirect links between the same population. For example, you can derive a graph of people that purchase similar items and a graph of products that are often sold together. The strength of the links in each bipartite graph tells you how often the two nodes are linked to a same node (of the other population) in the global graph.

Bipartite graphs can be used to cluster together populations, and you can use this information for further analysis or for recommendations.

Given the importance of this use case, a specific module has been added into SAP Predictive Analytics, the Recommendation module, which is described in depth in Chapter 13. As the details are outlined in that chapter, we won't replicate it here, but we want to highlight the fact that, to simplify the recommendation process, the Recommendation module has fewer functions and options than the Social Network Analysis module.

12.2.5   Proximity

When dealing with geographic information (latitude and longitude), you can build a graph linking people to places. If you also have time information, the graph can tell you who was where and when.

Using this functionality, Social Network Analysis tells you which nodes have been together at the same place and the same time. Because a place is a special type of node, with specific treatment and usage, the Social Network Analysis module has a dedicated interface for colocation analysis. This interface simplifies the workflow for creating geographical graphs to find people in the same location. An example of colocation analysis is provided in Section 12.5.1.

12.2.6   Path Analysis

Similarly to colocation, path analysis is the post-processing of a social graph using geographical information. With path analysis, you can determine the most typical paths that a person takes, and you can infer the next place a person will go.

Social Network Analysis provides a dedicated interface for path analysis to simplify the workflow. The output can be used to position new stores in a block or to understand why people go (or don't go) towards a specific place. For both colocation and path analyses, in your dataset, you'll need the coordinates of locations and the times when the subjects were at those locations.

An overview of path analysis is provided in Section 12.5.2.

12.3   Creating a Social Network Analysis Model

Now it's time to try building a Social Network Analysis model yourself.

In this section, you can follow along with the detailed steps using the sample datasets available with this book, you can use your own data, or you can use the sample data included in the SAP Predictive Analytics Automated Analysis installation in the ../../ ../Samples/KSN directory.

Sample Social Network Analysis Call Data and Workflow

The data used in our example is a simplified sample of a group of people who have had phone conversations.

The sample dataset can be downloaded at *www.sap-press.com/4491*.

Four files make up the dataset:

- The log of calls by phone number (*SNA_Calls.csv*)
- The customer ID related to each phone number (*SNA_Lookup.csv*)

- The customer relationship management (CRM) information for each customer (*SNA_Population.csv*)
- An application dataset (*SNA_Apply.csv*)

The data contains a log of phone calls between two families between January 1st, 2017 and February 28th, 2017. Two persons (Mary and Jane) in two different families talk with one another, as shown in Figure 12.1.

The dataset contains only information about phone calls; nothing is mentioned about the two families. You'll use the Social Network Analysis module on the data to understand who called whom and to look for communities. The Social Network Analysis will determine that there actually are two separate families and tell you that Jane and Mary have peculiar roles within each family.

In our dataset, we simulated that Mary changed her phone number and appears as two different nodes. You'll use the node pairing feature in Social Network Analysis to (re)discover that those two nodes are in reality the same person.

In the steps we describe next, we suppose that all three sample files are saved in a *C:\Predictive* directory on your machine.

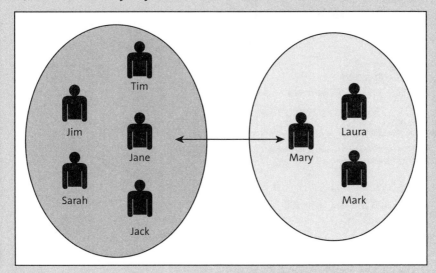

Figure 12.1 Sample Dataset: A Log of Calls between Two Families

To create the model hosting the Social Network Analysis, you'll follow these steps:

1. Upload (or connect) to the social information dataset.
2. Choose the graph type to create.

3. (Optional) Add additional graph analysis, as needed.

4. Specify what additional analysis you want to perform (communities, mega-hubs, node pairing).

5. Add additional information to the social data, and start the calculation.

Let's get started!

12.3.1   Starting the Module and Importing the Dataset

To start the workflow, launch the Automated Analytics interface, go to **Social** and select the **Create a Social Network Analysis** module.

The **Add Graph** page opens (Figure 12.2), where you'll select to **Build a Social Graph From a Dataset**. The two other options let you extend an existing graph in another model (**Extract a New Social Graph...**) or from a bipartite graph of this model (**Derive Graph from a Bipartite Graph**).

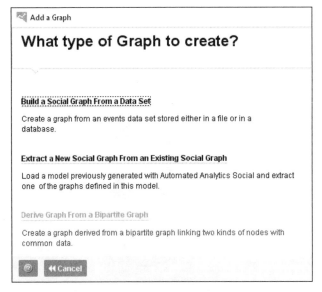

Figure 12.2 Adding a New Social Graph to the Model

Extracting a graph from another model is useful if you want to build a model based on an existing model for additional refining. Deriving a graph from a bipartite graph is used for recommendations and is described in detail in Chapter 13.

Now, select the file that contains the relationships between your nodes, for our scenario, the *SNA Calls.csv* file, as shown in Figure 12.3.

Figure 12.3 Loading the Events Data

The process to load the data is similar to the one described in Chapter 11, which you should refer to for a list of all the data-loading functionalities of the interface. Notice that you can get data not only from files but also from database tables.

Browse the file content with the loop button, and you'll see the following information:

- Source: the phone number making the call
- Target: the phone number receiving the call
- Duration: the duration in minutes of the communication
- Date: the date of the call

As we mentioned in Chapter 11, Section 11.2.1, you might want to look at the dataset's statistics. Notice that the Date field is interpreted as a string because the format of the date is not the default expected by SAP Predictive Analytics (YYYY-MM-DD). To change the default setting, click on the wrench button to edit the file settings (Figure 11.2); enter a slash symbol "/" in the **Date Separator** field and select **Day Month Year** from the **Date Order** dropdown list. If you now look at the statistics again, notice that the date field is correctly interpreted.

Go to the next page and click the **Analyze** button to have the dataset interpreted correctly for the analysis. The screen shown in Figure 12.4 will open.

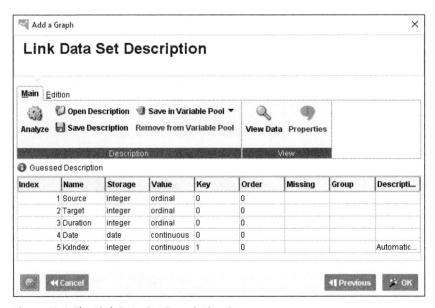

Figure 12.4 The Link Data Set Description Page

Now, click the **OK** button to enter the specific interface for Social Network Analysis.

12.3.2 Defining the Graph Model to Build

After you have defined the data structure, the **Graph Definitions** page opens, as shown in Figure 12.5.

Let's look at the different parts of this window, as follows:

- On the top left, the **Graph List** contains all of the graphs that will be generated by this model. By default, a **New Graph1** item is already available for you to define. You can add new graphs, duplicate existing ones, or filter through graphs using the buttons in the ribbon or by right-clicking on the appropriate graph. We will see in Section 12.3.3 how to use the **Temporal Duplication** functionality, but for now, this function is disabled in the interface.

Figure 12.5 The Graph Definition Page

- The right panel, **Graph Settings**, lets you define the type and content of the graph. This panel is primarily where you'll tell SAP Predictive Analytics how to build the graph.

  Five different types of graphs can be created (described in Table 12.2). Select the type in the **Graph Creation Type** dropdown list.

Graph type	Description
Contact	In this main graph type, nodes of the same population are directly linked to one another (e.g., "people" in phone calls). You can assign a weight to the link and filter out nodes by specifying a minimal weight or minimal number of links threshold. Use this graph type to analyze relationships between nodes of the same kind.
Transactions	This graph type creates a bipartite graph linking two populations (e.g., customers and products). You can specify a weight for the links. This graph is used mainly to derive each population graph and to build recommendations. The whole workflow of transaction graphs is described in Chapter 13 and will not be repeated in this chapter.
Proximity	This graph type links a population with a location expressed in latitude and longitude. Use this graph type to see if two nodes were at the same place at the same time or to identify common paths taken by multiple nodes. A specific workflow simplifies the whole definition of a proximity graph, so setting this value in the **Graph Settings** is not necessary; the option is available in this panel for backwards compatibility. We'll discuss colocation graphs in more detail in Section 12.5.1.
Nearest neighbors	This graph type looks at the distance between two nodes and defines a network based on the proximity of nodes. You can use this graph type to, for example, find persons who are "closer" together (either using a geographical "closeness" or a business one, i.e., by ordering people on a scale based on a business attribute such as revenue or expenses). To use this kind of graph, you'll need a specific column in your data containing the distance between two persons.
Links only	The links only mode is a subset of the contacts mode and won't be discussed here.

Table 12.2 The Five Different Graph Types

For our example, select the **Contact** graph type and fill the **Graph Setting** page, as shown in Figure 12.5. The description of each field is shown in Table 12.3.

Field	Description
Source Node	The ID of the node making the link action (e.g., making a phone call) or the first node of two being linked (e.g., A meets B).
Target Node	The ID of the node who receives or is the object of the link action or the second node of the two being linked.
Date Column	The date and time when the action (the link) takes place. The default format of this column is YYYY-MM-DD HH:mm:ss.
Links Type	**Directed**: The link has a precise direction—the source is taking an action towards the target (e.g., A calls B). **Undirected**: There is no direction in the action (e.g., A and B meet). Be sure you select the appropriate type, because defining communities largely relies on the direction (or not) of links.
Minimum Contacts Count	A link is retained only if it has a minimum number of occurrences. This filter is useful for reducing the size of the network by removing links that are rarely used.
Use a Weight Column	You can describe the strength of a link using this weight column. For phone calls, for example, a weight could be the duration of the call. The higher the weight, the stronger the link and the more the link will be taken into consideration when building the network of the node, its role, and the community to which it belongs.
Minimum Weight	This filter enables you to remove links with insufficient weight so to simplify the network.
Maximum Number of Connections	This filter limits the number of connections that are identified for a given node. Once this number of links has been found, no more links are added to nodes. You must not confuse this limit with the functionality to detect mega-hubs, which are removed from the network. The parameter in this field simply stops new links from being added to an already well-connected node.
Start Date	This filter keeps only the links whose date field is set from this date onwards. (The specific date is included in the selection.)
End Date	This filter keeps only links whose date field is set before this date. (The specific date is excluded from the selection.) You can use the **Start Date** and **End Date** fields to calculate the graph at different times and then compare their evolution.

Table 12.3 Fields for Defining a Contact Graph

Once you have filled in the information for the first graph, you could go on with the analysis. For our example, however, you'll create other time-based graphs so we can analyze their evolution.

12.3.3   Adding More Graphs

Now, we're going to duplicate the existing graph then filter the duplicate to a specific time period and automatically build other graphs for other time periods. The goal for our scenario is to build 4 biweekly graphs and 2 monthly graphs.

First, click on **New Graph1** in the **Graph List** panel and then, in the ribbon, select the **Duplicate Selected • Clone**. A copy of the graph appears in the list. For sake of readability, let's rename the graph, e.g., to "Temporal."

Go to the **Time Period** filters and set the initial date to January 1st, 2017, and end date to January 15th, 2017. The **Graph Settings** page should look like what's shown in Figure 12.6; all other fields will keep the same values as shown in Figure 12.5.

Figure 12.6 A Graph Filtered by Date

Now, you can automatically build the other graph (one for every 2-week period) by selecting the **Temporal** graph in the **Graph List** page and then, in the ribbon, selecting

Duplicate Selected • Temporal Duplication. In the small popup window that appears, set the values so as to build 3 additional graphs of 14 days each to cover the 2 months of data we have. Three more graphs will be created automatically, as shown in Figure 12.7.

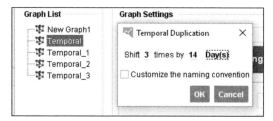

Figure 12.7 Making a Temporal Duplication of a Graph

If you now select each graph, you can see that their start and end dates have been automatically generated with the shift of 14 days for each graph.

Do the same workflow to build a new graph from January 1st to January 31st, 2017, and then use time duplication to create a graph for the month of February. The graphs should be called **JanuaryGraph** and **FebruaryGraph**, respectively.

To summarize, the **New Graph1** graph, when created, will contain all phone call records we have. The **Temporal** graphs will contain 14 days of conversations each. **JanuaryGraph** will contain all calls of January, and **FebruaryGraph** all calls in February.

From this interface, you could also add a filter on the social data for a specific set. For example, if the dataset has information about the type of contact (SMS, phone call, video call), you might want to create specific graphs for each of these types. To set the filter, select the graph and click on the **Add Column Filter** button on the ribbon. Notice that this filter removes rows of data but doesn't remove the filtered column. For our example, you don't need to add filters to the sample.

Now that you've defined the graphs to be created, click the **Next** button to go to the post-processing phase.

12.3.4   Setting Community, Mega-hub, and Node Pairing Detection

After the graph definition phase, you'll define the additional information you want to extract from existing relationships. The **Post-Processing** page (Figure 12.8) lets you choose in which graphs to identify communities and mega-hubs.

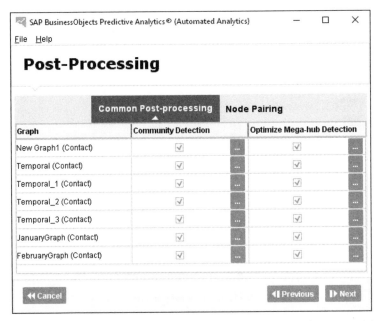

Figure 12.8 Post-Processing Page: Setting the Detection of Communities and Mega-hubs

By default, communities and mega-hubs are detected for all graphs, which can indeed be useful but is often time-consuming. For models that take a long time to run, consider disabling or limiting community detection (but keep the mega-hub removal). By checking or unchecking each box, you can turn on and off detection. Clicking on the three-dot button ▪▪▪ next to each box allows you to fine-tune the detection algorithm.

The detection of communities occurs with an iterative algorithm (Louvain algorithm), which finds the nodes that are more interrelated. At each iteration, the application measures a gain in the clustering represented by an Epsilon value. In general, these details about the algorithm aren't necessary, but might interest you if you are a data scientist.

In the communities detection configuration window (Figure 12.9), you can define the maximum number of iterations and an Epsilon value. We recommend keeping the default values or, to speed up the process, reducing the maximum number of iterations.

You can suggest an algorithm to derive communities from communities already found in another graph with the **Seed from graph** dropdown. This setting speeds up the recognition of communities and simplifies the comparative analysis of communities with the seed graph. Disabling supercommunities reduces the time it takes to build the model by excluding communities of communities. For our scenario, you can leave the default values.

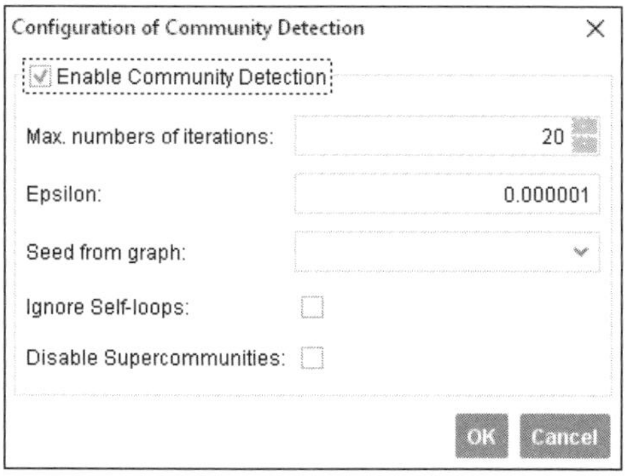

Figure 12.9 Configuring Community Detection

Mega-hubs are nodes that are abnormally connected to many other nodes. Call centers could be a mega-hub in a network of phone communications; best-selling books might be a mega-hub in a bipartite network of customers purchasing books. Often, removing mega-hubs from the graph is a good idea because they rarely carry valuable information and might hide other, more useful structures. For example, a bestseller doesn't need to be recommended because readers are already aware of and likely to buy the book. In a recommendation model, removing the best-seller from the recommendations decreases the risk of other recommended books going unnoticed.

Looking at the checked boxes in Figure 12.8, notice that mega-hubs are automatically detected and removed. You can fine tune their detection in each graph by clicking on the three-dot button ⬛; the window shown in Figure 12.10 will appear.

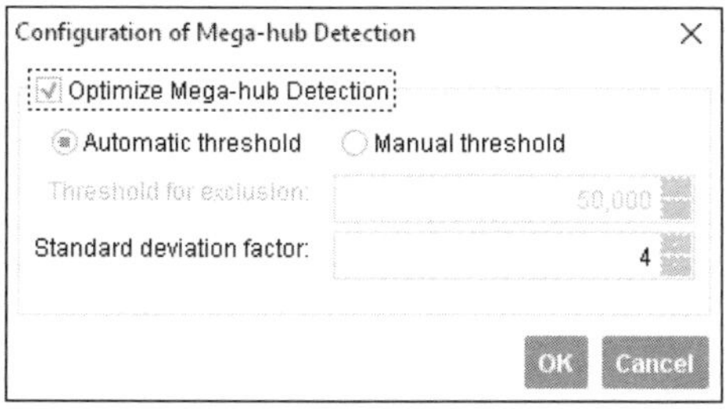

Figure 12.10 Mega-hub Detection Configuration Window

By default, automatic detection is enabled. This mechanism identifies as mega-hubs all nodes whose number of connection is above a calculated threshold, considering the distribution of the number of connections of each node:

connections mean + standard deviation × standard deviation factor

You can influence the threshold by changing the **Standard deviation factor** value in the interface. The lower the factor value, the lower the threshold for a node to be considered a mega-hub. If you enter "0," then all nodes with more connections than the mean are considered mega-hubs.

In some situations, manually setting the threshold by fixing the **Threshold for exclusion** value in the interface might be easier. By default, this value takes the **Maximum Number of Connections** that you fixed in the **Graph Settings** page shown in Figure 12.5. For our sample, just leave the existing values because no mega-hubs exist in our data.

Let's now detect if some nodes in the graph represent the same person using the node pairing feature. Go back to the **Post-Processing** window shown in Figure 12.8 and select the **Node Pairing** tab. The window shown in Figure 12.11 will appear.

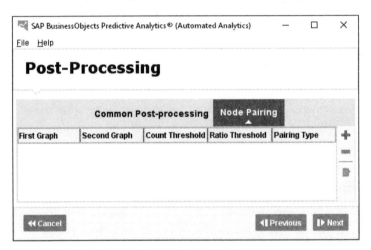

Figure 12.11 The Node Pairing Settings Interface

Your goal is to check the January and February graph to see if some nodes might actually represent the same person. Click on the blue plus icon ➕ to add a new node pairing analysis. The **Pairing Definition** page will open (Figure 12.12).

Figure 12.12 The Pairing Definition Page

On this page, you'll define how you want to identify node pairs.

For our task, select **JanuaryGraph** and **FebruaryGraph** in the **First Graph** and **Second Graph** fields, respectively. This action specifies the graphs will be checked for paired nodes. Give a name to the output graph that will contain the analysis, for our example, by entering "Paring_Jan_Feb."

The **Minimum Common Neighbors Count** field defines the minimum number of common neighbors for two nodes to be considered paired. As our graph is rather small, change the default value of "4" to "2." In general, your business knowledge should tell you what value is most appropriate for this field.

The **Keep Top N field** field lets you specify how many pairs you want to keep at most. (If too many pairs exist, then you may want to limit your analysis.) Leave the field as "0," which indicates that you don't want to apply the filter.

Click on the **Minimum Common Neighbors Ratio** checkbox and add a value to set an additional threshold. The application will retain only pairs that are above the ratio value calculated with the method chosen in the **Pairing Type** field. As detailed information about pairing types goes beyond the scope of this book, refer to the public user guide *Getting Started with Social* published by SAP and available at *http:// help.sap.com*.

When you've entered the values as shown in Figure 12.12, click **OK** to go to back to the **Post-Processing** page. Then, click **Next** to move to the next step where you'll add more information to the nodes.

12.3.5 Providing Descriptions of Nodes

At the moment, all the information you have about the node just identify the fields in the **Source** and **Target** columns of your dataset. In our example, those fields are the phone numbers of each person.

In real scenarios, you'll have much more information about your nodes (e.g., age, name, birth city, etc., for people). For better analysis, the Social Network Analysis module lets you, optionally, decorate your nodes with all the information you have about your population. Usually the identifiers of your population in your CRM system are different from the ones you use for social analysis. Social Network Analysis provides you an additional step to convert identifiers from one system to the other.

First, you'll convert the phone numbers to the customer ID of your population, and then, you'll upload a file that includes the birth year, phone brand, city, etc., for each customer. This information will be used later in the analysis output. The first (optional) step is to convert the identifiers you have in your social analysis dataset into the customer IDs of your information dataset.

After you moved away from the **Post-Processing** page, the **Identifiers Conversion** page will open, as shown in Figure 12.13.

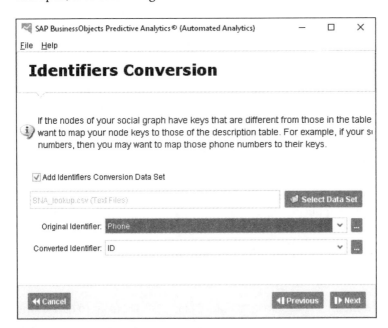

Figure 12.13 The Identifiers Conversion Page

Select the **Add Identifiers Conversion Data Set** checkbox to enable all the other fields. Using the **Select Data Set** button, browse and select the *SNA_Lookup.csv* file provided in the sample data. (The interface is the usual one for data upload, similar to the one shown in Figure 12.4.) Look at the data, and you'll see that there are just two columns: the phone number of the person and its ID in the CRM system. Remember to **Analyze** the file to enable its upload.

You must set up the conversion by setting the **Original Identifier** (in your social analysis data) to the Phone column and the **Converted Identifier** to the ID column (Figure 12.14). Now, the system knows how to find the ID in the information file about your population and how to relate it to the social data.

Click **Next** and the **Descriptive Attributes** page will open, as shown in Figure 12.14.

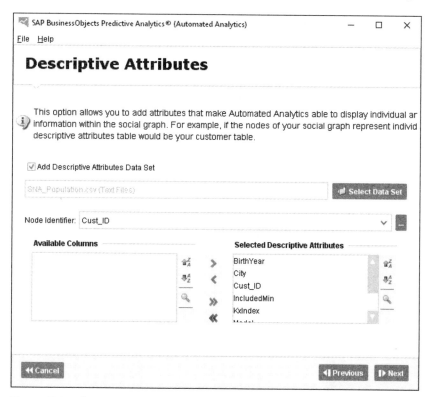

Figure 12.14 The Descriptive Attributes Page

In this (optional) page, you'll define which dataset contains the descriptive information about your population (your nodes).

After selecting the **Add Descriptive Attributes Data Set** checkbox, select a file with the **Select Data Set** button. For our example, select the *SNA_Population.csv* file.

In the **Node Identifier** field, enter the ID of the node (either from the unconverted social dataset or the converted identifier value). Finally, add descriptive columns to the model output. In our sample, you can add all of them by moving them in the **Selected Descriptive Attributes** list.

These values help you better understand the graph and can be used when applying the model to add more information for a subsequent classification, regression, or clustering on the nodes.

When you are done, click the **Next** button.

At this point, you've completed the definition of the graphs; the summary page (Figure 12.15) gives you an overview of what will be built.

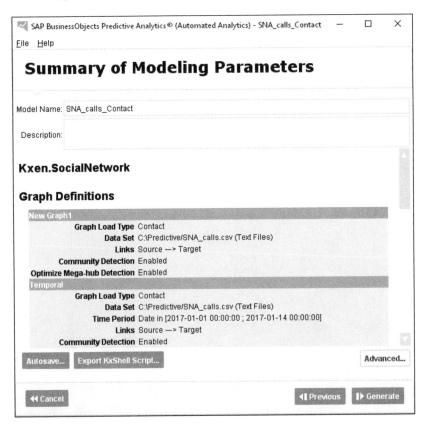

Figure 12.15 Summary of Modeling Parameters

On this page, you'll see a list of all the graphs to be created and their main properties. You'll also see if you added a converter and attributes information and if you requested node pairing, community detection, and/or mega-hub detection.

As the process of calculating the model can take some time (you might have thousands or even millions of links), we recommend having the system save the model automatically as soon as it is calculated to prevent inadvertently canceling the model calculation after it has been performed. To set this functionality, click the **Autosave** button and define where you want to save the calculated model (in a file or directly into a database).

If you want to execute the model via the scripting language, you can export the definitions via the **Export KxShell Script...** button. Chapter 16 provides examples of this script functionality.

Click the **Generate** button to start the model calculation. When completed, you can start the analysis.

12.4   Navigating and Understanding the Social Network Analysis Output

Now, it's time to look at the results and start interpreting them. While these steps don't necessarily follow a sequence, nor are they all required, a typical workflow involves these steps:

1. Check the overall model results.
2. Look at how nodes are linked together, as follows:
   - Navigate between nodes and links
   - Identify the existing communities
   - Check if node pairings exist
3. Apply the model to create a detailed output dataset.

Let's start with the global analysis.

12.4.1   Understanding Model Quality from the Model Overview

When the model calculation is completed, you'll see the **Model Overview** page (shown in Figure 12.16).

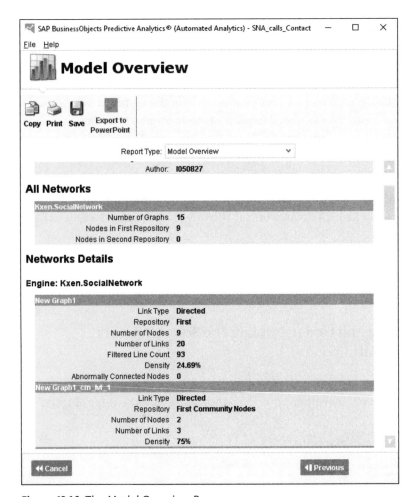

Figure 12.16 The Model Overview Page

Let's look at the information you can find on this page, as follows:

- In the **All Networks** section, you'll see how many graphs were created. Usually more graphs than what you asked for will be built because the solution also creates graphs for communities and communities of communities. In this section, you'll see how many nodes were identified. The nodes in the second repository appear when you create a bipartite graph associating populations of different types (e.g., people and products).

  Notice that our network is rather small (9 nodes). We kept our example simple to better globally visualize the results. You may already see an anomaly that should pique your curiosity: In our sample data, we talked about 8 persons—why do we have 9 nodes? We'll find out when studying the node pairing. In general, if you know how many items are in your population, you can check the number of nodes on this page to determine if a misalignment needs to be investigated.

- In the **Network Details** section, you'll see specific information for all graphs that have been created. Graphs with a _cm_ extension are graphs of automatically created communities. For each graph, we'll find the information described in Table 12.4.

Value	Description
Link Type	For each created graph, this value indicates if the graph was created with a directed or an undirected set of links.
Repository	The First repository contains all nodes of the same population; the second repository, the nodes of the target population in a bipartite graph; and the community repository, graphs of communities.
Number of nodes	This value indicates how many nodes belong to the graph. This number is useful for checking the evolution of a graph over time (you can compare the number nodes at different times). If the number is 0, then no nodes were found for this graph, which might interest your business or which might just indicate that you didn't define the graph correctly.
Number of links	This value indicates the number of links found in the graph. This number allows you to compare the same network over time or to check for incorrect graph if the value is 0.
Filtered line count	This value indicates the number of records in the social dataset used to define this graph. When building a graph, only the appropriate dates are taken into account, and only the records that satisfy all filters are put in place. This information is not available for community graphs.
Density	This value is the ratio between the number of links found and the total possible number of links in the network. Low numbers are symptoms of a sparse network; high numbers, of a dense network (a lot of people talking to a lot of people). Density is more or less the measure of the activity in the network; you can monitor changes in density over time for the same graph to see if activity increases or decreases. Also, in dense networks, we can expect that information and influence move more quickly than in sparse networks. Increasing density might be one of your business targets.

Table 12.4 Graph Information in the Model Overview

Value	Description
Abnormally connected nodes	The number of mega-hubs found in the graph (and removed from it). Be sure to check this value to determine if you are looking at the real network or at a simplified version of it. This information is not available for community graphs.

Table 12.4 Graph Information in the Model Overview (Cont.)

- In the **Network Communities** section, you'll see more information about the communities identified in each graph (Table 12.5).

Value	Description
Number of communities	This value indicates the number of communities found in the graph.
Modularity	This number measures the quality of the identification of the community: Links within the communities are compared with a random distribution of links in a network without communities. Modularity shows how much structure is found in the real network, in other words, the level of confidence that the group of nodes is a real community and not a random set of nodes. In general, values above 0.6 are good, and you can trust the results; below 0.5, and you should do more investigation. In our example, we have low modularity because, for sake of simplicity, we didn't put many conversations in our data. Nevertheless, you'll see that the two communities (the two families) are correctly identified.
Intra links median	This value is the median of the number of links within the community.
Inter links median	This value is the median of the distribution of the number of links from the community to other communities. The intra-and inter-median values are used to understand the role of a node: Nodes above the median tend to be social (within the community or externally); nodes below the median tend to be passive. Looking at those numbers will indicate if the communities tend to be closed (high intra-links and low inter-links) or open to other ones (high inter-links). The two values together indicate if a network is made up of separate groups or of groups with a lot of interactions.

Table 12.5 Global Information about Communities

For more detail, click on the **Next** button at the bottom of the page, which will bring you to the main **Social Network Analytics Options** page.

Be sure you select the **Display** tab on the left to see the various information options. The **Model Overview** link brings you back to the model summary page, but let's stay on this screen for now. For a detailed view of the global results of the model, click on the **Debriefing Tables** link; the **Statistical Reports** page will open (Figure 12.17).

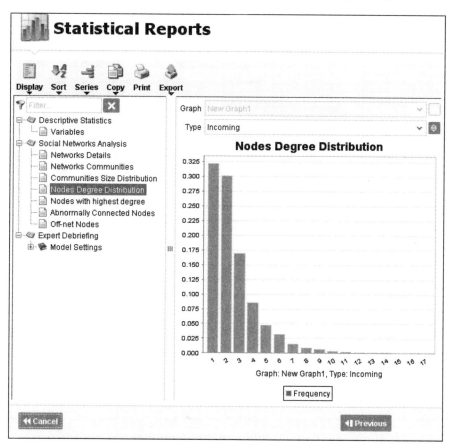

Figure 12.17 Statistical Reports Page

Select a report on the left panel by double-clicking on it. Various reports simply detail what is available in the summary page. Four reports are worth analyzing here, as detailed in Table 12.6.

Report	Description
Communities size distribution	This report shows a chart with the number of communities of a certain size. From this chart, you can see if you have many equivalent communities or if you have a mixed distribution of both large and small communities. Using this information, you can decide which kind of community to target for analysis.
Nodes Degree Distribution	The degree is the number of links of a node. In this chart, you'll see the frequency of nodes with a given degree. The typical distribution is the one shown in Figure 12.17 with many nodes having just one link (first column) and a few nodes with many links. Checking this representation, you'll see if an abnormal distribution of links exists in your community, which should be analyzed. (Note that the screenshot is not taken on the social dataset of the sample.)
Nodes with highest degree	You'll see here which nodes are most connected in your graph. This information is useful to quickly see the most influential persons in a network. You can also use it to identify a new threshold for mega-hubs.
Abnormally connected nodes	This list consists of mega-hubs that have been identified and removed from the graph.

Table 12.6 Some Useful Reports in the Detailed Debriefing

This detailed information in addition to the overview can help you understand if you'll find useful information in the model. Now let's move ahead and start looking how nodes are connected together.

12.4.2   Navigating into the Social Network

Going back to the main display page (**Social Network Analytics Options**), click on the **Nodes Display** link to open the navigation page (shown in Figure 12.18).

The **Node Display** page is divided in three areas:

- The ribbon is where all menu items appear. As menu items are context sensitive, when you open a page for the first time, only a few actions are available.
- The graph display panel is the main area of the page and displays the nodes, links, and communities.

- The reports panel shows detailed information of any node or community selected in the graph display panel.

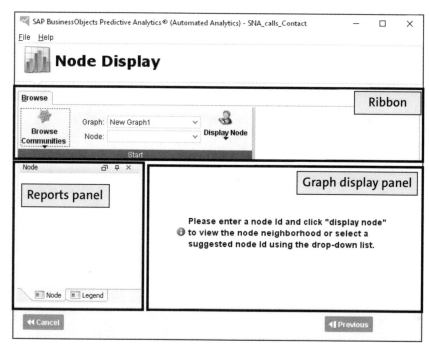

Figure 12.18 The Node Display Page

In the following sections, you'll learn how to navigate among the graphs, display the information you need, and perform a node pairing analysis to compare two different graphs.

Navigating among the Nodes

Using the sample dataset, let's start by selecting node 5. Go to the **Browse** ribbon tab, set a value in the **Node** dropdown list, and click the **Display Node** button. The display should look like Figure 12.19.

The graph now displays node 5 and all its direct links (its neighbors). Each node is represented by a small blue pawn.

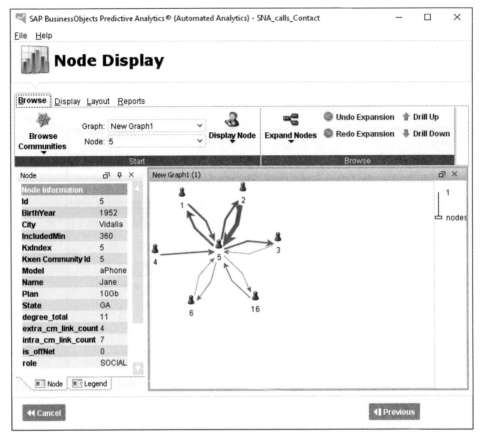

Figure 12.19 The Neighborhood of Node 5 in the Sample Dataset

On the top right of the graph display panel, you'll see a slider showing the **1** and **nodes** levels. This indicator tells you if you are seeing a graph of nodes (when the slider is on the **Nodes** level) or if you are looking at a community. The number gives you the level of the community. (In our sample, we have only one level, but in more complex graphs with communities of communities, you'll have multiple levels). Note that this indicator is read-only, you cannot move the slider.

In the reports panel, you'll see all the information related to the selected node. Data such as BirthYear and City come from the attributes dataset that you loaded; data like the links within or outside the community (intra_cm_link_count and extra_cm_link_count) are calculated by the model.

In the ribbon, the **Browse** group of commands (Table 12.7) lets you navigate into the graph.

Command	Description
Browse Communities	This button allows you to navigate among the communities and provides you more information on their evolution over time.
Graph	In this field, you can select which graph you want to visualize.
Node	In this field, you can select which node you want to visualize in the selected graph. The dropdown list shows the most connected nodes—not all nodes! If the node you want to visualize doesn't appear in the list, then you can manually enter its ID in the field. Note that the ID here is either the ID of the original social data file or the ID in the conversion file, if a conversion was used.
Display Node	Once you have selected a graph and a node, you can display it with this command. You have two choices: ■ **Display Node:** displays the node and its neighbors ■ **Display Community:** displays the node and all the nodes of its community
Expand Nodes	This command has three choices: ■ **Expand Selected Nodes:** adds the nodes directly linked to the one you selected to the graph. ■ **Expand All Nodes:** adds all nodes of the network to the graph. This command might return many nodes, and you'll be warned if the number of nodes is very large. ■ **Expand Community of Selected Nodes:** adds all nodes in the same community as the selected node to the graph.
Undo Expansion, Redo Expansion	These commands are used to undo or repeat the last expansion action.
Drill Up	When you select a node (or a community), this action creates a new graph that shows the community of the node (or the supercommunity of the community).
Drill Down	When you select a community, this action creates a new graph that shows all nodes (or subcommunities) of the community.

Table 12.7 The Browse Actions in the Ribbon

Note that these actions are also available by selecting a node and right-clicking in the graph display area.

Customizing the Display of the Nodes

Notice that nodes always show the same pawn icon and ID. You can customize the appearance of nodes to highlight the information you need for your analysis. Click on the **Display** tab of the ribbon (shown in Figure 12.20) to see what actions you can take.

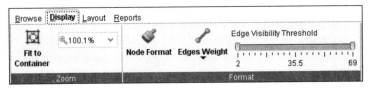

Figure 12.20 The Display Tab of the Ribbon

A detailed list of actions in the **Display** tab can be found in Table 12.8.

Command	Description
Fit to container	This button automatically adapts the visualization of the network so that the whole network is displayed within the graph display panel.
Zoom	You can change the zoom on the graph by selecting a percentage here. (However, an easier way would be to click in the graph display panel and use the center mouse wheel.)
Node Format	The most important command, this action opens the format window where you can set the specific way to display nodes. We'll dig into its functionality soon.
Edges Weight	This option lets you choose how to display the weight of the links as its width or color or as a label.
Edge Visibility Threshold	This command identifies links with a given weight interval. You can isolate, for example, only strong connections or weak ones.

Table 12.8 The Commands of the Display Ribbon

The **Node Format** action (which opens the **Display Settings** window shown in Figure 12.21) gives you a lot of freedom to customize how the nodes are displayed. Let's look at a few possibilities.

Figure 12.21 The Display Settings Window for Node Formatting

The **Display Mode** dropdown list at the top lets you choose how the nodes will be visualized in the graph. The **Custom** option let you define exactly what you want to see in the section below. The **Community** setting automatically displays nodes using the same icon for nodes of the same community.

Keeping the **Custom** setting and **Simple Formatting** option, you can choose if the size and color of the node should be related to the value of an attribute. With **Conditional Formatting**, you can define complex rules to define how a node should be displayed.

If you click on the **Label** or **Tooltip** entries on the left, you can specify the attribute that will determine how the node is displayed (by default, the node's ID) as well as the tooltip that should be displayed when the mouse cursor hovers over a node.

Going back to the main page, if you click on the **Layout** tab of the ribbon (Figure 12.22), you'll find a useful system for organizing nodes.

Figure 12.22 The Layout Tab of the Ribbon

The **Refresh Layout** button just refreshes the display; the **Scattering** slider shows nodes closer or farther one to another. The **Clustering Attribute** dropdown list lets you select an attribute of the population: When you refresh the display, the nodes will be reorganized so that nodes with the same or similar value in the selected attribute will be displayed closer to each other.

Playing with the display and layout options, you can rearrange and customize the display as you want to highlight specific information about your nodes. Let's now move a step and learn how to analyze communities.

Navigating into Community Information

You've seen how to use the **Drill Up** button and the **Node Display** command to show basic information about communities. If you want to go deeper with your analysis, use the **Browse Community** button in the ribbon. This button has two options.

Select **Browse Community • Display Top Level Community Graph** to create a new graph showing only communities of the highest level. From that graph, you can drill down into the community you want to analyze.

Select **Browse Community • Browse Community Tree** to open a tree hierarchy of communities (Figure 12.23), which gives you more control and more information.

Select a graph in the **Graph** field on top, and the communities of that graph will be displayed below. When you select a community, some details will be presented in the lower part of the window.

The **View Community • In the selected graph** button shows the community in the graph display panel (as a single dot that you can use as a starting point for drilling down or up). In our example, you'll notice that you have found two communities; these are the two families we had in our sample data.

Now that you've seen how to analyze communities, we want to point out two more features that can be quite useful in comparative analyses of your social networks.

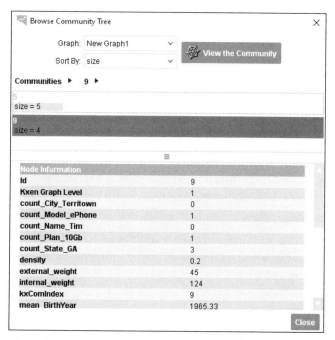

Figure 12.23 Browsing the Community Tree

Node Pairings and Graph Comparisons

As discussed in previous sections, node pairings help you discover which nodes represent the same physical item even if they appear multiple times in the network. If you display all of the `Pairing_Jan_Feb` graph that you created before, you'll see that it contains 2 nodes. Those nodes are actually the same person (which you can prove by displaying the name associated to the node using the display settings). The Social Network Analysis module found this pairing by searching for different nodes in the same neighborhood at different times.

By selecting each node, right-clicking on it, and opening it into `NewGraph1`, you'll obtain two new graphs. Using **Report** in the ribbon, you can run the **Compare** command on those two graphs. Notice that the two nodes have exactly the same neighborhood at different times.

In general, the graph comparison helps you see the differences (and similarities) between two graphs, analyze node pairings, see the evolution of or changes in a network over time, or filter information in different ways (e.g., differences when a node communicates with SMS or when it communicates via phone: Is this node talking to the same people? Are there SMS contacts that are never called by this person?).

Further advanced functionalities are available for exploring social networks, but at this point, you've gained the fundamental skills necessary to continue the journey by yourself. Next, let's look at the information that can be obtained by applying the model and generating an output dataset.

12.4.3   Applying the Model

For all the possible information about your nodes and communities, you'll have to apply the model to a dataset. When applying the model, you'll obtain all the details that could not be presented in the visual interface. The output is a tabular dataset that you can visualize with a business intelligence client tool or join to other datasets to add attributes to a classification, regression, or clustering model.

To apply the model, go to the main window, select **Run** and then **Apply Model.** The **Applying the Model** page will appear, where you'll set all the parameters for generating the detailed output file (Figure 12.24).

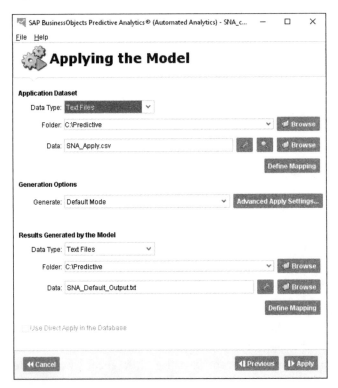

Figure 12.24 Applying the Model

In the interface, you'll select and adapt the application dataset, define the output format, and finally set the output dataset location. In our example, you'll always use files, but in a real-world scenario, you might want to apply the model directly to database. To apply a model to a database, you must save the model in the database and use a database table as the application dataset. In this case, make sure the **Use Direct Apply in the Database** checkbox is enabled for the supported data sources.

Choosing and Setting Up the Application Dataset

The application dataset needs to contain one column where you put a distinct list of the IDs of your nodes (your population). The ID is the value that appears in the node display interface as node identifier (hence, the ID in the social data file or in the converter file). If you have detected communities, you'll also need another column for the community ID. Usually, you'll create this column in your file (or database table) but leave the column empty. For our example, you can use the *SNA_Apply.csv* dataset.

In the **Application Dataset** section, use the **Browse** buttons to select the appropriate file. Then, select the **Define Mappings** button to map the source node ID and community ID to the correct fields in the model (called Source and kxComIndex).

Choosing the Generation Options

In the **Generation Options** section, use the **Generate** field to choose which information you want to add to the output dataset. Notice that the dataset can be quite large as it is proportional to the number of nodes and of graphs. To avoid unnecessarily large datasets, make your generation choice carefully, based on the output you really need. You have the choice between seven predefined modes and a customizable one (listed in Table 12.9).

Mode	Description
Default	This mode results in a typical output format providing information about each node's neighbors and its communities in each graph. You use this output to feed into another model for classification, clustering, or regression models to improve their quality.
Circle	This mode restricts the analysis to only show how much a node is connected to its direct neighbors in each graph. Information about communities is not reported.

Table 12.9 Generation Options

Mode	Description
Centrality	This mode returns indicators as the **Circle** mode aimed at understanding how much a node is central to the graph.
Neighbors	For each node, you'll see each directed link, the weight of the link, the ID, and the degree of the neighbor. This dataset contains one line per (directed) link and per graph. You can use this mode to analyze if the sociality of a node has changed (more or less links, more or less weight on a link) in different graphs (e.g., different times). You can also determine the most appropriate paths between nodes, that you can manage to the most connected nodes in the graph.
Describe	This mode returns the information you added in the Additional Attributes dataset with some general information of the node in the network (e.g., the degree, the links within and external to the community).
Community	Use this mode to see information about each node's community in each graph. The information is the same for nodes in the same community.
Node Pairing	This mode returns the incoming and outgoing links and their weights for node pairs only. Use this mode to filter your analysis to paired nodes only.
Advanced Apply Settings	Use this mode to manually set the output information graph by graph using the **Advanced Apply Settings...** button. This mode can be used to limit the extraction to only the detail you need. For example, you might want to know only the social pressure on each node from neighbors using the zPhone phone brand and only for the month of January.

Table 12.9 Generation Options (Cont.)

Depending on your choices, hundreds of different columns could be created for you to get lost in. Fortunately, the Social Network Analysis engine uses a naming convention to help you understand what you are looking at. The system builds the name of the output variable by concatenating various smaller strings, always in the same order:

- "sn": All variables start with this two-letter code.
- *Name_of_the_graph*: This optional entry shows the name of the graph where the variable is calculated.

- "n" or "cm": This part indicates if you are looking at a variable for a node ("n") or a community ("cm"). Note that the "n" sometimes is not used, when you don't see either of those two then consider the information as related to the node.

- "i" or "o": This optional entry indicates if the variable is about incoming or outgoing links for directed connections.

- "c," "m," or "r": Explains the calculation used to obtain this variable: "c" is the weighted count of neighbor nodes that verify the variable definition, "m" is the average value of the neighbor nodes, and "r" is the ratio of nodes that verify the variable definition over the total number of neighbors.

- "c0," "m0," or "r0": Count, average, or ratio as above but not weighted.

- "d": A description string, optional.

- "n": An identificatory label, optional.

- "dg": Degree of a node, optional.

- "sz": Size of a community, optional.

- *Name_of_the_Attribute*: Optional, the name of the attribute variable.

- *Value_of_the_Attribute*: Optional, the value of the attribute being analyzed.

At first, this convention might seem complex, but after a while, you'll easily remember their values. Let's look at two examples from the dataset:

- sn_New Graph1_i_c_Name_Sarah: This is the weighted count of incoming communications between the node we are looking at and all its neighbor nodes whose Name is Sarah in New Graph1.

- sn_New Graph1_cm_c0_Model_ePhone: The quantity of nodes with an ePhone Model in the community of New Graph1 of the node being analyzed.

After selecting the kind of output information you want, choose the dataset to be generated, using the window shown in Figure 12.24.

Choosing the Dataset Output Location

In the **Results Generated by the Model** section of the page shown in Figure 12.24, use the browse buttons to define the place and name of the output dataset (in a file or in a database). The **Define Mapping** button opens the **Mapping Definitions** page where you can change the names of the generated columns if you want to adapt them to an existing file format.

When you are finished, you click the **Apply** button. At this stage, the file will be generated, and you can view its output and use it in other tools.

At this point, you've now seen how to run a Social Network Analysis project, from getting the data to define the model to understanding and applying the model to get more details about your network.

Social Network Analysis is a rather large solution that enables other business cases that are beyond the scope of this book. Its main use—recommendations—will be discussed in detail in Chapter 13. Before we finish this chapter, though, we want to provide a short overview of graphs based on geographical nodes.

12.5   Colocation and Path Analysis Overview

The Social Network Analysis module offers two workflows specifically designed to run a social analysis on networks where one of the nodes is a location defined in terms of latitude and longitude:

- The first workflow, *colocation analysis*, helps you find if two items in a populations were in the same place at the same time. You can use colocation analysis, for example, in security situations or to check if customers (or potential customers) are attracted by the same locations.

- The second, *frequent path analysis*, finds if common paths exist that are often used by the population you are studying. A business usage is to position your business in the best location or to predict what the next shop a potential customer will visit.

You can start both workflows from the main Social Network Analysis start page. In the following sections, we'll highlight the differences between a regular Social Network Analysis and the geography-enabled analysis.

In the following examples, we'll use a dataset containing locations of vehicles over time.

12.5.1   Colocation Analysis

In the workflow, you'll select a dataset, set the analysis parameters, and then analyze the results. To begin, in the Automated Analytics client, go to **Social** and click the **Colocation Analysis** link. Next, select an input dataset. This dataset needs at least 4 entries:

- The ID of the items of your population
- A latitude
- A longitude
- A date-time value that indicates when the item was at the given latitude and longitude (usually in the format YYYY-MM-DD HH:MM:SS)

When the data is analyzed, you'll have to store the longitude and latitude values as type angle (an example is shown in Figure 12.25). This information tells the system that they are the geographical data.

Figure 12.25 Importing a Geographical Dataset

When you click **Next**, a new window will appear (Figure 12.26) where you'll assign the two geographical values to a new group of type Position and give it a name ("Item-Location" in our example). Click **OK** to validate your choice.

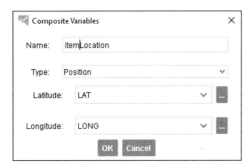

Figure 12.26 Setting the Position Coordinates

Go back to the **Transaction Data** page (Figure 12.25) and select **View Data,** which will visualize the items directly within Google Earth. On the next page, set the parameters for the analysis as shown in Figure 12.27.

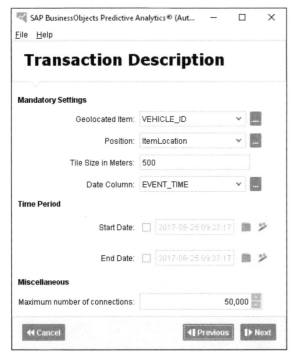

Figure 12.27 Setting the Parameters for Geographical Analysis

Mare sure that you select the correct ID of your population in the **Geolocated Item** field (**Vehicle_ID** in our example).

The geolocation algorithm divides space into square tiles considered as single nodes. You can define the size of the tile in this page by modifying the **Tile Size in Meters** field. All points within the tile are considered "in the same location." The other fields are the same as our earlier Social Network Analysis (Figure 12.5).

Click **Next** to go to the page for setting the colocation interval (Figure 12.28).

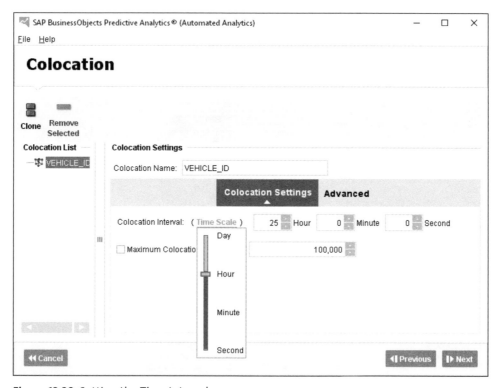

Figure 12.28 Setting the Time Interval

Click on the **Time Scale** field to choose the most appropriate time granularity. All events that happen within the same interval are considered to be happening "at the same time."

By setting the tile size and the time interval, you've essentially defined what "at the same place and at the same time" means. Click **Next** to start the analysis of the data; Automated Analytics will position your population in time and space and find colocations.

After the model has been built, analyze the model as we did earlier. The main difference in colocation analysis is that you'll have direct access to the list of colocated items and the places where they met.

To see the list, click on the **Colocations** link of the **Display** page, enter the ID of the item to analyze, and click the **List the Colocations** button. The result is a list of items colocated with the node you selected, as shown in Figure 12.29.

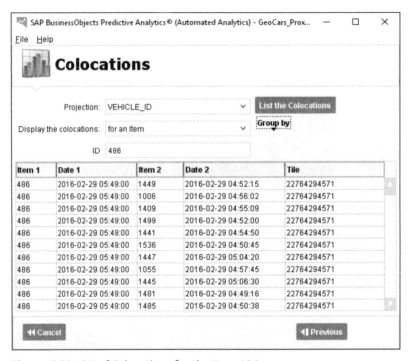

Figure 12.29 List of Colocations for the Item 486

Use the **Group By** button to simplify the view to show how many times two nodes met or how many times a specific tile was the meeting point for a specific node.

12.5.2   Frequent Path Analysis

The workflow to define a frequent path analysis (finding the typical paths taken by your population) is similar to the workflow for colocation. The dataset input process is exactly the same. You'll start the workflow in the Automated Analytics client and then go to **Social** and to **Frequent Path Analysis.** After the model has been calculated, analyze the frequent paths by clicking on **View Sequences** in the **Display.** The **Sequences Visualization** page will open (Figure 12.30).

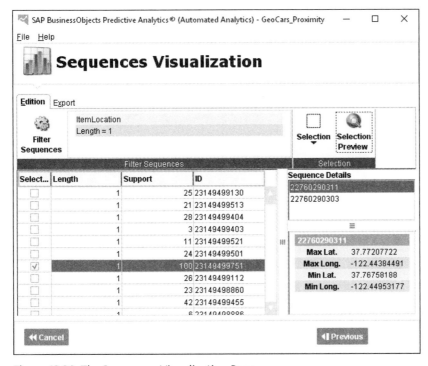

Figure 12.30 The Sequences Visualization Page

This page lists all the frequent paths that have been identified. The **Length** field tells you how many steps are in the path (moving from one tile to another is one step), and the **Support** column displays the number of occurrences of that path.

The **Selection Preview** button opens all selected paths directly in Google Earth. Finally, you can export the resulting paths as *kml* or *gml* files using the **Export** tab in the ribbon.

When you visualize a path on a map, you can, for example, identify which shops are being visited and in which order, which can help you decide where to install your next business.

12.6 Conclusion

In this chapter, you learned what Social Network Analysis is and how to use the Social Network Analysis module in SAP Predictive Analytics. We covered the module's general functionality and some of the most important analysis approaches. You've also seen a high-level workflow for the geographical analysis of a social model for colocation and path analysis.

One important business use of social networks is for recommendations, and because of its widespread importance, we've dedicated the whole next chapter to recommendation medels.

Chapter 13

Automated Predictive Recommendation Models

Recommendation models have become pervasive in our daily lives, whether we listen to music or look for new relationships. This chapter covers creating and applying recommendation models using Automated Analytics' powerful yet simple technology.

Whether you are listening to music online, looking for a brand-new movie or TV series, shopping on Amazon, or looking for new connections on LinkedIn, you are in fact guided by recommendation models. These models guide you towards what or whom you are most likely to be interested in.

Recommendation models help companies personalize the consumer experience and maximize engagement with customers. Using SAP Predictive Analytics and the Automated Predictive Library (APL), you can analyze customer transactions and generate recommendations in an easy and effective way.

Each time a customer expresses interest for a product, buys it, rates it, or clicks on it, a new transaction is generated in the database. Based on the analysis of these transactions, multiple applications are possible:

- You can suggest products that your customer might be interested in, based on the interest from other customers, which is how Amazon and Netflix make recommendations. Known as a *collaborative-filtering approach*, you'll make predictions about the potential interest of a user based on the interests of other similar users, usually by common tastes.

- You can suggest other users that your customer might be interested in based on common interests among users. How LinkedIn, Facebook, and Twitter work, in this application, the products are actually you and me.

- You can optimize product placement in retail, for example, by placing similar products close one to one another for the customer's convenience. Conversely, you can place similar products far away from each other to get your customers to follow certain routes inside your store.

- In manufacturing, you can use the same techniques to analyze which errors occur often at a similar time, giving the quality engineer helpful information to maintain machines and prevent breakdowns.

In this chapter, we'll first introduce the basic concepts, datasets, and techniques for generating recommendations. Then, we'll guide you through creating a recommendation model using the Social Network Analysis and Recommendation modules in Automated Analytics. We'll also briefly cover the options offered by the Automated Predictive Library.

13.1   Introduction

In this section, we'll introduce some basic concepts. Then, we'll describe the structure of the datasets that are generally used as sources for recommendation models. We'll present the sample dataset that you'll use in this section. Finally, we'll summarize the different approaches that can be used to create recommendation models with Automated Analytics and the Automated Predictive Library.

13.1.1   Basic Concepts

Before jumping into the steps for creating recommendation models, we need to recall a few basic concepts described in Chapter 12 and introduce some new concepts for this chapter:

- A *node* simply represents the different users (customers) or items (products).
- A *link* relates two nodes together. For instance, a purchasing link relates a customer node and a product node.
- The *weight* of a link is the relative importance of the link compared to another links.
- A *graph* is a collection of nodes related through links.
- A *rule* represents a condition and its consequence. An example of a rule would be Product A → Product B; in other words, Product A leads to Product B.
- The *antecedent* of a rule is the first term of rule. In our example, Product A → Product B, the antecedent is Product A.

- The *consequent* of a rule is the second term of rule. In our example, Product A → Product B, the consequent is Product B.

Different metrics can be used to evaluate a rule:

- The *support* of a rule is the number of times a rule is found in the dataset.
- The *confidence* in a rule is the percentage of transactions verifying the consequent (recommended product) among those verifying the antecedent (purchased product). In our example, Product A → Product B, when we look only at baskets (shopping carts) that included Product A, the confidence corresponded to the percentage of baskets that also included Product B (in addition to Product A).
- The *predictive power* of a rule corresponds to the proportion of information contained in the consequent that the antecedent is capable of explaining. This concept can also be understood as the relevancy of the rule regarding the whole dataset. For a detailed definition of predictive power, refer to *http://bit.ly/2xXCI3C*.

Finally, a *best-seller* is a product that sells very well. How you define a best-seller is based on a specified transaction volume threshold and varies by use case.

13

13.1.2   Datasets

A recommendation dataset usually has the following structure (Figure 13.1):

- The dataset must contain a *user* or *source* (customer) column.
- The dataset must contain an *item* or *target* column (typically a product).
- The dataset might contain a *weight* column. For instance, a weight column can represent the number of products that the customer has purchased or the amount spent on a product. The weight column enables you to give more or less importance to each transaction.
- The dataset might contain a *date* column. Adding a date column enables you to filter transactions by date, thereby restricting the transaction history that recommendations are based on. This restriction can be helpful, for instance, for seasonal products, so that recommendations only take into account the most recent transactions.
- The dataset might contain other columns as well, usually related to the transaction.
- Each row in the dataset represents a transaction relating a user with an item. For instance, a row could represent a purchase, a rating, a click on the website, etc.

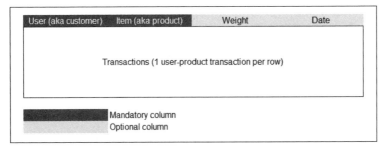

Figure 13.1 Basic Structure of a Recommendation Dataset.

The dataset we'll use in our example (*movies and ratings.csv*) contains movie rating from MovieLens, a movie recommendation service. This dataset and the other datasets we'll use for model application are available for download at *www.sap-press.com/4491*. Please copy these files to a local folder.

The dataset contains 100,004 ratings across 9,066 movies. These ratings were submitted by 671 users between January 9, 1995, and October 16, 2016. The dataset was generated on October 17, 2016. All selected users have rated at least 20 movies. The dataset contains the following fields:

- *User*: This field contains an anonymized user's identifier and will be our *User* field.

- *MovieID*: This field contains is the movie's identifier in the MovieLens database.

- *MovieRating*: This field contains the rating of the movie. Ratings are made on a 5-star scale, with half-star increments (0.5 stars to 5.0 stars). This field will be our *Weight* field.

- *Date*: This field contains the date corresponding to the user's rating of the movie. This field will be our *Date* field.

- *MovieTitle*: This field contains the title of the movie. This field will be our *Item* field.

- *MovieGenres:* This field contains the different genre(s) of each movie in pipe-separated (|) lists.

Note

We are grateful to the GroupLens research lab (*https://grouplens.org/about/what-is-grouplens/*) for providing this dataset, and we would like to cite the related research paper:

F. Maxwell Harper and Joseph A. Konstan. 2015. The MovieLens Datasets: History and Context. *ACM Transactions on Interactive Intelligent Systems (TiiS)*, Volume 5, Number 4, Article 19 (December 2015), 19 pages. *http://dx.doi.org/10.1145/2827872*.

13.1.3 Recommended Approaches

Automated Analytics and the Automated Predictive Library offer multiple ways to create recommendation models. The two techniques that should be used in priority are as follows:

- To create powerful recommendation models in a user interface, use the Social Network Analysis module of Automated Analytics. This module can detect communities and refine the recommendations based on communities. We'll talk more about communities in Section 13.2.

- If you are using SAP HANA, you can leverage the Automated Predictive Library (APL) 3.2 SQL-based recommender, especially if you require good performance on very large data volumes and real-time recommendation based on basket content. We'll describe this approach in more detail in Section 13.4.

In general, we don't recommend using the Recommendation module because the Social Network Analysis module offers better models and more flexibility. Nevertheless, we'll briefly cover using the Recommendation module in Section 13.3.

One last option is the Association Rules module of Automated Analytics. We don't recommend using it and will not cover it in detail in this book.

> **Note**
>
> Throughout this chapter, we'll describe the different ways recommendation rules can be obtained using Automated Analytics and the Automated Predictive Library, and we'll recommend which techniques should be prioritized.

Technique	Social (Bipartite) Graphs (Automated Analytics, APL)	Recommendation (Automated Analytics, APL)	SQL-Based Recommender (APL)	Association Rules (Automated Analytics)
Rule Support & Confidence	✓	✓	✓	✓
Rule Predictive Power	✓	✓	✓	✓
Graphical display of rules	✓	✓	N/A	✓

Table 13.1 Comparison of Recommendation Techniques

Technique	Social (Bipartite) Graphs (Automated Analytics, APL)	Recommendation (Automated Analytics, APL)	SQL-Based Recommender (APL)	Association Rules (Automated Analytics)
Best-sellers	✓	✓	✓	
Rule Weight	✓	✓		
Community of Customer	✓			
Community of Products	✓			
Role in network	✓			
Performance	Faster	Faster	Faster	Slower, does not scale
Implementation	One-shot model application using KxShell Script; direct use in SAP HANA SQL (APL functions)	One-shot model application; export rules in SQL code KxShell Script	Direct use in SAP HANA SQL (APL functions)	One-shot application using KxShell Script
Recommendation	**Recommended.** Use this technique to detect communities and roles in network or to customize the model. Use this technique also for basic scenarios.	Not recommended except for basic scenarios. This technique is a packaged workflow and is not very flexible.	**Recommended.** Use this technique if you need performance on very large data volumes and real-time recommendation based on basket content in SAP HANA.	Not recommended.

Table 13.1 Comparison of Recommendation Techniques (Cont.)

13.2   Using the Social Network Analysis Module

In this section, we'll walk you through creating, understanding, and using a recommendation model using the Social Network Analysis module of Automated Analytics.

13.2.1   Creating the Model

Recommendation models can be created using the Social Network Analysis module of Automated Analytics (either the client or the desktop version) by clicking on the **Create a Social Network Analysis** link (Figure 13.2). The Social Network Analysis module was described in detail in Chapter 12, but in this chapter, we'll focus on how the module supports recommendation models.

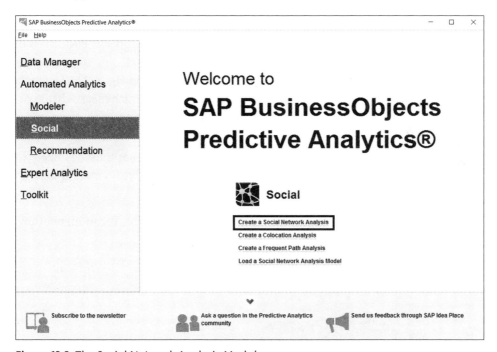

Figure 13.2 The Social Network Analysis Module

Creating a recommendation model is a two-step process:

1. First, you'll create a graph relating users to items. In our example, we'll relate users rating movies to the movies themselves. The product creates a "customers to

products" graph (Figure 13.3). Called a *bipartite graph* or a *transactions graph*, essentially, two nodes of different natures are connected. In our example, the intensity of the relationship, known as the *weight*, between the user and the product depends on the value of the movie rating.

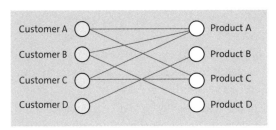

Figure 13.3 Customers to Products Graph

2. Then, you'll create a derived graph (from the earlier bipartite graph) that relates products together, for instance, if some products have a number of customers in common (Figure 13.4), or that relates clients together if some clients have a number of products in common (Figure 13.5). In the example shown in Figure 13.5, Products A and C are connected with the comment of "2 customers," which means that 2 customers have purchased both Product A and Product C. No customer has purchased Product A and Product B together; thus, these two products are not connected.

3. In our example, let's say we want to predict the movies that a user is likely to appreciate (and rate highly). To make these predictions, we'll create a derived graph for movies (products).

Once the Social Network Analysis module creates these graphs, recommendations can be derived.

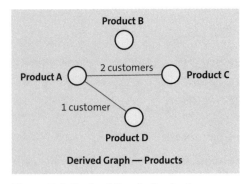

Figure 13.4 Derived Graph: Products

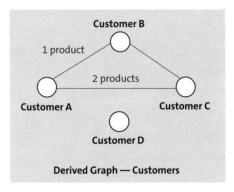

Figure 13.5 Derived Graph: Customers

Creating the Bipartite Graph

Because we covered the Social Network Analysis interface in Chapter 12, in this section, we'll only describe the specific steps for our sample workflow without a complete description of all fields. Please refer back to Chapter 12, Section 12.4, for a more details.

1. First, select the **Build a Social Graph From a Data Set** option (Figure 13.6).

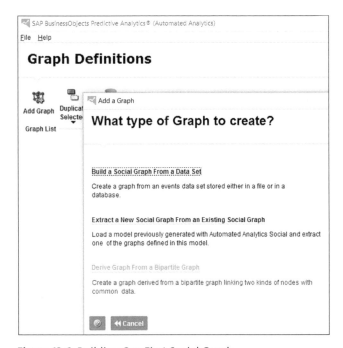

Figure 13.6 Building Our First Social Graph

2. In the next screen, **Extract Graph From a Data Set**, select the dataset *movies and ratings.csv* and then click **Next**.

3. Next, in the **Link Data Set Description** screen, analyze the dataset by clicking the **Analyze** button. Then, click **OK** to work on this dataset file.

4. In the **Graph Definitions** screen, maintain the following fields (Figure 13.7):

   – Enter "Users-Movies" in the **Graph Name** field.

   – Select **Transactions** from the **Graph Creation Type** dropdown list.

   – The graph is a **Transactions** graph that relates objects of different nature (users and movies). In the previous chapter, we described the other graph types.

   – The **Source Node** is the field **User**.

Figure 13.7 Setting the Right Parameters to Create the Bipartite Graph

- The **Target Node** is the field **MovieTitle**.
- The **Date Column** is the field **date**.
- Keep the **Target** and **Target Key** fields empty.
- Select the **MovieRating** field from the **Use a Weight column** dropdown list.
- Keep the **Maximum Number of Connections** as "50000." This value specifies the maximum number of connections that can be created for one node.

5. Next, create a filter by clicking **Add Column Filter** in the toolbar. Keep only ratings in the desired range [3.5;5], which are considered positive ratings, by setting the **Filtered column** field to **MovieRating** and setting the **Minimum** to 3.5 and the **Maximum** to 5.

Your first graph has now been defined but not yet calculated. Immediately specify the second graph (derived graph) by clicking on **Add Graph**.

Creating the Derived Graph

This time, select the **Derive Graph from a Bipartite Graph** option. The graph that you want to create is the derived graph for movies. Use the following settings (Figure 13.8):

- The **Graph to Derive from** dropdown should be set by default to **Users-Movies**.
- Select **MovieTitle** from the **Entity** dropdown list..
- Leave the value of the **Minimum Support** as "2." The minimum support value represents the minimum number of links necessary for a node to be added to the graph. In our example, the new graph will contain only movies that have been rated positively by at least two users.

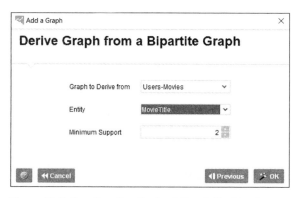

Figure 13.8 Creating the Derived Graph for Movies

Once you've completed the parameters on this screen, you click **OK**. You'll be navigated back to the **Graph Definitions** screen. Click on the **Next** button four times, which takes you through the following screens:

- The **Post-Processing** screen (please note communities will be detected for the derived graph)
- The **Identifiers Conversion** screen (our example does not use this option)
- The **Descriptive Attributes screen** (our example does use this option)

Finally, you'll reach the **Summary of Modeling Parameters** screen (Figure 13.9). Click on **Generate** to create the Social Network Analysis model.

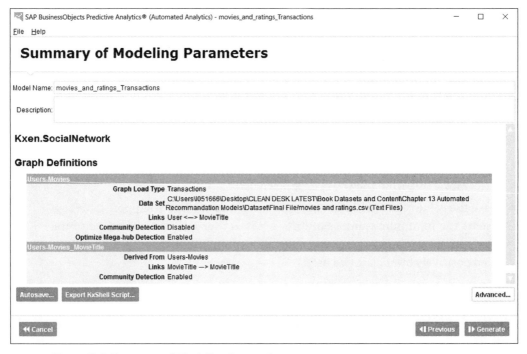

Figure 13.9 Summary of Modeling Parameters

13.2.2   Understanding the Model

Once you've generated the model, you'll be presented with the **Training the Model** screen and the **model overview** report. Click **Next** to go to the **Display** tab, where you can access various options. In this section, we will focus specifically on the **Model**

Overview, the Nodes Display, and the Recommendations. Refer back to Chapter 12, Section 12.4.1, for more information on the Debriefing Tables option.

Model Overview

Click on the Model Overview option. Following the model overview itself, a table named All Networks (Figure 13.10) will present the number of graphs created and the number of nodes in the bipartite graph (users and movies). In our case, we have four graphs, the bipartite graph Users-Movies, the derived graph Users-Movies_MovieTitle, and two graphs (Users-Movies_MovieTitle_cm_lvl_1 and Users-Movies_MovieTitle_cm_lvl_2) corresponding to the two levels of communities that were found.

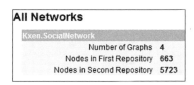

All Networks

Kxen.SocialNetwork	
Number of Graphs	4
Nodes in First Repository	663
Nodes in Second Repository	5723

Figure 13.10 The All Networks Table

In addition to the usual graph information presented in Network Details, you'll find specific data about the bipartite graph we generated (Figure 13.11). This bipartite graph connects 663 users to 5,723 movies, through 41,401 links, which represents a density of 1.09%. Notice that the graph is not very dense, which indicates that the rating frequency is not high in general.

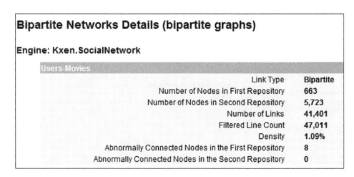

Bipartite Networks Details (bipartite graphs)

Engine: Kxen.SocialNetwork

Users-Movies	
Link Type	Bipartite
Number of Nodes in First Repository	663
Number of Nodes in Second Repository	5,723
Number of Links	41,401
Filtered Line Count	47,011
Density	1.09%
Abnormally Connected Nodes in the First Repository	8
Abnormally Connected Nodes in the Second Repository	0

Figure 13.11 Bipartite Graph Information

Node Display

The Node Display screen, accessible from the Display tab, visualizes various graphs. We covered navigating these graphs in Chapter 12, Section 12.4.2.

For instance, looking at the bipartite graph **Users-Movies**, let's focus on a specific user—for example, user 367 (Figure 13.12). Let's see which movies have been rated by this user and get the exact ratings on the links (the width of the line corresponds to the value of the rating). Enter the value "367" in the **Node** field and then click **Display Node**.

Two points should be noted:

- When a node has many connections, display the graph in the user interface may take some time. You'll see a warning if this might be the case.

- The representation you get won't be identical to what's shown in Figure 13.12 because node and link positions vary over time. However, the connections between users and movies should remain exactly the same.

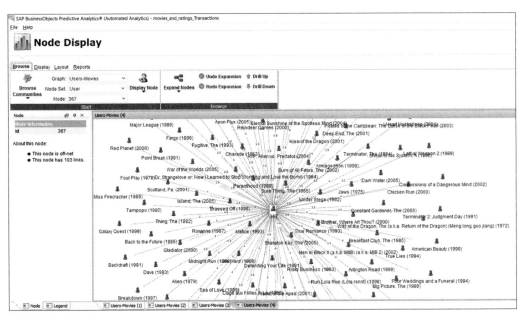

Figure 13.12 Movies Rated by the User 367

Change the value in the **Graph** dropdown to **Users-Movies_MovieTitle**, enter the value "Mean Streets (1973)" in the **Node** field (Figure 13.13), and then click **Display Node**.

Now, you'll see which movies are the most related to the movie *Mean Streets* in terms of common user ratings. The intensity of the relationship is represented by the width of the link. You can change the way weights are represented in the **Display** tab, using the **Edge Weights** command.

In our example, notice that movies produced in the same decade are usually picked by users, for instance, the movie *Manhattan*. Again, please note that your screen may not be identical to Figure 13.13 because node and link positions may vary over time. However, the connections between movies should remain exactly the same.

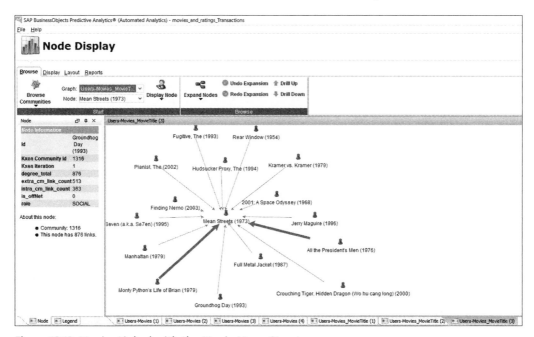

Figure 13.13 Movies Linked with the Movie Mean Streets

You can also visualize communities and understand the roles of the different items in communities by following the menu path **Browse Communities • Browse Community Tree**.

A tree of communities will be displayed that you can sort based on different criteria. Select one that you would like to view.

The default display shows the first level of communities, with three communities displayed. Click on the horizontal arrow on the line corresponding to community 1495, select community 1170, and then click **View Community** (Figure 13.14).

You'll see a screen that displays communities 1170 and 1316. Select the bubble corresponding to community 1170, then click on the command **Drill Down** in the toolbar.

You can visualize the organization of the community (Figure 13.15). Community 1170 is organized around a bridge node representing the movie *The Silence of the Lambs*.

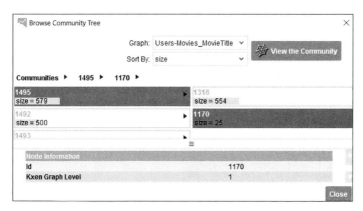

Figure 13.14 Viewing Community 1170

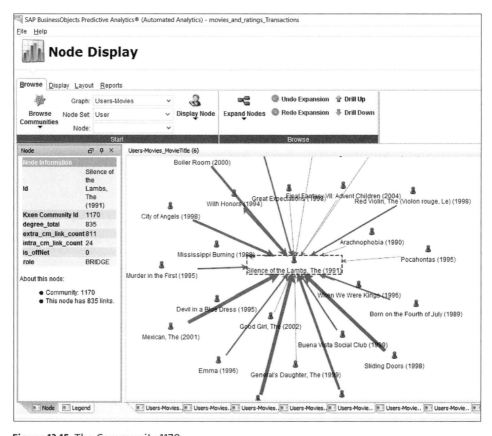

Figure 13.15 The Community 1170

Community 1170 is made of 25 nodes. A bridge node connects to 24 intra-community members and to 811 extra-community members. Defining bridge nodes and the other roles were described in Chapter 12, Section 12.1.

Recommendations

To make recommendations for a single user, click on the **Recommendations** link on the **Display** tab, and you'll be navigated to the **Recommendation** screen (Figure 13.16). While this screen can be useful for familiarizing yourself with recommendations, you will not use this screen in production.

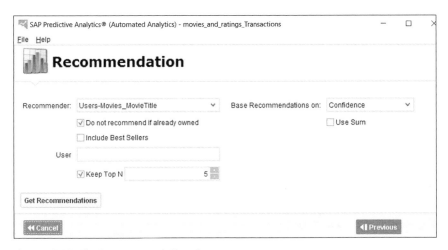

Figure 13.16 The Recommendation Screen

Different options can be selected in this screen, as follows:

- **Do not recommend if already owned**
  If you select this checkbox, products already related to a user will not be proposed. For instance, you will not propose that he rate movies that he has already rated.

- **Include Best Sellers**
  If you deselect this checkbox, best-selling products will not be proposed. The determination of best-selling products is not linked to specific users but instead is done globally. Check this option if you want best-sellers to be considered as part of the recommendations.

- **Keep Top N**
  Select this checkbox and set the number of recommendations you want to generate or uncheck it to get all possible recommendations.

■ **Base Recommendations on**
Different metrics can be used to sort recommendations. By default, recommendations are sorted by the rule's confidence. However, you can select a different metric, for instance, the rule's support, the rule's predictive power, or more sophisticated indicators like the **Combined Confidence** or the **Cosine**. The definitions and formulas for these different metrics are presented in the documentation at *http://bit.ly/2AJCksm*.

Once you've configured this screen, enter a specific user ID in the **User** field and click **Get Recommendations** to get recommendations corresponding to this specific user. Enter the number "367" but do not change any other settings. Then, click **Get Recommendations**. Recommendations will be presented in a table that contains:

■ The name of the recommendation

■ The value of the metric chosen in the **Base Recommendations on** dropdown list, for instance, **Confidence** or **Support**

■ The role of the recommended node in the community he belongs to

■ The community that the node belongs to. Communities are a great asset to generate tailored recommendations

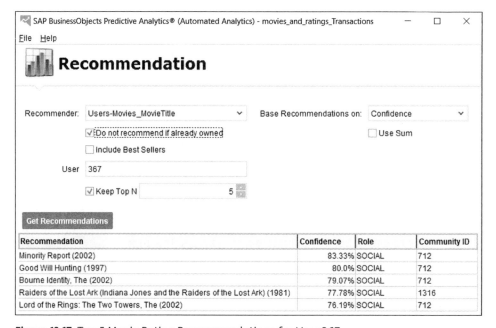

Figure 13.17 Top 5 Movie Rating Recommendations for User 367

Figure 13.17 shows the top 5 recommendations for user 367, sorted by confidence. The number 1 recommendation is the movie *Minority Report*.

13.2.3   Applying the Model

We described in detail the general process of applying a social model to a dataset in Chapter 12.

However, for the Recommendation model, a few high-level guidelines determine how the **Applying the Model** screen is typically used to perform product recommendations:

- The application dataset you need to use typically contains three columns. The first column is the product and contains the list of all distinct products. The second column corresponds to the user and can be filled with one single user (this column is not really used in the application process). The third column corresponds to the community identifier. Usually, you'll create this column but leave it empty.

- You'll need to apply the model to this dataset using two different modes in succession.

  First, select the **Neighbors Mode** in the **Generate** dropdown list, which will create an output table in your database that lists the rules relating products.

  Second, select the **Community Mode** in the **Generate** dropdown list, which will create an output table in your database that contains community-related information for each node.

- You can now combine these two output tables through scripting, both in terms of combining the information stored in the two database tables and in terms of combining the rules properties that generate the most appropriate recommendations. As a result, business rules and customizations, like checking if a recommended product is available in stock, are included.

The Social Network Analysis module's apply mode was described in Chapter 12, but in the Recommendation model, an additional functionality is available when creating a bipartite graph: batch recommendations. You can use this feature to create recommendations in a batch for multiple users. Batch recommendations create a more scalable model: What we have done for one user, now we do for all users.

In the **Run** tab of the Social Network Analysis module, click on the **Batch Recommendations** link (Figure 13.18).

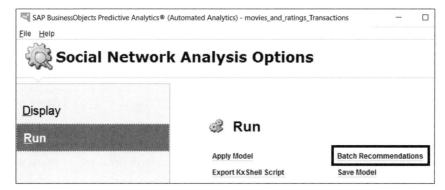

Figure 13.18 Batch Recommendations Option

The screen shown in Figure 13.19 will open, where you can generate a list of recommended products for each customer in your dataset.

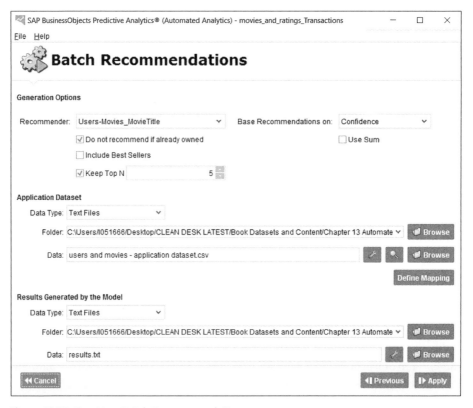

Figure 13.19 Creating Batch Recommendations

For our example, you'll apply the model to *users – application dataset.csv*.

To apply a social model to a dataset, it must contain the following variables:

- One variable for each population, for example, one for customers and one for products.

- The kxComIndex variable, which contains community identifiers, should be a nominal integer. This variable can be applied on the community graphs, and you can use this column to provide a list of community identifiers on which you want to compute metrics. If not applying on community graphs, you should leave this variable empty or, in the case of a database, fill the variable with a dummy value, which won't be used.

Follow these steps:

- Select the file *users – application dataset.csv* in the **Data** field in the **Application Dataset** section.

- Enter a file name, for instance, "results.txt" in the **Data** field in the **Results generated by the model** section.

- Click **Apply**.

For each user, you'll get the top 5 recommendations (Figure 13.20).

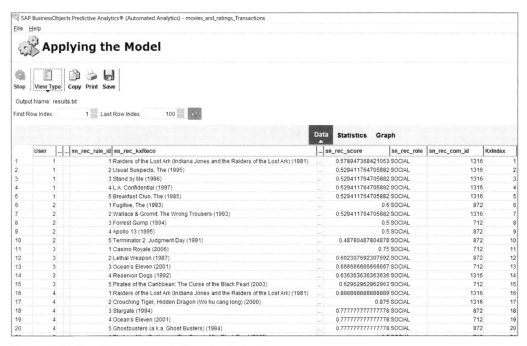

Figure 13.20 Top 5 Recommendations for Each User

13.3   Using the Recommendation Module

You can also create recommendation models using the Recommendation module in Automated Analytics. Getting recommendations using the Recommendation module involves fewer steps than using the Social Network Analytics module, which we discussed in the previous section.

However, some options cannot be configured (for instance, you cannot apply filters based on the values of ratings, which is available in the Social Network Analysis module), and communities (explained in Chapter 12) are not generated and therefore cannot be used to make product recommendations. Therefore, we recommend using the Social Network Analysis module in Automated Analytics, as described in Section 13.1.3.

13.3.1   Creating the Model

In this section, we'll create a recommendation model, using the Recommendation module, on the same dataset we used earlier. From the main screen, select the **Create a New Recommender** option in the Recommendation module. Then, load the file *movies and ratings.csv* and click **Analyze** and then **Next**.

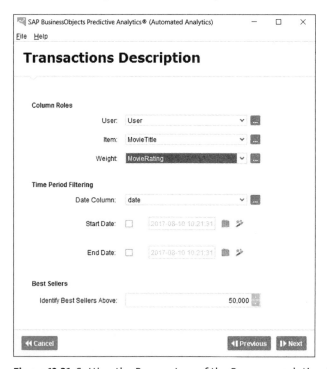

Figure 13.21 Setting the Parameters of the Recommendation Model

On the **Transactions Description** screen, enter the parameters as shown in the Figure 13.21. Then, click **Next** and **Next** again in the **Recommenders** screen. In the **Summary of Modeling Parameters** screen, click **Generate**.

Your model has now been trained, and you'll see the results of the training in the **Training the Model** screen (Figure 13.22).

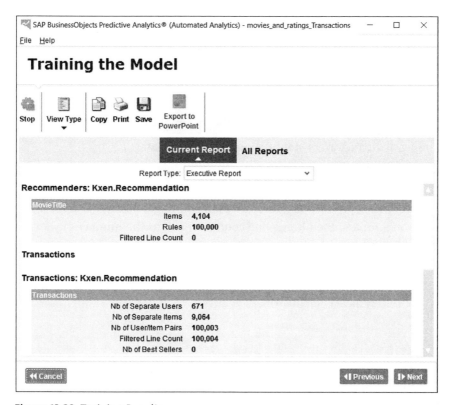

Figure 13.22 Training Results

13.3.2 Understanding the Model

Once the model has been generated, the following screens are visible in the **Display** tab:

- Model Overview
- Nodes Display
- Debriefing Tables
- Recommendation

Model Overview

The Recommendation module presents the recommendation models in a somewhat different format compared to what you get in the Social Network Analysis module.

For each recommendation model, you'll see the following information in the **Recommenders** table (Figure 13.23):

- The number of products (**Items**) corresponding to the parameters set for the recommender.
- The number of **Rules** found by the recommender. The maximum number of rules found by the recommender depends on the value of the parameter **Max Top Nodes**, set during the model parameterization phase.

In the **Transactions** table, you'll see the following information:

- The number of distinct users identified in the training dataset.
- The number of distinct products identified in the training dataset. In our case, this corresponds to the number of movies.
- The number of user/product pairs, defined as the number of unique links between a user and an item and the filtered line count, defined as the number of transactions after filtering.
- The number of best-sellers, defined as products that appear more often in the transactions as the threshold set during the model parameterization. In our example, no best-sellers have been identified.

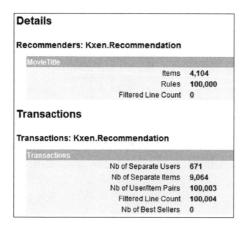

Figure 13.23 Overview of the Recommendation Model

Nodes Display

The **Node Display** screen visualizes "user to product" links or "product to product" links. The only difference with the equivalent screen in the Social Network Analysis module, which we discussed in Section 13.2.2, is that you cannot visualize a community because communities are not calculated. So, for a given node, only its degree (number of links) will be displayed.

Debriefing Tables

As we described in Section 13.2.2 for the Social Network Analysis module, the **Debriefing Tables** are mostly intended for expert debriefing. The specific recommendation reports available are:

- **Rule Distribution**
  Displays the distribution of the rules, based on the number of connections per rule, in absolute value and frequency

- **Item Connectivity**
  Shows for each product how many users are connected to it

- **User connectivity**
  Shows the number of products that are connected to users

- **Highest number of rules**
  Shows the top 500 products with the most connections to other products

- **Highest Connections (Items), Highest Connections (Users)**
  Shows the top 500 products with the most connections to items and the top 500 items with the most connections to products

- **Best Sellers**
  Is displayed if a product exceeds the threshold for best-sellers and presents items that are extremely well connected

Recommendations

This screen is similar to the one that we described in the Social Network Analysis module in Section 13.2.2. The main difference is that recommendations are by default based on confidence, which cannot be changed by the user. No community-related information is displayed because communities are never computed by the Recommendation module.

13

13.3.3   Applying the Model

Using the Recommendation module, you'll apply the model to a dataset to generate recommendations for users.

To apply the model to a dataset, the dataset must contain one variable for the users and one variable for the products. The values of the user variable should be filled.

For example, let's apply the model you created to a new dataset named *users and movies - application dataset.csv*, using the parameters shown in Figure 13.24. Applying the model will create movie recommendations for each user.

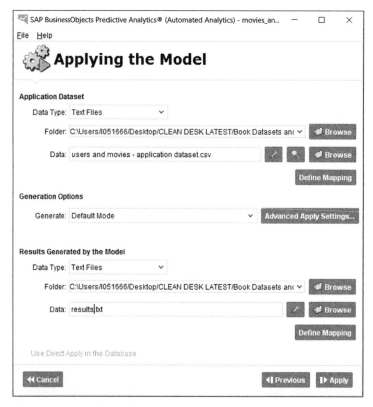

Figure 13.24 Applying the Recommendation Model

The results of the model application are presented in Figure 13.25:

- No recommendations were found for user 1 (no rules may have been applicable). You might consider recommending best-sellers to such users.

- The recommendations are sorted by decreasing *confidence*, which is expressed as a percentage and presented in the column **sn_rec_score**.

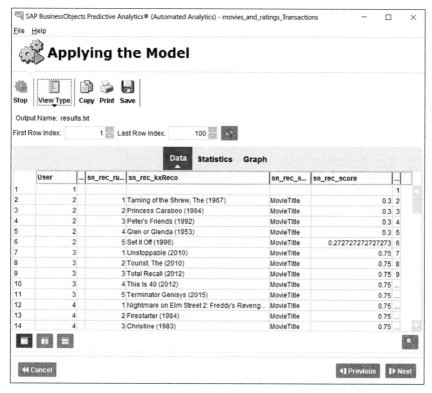

Figure 13.25 Results of Applying the Model

Three additional options are also available in the **Run** tab:

- **Generate SQL code**
  The recommender's logic can be exported as SQL code, using the specific syntax of multiple databases or in a standard ANSI format.

- **Export KxShell Script**
  This option makes enables you to save the recommendation model's logic in KxShell Script.

- **Save Model**
  The recommendation model can be saved for later use.

13.4   Using the Automated Predictive Library

Since SAP Predictive Analytics 3.2, an SQL-based recommender has been included as part of the Automated Predictive Library (APL), which is an Application Function Library (AFL) that can be installed on top of SAP HANA and provides automated predictive functions.

If you need a solution that can handle very large data volumes effectively, then you should use the SQL-based recommender, which, thanks to the APPLY_RECOMMENDER_TO_ BASKET procedure, can provide real-time recommendations based upon the actual items in a basket.

However, if you need to detect communities or weights, then you should use the graph-based social model.

> **Related Resources**
>
> SAP HANA Automated Predictive Library Reference Guide: *http://bit.ly/2zE2X2R*
>
> Empower your business with the SQL-Based Recommender: *http://bit.ly/2ih3mP2*

The SQL-based recommender is based on the principles of the *Apriori algorithm*.

APL 3.2 comes with three new procedures. The following procedures are not based on the application function library but instead are SQL-based:

- *CREATE_RECOMMENDER*: This procedure creates a recommendation model based on a transaction table relating users and products.
- *APPLY_RECOMMENDER_TO_USERS*: This procedure applies the recommendation model to a set of users and generates product recommendations for the selected users.
- *APPLY_RECOMMENDER_TO_BASKET*: This procedure applies the recommendation model to a given's user basket (list of products) and generates product recommendations.

These procedures can be found in the SAP HANA system by following the menu path **Catalog • Sap_pa_Apl • Procedures - Filter: *recommender* • Table Types**.

The following APL functions enable you to create and apply recommendation and social models using an AFL-based approach:

- *CREATE_RECO_MODEL_AND_TRAIN*
- *APPLY_RECO_MODEL*

- *PARALLEL_APPLY_RECO_MODEL*
- *EXPORT_APPLY_CODE_FOR_RECO*
- *CREATE_SOCIAL_MODEL_AND_TRAIN*
- *APPLY_SOCIAL_MODEL*
- *PARALLEL_APPLY_SOCIAL_MODEL*

To learn more on using these functions, refer to the APL documentation.

13.5   Summary

In this chapter, we covered various techniques to efficiently create recommendation models that perform well and generate concrete value for your business operations. Besides describing these techniques, we compared several different approaches, their related use cases, strengths, and weaknesses. The next chapter covers the topic of data preparation, a key step in any predictive project.

13

Chapter 14

Advanced Data Preparation Techniques with the Data Manager

In this chapter, we'll show you how to use the Data Manager to define datasets. We'll start first with a description of the different types of datasets that may be required in a predictive analytics project and how to implement these datasets using the Data Manager.

Data preparation is the process of defining a dataset to answer a business question and is the cornerstone of Automated Analytics. In automated model building, having a good initial dataset is more important than when using more manual approaches.

With the ability to schedule the whole process—model building, batch production of the results, control of model quality, and model retraining—handled by the Predictive Factory, you'll need to provide the right dataset for each step. The Data Manager is a component of Automated Analytics to help you in this process.

The concept of the time dependency of datasets—right now for production, sometime in the past for controlling and retraining—is key to the Data Manager's design. The Data Manager methodology helps you define those datasets. In this chapter, we'll discuss data preparation in the context of SAP Predictive Analytics, the methodology you'll use to build a predictive analytics dataset, and the steps to actually create that dataset. We'll also discuss some additional functionality provided by the Data Manager and how to use it to manage metadata.

14.1 Data Preparation for SAP Predictive Analytics

Without datasets, there is no predictive analytics. Defining datasets is necessary for answering business questions. Datasets are used at every step of the predictive analytics process—at training, to produce results, during model control, and for retraining. In a Predictive Factory context, since batch producing results, model control and retraining are performed automatically, the production of the datasets must also be done automatically. For efficiency and to avoid breaks in the process, datasets should be pulled from the process and not pushed to it. In other words, the production of the dataset, although a database job, must be triggered from the SAP Predictive Analytics platform.

The job of the Data Manager is exactly this process: delivering all required datasets when needed by the process. The Data Manager comes in two flavors:

- Data manipulation, which starts from a given table that is then is "decorated" by joins and aggregates
- Analytic data, which uses data manipulation capabilities to provide a methodology to build datasets

However, certain constraints exist: SAP Predictive Analytics does not have a proprietary data repository for manipulating data. Therefore, no consolidation layer for the data is provided. SAP Predictive Analytics does not have a data manipulation engine either, so it relies on the database it's connected to to handle data transformations. Moreover, to avoid performance issues in delivering datasets, heterogeneous queries on multiple databases are not possible.

As a result, data transformations in the Data Manager only rely on one database, where data has been previously consolidated. The consolidation of data into this database is not the job of SAP Predictive Analytics. Consolidation is an IT process handled with an extract, transform and load (ETL) tool. If you connect to SAP HANA, you can use the virtualization capabilities in SAP HANA to serve as a consolidation layer.

The Data Manager pushes SQL code to the underlying database and can serve as a semantic layer between database schemas and datasets. However, Data Manager objects, as defined in the next section, are not stored as SQL code but in a proprietary format in a metadata repository.

The principle is that a combination of a data source (through ODBC) and a metadata repository are linked to a data transformation. Therefore, the Data Manager's objects are specific to a data source. We'll describe the mechanism for transferring metadata to a different data source in Section 14.6.

Additionally, with SAP HANA, data transformations can use objects other than just pure SQL objects (views and tables). SAP HANA provides specific views using the OLAP engine. These views behave differently from normal database objects and therefore should be treated differently in SAP Predictive Analytics.

14.2   Building Datasets for SAP Predictive Analytics

In the following subsections, we'll describe how to build a dataset for use in SAP Predictive Analytics. First, we'll discuss the various types of datasets before moving on to an overview of the methodology.

14.2.1   Datasets

Globally, three types of datasets can be defined to address predictive analytics questions:

- **Snapshots of entities at a certain time-stamp**
  This first type is typically used in business-to-consumer (B2C) scenarios, where a large number of objects need to be viewed simultaneously, typically required in marketing and risk management. The keys of the dataset are the ID of the entity (customer, contract, etc.) and a given time-stamp. For producing results from a model, the time-stamp is "Now," or a transformation of "Now"; for model training and control, the time-stamp is a date in the past where the target variable can be measured. Figure 14.1 shows the time axis used and how, from the definition of the target from the production perspective, the dataset is simply shifted in time for the training and control datasets. These datasets are extended when IDs appear at a date that corresponds to the same event for each ID. For example, to predict customer value 3 months after becoming a customer, the start date is shifted by 3 months.

  Snapshot datasets are designed according to the result to be produced and according to which business processes will use the results and how. At production, the reference date is "Now" or a transformation of "Now" (the 1st of the month, etc.). The target definition includes the prediction time frame ("Target Period") and potentially a "Lag." It's the only part of the dataset that is designed in the future. No other information is known, and as a result, having "No Information" after "Now" can be included in the predictors as they would be unknown by definition. Filters on the population can also only apply to data in the past.

  For model training, everything is shifted to a point in the past where the "Target" can be measured. That "Training Date" is what was "Now" at that time. Because all time-dependent elements of a data transformation are built according to a reference date (provided by a prompt), the right dataset can be built at any moment. Time is the main parameter of the data transformation to provide the right dataset. In Figure 14.1, the rectangle containing yellow blocks represents the description of the entity. The yellow blocks correspond to different periods of description.

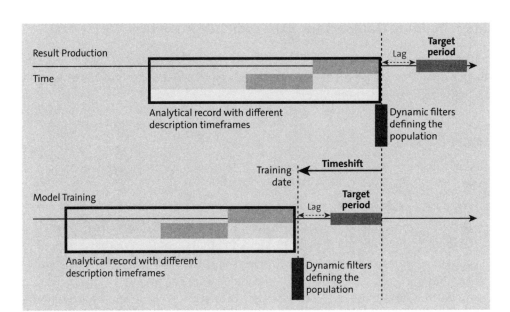

Figure 14.1 Time Shifting between Production and Training

- **Transaction datasets**
  Transaction datasets correspond to keys of the dataset (in this case, transaction IDs) and the time-stamp (the date of the transaction). Transaction datasets are used, for example, in fraud detection datasets.

- **Time series datasets**
  Time series datasets are used for time series forecasting models and for predictive maintenance and quality management in manufacturing contexts. One or several entities (for example, a machine or a set of machines of the same type) are the entity. The dates associated to this entity correspond to the dates at which results should be delivered, for example every minute.

Among these three types of datasets, the first two can be handled with the Analytic Datasets methodology, as described in the next section. To address time series datasets, you should use the data manipulation capabilities and perhaps perform some additional database work.

14.2.2   Methodology

The Analytic Datasets methodology used in the Data Manager decomposes the dataset into bricks, which once combined define the dataset. You access it by launching

Automated Analytics, clicking on the **Data Manager** link on the left tab, and then selecting the **Create and Manage Analytic Datasets** link.

The first object is the *entity*, which defines the row of the dataset. This entity is then combined with a date to create the *time-stamped population*. The nature of the date is by default a unique date coming from a prompt. The time-stamped population, therefore, defines a set of IDs as seen at a certain point in time. The definition of the date (called KxTimeStamp) can also be changed so that each ID has its own date, which might be the case to capture when customers first became customers or for transactions (e.g., the transaction date itself).

The time-stamped population can be used to define the business question the dataset answers by defining the population that should be considered and the target. For example, "the active customers over the last year" are customers of interest, and the target action is "buys a certain product next month."

The other object is the *analytical record*, which defines the set of attributes (predictors) used to create the model and is linked to the entity.

Additional Guidelines for Building Relevant Datasets

Starting with the production process and how results will be used by your business is key. The most important elements are the definition of the target, the definition of the population of interest, and the frequency at which results must be delivered. The frequency at which results must be delivered defines the smallest temporal aggregation that can be used. For example, if results need to be produced every week, weekly aggregates are the smallest aggregates that can be used.

The definition of the target is also usually an aggregate, such as problem in 10 minutes for a minute or churn in a week for 2 weeks. The time frame is independent from the frequency of production. A lag corresponds to the amount of time required to get data and/or to the time needed to execute the business process (send a campaign, for example).

14.3   Creating a Dataset using the Data Manager

To demonstrate the Data Manager's capabilities, throughout this chapter, we'll use a public database available at *https://blogs.sap.com/2015/11/05/hands-on-tutorial-sap-predictive-analytics-automated-mode-data-manager/*. Figure 14.2 illustrates the database schema of tables we'll use to build datasets.

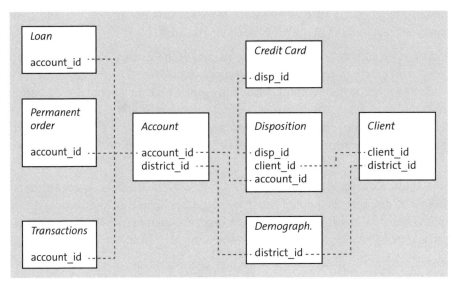

Figure 14.2 Database Schema Used in This Chapter

First, we need to define a business question to answer. For our example, let's try to identify the bank active customers likely to sign up for a credit card in the next 3 months. An "active" customer is a customer who has conducted at least 1 transaction in the last 3 months. Results will be produced monthly, based on the first of each month.

This business question provides us all the elements we need for creating the dataset to answer the question. The entity will be the customer. The time-stamped population will be filtered by activity and whether or not they already have a credit card. Our minimum time frame for temporal aggregates will be monthly. What we want, the result, will be a snapshot of customers to target. We can use the Analytic Dataset methodology.

To begin, launch Automated Analytics, go to the Data Manager page, and select **Create or Edit Analytic Data**.

As described earlier, the Data Manager must be connected to a relational database because SQL code will be pushed to the database to create the required datasets. The database connection must be an ODBC connection. You'll make these settings at the top of the screen shown in Figure 14.3. For our example, we'll use an SAP HANA Express instance and the ODBC connection is called "LOCAL_HANA."

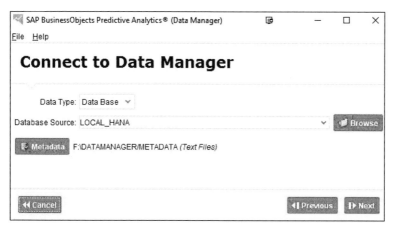

Figure 14.3 Create or Edit Analytic Data Landing Page

Everything defined in the Data Manager is stored as metadata. Therefore, a metadata repository must be defined as well. By default, the repository is the relational database that the Data Manager is connected to. However, in this case, all objects are stored in the schema of the database user. To allow more flexibility in managing metadata, we recommend using folders on the SAP Predictive Analytics server. Once you've defined the connection, click **Next**.

Note

To change the metadata repository, click on the **Metadata** button.

Let's now jump into our first step: creating Data Manager objects.

14.3.1   Creating Data Manager Objects

To create a Data Manager object, you'll take four main steps:

1. Create the entity.
2. Edit the time-stamped population.
3. Create complex time-stamped populations (optional).
4. Create the analytical record.

Let's look at each of these steps next.

Creating the Entity

To create an entity, follow these steps:

1. Define the **Entity** by clicking on the plus **+** button and then **Entity**. The screen for defining an entity will open, as shown in Figure 14.4.

Figure 14.4 Defining an Entity

2. Give the **Entity** a name; here, we'll enter "Customer."

3. Select the table that contains the list of unique IDs to be used to define the entity, as shown in Figure 14.5. When connected to SAP HANA, this table can be a file, a view, or an SAP HANA view. First, select the schema in which they are present. Tables and views are in the **Catalogue** folder; SAP HANA views, in the **Content** folder.

4. Select the field of the table or view that will define the entity. If a key already exists, it is selected by default.

5. Click on **Next**, and the default time-stamped population is generated. By default, the reference date format is set to **Date and Time**. In rare cases, you may need to specify a different format if the database that SAP Predictive Analytics is connected to does not support joins between **Date Only** and **Date and Time** formats and if all dates in the database are stored as **Date Only**, as shown in Figure 14.6.

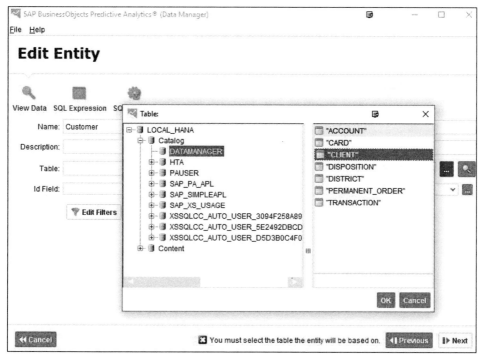

Figure 14.5 Creating an Entity: Selecting the Table Containing Unique IDs

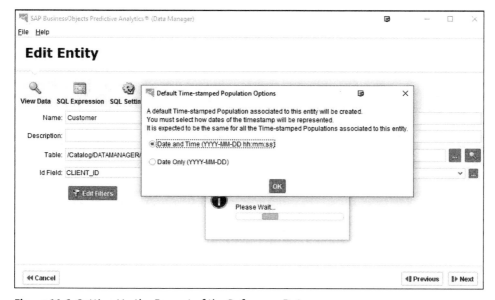

Figure 14.6 Setting Up the Format of the Reference Date

6. The results will be displayed on the screen shown in Figure 14.7.

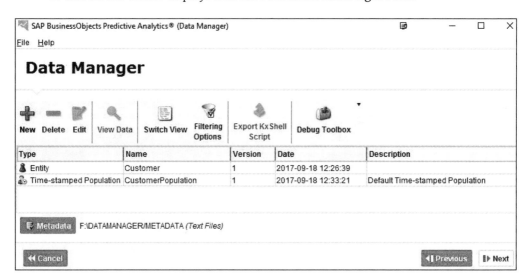

Figure 14.7 Entity and Default Time-Stamped Population

Editing the Time-Stamped Population

Once an entity is defined, the main screen of the Data Manager now shows two new objects: the entity and the default time-stamped population. The default time-stamped population should be edited to define the question asked to the data—in our example, we will apply filters on the population of interest and define the target.

In the methodology, the population of interest must only be filtered using the time-stamped population. After creating the right filtering fields (to filter by activity, for example), the filter is defined using the **Filter** button. Then, you can apply filters to the population by clicking the **Filter** button and then the **New Condition** (Figure 14.8).

Two ways of combining filters are available: **AND (Match All of the Following)** and **OR (Match any of the Following)**. A more complex filter, e.g., using AND/OR operators, can also be set up using the Formula Editor. See Section 14.3.4 for more information.

When setting up filters, you can also define sampling of the dataset. The subsampling can be on the first *n* lines or randomly (Figure 14.9). When random, you'll enter a random seed and a percentage of lines to be kept.

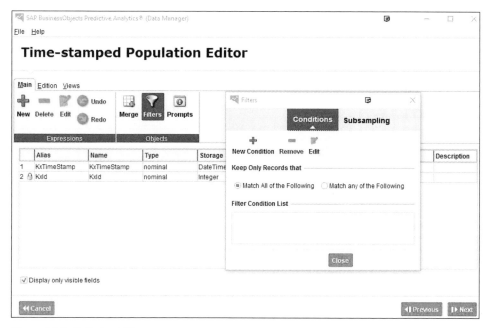

Figure 14.8 Defining Filters

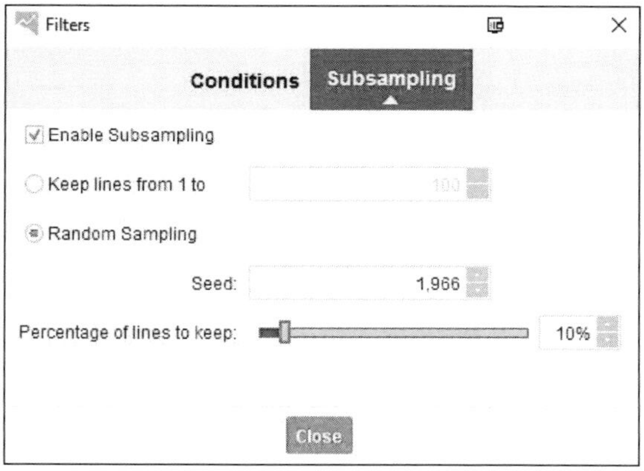

Figure 14.9 Subsampling

To ensure a seamless flow for each step in the modeling and deployment process, the target variable must be identified. After defining the target variable in the time-stamped population, click **Next** to leave the **Edit Filters** interface and then click on the **Target** button next to **Settings** (Figure 14.10).

Figure 14.10 Stratified Sampling

When defining the target, stratified sampling is also available. For performance reasons, we recommend using stratified sampling on the dataset by separating positive and negative cases when doing classification. A good example is fraud detection: Let's say our dataset shows a fraud rate of less than 1/1,000. In order to get enough positive cases (1,000 for example), the dataset will require than 1,000,000 cases. Because training time increases with the number of lines in Automated Analytics, reducing the size of the subsample reduces overall computation time by, for example, randomly selecting a subset of negative cases. Instead of having a 0.1 to 99.9% distribution subsample, focusing only on the negative cases results in, for example, a 2% to 98% distribution—in other words, 1,000 positive cases and 50,000 negative ones.

Stratified sampling can be achieved by first estimating the target rate by clicking on the **Define initial proportion** button. Then, a new proportion can be set. If you select the **Enable Weight** checkbox (see Figure 14.10), a new column will be created containing the value "1" for positive cases and containing the sampling factor for negative cases. This new column can be used in the modeling process to consider negative cases in their initial proportions.

Creating Complex Time-Stamped Populations

Sometimes, a simple time-stamped population (just filtered IDs at a given time) is not enough to answer a business question, usually because of one of the following situations:

- Seasonalities
- Not enough positive cases for a given period

In both cases, it would be interesting to UNION datasets as of different reference date. So far, we've edited the default time-stamped population, but we can also create new time-stamped populations.

In principle, you can UNION (concatenate), INTERSECT, or calculate the DIFFERENCE between predefined time-stamped populations. For example, by editing the KxTime-Stamp variable and shifting it to 1 month before the prompt value. Then, if you UNION the initial and transformed time-stamped populations (by shifting the definition of KxTimeStamp), the defined dataset will be a union of the two time-stamped populations. For a further UNION, you'll have to add more operators (Figure 14.11).

Time-stamped populations can also be sampled.

Figure 14.11 Creating a Compound Time-Stamped Population

Creating the Analytical Record

The next step is to define the analytical record, which is the set of attributes that describe an entity when creating models. Create an analytical record by clicking on the plus (+) button and then **Analytical Record**. Enter a name for the analytical record and select the entity that will be the basis for the analytical record. Within a same metadata repository, several entities can be defined. The one corresponding to the analytical record must be set (Figure 14.12).

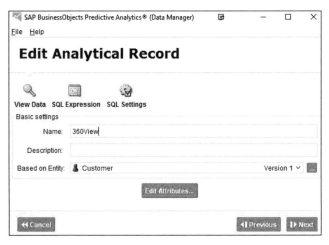

Figure 14.12 Creating an Analytical Record

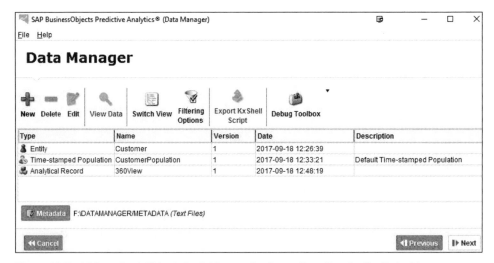

Figure 14.13 All Required Objects to Address a Business Question in the Data Manager

Now that we've walked through creating Data Manager objects (Figure 14.13), let's look at the main data transformations available. We'll illustrate these options through a workflow for creating a dataset that picks up on the question we asked in Section 1.3.1: Who among our bank active customers is likely to sign up for a credit card in the next 3 months? Recall that an active customer is a customer who has at least 1 transaction in the last 3 months and that results will be produced monthly, on the first of each month.

14.3.2   Merging Tables

If a 1:1 or *n*:1 cardinality exists between the default time-stamped population and a table containing additional data about our entities on the KxId and/or KxTimeStamped columns, a join can be performed. The constraint is to keep the number of lines of the dataset unchanged by using the **Merge** button. A left outer join is always performed.

Let's do merge tables in the analytical record we created in the previous section, as follows:

1. First, step is to **Edit** the analytical record and then click on **Edit Attributes** (Figure 14.14). The only two fields available in the analytical record when first created are KxId and KxTimeStamp. KxId corresponds to the IDs defined in the entity, while KxTimeStamp is the reference date to be used when defining the time dependency. When we create the question with a specific time-stamped population, we'll see how we can change its definition.

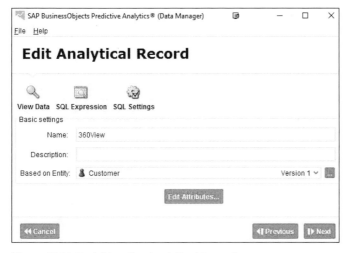

Figure 14.14 Enriching the Analytical Record

2. With the provided database schema, let's join the CUSTOMERS table with the DISPOSI-TION table. We click on the **Merge** button and then the plus **+** button.

3. Select the table to join, in our case, **"Disposition"** as shown in Figure 14.15.

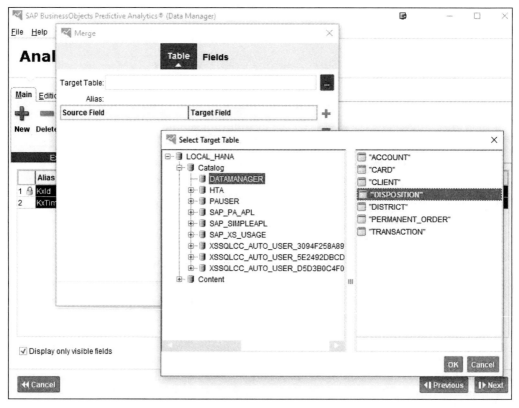

Figure 14.15 Selecting a Table to Join

4. Once the table is selected, define the join key or keys by clicking on the plus **+** button (Figure 14.16 and Figure 14.17).

5. The KxId (the alias for Client_ID) is used with Client_ID for the Disposition table. Click on **OK** and then **OK and Close**, which takes us back to the main data manipulation screen.

The analytical record now contains the new fields brought in by the join (Figure 14.18).

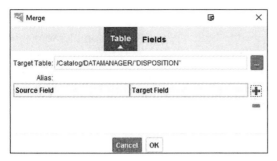

Figure 14.16 Defining the Join Key: First Screen

Figure 14.17 Defining the Join Key: Second Screen

14

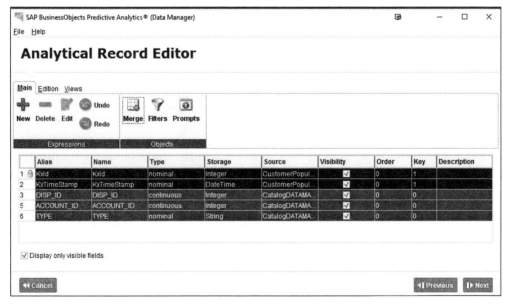

Figure 14.18 Joined Fields

14.3.3   Defining Temporal Aggregates

When cardinality is 1:*n* or *n*:*m*, you'll need to build aggregates. To complement this analytical record, let's build some aggregates. As we want monthly results, the minimum aggregate time frame is 1 month. Follow these steps to build monthly aggregates from a transaction table:

1. Click on the plus **+** button and then **New Aggregate**, which will open the screen shown in Figure 14.19 where you can define aggregates.

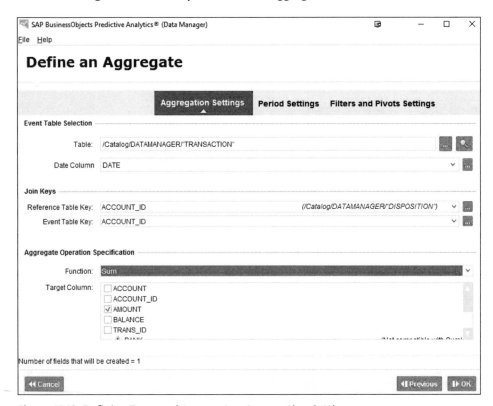

Figure 14.19 Defining Temporal Aggregates: Aggregation Settings

2. First, select the table on which to build aggregates. Define the Date that will be used by the aggregation from the transaction table if you are building a temporal aggregate. The **Join Keys** define on which IDs the aggregated data will be joined to the existing analytical record and also defines the aggregation level. Select the **ACCOUNT_ID** for both tables.

3. Then, specify the **Aggregate Operation Specification** parameters, i.e., the aggregation **Function** and the **Target Column** it applies to. In our case, we would like the **Sum** of the **AMOUNT**.

4. Then, open the **Period Settings** tab (see Figure 14.20), where you'll define the temporal part of the aggregates based on the date provided in the transaction table. If no date is provided, this tab is not available. Two options are available here:

   – **Single Period**

   – **Successive Periods**

   For our example, we'll use multiple periods, which is the easiest way to define the temporal part of the aggregates. Let's build aggregates on 2 periods of 1 month each. We only want aggregates in the past (before the reference date represented by KxTimeStamp). Therefore, we'll need aggregates starting 2 months before that date.

Figure 14.20 Defining Temporal Aggregates: Period Settings

5. On the **Filters and Pivot Settings** tab (Figure 14.21), define the following:
    - **Filter Transaction Table**
    - **Filter Reference Table**
    - **Pivot**

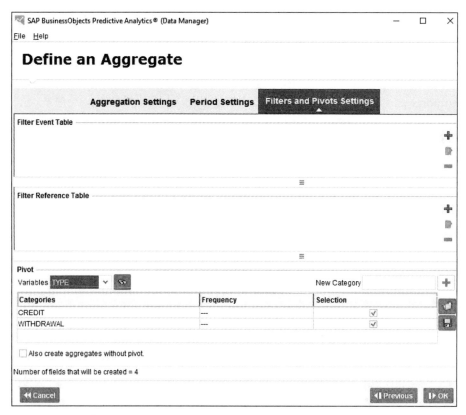

Figure 14.21 Defining Temporal Aggregates: Filters and Pivots Settings Tab

Filtering the transaction table allows you to create only one aggregate for a subset of the transaction table. Filtering the reference table is something that we cannot use with analytic data because, in the methodology, the filtering of a population is handled in the time-stamped population. However, you can filter a population through data manipulation.

Pivot is the most used functionality. This option allows you to multiply the number of existing aggregates by the number of categories contained in the **Pivot** column. The pivoting column must be defined as well as the pivoting categories of this column. The binoculars button shows you a list of available categories for all the columns in the transaction table but might be slow. One trick to speed up the calculation is to push SQL to the underlying database using the **Open** button at the right-hand side of the **Pivot** area.

Enter the following SQL code:

```
Select distinct TYPE from DATAMANAGER.TRANSACTION
```

When doing this, be sure you select the right column, in our case, **TYPE**, as the pivot column. A user-defined prefix is added to the names of the resulting columns. The following naming convention is used:

```
prefix_perioddefinition_pivotcolumn_pivotcategory_operator_period_variable
```

where the prefix provided by the user, `perioddefinition` is composed of 4 letters (**2M2B**, meaning starting 2 months before), `pivotcolumn` is the pivoting column (**TYPE**), `pivotcategory` is the category on which this specific variable is pivoted, the `operator` is the calculation performed (**sum**), period is the rank of the period starting at 0 with the first in time, and variable is the variable on which the aggregate is calculated (**Amount**) (Figure 14.22).

Figure 14.22 Aggregates Defined in the Data Manager

14.3.4   Using the Formula Editor

The Formula Editor can be used to create calculations between columns. A broad set of operators are available: **Arithmetic Operators** (transformation of a number into a number); **Boolean Operators** (the result is a TRUE/FALSE flag); **Conversion Operators** (to change field format); **Date Operators** (to transform date and date-time variables); **Miscellaneous Operators** (e.g., coalesce); and **String Operators** (extracting parts of strings, concatenation, etc.).

The fields that can be used in Expression Editor are available on the right side of the screen, as shown in Figure 14.23.

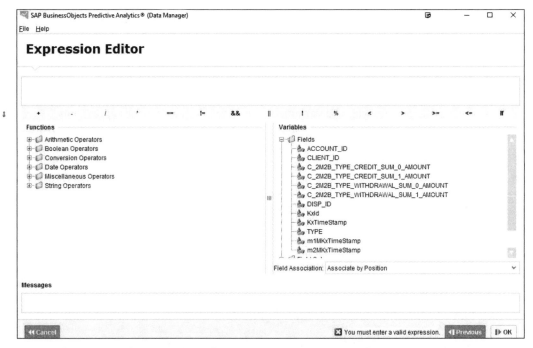

Figure 14.23 The Expression Editor

Another capability of the Formula Editor is the ability to define variables en masse. This function relies on two mechanisms:

- **Field Sets** (i.e., set of variables)
- Wildcards

Field Set definition is located below **Available Fields** (Figure 14.24).

Figure 14.24 Field Set Definition

Filters are available to ease field set definition. Ordering by **Name**, **Type**, or **Storage** is possible. Fields in a field set are all transformed at the same time.

Wildcards offer another way to design data transformations easily. Three wildcards are available: @, $, and #. Unlike other software, where the same wildcard is used to define the common elements to be used, here a different wildcard must be used in each location. For example, to create the ratios of the aggregates we created in the analytical record, we can write the following:

```
C_2M2B_TYPE_#_SUM_O_AMOUNT/C_2M2B_TYPE_@_SUM_1_AMOUNT
```

The mapping of the wildcards can be done one of in two ways:

- Association by position
- Association by value

Association by position means the system will not check for matches on the values of wildcards. Instead, matches are made in the order found in the list of fields. To ensure no errors arise, the name includes all wildcard values. Association by value checks the match between the wildcard values. The name contains only the checked value of the wildcards.

Using this formula creates two additional fields.

14.4   Additional Functionalities

This section covers additional functionalities that help you define data transformations, as follows:

- Visibility and values
- Prompts
- Domains

We'll also cover functionalities that help you review data transformations, as follows:

- Documentation
- Data previews and statistics
- Generated SQL code

14.4.1   Visibility and Value

Once the various columns are built, you can define subsets of columns to be used by setting the **Visibility** of each column. By default, only visible columns are displayed.

In our example shown in Figure 14.25, the **Display only visible fields** checkbox is not selected. As a result, all columns are displayed. By default, columns used only in intermediate calculations are not visible.

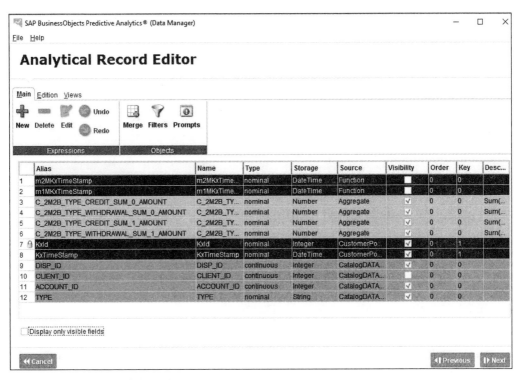

Figure 14.25 Visibility of the Columns

Values must also be verified. For example, in Figure 14.25, the aggregates that were created in the analytical record are numbers, but they've been defined as **nominal** values when they should be **continuous**.

14.4.2 Domains

When creating large numbers of variables, even if a naming convention is used, getting lost is rather easy. To help you manage variables, *domains* are groups of variables that you can define to help you debrief models. In the Data Manager, domains are streamlined in the modeling phase.

By default, columns coming from a merge are assigned to a domain whose name is the joined table name. You can create new domains and assign any variable to them (Figure 14.26).

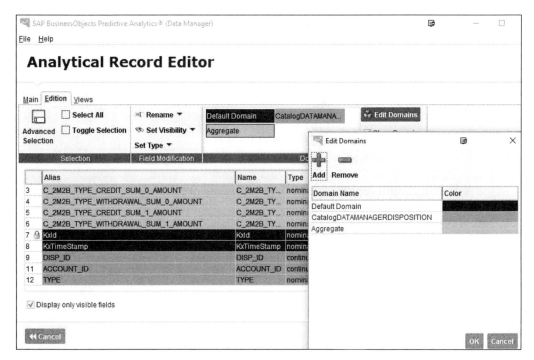

Figure 14.26 Domains of Data

14.4.3   Documentation

The Data Manager documents the data transformations you've designed, and this documentation is available under **Views • Documentation**, as shown in Figure 14.27.

The documentation contains a graphical summary (a flowchart of data transformations), visible and invisible fields, prompts, and detailed expressions of the columns. This information is available for all users with access to the Data Manager's objects.

You can export the documentation in HTML, PDF, TXT, and RTF formats.

Figure 14.27 Documentation

14.4.4   Data Preview and Statistics

At any time, you preview the data and calculate statistics on the Data Manager object under **Views Data and Statistics.**

To preview a time-stamped object, such as a time-stamped population or an analytical record, enter the time-stamp of the target object (Figure 14.28).

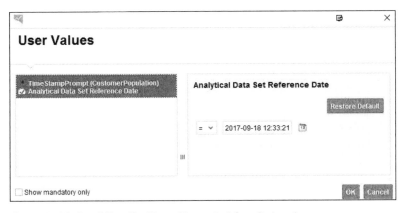

Figure 14.28 Providing the Time-Stamp to View Datasets

Before launching the execution of the SQL code to the database, you'll have to confirm that you're ready by refreshing after you receive the message instructing you to click the "refresh button to review the data."

The view data is performed on the 100 first lines by default, but you can request more by entering a higher number in the **Last Row Index** field (Figure 14.29).

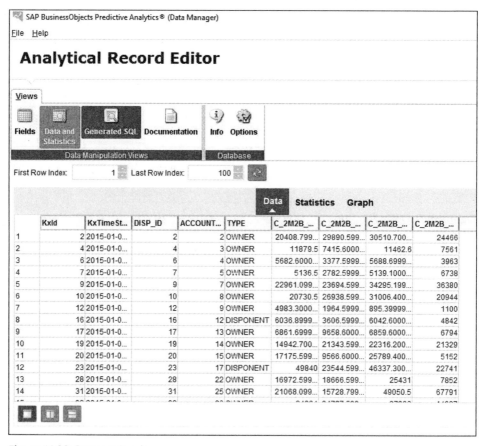

Figure 14.29 Dataset Preview

Statistics can also be calculated to include category frequency and statistics on continuous variables (Figure 14.30 and Figure 14.31). You can generate statistics about whole datasets or samples within a dataset. To randomly select rows for use in statistics, click the **Advanced** button.

Figure 14.30 Defining Statistics Computations

Figure 14.31 Statistics Computation Results

14.4.5   Generated SQL

You can view the SQL code generated by the Data Manager, but you cannot modify it because the code is generated on the fly when requested and is specific to the underlying database (Figure 14.32).

Playing with the options allows you to change the structure of the generated code to improve execution performance. The SQL generated can be a single statement or a script with intermediate, temporary tables.

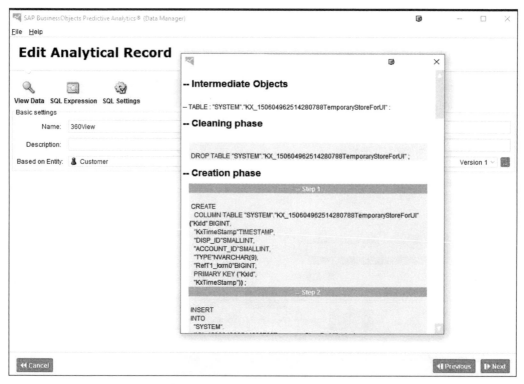

Figure 14.32 Example of Generated SQL Script

14.4.6   Prompts

Because datasets are designed to be executed dynamically, you can add even more flexibility. For example, in a manufacturing context, you may want to define how far into the future we can predict reliably. When defining the target, you can add a lag so that the start date of the target is not the reference date but instead sometime later. To determine most suitable future date, you may want to create several models with different lags. Defining a prompt will help because the lag can be defined with reference to this prompt.

In the time-stamped population, a default prompt is created which, if not changed, defines **KxTimeStamp**.

You must give the prompt a **Name**, a **Type**, a **Default Value**, and a **Prompt Heading** (a description), as shown in Figure 14.33. In the methodology, if the prompt used as a filter or to define a population, the only place the prompt can be defined is the time-stamped population.

Figure 14.33 Defining a Prompt

14.5   Using Data Manager Objects in the Modeling Phase

Once created, Data Manager objects can be used during the modeling phase.

You can use Data Manager objects in classification models. After launching the classification module, select **Use Data Manager** under **Select a Data Source** (Figure 14.34). The analytical record and time-stamped population must be defined. Then click **Next**; a new dialog box will open where you can set the reference date on which the model will be built. The remaining steps of this process are the same as when not starting from Data Manager objects.

Figure 14.34 Using Data Manager Objects to Build a Model

14.6   Managing Metadata

Metadata contains the definitions of data transformations created by the Data Manager. They are linked to an ODBC connection.

If you have a development environment and a production environment, you won't want to define transformations twice. Instead, you can use a transfer mechanism to avoid duplication: the **Data Transfer** functionality of the **Toolkit**. When you define a Data Manager object as the source in a transfer (Figure 14.35), you can either **Transfer the Data** or **Transfer the Definition**. To transfer metadata, you'll choose the second option (Figure 14.36).

Figure 14.35 Selecting Objects to be Transferred

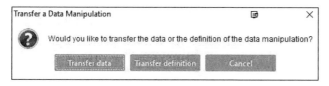

Figure 14.36 Transferring a Definition

Data Manager objects must be transferred in a logical order: entity first, then the default time-stamped population, all other time-stamped populations, and finally analytical records.

Define a target database and metadata repository, as shown in Figure 14.37.

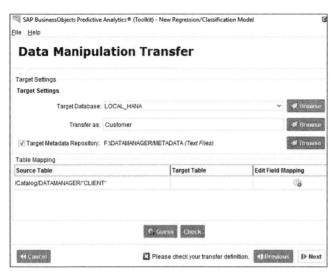

Figure 14.37 Defining Where and What to Transfer

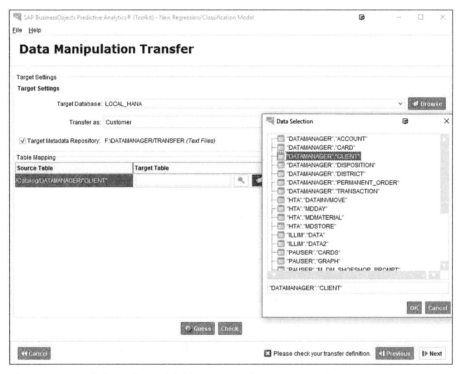

Figure 14.38 Defining What Table(s) to Use in the Target Database

For simplicity, only the **Metadata Repository** has been changed. However, in a real environment, mapping the tables constituting the objects must be performed. Table names can be different, as can the names of fields in the tables. But tables in two databases must have the same structure (Figure 14.38).

The current mapping of fields is displayed on the right in the **Data Selection** window. Clicking the **Check** button will result in a match based on names first. You'll have to check the overall mapping again before clicking the **Next** button to perform the transfer.

14.7   SQL Settings

SQL settings are parameters you can play with to alter the structure of the generated SQL code. Access these settings by clicking on the **Views** tab and then **Options** (Figure 14.39).

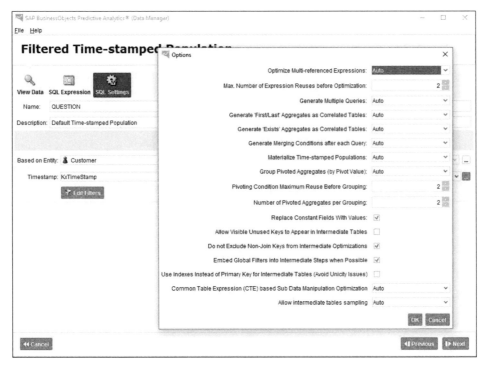

Figure 14.39 SQL Settings

Default values are given for each database (Figure 14.39). Some settings default to **Auto**: These settings automatically adapt to the underlying database being used. A comprehensive description of the impact of each parameter is available in the documentation.

14.8   Summary

In this chapter, we described how to use the Data Manager to define datasets. We discussed the methodology underlying the dataset requirements for successful SAP Predictive Analytics projects. This chapter also described the steps to build datasets according to this methodology and how to create and use objects in the modeling phase of the project. Finally, we described the additional functionalities that make the Data Manager a robust tool for creating datasets.

PART IV

Advanced Workflows

Chapter 15
Expert Analytics

The automated approach for creating predictive models with SAP Predictive Analytics complements the more manual approach in Expert Analytics. With expertise in conventional algorithms, users can graphically define analytical workflows to implement quite specific requirements.

As a data scientist or statistician yourself, you probably learned about many different predictive algorithms—probably hundreds, possibly more. You may have spent a lot of time comparing how different algorithms perform on certain tasks, and you may have your personal favorites. If you need to use such algorithms in your project, then Expert Analytics is a graphical interface designed for you.

In this chapter, we'll introduce the purpose behind and user interface in Expert Analytics. We'll show you how to create a project using built-in-components and how to extend the available functionality.

15.1 When to Use Expert Analytics

Before we go into detail about Expert Analytics, we'd like to refer you back to our recommendation in Chapter 4, Section 4.2.4, on how to choose which modeling approach to use with SAP Predictive Analytics.

We believe in benefitting from the scalability of the automated approach whenever possible, whether via the browser-based Predictive Factory or with Automated Analytics locally installed. Even if you are comfortable with the complexity of manually crafting predictive models, please consider whether the automated approach might be more effective.

However, you may encounter business requirements where using a more conventional approach with Expert Analytics is the best way forward. Sometimes, for example, certain industry regulations can require you use specific algorithms. So, even if the automated approach might be more efficient, if you need to use specific algorithms, then Expert Analytics is your friend.

15.2   Navigating the Expert Analytics Interface

While the automated approach is designed for the use by both data scientists and more casual users, Expert Analytics is clearly made for users who are happy to dig deep. Therefore, the interface is quite different from what we have seen so far in this book. Before explaining the workflow of Expert Analytics in more detail in the following sections, let's introduce the most important navigation techniques first.

The main interface is a graphical workbench, shown in Figure 15.1. Each individual functionality or algorithm is represented by a graphical node. On the right-hand side, all available components are listed, grouped by their overall purpose.

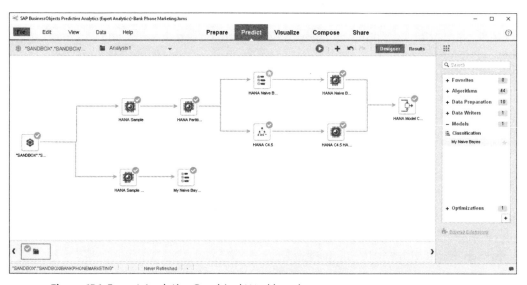

Figure 15.1 Expert Analytics Graphical Workbench

To add a component to the canvas on the left, first click on the existing node on this canvas where the new node should be added. Then, select the node you want to add on the right-hand side and either drag and drop this new node onto the canvas or double-click the node. The node will be added right after the existing node you selected earlier. A single node can be followed by more than one node, thereby creating different execution streams.

Note that the canvas is never completely empty. The canvas is only accessible after a data source is selected, whose node is always shown.

To execute the full chain you just put together, click the green play button above the canvas.

You can also execute the chain only up to certain point. Just click the cogwheel of the last node you want to be triggered and then then select **Run up to Here**, as shown in Figure 15.2.

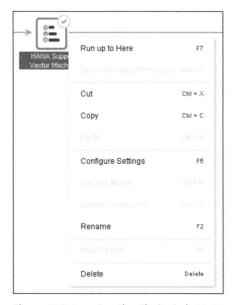

Figure 15.2 Running the Chain Only Up to a Specific Node

You are now familiar with the most important aspects of navigating the graphical interface in Expert Analytics.

15.3   Understanding a Typical Project Workflow

Now, let's look at some common steps to create a typical project. Not every step listed in this section is required in every project, however.

First, open Expert Analytics, launch SAP Predictive Analytics, and then in the main menu on the left, go into **Expert Analytics**. Then, click **Expert Analytics** on the right-hand side, as shown in Figure 15.3.

We'll now show you how to connect a data source and how to explore and understand its content. The data can then be used to train and apply a predictive model, which can then be productionized.

Figure 15.3 Navigating to Expert Analytics

15.3.1   Selecting Data Source

Each project starts by selecting a data source. Expert Analytics can connect to a wide range of data sources. Follow the menu path **File • New**; a number of possible data sources will be listed, as shown in Figure 15.4.

The most important option for us is **Connect to SAP HANA**. With this option, you'll create an analytical model chain using data in SAP HANA without downloading the data onto your desktop. Furthermore, additional predictive libraries that can be installed on SAP HANA will become available in Expert Analytics' graphical interface. You can then leverage the algorithms in SAP HANA that come with the Predictive Analysis Library (PAL) and the Automated Predictive Library (APL). We mentioned these advanced components at the beginning of Chapter 3, but you can learn more in the product documentation (*https://help.sap.com/pa*).

In addition, if you require even further functionality, you can leverage the open-source language R. When using the **Connect to SAP HANA** option, an R server must have been installed alongside SAP HANA. Remember, with this connectivity type, data is not downloaded onto your desktop, so the R server is necessary. When using the other connectivity options, data will be downloaded onto your desktop where you can also use an R environment to extend the functionality of Expert Analytics. In Section 15.6, we'll explain how to create new nodes to extend the standard functionality.

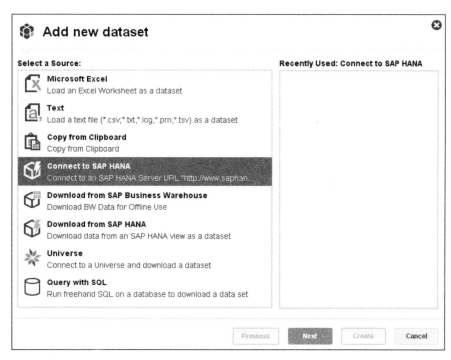

Figure 15.4 Some Available Data Sources

When connecting to SAP HANA, specify SAP HANA's server name or IP address and the SAP HANA instance number.

However, if the list of options shown in Figure 15.4 is not sufficient, further data sources can be made available. Follow the menu path **File • Preferences** and go into the **SQL Drivers** section. Many more potential data sources are listed, from Apache to Teradata, as shown in Figure 15.5.

When you go through the individual sources on that screen, some will show a red icon, indicating the source's driver has not been found in your installation. If you want to make such a connection available, please see the "Installing Data Access Drivers" section of the official documentation of SAP Predictive Analytics.

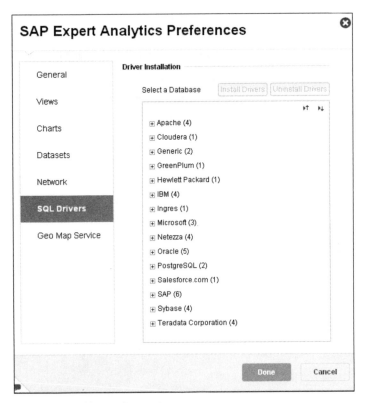

Figure 15.5 Additional Data Sources

15.3.2   Data Explorations

The data exploration capabilities in Expert Analytics depend on whether you are working with data that remains in SAP HANA (whether you selected the **Connect to SAP HANA** option or not). In both cases, you'll have access to the **Prepare** tab, where you can see, for instance, the different values stored in each column, as shown in Figure 15.6.

If you are not connected to SAP HANA, you'll have additional functionalities for preparing the data. For instance, you can manually address data quality problems, e.g., by correcting typos in the data. Not all transformations, however, will be recognized when creating a predictive model. For instance, filtering on the **Prepare** tab does not filter the data in the actual analytical workflow. You'll need to create a filter in the workflow itself.

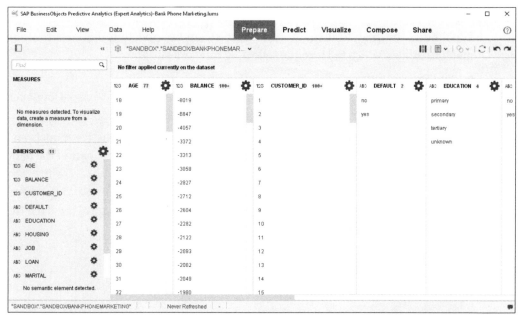

Figure 15.6 The Prepare Tab

Select the **Visualize** tab to explore the data further. The interface might look familiar to you because this tab is an integration of SAP Lumira 1.25 directly into Expert Analytics, as shown in Figure 15.7.

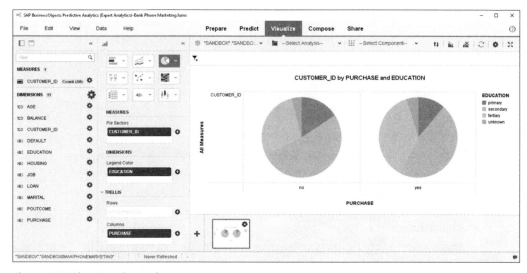

Figure 15.7 The Visualize Tab

15.3.3   Graphical Components

You'll build the analytical chain in the **Predict** tab by modeling the logic through graphical nodes, which fall into the following categories:

- **Data Preparation**

  Includes typical functionality required for preprocessing and postprocessing, such as **Data Type Definition**, **Filter**, and **Binning**, but also data partitioning.

  The **Partition** node makes it easy to split the data to train predictive models and test their performance on unseen data. In the **Partition** node, one part of the data, the **Train Data Set**, is assigned to "train" a new model. This model can be tweaked for best performance on the second part of the data, the **Test Data Set**. The performance of the different models is then evaluated on the third part of the data, the **Validate Data Set**, as shown in Figure 15.8.

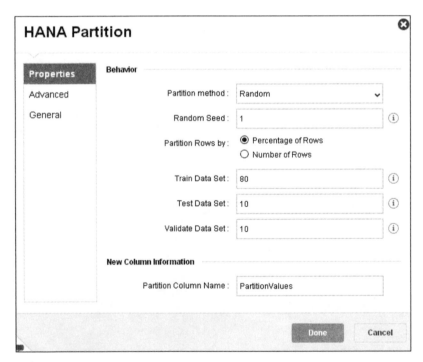

Figure 15.8 Splitting the Data

- **Algorithms**

  Provides core functionality to analyze the data. Thanks to the Predictive Analysis Library (PAL) and the Automated Predictive Library (APL), a broad range of functions are available. These functions can be used, for instance, to estimate missing values, train models, carry out predictions, identify outliers, find associations, etc. The available functions are listed in Section 15.5. You can also extend the functionality of Expert Analytics by leveraging the R programming language, which we'll discuss in more detail in Section 15.6. The graphic representation of a trained decision tree is shown in Figure 15.9.

If you do not have access to SAP HANA, you can still use a smaller set of algorithms that are included in a local SAP Predictive Analytics installation.

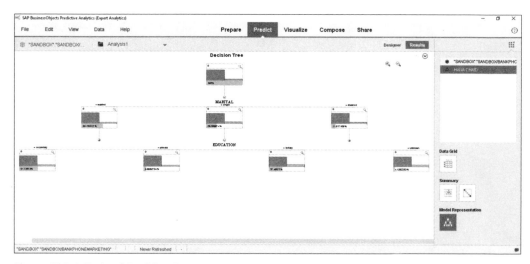

Figure 15.9 A Trained Decision Tree

- **Models**
  If a predictive model has been trained, it can be saved as a new graphical node. To apply the model, just drag it into your analytical chain.

- **Data Writer**
  To persist the output of your analysis, data can be written into an SAP HANA table. If you are not connected to SAP HANA, the data can be saved either via a JDBC to a database or in a text file.

- **Optimizations**
  Provides a graphical interface to the optimization logic in SAP HANA. You can minimize or maximize a function under one or more linear constraints. Functions can be solved immediately; they cannot be added as node into the analytical chain.

15.3.4   Applying a Trained Model

A trained model can be transformed into a new graphical node using the **Save as Model** option (see Figure 15.10). The new graphical node will appear on the right-hand side in the library of components under **Models**. You'll drop the model into the current analytical chain to produce forecasts on new data.

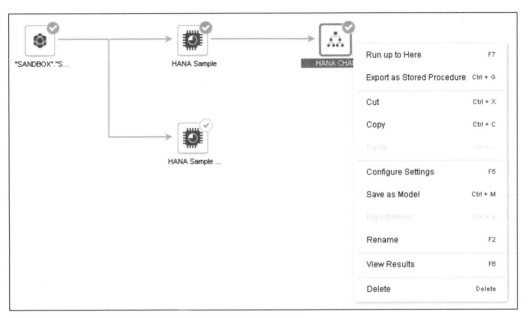

Figure 15.10 Saving a Trained Model

A saved model is available only within the context of the current document. If you want to use the model in another document, you can export the model from the current document and import it into a new document. For the initial export, simply select the saved model in the library on the right-hand side and click **Export Model**. Choose the **Expert Analytics Archive** option and save file, which will have the file extension .spar. Then, open a new document and click the **+** sign below the library on the right-hand side (Figure 15.11). Choose **Import Model/Extension** and select the file containing the saved model. Now, the model will be available in the library.

Figure 15.11 Importing a Saved Model

15.3.5   Productionize

A number of options are available for bringing the output of an analytical chain into your processes. You can either manually share the output, or you can set a regular schedule for integrating analytic outputs into your processes.

Manually

When working in Expert Analytics' graphical interface, the analytical chain can be manually triggered, either in full or in part. This option is particularly helpful when setting up a new chain and you need to test its functionality.

Maintained by the Predictive Factory

If the model needs to be updated more frequently, the manual approach may not suffice. An analytical chain created in Expert Analytics based on SAP HANA can be imported into the Predictive Factory, which can automatically retrain and apply the model as needed.

The chain is passed to the Predictive Factory by exporting it first to a file via the **Export as Model Chain** option (see Figure 15.12).

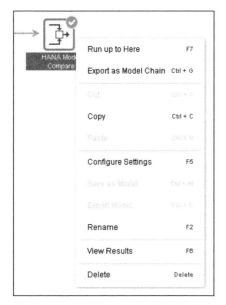

Figure 15.12 Exporting a Model Chain

This exported file can then be imported into a project in the Predictive Factory using the **Predictive Pipeline from File** option. Note that, for this option to be available, the data connection in the project in the Predictive Factory must use an SAP HANA server as the modeling server (see Chapter 3, Section 3.4.4). This model can then be retrained and applied on a regular schedule by the Predictive Factory If the modeling server is an Automated Server, the import option is not available.

Stored Procedure in SAP HANA

The model chain can also be turned into a stored procedure within SAP HANA. When exporting the model chain, you can choose a name for the stored procedure, which Expert Analytics will create for you. This stored procedure is connected to the source of your analytical chain and can be called to produce a prediction for all records found in that source. This stored procedure can be used most easily through a column database view, which can also be created for you. We'll describe this function in more detail in Section 15.4.3.

Predictive Modeling Markup Language (PMML)

Once a model has been trained and saved as new node into the library on the right-hand side, the model can also be exported to Predictive Modeling Markup Language

(PMML). PMML is a common XML format for describing and exchanging predictive models. Select the node of the trained model in the library, click **Export Model,** and choose the option for PMML as shown in Figure 15.13. When specifying the file name, change the extension from .pmml to .xml so that other applications supporting PMML can use the file.

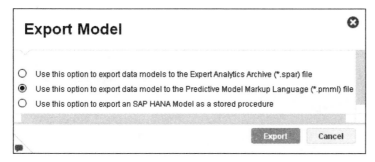

Figure 15.13 Export to Predictive Model Markup Language

We won't discuss the **Compose** and **Share** tabs in Expert Analytics in this book; these tabs mainly provide legacy functionality for SAP Lumira.

15.4   Creating an Expert Analytics Predictive Model

For some hands-on practice with Expert Analytics, in this section, we'll show you how to create two different classification models, compare them, and put the preferred one to use. In our example, we are connected to an SAP HANA system. If you don't have access to an SAP HANA installation, you won't have all the algorithms we mention available. A similar analysis, however, can be carried out with a flat file as a data source, or you can check out SAP HANA, express edition.

> **SAP HANA, Express Edition**
>
> For more information about SAP HANA, express edition, see *https://www.sap.com/developer/topics/sap-hana-express.html.*

Our sample data comes from a bank promoting a certificates of deposit (CDs). Over 45,000 customers were contacted by telephone. For each contact, we know certain information, such as the customer's age and balance on account, and whether the person signed up for the product. We want to understand which customers are likely to be interested in that product. So, we'll predict their purchasing affinity. The original data is available online at *https://archive.ics.uci.edu/ml/datasets/bank+marketing* and comes from S. Moro, P. Cortez, and P. Rita. *A Data-Driven Approach to Predict the Success of Bank Telemarketing. Decision Support Systems*, Elsevier (June 2014).

For our example, we reduced the data slightly to help focus on the core workflow of creating a predictive model in Expert Analytics.

The available information about our customers is described in the Table 15.1.

Column Name	Description
AGE	The person's age.
JOB	The person's job.
MARITAL	The person's marital status.
EDUCATION	The person's education.
DEFAULT	Value of "1" if the person has a credit card in default (i.e., an overdue amount); "0" otherwise.
BALANCE	The person's balance on their account.
HOUSING	Value of "1" if the person has a mortgage; "0" otherwise.
LOAN	Value of "1" if the person has a personal loan (i.e., consumer credit); "0" otherwise.
POUTCOME	Outcome of a previous marketing campaign (how did the person respond then?).
PURCHASE	Value of "1" if the person bought the term deposit (the target variable); "0" otherwise.

Table 15.1 Columns in Our Example Dataset

15.4.1   Load Data into SAP HANA

To load the data for our example into SAP HANA, follow these steps:

1. Obtain the *BANKPHONEMARKETING.csv* file from *www.sap-press.com/4491*.

2. In SAP HANA Studio, follow the menu path **File • Import • SAP HANA Content • Data from Local File**. Click **Next** and select the SAP HANA system to import the data into. Click **Next** again.

3. Select the file *BANKPHONEMARKETING.csv* and set the **Field Delimiter** to **Semi Colon**. Select the **Header row exists** and **Import all data** checkboxes. Next, select the database schema to load the data into. Specify the table name as "BANKPHO-NEMARKETING." The screen should look similar to the one shown in Figure 15.14.

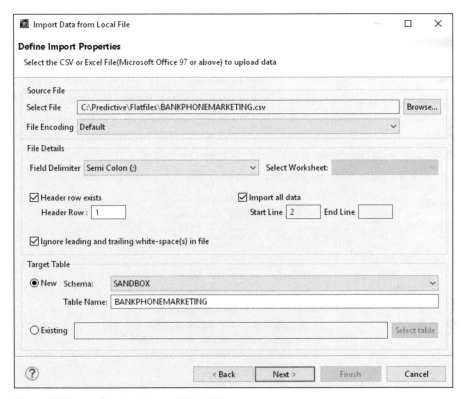

Figure 15.14 Loading Data into SAP HANA

4. Click **Next**. On the following **Manage Table Definitions and Data Mappings** screen not all proposed data types are supported by the algorithms we will use. Therefore, set the **Data Type** of the CUSTOMER_ID, AGE, and PURCHASE columns to **Integer**. Click **Next** and then **Finish**.

Congratulations! The data has been loaded.

Supported Data Types

See SAP Note 2373381 for supported data types.

15.4.2   Create a Predictive Model

To create a predictive model in Expert Analytics desktop, follow these steps:

1. From the initial screen of SAP Predictive Analytics desktop, first click on **Expert Analytics** in the menu on the left hand side. Then, click on **Expert Analytics** in the center of the screen to open the graphical interface.

2. Follow the menu path **File • New** and then click on **Connect to SAP HANA**. This connectivity option is preferred, so that the data remains in SAP HANA and does not need to be downloaded. Enter your SAP HANA credentials and then click **Connect**.

3. You'll then see the database schemas available in SAP HANA. Open the schema into which the data was loaded. Select the table name and click **Next**. You'll see a list of the columns found in the table. If you want to ignore some columns, deselect them. For our example, however, we'll keep the default settings.

4. Finally, click **Create**, and the **Visualize** tab will open, as shown in Figure 15.15.

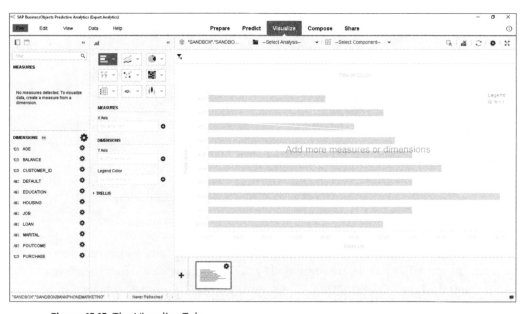

Figure 15.15 The Visualize Tab

5. To explore the data graphically, you'll need to create a measure. Click the cogwheel next to **CUSTOMER_ID** and select **Create a measure**. A measure is created with the

default aggregation of type **Sum**. Turn this sum into a count by clicking the cog-wheel next to the newly created measure. Change the aggregation type to **Count (All)**. Now, you'll be able to drag the measure and its dimensions to the right-hand side and graphically explore the data. As shown in Figure 15.16, for example, students constituted a higher-than-average proportion of those taking up the offer.

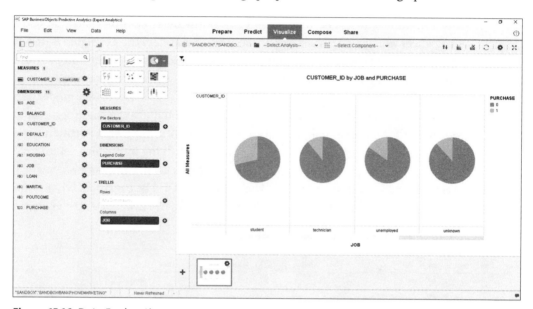

Figure 15.16 Data Exploration

6. Go into the **Prepare** tab to further explore the data. Notice, for example, which values are found in each column.

7. Now, go to the **Predict** tab to create a prediction. For our example, we want to use more than one algorithm to train a model to determine if a customer would be interested in a term deposit offer promoted by phone.

8. On the left-hand side, notice our data is represented by a graphical node. Otherwise, the canvas is still empty. First, we'll need to split the dataset to separate rows to train the models and to test their performance. In the library on the right-hand side, look for the **HANA Partition** component and either double-click it, or drag and drop it onto the canvas on the left. Your screen should look similar what's shown in Figure 15.17.

Figure 15.17 Partition Node

9. To see how the data will be split, move your mouse over the **HANA Partition** node. A cogwheel will appear, which you'll click and then select the **Configure Settings** option. Notice that the data is split into three parts. Models are trained on the **Train** subset. You can try to improve the trained model's performance using the **Test** dataset. The **Validate** subset can be used to assess how well a chosen model performs on yet another unused set of records. You could change these settings of course, but for our example, we'll stick to the defaults. The **HANA Partition** node adds a column, PartitionValues, to the dataset, specifying into which set an individual record was placed. This can be accessed by clicking the node's cogwheel again and choosing **Run up to Here**. The node's logic will be executed. When complete, you'll receive a notification, which you confirm by clicking **OK**. The enriched dataset is shown in Figure 15.18.

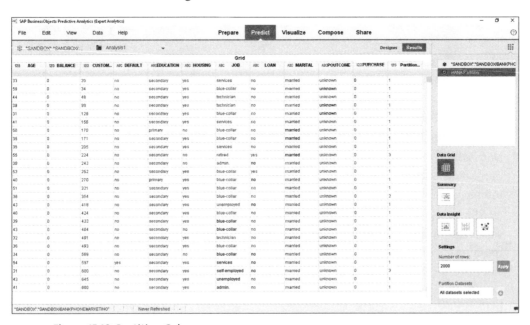

Figure 15.18 Partition Column

10. Return to the analytical chain by clicking on **Designer**. Now, add two classification nodes directly after the **HANA Partition** node. Drag the **HANA Naïve Bayes** and **HANA Auto Classification** nodes on top of the **HANA Partition** node. Configure the settings of both nodes. Set **Target Variable** to PURCHASE. The **Features** option specifies which columns should be considered for training the model. Select all columns except CUSTOMER_ID, PURCHASE, and PartitionValues. Your chain should look similar to what's shown in Figure 15.19.

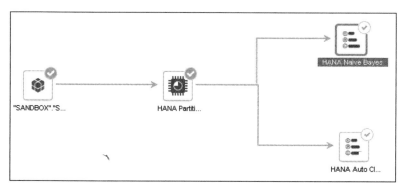

Figure 15.19 Analytical Chain with Classification Nodes

11. You can train each of the two new nodes by clicking their cogwheels and then selecting **Run up to Here**. After the execution, a prompt will ask if you want to go into the **Results** view, which shows the prediction columns added to the dataset. Also, some charts will show information about the model's performance.

12. Further information on the model's performance is available through the **HANA Model Statistics** node. Drag individual nodes from the library on the right on top of both trained classification nodes. These new nodes have to be configured. For both, set **Target Column** to PURCHASE and **Predict Column** to PredictedValues. Execute both nodes with the **Run up to Here** option. For each of the **Model Statistics** nodes, the model's performance is shown through charts on the **Results** tab. The performance is shown individually for the **Train**, **Test**, and **Validate** subsets, as shown in Figure 15.20.

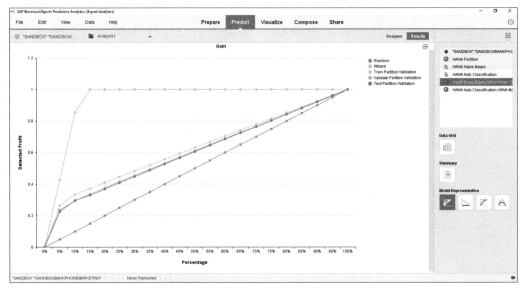

Figure 15.20 Model Performance

13. Since we want to compare the performance of multiple models, add the **HANA Model Compare** node to the analytical chain. First, drag the node onto one of the **HANA Model Statistics** nodes. Then, drag the same node from the canvas on top of the second **HANA Model Statistics** node. Your chain should be similar to what's shown in Figure 15.21.

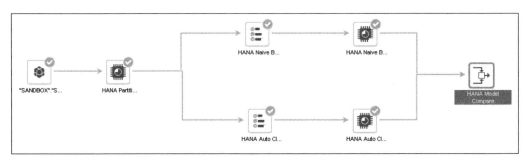

Figure 15.21 Comparing Nodes Models in the Analytical Chain

14. Now, configure the **HANA Model Compare** node. In its properties, you can select the criteria for comparing the models based on quality. The symbol "KI" refers to

predictive power and "KR" to *prediction confidence*. You might remember this terminology from earlier chapters. Further criteria such as area under the curve, lift, or gain are also available. If the columns from the different models have different names, then the columns can be mapped in the **HANA Model Compare** node, but in our case, the columns are identical. However, only the **HANA Classification Node** outputs a **Probability** column. Delete this column at the bottom of the **Column Mapping** option, as shown in Figure 15.22.

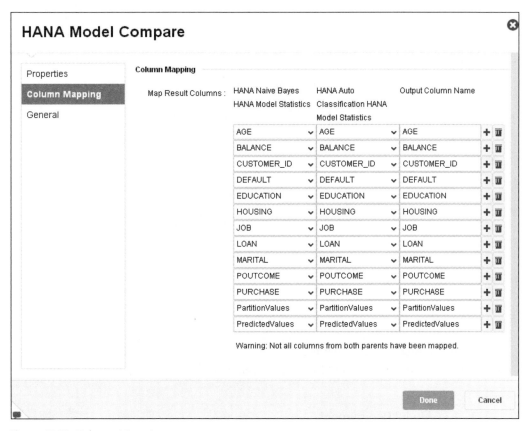

Figure 15.22 Column Mapping

15. Execute the **HANA Model Compare** node. On the **Results** tab, the **Summary** option will show you how the two models compare on the chosen criteria. The winning model is marked with a blue star, as shown in Figure 15.23.

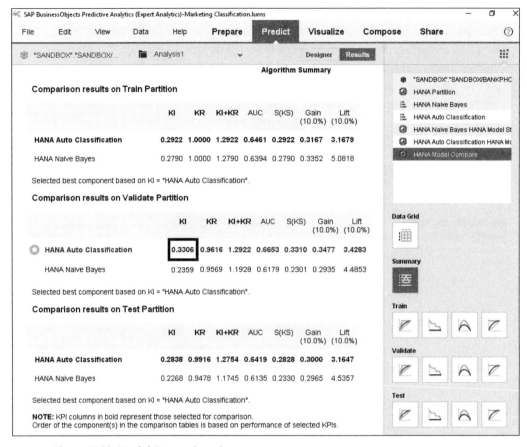

Figure 15.23 Model Comparison Summary

The same blue star is also shown in the analytical chain on top of the winning model's node. You have now trained and compared two models.

15.4.3   Model Deployment

The winning model can now be deployed. For all deployment options, see Section 15.3.4 and Section 15.3.5 as well as the official product documentation for a broader overview.

Let's conclude our example by leveraging our trained model as a stored procedure in SAP HANA, so that any business process that requires predictions can have predictions created. Click the cogwheel of the **HANA Model Compare** node and select **Export as Model Chain**. Set the name to "MyPurchasingModel." Select your database schema and set the procedure name also to "MyPurchasingModel," as shown in Figure 15.24. Notice that these settings will also create a view on top of the procedure, which we will make use of.

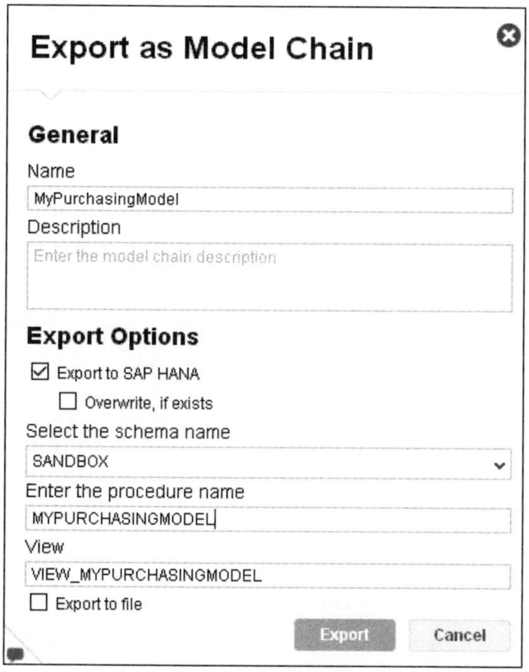

Figure 15.24 Export as Model Chain

Click **Export**, and you should receive a confirmation message. Now, open the SAP HANA Studio, where you'll see a number of new stored procedures that have been created as well as a database column view, as shown in Figure 15.25.

Leveraging the trained model is easiest by calling the view. The following command will score all rows kept in the source table of our analytical chain. New rows can be added to this table, and the view will return the people's purchasing affinity, as follows:

```
SELECT * FROM "SANDBOX"."VIEW_MYPURCHASINGMODEL"
```

Figure 15.25 SAP HANA Studio

You can save the analytical chain itself onto your local drive. The document is saved in the folder *SAP Predictive Analytics Documents* within your personal *Documents* folder.

15.5   Exploring the Available Algorithms

The algorithms that are available out-of-the box depend a great deal on the connectivity type. For a list of algorithms that can be extended using the open-source language R, see Section 15.6. In this section, we'll only list the most important algorithms. Any functionality related to the Data Preparation or Data Writer components is not described in this section, but you can refer back to Section 15.3.3. The auto classification, auto regression, and auto clustering algorithms contain the core functionality of the automated approach of creating models introduced earlier in the book. Note that, in Expert Analytics, configuring or interpreting the automated model is not really possible. However, the automated algorithms available in Expert Analytics can be useful for high-level model comparison, for instance.

15.5.1   Connected to SAP HANA

We prefer to use the **Connect to SAP HANA** connectivity type, which leverages the functionalities available in SAP HANA. With this connection type, data will not be downloaded onto your computer. The following algorithms are available to you in

Expert Analytics as graphical nodes (if SAP HANA has the Predictive Algorithm Library (PAL) and Automated Predictive Library (APL) installed).

Any algorithm starting with "HANA R-" requires that SAP HANA be connected to an R server. SAP HANA will automatically delegate the logic to that server, but the data will not be downloaded onto your local desktop.

- **Association**
  - HANA Apriori
  - HANA R-Apriori
- **Classification**
  - HANA ABC Analysis
  - HANA Auto Classification
  - HANA KNN
  - HANA Naive Bayes
  - HANA R-Bagging Classification
  - HANA R-Boosting Classification
  - HANA R-Random Forest Classification
  - HANA Support Vector Machine
  - HANA Weighted Score Analysis
- **Clustering**
  - HANA Auto Clustering
  - HANA DBScan
  - HANA K-Means
  - HANA R-KMeans
  - HANA Self-Organizing Maps
- **Decision trees**
  - HANA C4.5
  - HANA CHAID
  - HANA R-CNR Tree
- **Outliers**
  - HANA Anomaly Detection
  - HANA Inter-Quartile Range Test
  - HANA Variance Test

15

- **Regression**
  - HANA Auto Regression
  - HANA Exponential Regression
  - HANA Geometric Regression
  - HANA Logarithmic Regression
  - HANA Logistic Regression
  - HANA Multiple Linear Regression
  - HANA Polynomial Regression
  - HANA R-Multiple Linear Regression
  - HANA R-Random Forest Regression
- **Time series**
  - HANA Demand Forecasting (might require an addition license for SAP Customer Activity Repository)
  - HANA Single Exponential Smoothing
  - HANA Double Exponential Smoothing
  - HANA Triple Exponential Smoothing
  - HANA R-Triple Exponential Smoothing
- **Optimization**
  - Custom optimization function can be solved under specified constraints.

15.5.2   Other Connectivity Types

The other connectivity types download data onto your local computer, and algorithms from SAP HANA will not be available. Make sure that the open-source language R has been downloaded and configured to have all available functionalities. We don't recommend installing R manually—simply have Expert Analytics install and configure R for you. First, make sure your computer is online. Then, go to **File • Install & Configure R** and click **Install R**. Wait for the download and installation to complete. Next, ensure that, on the same screen in the **Configuration** submenu, that the **Enable Open-Source R Algorithms** option is selected. Any algorithm starting with the prefix "R-" requires the R configuration.

- **Association**
  - R-Apriori
- **Classification**
  - Auto Classification
  - R-Bagging Classification
  - R-Boosting Classification
  - R-Random Forest Classification
- **Clustering**
  - Auto Clustering
  - R-K-Means
- **Decision trees**
  - R-CNR Tree
- **Neural networks**
  - R-MONMLP Neural Network
  - R-NNet Neural Network
- **Outliers**
  - Inter Quartile Range
  - Nearest Neighbour Outlier
- **Regression**
  - Auto Regression
  - Exponential Regression
  - Geometric Regression
  - Linear Regression
  - Logarithmic Regression
  - R-Exponential Regression
  - R-Geometric Regression
  - R-Linear Regression
- **Time series**
  - R-Single Exponential Smoothing
  - R-Double Exponential Smoothing
  - R-Triple Exponential Smoothing
  - Triple Exponential Smoothing

15

15.6   Extending Functionality with R

If you require additional functionality in Expert Analytics, further nodes can be created with the open-source language R. An expert familiar with R can create a graphical node that other users can then leverage without being exposed to the complexity of R.

A collection of such extensions is listed in SAP's App Center, which can be opened by clicking **Browse Extensions** under the library of algorithms in Expert Analytics.

We recommend going through the following steps when creating a new extension:

1. Develop the desired functionality in your preferred R editor outside SAP Predictive Analytics.
2. Encapsulate that functionality in an R function as required by Expert Analytics.
3. Use this function as the foundation for a new node in Expert Analytics.

Remember that the graphical nodes available for your analysis depend on how you are connecting to the data source (whether **Connect to SAP HANA** or another connectivity type was chosen). The same principle applies to these extensions. An extension created while connected to SAP HANA executes on an R server connected to SAP HANA. If you are not connected to SAP HANA, this extension will not appear in the library. Similarly, an extension created while connected to any other source will not show up when working with **Connect to SAP HANA**.

15.6.1   Developing in an R Editor

We assume you are already familiar with R if you are reading this section. To get started, we'll introduce the concept of extending Expert Analytics by creating a new node, which displays a boxplot for a variable chosen by the end user. In our example, we'll create a node with the **Connect to SAP HANA** connectivity type. The same steps apply also when working with different connectivity types. To develop your new node, follow these steps:

1. Start by opening your preferred R editor. We use RStudio Desktop, but any editor is absolutely fine but we recommend that your R editor use the same R environment as used by Expert Analytics, which means that R packages installed in your editor will also be available in Expert Analytics. Therefore, take note of the installation path of the R environment of Expert Analytics.

2. In Expert Analytics, follow the menu path **File • Install and Configure R,** and on the
   Configuration tab, you will see a folder, for example *C:\Users\Public\R-3.3.0*. Point
   your R editor to this installation. In RStudio Designer, navigate to **Tools • Global
   Options** and enter the file path for that folder into the **R version** field, as shown in
   Figure 15.26.

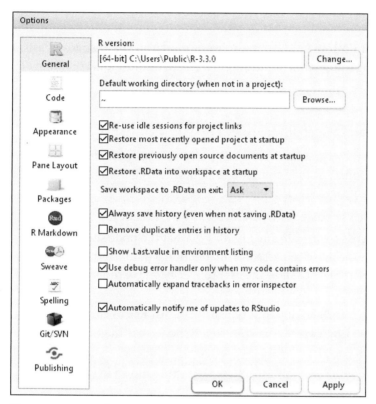

Figure 15.26 Specifying R Version in RStudio Designer

3. To illustrate the next steps, we'll use the ubiquitous iris dataset for creating the initial chart in R. This dataset contains 150 measurements of the petals of three different flower species and is commonly used for introductory purposes in R.
   Download the dataset at *http://archive.ics.uci.edu/ml/datasets/Iris*. The syntax
   shown in Listing 15.1 creates a fairly simple boxplot in your R editor. So far, no component of SAP Predictive Analytics is being used.

```
library(ggplot2)
ggplot (iris, aes_string(x="1", y="Petal.Width"))+
  geom_boxplot() + xlab("") +  ylab("") +
  scale_x_discrete(breaks=NULL) +
  coord_flip()
```

Listing 15.1 Example of R Syntax Used Directly in R Editor

The name of the data frame is `iris`. The column shown in the boxplot is called `Petal.Width`. Changing the column name to `Petal.Length` would show a different column in the plot.

15.6.2   Developing an R Function

For the R syntax to fit into a graphical node in Expert Analytics, you'll need to provide the syntax as an R function that complies with several requirements. The most important requirements include the following:

- The data frame must be passed as a parameter into the function.
- If the user is expected to provide any input as to what the node should carry out, then this information must be passed as an additional parameter into the function. A common example is to allow the user to specify one or more columns from the dataset.
- The function must return an object of type list. This list has to contain a dataset, which can be passed by Expert Analytics to any node that might follow in the chain.
- Rearranging our code accordingly, we obtain the syntax shown in Listing 15.2.

```
myBoxPlot <- function(myData, strColName)
{
library(ggplot2)
myPlot <-ggplot (myData, aes_string(x="1", y=strColName))+
    geom_boxplot() + xlab("") +  ylab(strColName) +
    scale_x_discrete(breaks=NULL) +    coord_flip()
    print(myPlot)
return(list(out=myData))
}
```

Listing 15.2 Example of Rearranged R Syntax as a Parameterized Function

This function takes the dataset as a parameter and returns the same data without modification. A parameter specifies which column should be shown in the boxplot.

Notice that this function is quite generic and does not make any reference to a specific dataset or column. This independence provides the flexibility that the function can be used on rather different datasets and columns.

We can now call this function in R, passing a dataset and the name of the column to plot, as shown in Listing 15.3. We can use different columns from the iris dataset or a completely different dataset.

```
myBoxPlot(iris, "Petal.Length")
myBoxPlot(iris, "Petal.Width")
myBoxPlot(mtcars, "hp")
```

Listing 15.3 Calling the Parameterized Function in an R Editor

15.6.3   Creating an R Extension

The code is now ready for Expert Analytics. You'll create an R extension from the **Predict** tab, which can be accessed only after some data is made available. To begin, follow these steps:

1. Open the analysis saved in Section 15.4. If this analysis is not available, just connect to the data as described in that section. If you do not have an SAP HANA system available with an R server connected to it, you can also connect to a flat file directly, using the source type **Text**.

2. Go to the **Predict** tab, click the plus + sign under the algorithm library, and select **R Extension**. A new window will open where you can name the extension. Enter "Boxplot Single Variable" and select the **Make editable when shared** checkbox. These settings ensure that you can see the underlying R syntax when sharing the component with others. Click **Next**.

3. Copy the function from Section 15.6.2 into the Script Editor. Select **myBoxPlot** from the **Primary Function Name** dropdown. This selection tells the tool which function to call when the node is executed. If you want to enter more complex R code with subfunctions, select the function that should be called initially.

4. Next, select **MyData** from the **Input DataFrame** dropdown. This selection passes the data of the previous node to that variable. In the **Output DataFrame** field, enter "out," which is the name of the variable that contains the output dataset in the list the function is returning. In your own functions, you can specify a different name.

15

Also select the **Show Visualization** checkbox; otherwise, our new chart will not appear. The screen should look like what's shown in Figure 15.27.

Figure 15.27 Creating a New R Extension

> **Note**
>
> We won't discuss any of the other options shown in Figure 15.27 in this simple example. Much more complex requirements can be implemented. When adding a new algorithm to train a model, for example, you could provide two different functions, one for training the model and a second for applying the model. At the end of this section, we'll provide two links for examples to help you get started with more complex extensions.
>
> An R extension can also display multiple plots. Please see the product documentation for such requirements.

5. To continue, click **Next**. If the button is not active yet, click into the code window, which should make the option clickable. You'll see a screen where you can specify,

in the upper section, the data output columns if the output data structure will be different from the input structure. Since we are only creating a plot without changing the data structure, we'll leave the upper section unchanged.

6. In the lower section, notice that the editor shows the function's parameter: strColName. You'll need to configure how this parameter from our function should be presented to the user. The **Property Display Name** option allows you to present the prompt with a meaningful name. Enter "Variable."

7. So that users do not have to type column names manually, select **Column Selector (Single)** as the **Control Type**. Now, the user will be able to select the column to be displayed in the boxplot from a dropdown list.

8. Click **Finish**, and the extension will be created. You'll find the new extension in the library as **EXT Boxplot Single Variable**. Drag the extension onto the analytical chain, right on top of the first node on the left. Configure its settings and select the variable **BALANCE** from the dropdown list as shown in Figure 15.28.

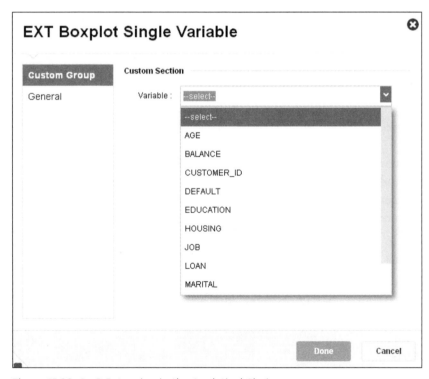

Figure 15.28 An R Extension in the Analytical Chain

Execute the node with **Run up to Here**. Once completed, you'll see a chart on the **Results** tab. Congratulations! You have extended Expert Analytics' functionality! An end user can now leverage the R logic, without being exposed to the complexity of the R syntax.

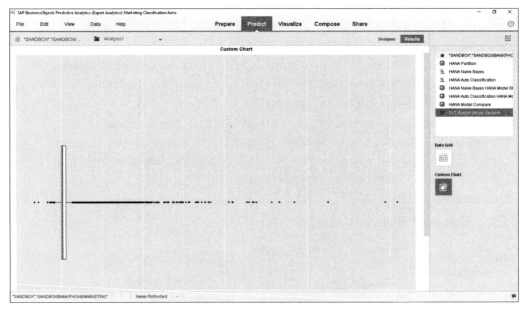

Figure 15.29 Plot from R Extension

These R extensions can also implement much more complex requirements. If you want to implement an algorithm that trains and applies a predictive model, for instance, we've provided a template for logistic regression to help you get started, available for download at *www.sap-press.com/4491*.

- Connection to SAP HANA with R server configured:HANA Logistic Regression as Template.spar
- Connection to any other data source (data gets downloaded, the local R runtime is being used):Logistic Regression as Template.spar

15.7   Summary

You are now familiar with Expert Analytics' workbench. If you have requirements that are unsuitable for an automated approach, which was introduced earlier in the book, you can leverage the flexibility of graphically creating analytical chains. Most algorithms are available when connecting to SAP HANA. However, you can also connect to a broad range of other data sources. If you need to go beyond the standard functionality, then additional logic can be added through R extensions.

15

Chapter 16

Integration into SAP and Third-Party Applications

This chapter explains how SAP Predictive Analytics can be embedded in third-party applications. In this chapter, we'll cover exporting models as third-party code, in-database integration, scripting language, and APIs.

SAP Predictive Analytics, before SAP acquired KXEN, was designed to embed predictive analytics into business processes. This same philosophy has been retained after KXEN was acquired by SAP.

The integration of SAP Predictive Analytics capabilities with SAP HANA applications used to be handled by a component called the Predictive Analytics Integrator. This chapter does not describe using the Predictive Analytics Integrator because it is not performed with SAP Predictive Analytics. Integration with SAP HANA can also be performed using SQL scripts that call the Automated Predictive Library (APL). Again, because this process does not use SAP Predictive Analytics, we will not describe it in this book.

Other methods for integrating SAP Predictive Analytics into your business processes are as follows: exporting models as third-party code, in-database integration, scripting language, and APIs. While, this chapter is not a course on scripting and APIs, we'll provide you with a basic overview that can be further developed in more advanced, dedicated courses.

16.1 Exporting Models as Third-Party Code

Models built with Automated Analytics (except for time series forecasting models) are fully expressible in programming languages. Therefore, the ability to transform models into third-party code to be executed outside of the application (if the right input data has been fed into this code), has been a long-standing capability that's been enriched over time and is still evolving.

This functionality is provided in the modeler, once the model has been built. To access the modeler, follow the menu path **Save/Export • Generate Source Code**. The screen shown in Figure 16.1 will open.

Figure 16.1 Generating Code

For this example, we'll use the census dataset available for download on this book's website at *www.sap-press.com/4491*. First, if several models are built in parallel, the right model must be chosen by selecting the target to be used. Then, the **Information to be generated** must be chosen. For classification, your options are **Score**, **Error bar**, or **Probability**. **Value** and **Error** are your options for regression, and **Segment value**, for clustering. The **Code Type** is then set, which defines SQL codes for various databases, such as the following:

- SAP HANA
- SAP IQ
- SAP Vora
- Oracle
- IBM DB2 and Netezza
- Teradata
- Microsoft SQL Server
- HP Vertica
- PostGreSQL
- HIVE and Spark SQL

A list of supported databases and their versions is available in the Product Availability Matrix (PAM). SQL code in ANSI format can also be generated. CCL code for SAP HANA smart data streaming is provided.

User-defined functions (UDFs) for several databases are also available. UDFs are compiled in databases and called in SQL statements, thus facilitating integration. SAP HANA, SAP IQ, Oracle, Teradata, and IBM DB2 UDFs can be generated. Other codes are also available, such as Awk, C, C++, PMML, Java, JavaScript (HTML), SAS, and VB.

Scorecards can also be exported to HTML format with detailed equations for each variable.

Once you click **Generate**, the code is written into a file (or into a database by selecting a target database as a folder). The generated code can be viewed in the interface but not edited.

You'll be prompted for the name of the input table and the key of the input table (except for .csv export), as shown in Figure 16.2.

Figure 16.2 Entering Dataset and Key

Listing 16.1 shows sample code to illustrate its structure. This code generates probabilities using a classification model. If you create a model corresponding to the census dataset with rr_class as the target, you will get this code, which is divided in two parts: the score computation and the probability computation.

```
SELECT $Key, "rr_class", CAST( (CASE
WHEN "rr_class" < -2.045621060666e0 THEN 0.0e0
WHEN "rr_class" <= -5.466210477908e-1 THEN 0.0e0
WHEN "rr_class" <= -5.456210606654e-1 THEN ( 1.39588620152e-3*"rr_class"+
7.63020778073e-4 )
...
WHEN "rr_class" <= 4.652748985038e-1 THEN ( 1.889654885587e2*"rr_class"-
8.696771525781e1 )
WHEN "rr_class" <= 9.272834616826e-1 THEN ( 1.893439871891e-4*"rr_class"+
```

```
9.530951548639e-1 )
WHEN "rr_class" <= 9.282834617301e-1 THEN  ( 8.747853931279e-2*"rr_class"+
8.721533276549e-1 )
WHEN "rr_class" > 9.282834617291e-1 THEN 9.533582089552e-1
ELSE 9.533582089552e-1
END) AS DOUBLE )
AS PROBA0
```

Listing 16.1 Example Code

Listing 16.1 corresponds to the probability calculation. We removed some parts, but the structure involves each band of a score having a regression that provides the probability value. The bands of scores correspond by default to bins of roughly 5% of the population ordered by increasing score. This calculation uses rr_class, computed in the second part of the code, which corresponds to the score (see Chapter 6, Section 6.5.1, on regressions).

Listing 16.2 corresponds to the score calculation, which uses each category/band of values of the variables to calculate its score value. Their sum provides the score, which is then fed into the probability computation.

```
FROM
(
SELECT $Key,
(
 ( CAST( (CASE
WHEN ( "age" IS NULL ) THEN 1.308700553736e-2
WHEN "age" <= 1.7e1 THEN -9.061039302303e-2
WHEN "age" <= 1.899800002575e1 THEN  ( 4.776918189201e-4*"age"-
9.873115394457e-2 )
WHEN "age" <= 1.9e1 THEN  ( 5.34884620677e-1*"age"-1.025139400215e1 )
WHEN "age" <= 2.168924224032e1 THEN  ( 8.751272307016e-4*"age"-
1.052136266709e-1 )
...
WHEN "hours-per-week" <= 5.883355459675e1 THEN  ( -1.48815405563e-3*
"hours-per-week"+1.288783536937e-1 )
WHEN "hours-per-week" <= 6.4e1 THEN  ( -1.48815405563e-3*"hours-per-week"+
1.288783536929e-1 )
WHEN "hours-per-week" <= 6.403500000166e1 THEN  ( -2.619672891509e-1*
"hours-per-week"+1.679954299979e1 )
WHEN "hours-per-week" <= 9.9e1 THEN  ( 2.884935451665e-4*"hours-per-week"+
```

```
5.993954411679e-3 )
WHEN "hours-per-week" > 9.9e1 THEN 3.455481538316e-2
ELSE 3.455481538316e-2
END) AS DOUBLE) )
) AS "rr_class" FROM $Dataset
) TMPTABLE0
```

Listing 16.2 Score Calculation

Under **Advanced Settings** (see Figure 16.3), you can set export parameters, such as whether to use Unicode, whether to generate all variables or only the ones used by the model, and which separator to use.

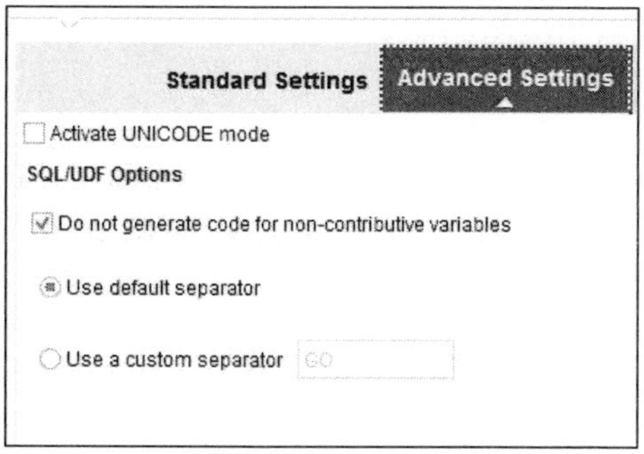

Figure 16.3 Advanced Settings

16.2   In-Database Integration

In SAP Predictive Analytics, in-database integration is only available if a database is the data source and the **In-Database Apply** option has been checked under **Apply Settings**. In the background, SAP Predictive Analytics will generate the SQL code for the database it is connected to. The code is wrapped up with table creation/update and pushed to the database through ODBC. The code is executed in the database, and results are written into the table. This process is also triggered by the Predictive Factory when batch processing is scheduled.

You can also directly integrate code in a database, but you'll have to export the right code (SQL or UDF). SQL code can be transformed, for example, into a database view that would execute when called in an SQL statement. In the same way, a UDF can be created in a database and executed in an SQL statement.

When using the second integration path, we must be careful to provide the right input into the UDF. Of course, these inputs are handled for the user when piloted by SAP Predictive Analytics. Using the **In-Database Apply** option on batches of models is much easier than integrating code yourself.

16.3 Scripting

SAP Predictive Analytics' scripting capabilities allow you to run scripts for any task that can be run with the software. This functionality offers even more parameters than the user interface does. In the following sections, we'll run through an example of how scripting can be used in SAP Predictive Analytics. Scripts can be launched from the Predictive Factory as external executables to broaden the capabilities of the Predictive Factory.

16.3.1 Getting Started

All information about the model is stored in SAP Predictive Analytics as a parameter tree. To access the parameter tree, navigate to **Preferences • General** and then select the **Display the Parameter Tree** checkbox as shown in Figure 16.4. Then, a new entry, **Model Parameters**, is available in the **Display** tab in the modeler. The Automated Analytics client needs to be restarted to access the parameter tree.

Figure 16.4 Displaying the Parameter Tree

The parameters displayed in the parameter tree (see Figure 16.5) correspond to both the settings for the model and the results. You set the parameters with a `changeParameter` command and to get the results with a `getParameter` command.

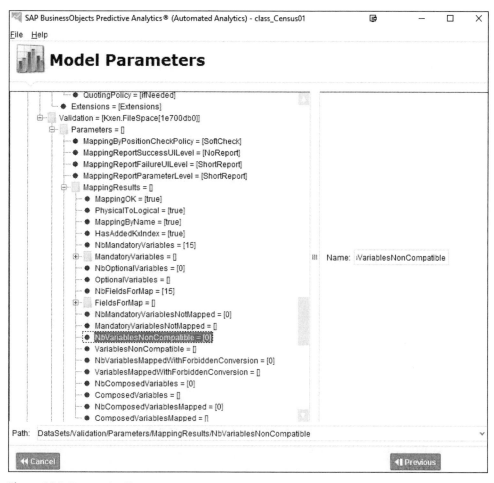

Figure 16.5 Parameter Tree

We'll concentrate on model building and deployment using the Census example we mentioned earlier. When a model is built or applied to a dataset, you can export the script corresponding to its training by following the menu path **Save/Export • Export KxShell Script**.

The destination and name of the **Folder** and **File** must be set (Figure 16.6).

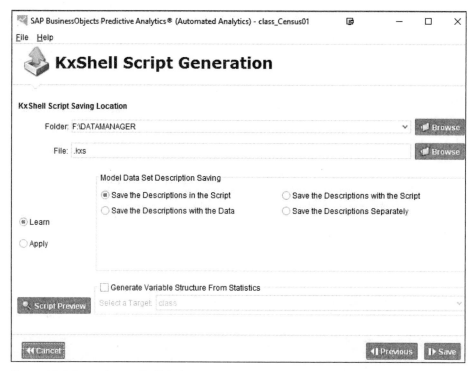

Figure 16.6 Exporting KxShell Script

16.3.2   KxShell Script

The generated code looks similar to what's shown in Listing 16.3. The first block, where each line starts with default, defines default parameters, such as database user and password, data source, etc.

```
#
# KxShell Script
# generated on 2017-09-26 09:14:57
# by SAP BusinessObjects Predictive Analytics® 3.2.0
#

set echo on
set utf8in on
```

```
default STORE_USER ""
default STORE_PWD ""
default DESC_USER ""
default DESC_PWD ""
#Declaring the 'TRAINING' store and space
default TRAINING_STORE_TYPE "Kxen.FileStore"
default TRAINING_STORE_NAME "../../../Samples/Census"
default TRAINING_STORE_USER $STORE_USER
default TRAINING_STORE_PWD $STORE_PWD
default TRAINING_STORE_ALIAS myTrainingStore
default TRAINING_SPACE "Census01.csv"
default TRAINING_SEED 1960

default MODEL_SAVE_STORE_TYPE "Kxen.FileStore"
default MODEL_SAVE_STORE_NAME "."
default MODEL_SAVE_STORE_USER ""
default MODEL_SAVE_STORE_PWD ""
default MODEL_SAVE_NAME "class_Census01"
default MODEL_SAVE_SPACE "class_Census01.kxen"
default MODEL_SAVE_COMMENT "The model 'class_Census01' has been saved"
```

Listing 16.3 Defining Default Parameters

Then, the parameters of the models are set in the createModel section, as shown in
Listing 16.4.

```
createModel Kxen.SimpleModel m
m.getParameter ""
m.changeParameter Parameters/CutTrainingPolicy "random with no test"
if $FORCE_CODINGSTRATEGY ne "" then m.changeParameter Parameters/
CodingStrategy "9.0.1"
m.setName "class_Census01"
m.validateParameter

m.bind protocol Default p
p.getParameter ""
p.changeParameter "Parameters/StrangeValueLevel" "12"
p.changeParameter "Parameters/SmallTargetThreshold" "5"
p.changeParameter "Parameters/CopyTarget" "true"
p.changeParameter "Parameters/UseDateCoder" "true"
```

```
p.changeParameter "Parameters/ApplyInDataBase" "true"
p.changeParameter "Parameters/ModellingInDataBase" "false"
p.changeParameter "Parameters/IDBAFallbackToRegularApply" "true"
p.changeParameter "Parameters/SoftMode" "true"
p.changeParameter "Parameters/WeightInformation" ""
p.validateParameter
delete p

m.pushTransformInProtocol Default Kxen.RobustRegression
m.pushTransformInProtocol Default Kxen.ConsistentCoder

-delete $TRAINING_STORE_ALIAS
m.openNewStore $TRAINING_STORE_TYPE $TRAINING_STORE_NAME $TRAINING_STORE_
USER $TRAINING_STORE_PWD $TRAINING_STORE_ALIAS
m.newDataSet Training $TRAINING_SPACE

bind m DataSet Training t
t.getParameter ""
t.changeParameter Parameters/RandomSeed $TRAINING_SEED
t.changeParameter Parameters/RandomMax 1.0
t.changeParameter Parameters/RandomMin 0.0
t.changeParameter Parameters/SkippedRows 0
t.changeParameter Parameters/LastRow 0
t.changeParameter Parameters/HeaderLines 1
t.changeParameter Parameters/Locale ""
t.validateParameter
delete t
bind m DataSet Training s
s.startDescription
s.addVariableDesc "age" number continuous 0 0 "" "" ""
s.addVariableDesc "workclass" string nominal 0 0 "?" "" ""
s.addVariableDesc "fnlwgt" number continuous 0 0 "" "" ""
s.addVariableDesc "education" string nominal 0 0 "" "" ""
s.addVariableDesc "education-num" number ordinal 0 0 "" "" ""
s.addVariableDesc "marital-status" string nominal 0 0 "" "" ""
s.addVariableDesc "occupation" string nominal 0 0 "?" "" ""
s.addVariableDesc "relationship" string nominal 0 0 "" "" ""
s.addVariableDesc "race" string nominal 0 0 "" "" ""
s.addVariableDesc "sex" string nominal 0 0 "" "" ""
```

```
s.addVariableDesc "capital-gain" number continuous 0 0 "99999" "" ""
s.addVariableDesc "capital-loss" number continuous 0 0 "" "" ""
s.addVariableDesc "hours-per-week" number continuous 0 0 "" "" ""
s.addVariableDesc "native-country" string nominal 0 0 "?" "" ""
s.addVariableDesc "class" number nominal 0 0 "" "" ""
s.endDescription
delete s


m.checkMode learn


m.bind protocol Default p
p.getParameter ""
p.changeParameter "Variables/relationship/Role" input
p.changeParameter "Variables/relationship/UserEnableCompress" true
p.changeParameter "Variables/race/Role" input
p.changeParameter "Variables/race/UserEnableCompress" true
p.changeParameter "Variables/education/Role" input
p.changeParameter "Variables/education/UserEnableCompress" true
p.changeParameter "Variables/hours-per-week/Role" input
p.changeParameter "Variables/hours-per-week/UserBandCount" 20
p.changeParameter "Variables/hours-per-week/UserEnableCompress" true
p.changeParameter "Variables/education-num/Role" input
p.changeParameter "Variables/education-num/UserBandCount" 20
p.changeParameter "Variables/education-num/UserEnableCompress" true
p.changeParameter "Variables/sex/Role" input
p.changeParameter "Variables/sex/UserEnableCompress" true
p.changeParameter "Variables/workclass/Role" input
p.changeParameter "Variables/workclass/UserEnableCompress" true
p.changeParameter "Variables/capital-loss/Role" input
p.changeParameter "Variables/capital-loss/UserBandCount" 20
p.changeParameter "Variables/capital-loss/UserEnableCompress" true
p.changeParameter "Variables/class/Role" target
p.changeParameter "Variables/class/TargetKey" 1
p.changeParameter "Variables/class/UserEnableCompress" true
p.changeParameter "Variables/age/Role" input
p.changeParameter "Variables/age/UserBandCount" 20
p.changeParameter "Variables/age/UserEnableCompress" true
p.changeParameter "Variables/capital-gain/Role" input
p.changeParameter "Variables/capital-gain/UserBandCount" 20
```

16

```
p.changeParameter "Variables/capital-gain/UserEnableCompress" true
p.changeParameter "Variables/occupation/Role" input
p.changeParameter "Variables/occupation/UserEnableCompress" true
p.changeParameter "Variables/fnlwgt/Role" input
p.changeParameter "Variables/fnlwgt/UserBandCount" 20
p.changeParameter "Variables/fnlwgt/UserEnableCompress" true
p.changeParameter "Variables/marital-status/Role" input
p.changeParameter "Variables/marital-status/UserEnableCompress" true
p.changeParameter "Variables/native-country/Role" input
p.changeParameter "Variables/native-country/UserEnableCompress" true
p.validateParameter
delete p

m.bind TransformInProtocol Default 0 t
t.getParameter ""
t.changeParameter Parameters/Order 1
t.changeParameter Parameters/VariableExclusionSettings/ExcludeSmallKR System
t.changeParameter Parameters/MaximumKeptCorrelations 1024
t.changeParameter Parameters/LowerBound 0.5
t.changeParameter Parameters/ContinuousEncode true
t.changeParameter Parameters/K2RMode "Standard Mode"
t.changeParameter Parameters/RiskMode false
t.changeParameter Parameters/RiskMode/PDO 15
t.changeParameter Parameters/RiskMode/GBO 9
t.changeParameter Parameters/RiskMode/RiskScore 615
t.changeParameter Parameters/RiskMode/RiskFitting Frequency_Based
t.changeParameter Parameters/RiskMode/RiskFitting/NbPDO 2
t.changeParameter Parameters/RiskMode/RiskFitting/MinCumulatedFrequency 0.15
t.changeParameter Parameters/RiskMode/RiskFitting/UseWeights true
t.changeParameter Parameters/Strategy WithOriginalTargetEncoding
t.changeParameter Parameters/DecisionTreeMode false
t.changeParameter Parameters/ScoreUserBoundCount 20
t.changeParameter Parameters/VariableSelection true
t.changeParameter Parameters/VariableSelection/DumpIntermediateSteps true
t.changeParameter Parameters/VariableSelection/SelectionMode/
Mode ContributionBased
t.changeParameter Parameters/VariableSelection/SelectionMode/
NbVariableRemovedByStep 1
t.changeParameter Parameters/VariableSelection/SelectionMode/
```

```
PercentageContrib 0.95
t.changeParameter Parameters/VariableSelection/StopCriteria/
QualityCriteria KiKr
t.changeParameter Parameters/VariableSelection/StopCriteria/
MinNbOfFinalVariables 1
t.changeParameter Parameters/VariableSelection/StopCriteria/
MaxNbOfFinalVariables -1
t.changeParameter Parameters/VariableSelection/StopCriteria/
FastVariableUpperBoundSelection true
t.changeParameter Parameters/VariableSelection/StopCriteria/QualityBar 0.05
t.changeParameter Parameters/VariableSelection/StopCriteria/
SelectBestIteration true

# Gain Chart Settings
t.changeParameter Parameters/GainChartConfig/Learn false
t.validateParameter
delete t

m.bind TransformInProtocol Default 1 t
t.getParameter ""
t.changeParameter Parameters/Compress true
t.validateParameter
delete t
```

Listing 16.4 Model Parameters

The model is then trained, using the code in Listing 16.5.

```
m.sendMode learn

m.openNewStore $MODEL_SAVE_STORE_TYPE $MODEL_SAVE_STORE_NAME $MODEL_SAVE_
STORE_USER $MODEL_SAVE_STORE_PWD
m.saveModel $MODEL_SAVE_SPACE $MODEL_SAVE_COMMENT $MODEL_SAVE_NAME
print Model class_Census01 has been saved.
delete m

exit
```

Listing 16.5 Training and Saving the Model

All parameters of the script can be defined by the user.

16.3.3   Executing Scripts

The engine used to execute scripts is located in *C:\Program Files\SAP BusinessObjects Predictive Analytics\Server\EXE\Clients\CPP* by default. To execute the script, you'll need to run *KxShell.exe*. If you run *KxShell.exe* in the Windows command prompt, you'll see the screen shown in Figure 16.7.

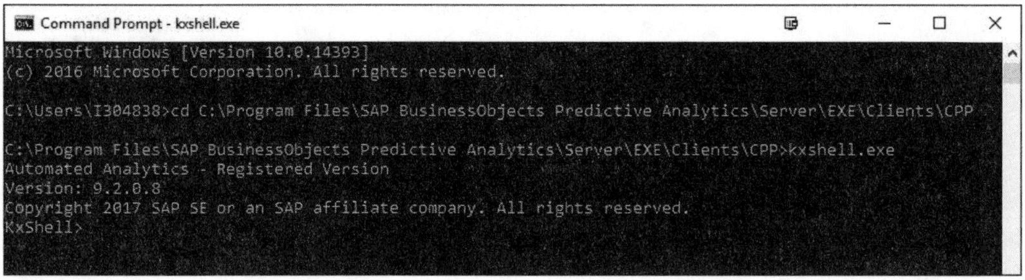

Figure 16.7 Executing KxShell.exe

Now, you can write commands. However, the KxShell engine is not usually used in this way. We'll launch the KxShell engine and then feed it the following script (which can be exported from the model training as shown in Section 16.3.1): *C:\Program Files\SAP BusinessObjects Predictive Analytics\Server\EXE\Clients\CPP>kxshell.exe script.kxs.* This script will work if *script.kxs* was saved in this file path.

You can change the model settings to change model training. Add -DPARAMETERNAME = "value", where PARAMETERNAME is the name of the parameter that needs to be changed and "value" is the new value passed to the script.

If exporting a model built using the Data Manager, the parameters of the Data Manager are exposed. Of course, KxTimeStamp is one. If prompts are set to further define the dataset, they are also exposed. For example if we want to predict a likelihood to purchase by categories of products and if a prompt is used to define which category in the Data Manager, then you can run the script with the different prompt values to create all the required models. As a result, the command kxshell.exe script.kxs -DPARAMETER = "value" is included into a loop where the value of the parameter is pushed to the script.

We've only provided a glimpse of all that can be achieved using scripts. Formal training is required to go further.

16.3.4 APIs

Automated Analytics in SAP Predictive Analytics includes a C++ API and a Java API. How you integrate with either API depends on the software you want to use, and therefore, we won't be able to describe this activity in detail.

Programming an API follows the same principles as scripting. You'll define model parameters in the parameter tree and get these parameters once the model has been trained.

Using APIs is oriented towards integrating external applications from third-party vendors and specific training is available from third-party partners.

16.4 Summary

This chapter covers how to integrate SAP Predictive Analytics by describing how models can be exported as third-party code that can then be integrated into a database or into software. We also showed you how this code can be used when integrating SAP Predictive Analytics to relational databases. This mechanism is used by the Predictive Factory. Finally, we described the principles behind scripting, how to export scripts, and the available APIs.

16

Chapter 17
Hints, Tips, and Best Practices

In this chapter, we've collected further information that we think will be useful for you to get the most out of SAP Predictive Analytics. Building on the earlier chapters, we hope to give you further confidence when implementing your own predictive projects.

We hope that this book helps you become confident in improving your business processes through SAP Predictive Analytics. Following the CRISP-DM approach, as described in Chapter 4, you can define use cases, prepare the data, produce predictive models, and put your predictions into productive use.

However, the best understanding of any process or tool comes through experience, which you will build up with your own projects. We hope that the experiences and best practices we share in this chapter will help you become truly comfortable and productive with SAP Predictive Analytics.

In this chapter, we'll provide further advice on improving the quality of your models, and we'll point you to additional resources that we think might come in handy.

17.1 Improving Predictive Model Quality

You have many options to improve the predictive quality of a model. Some concepts might be common and obvious; others might be less well known and easily overlooked. This section gives an overview of which options are the most important to consider.

17.1.1 Data Quality

Before looking at the specifics of improving the quality of a predictive model, let's remember the basics. It may seem obvious, but the better the quality of the data you feed into a predictive model, the better the chance of getting a high-quality model. Consider putting a data quality process into place to improve the data quality of your source systems. In a customer relationship management (CRM) system, perhaps the addresses of all current contacts in your system are validated and corrected if needed. SAP Data Services can help in this instance, but other tools are also available. Try not to make data quality processes just one-off activities; new data added to the CRM system should also be validated. In our example, the moment a new person is added to the CRM, their postal address should be validated and corrected, or data quality will deteriorate over time.

17.1.2   Data Description

The automated approach of creating predictive models can suggest data descriptions, which is convenient. However, we recommend that you get into the habit of verifying the suggested descriptions and adjust where needed. Your business understanding of the data is invaluable. Having these settings incorrect can hold back your predictive model. Please see Chapter 6 for more information on the correct settings.

17.1.3   Adding Predictors

To improve the predictive power (KI) of your model, try enriching your dataset with additional predictors. Adding such additional information for each entity can help your predictive model be more accurate. For example, in a marketing scenario where you want to predict a person's affinity for a specific product, think about what additional information could be relevant. For instance, try adding more columns that describe the product you want to promote or try adding additional information about the prospect.

Let's look at some common options to add new predictors to your project. These predictors can be obtained by enriching your dataset with new sources or by deriving new predictors out of the data that is already available.

Leveraging Additional Tables and Data Sources

Additional predictors can come from completely new data sources, e.g., from your call centers. How often did a person contact you in the past 12 months? What were the reasons for the calls? What were the outcomes? This kind of information can help hone your model.

The data sources you are already using may also hold further information that your predictive model does not yet use. A good practice is to check if further tables with relevant information can be used.

Deriving Additional Predictors

You should also consider creating new predictors out of already existing information. The Data Manager functionality introduced in Chapter 14 efficiently creates new predictors out of existing data. You might store a customer's sales history, for instance, and then use Data Manager to create columns such as the following:

- Previous year's revenue
- Revenue 2 years ago
- Change in revenue between the last 2 years

Such predictors can be created for many different time frames and individually for each product segment you sell. With just a few clicks, you can create hundreds of such predictors. The automated approach is designed to handle wide datasets with tens of thousands of predictors. Columns that do not contain values are discarded, but one or more of these columns might just hold important information for your predictive model.

17.1.4 Composite Variables

Imagine you are selling a product that sells well for younger customers in one region but sells better with older customers in another region. The value of one predictor (region) has an impact on how another variable (age) relates to the behavior we want to forecast. A single model will struggle to identify this particular combination.

When using SAP Predictive Analytics client or desktop, you can address such scenarios with composite variables.

A composite variable combines the values of one predictor variable with the values of another variable, thereby creating a more granular view. For instance, the variable might serve as a bucket representing German customers in their 30s and French customers in their 30s. This composite variable is then considered as additional predictor in the model finding phase. The model can now consider whether the combination of region and age has a stronger impact than when considering age and region separately.

Composite variables are created in the **Data Description** of Automated Analytics, as shown in Figure 17.1.

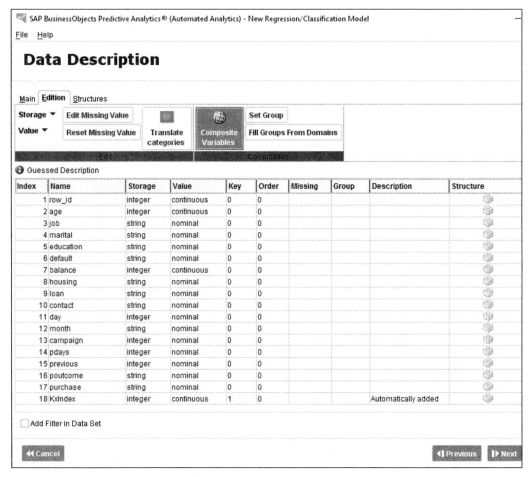

Figure 17.1 Composite Variables

1. Click the **Composite Variables** button. An empty window will open, as no composite variables have been declared yet.

2. Click on **Add**.

3. To create a single composite variable, set the **Type** to **Cross**.

4. Move the variables you want to combine to the right-hand side. You can select more than two columns, but be cautious. If too many variables are combined, the segments become too specific, and you might not have enough data for the model to find any particular pattern.

5. Give the new variable a name as shown in Figure 17.2 and then click **OK**.

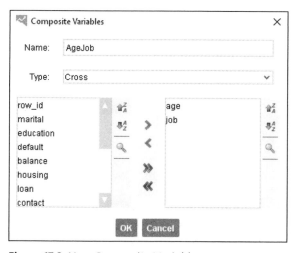

Figure 17.2 New Composite Variable

The composite variable has been created but will not show up as an additional line in the **Data Description** window. If you need to make any changes to the variable, or if you want to create further composite variables, just click the **Composite Variables** button.

When specifying variables for your predictive model, your composite variables will appear on the left-hand side as additional explanatory variables, as shown in Figure 17.3.

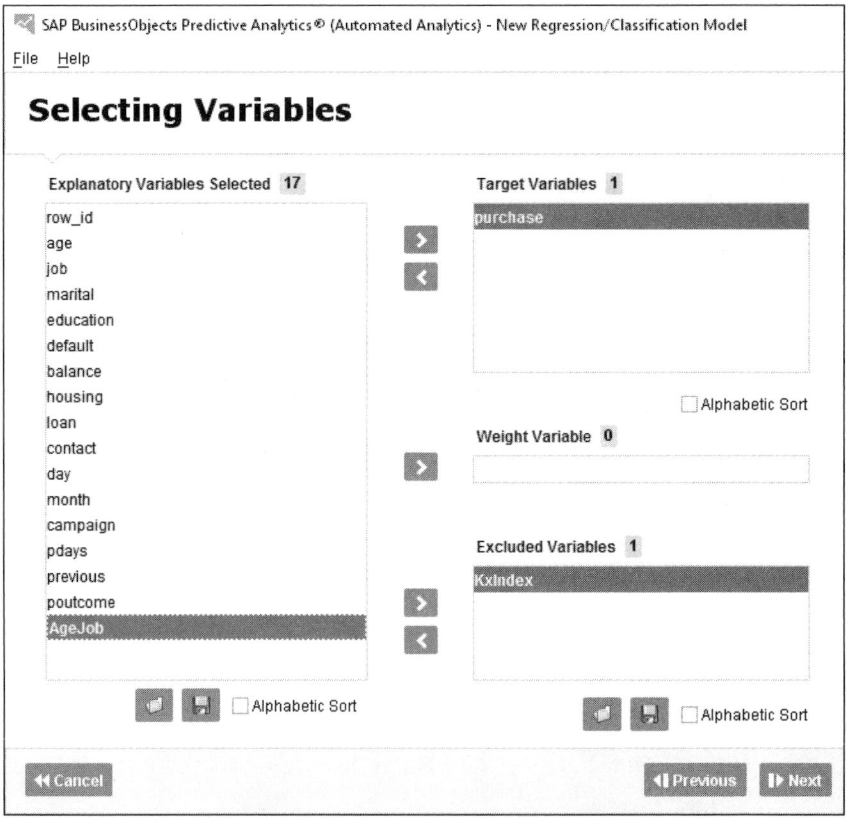

Figure 17.3 Selecting Variables

If you want to create many composite variables, you don't have to create each one manually as we just described. Imagine you have 5 variables, and you want to create composite variables for all possible pairs, so all combinations of 2 different variables, resulting in 10 different combinations. To create these composite variables efficiently, we can combine the concept of grouping variables with the mass production of composite variables, by following these steps:

1. In the **Data Description** window, highlight 5 variables, click **Set Group**, give the group a name, and press **OK**.

2. Now, create a new composite variable, but this time set the **Type** to **Mass Cross** and choose the newly created group as both **First Set** and **Second Set**, similar to the screen shown in Figure 17.4.

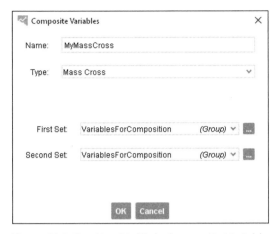

Figure 17.4 Creating Multiple Composite Variables

3. Click **OK** and the 10 different combinations of composite variables will be created.

Predictions as Predictors

The output of one prediction can be valuable input as a predictor for another model. So consider leveraging predictions that might already exist or create additional predictions. For example, try clustering your customers before predicting their behavior. The cluster a person has been assigned to might help a purchasing affinity model.

Feel free to create different clustering models as you can cluster your customers in many different ways. Automated clustering supports your clustering efforts through targeted clustering. Before clustering, the data can be encoded towards a specific target variable, allowing you to cluster the same group of customers, for instance, by the amount spent last year, by the number of different products purchased, or by the number of days since their last purchase from you.

Similarly, the output of a Social Network Analysis can produce many different variables that often improve predictive models.

Increased Polynomial Degree

The polynomial degree specifies whether a predictor variable is fed into the model without additional transformations (degree of 1) or whether exponentiated transformations are also considered as predictors (degree greater than 1).

By default, a polynomial degree of 1 is used in Automated Analytics. Set the polynomial degree to 2, and additional predictor variables are created by multiplying each input variable with every other single input variable, including itself. Similarly, with higher polynomial degrees, further variables exponentiated at a higher order are added.

The polynomial degree can be set in Automated Analytics for classification and regression modules. After selecting your variables, you'll see the **Summary of Modeling Parameters**, where you can go into the **Advanced Model Parameters** area to change the **Polynomial Degree**.

17.1.5   Adding Rows of Data

To improve predictive confidence (KR), try enriching rows of data to your dataset, particularly rows that contain the behavior you are trying to predict. A good rule of thumb is that 1,000 positive cases are needed to reliably create a model in Automated Analytics (assuming you have at least as many negative cases). Often, smaller numbers can suffice, however, especially when forecasting the behavior of machines or anything nonhuman. However, the more positive cases you have in the dataset, the better for your predictive confidence.

If you simply cannot obtain further positive cases for your predictive model, try leveraging the compounding concept introduced in Chapter 14. This concept creates a *union* of multiple datasets that address the same business question over a longer time period, thereby increasing the number of positive cases.

Alternatively, you can try adjusting the business question you are addressing; just make sure the new business question can still deliver the required business value. When predicting which customer will buy a product next month, you'll train the model on customers who purchased the product in the previous month. The number of positive cases can be increased by predicting who will purchase the product in the next 3 months, thus giving you a longer historical time frame (3 months instead of 1 month) with more positive cases to learn from.

17.1.6   Reducing the Historical Period

To increase the quality of a time series forecast, one apparent option is to try to increase the number of predictor variables. To forecast the demand of a product, the weather or other factors may increase accuracy. What may be less obvious, however, is that you can also try reducing the length of historical time frame from which you learn. If the structure of a time series has changed during the past, reducing the history can remove these now irrelevant patterns. The forecast can therefore become more accurate.

17.1.7 Uniform Target Encoding

This option is only applicable when carrying out an automated regression in the Automated Analytics interface on Windows but can be particularly useful if your target variable does not have a uniform distribution.

When activating the option **Uniform target encoding** in the **Advanced Model Parameters**, the following occurs:

- The models are not trained on the original target variable but on an encoded version, which is closer to a uniform distribution.
- After the model has been found and scores are forecasted, these scores are transformed back to the original distribution.

17.1.8 Segmented Modeling

The overall quality of the predictions might be improved by leveraging multiple individual models, as opposed to one model that tries to address everything. Sticking to our marketing example of promoting a product, you might have created one predictive model. Especially if you have a dataset with many positive cases, you can try targeting specific subsets of your customer base with dedicated models. If the purchasing behavior of customers in two geographical regions is totally different, for example, try creating individual models for each region to capture these specifics.

In the Predictive Factory, segmented time series can be created with a few clicks. Other models can be created either manually or using KxScript for automated models.

17.1.9 Changing the Modeling Approach

Sometimes a business question can be addressed with different predictive approaches. Forecasting the demand of a product in 3 months' time, for instance, can be done with time series forecasting or with a regression. While the time series approach may be

17

more common, experimenting with a regression or even a mix of both approaches can be worthwhile. Both forecasts could be produced and averaged. Be creative!

17.2   Additional Resources

Hopefully, this book can continue to serve as a valuable resource to help you get the most out of SAP Predictive Analytics. So, we'd also like to point out some additional useful resources, many of which we ourselves have consulted in the past.

17.2.1   SAP Community and Newsletter

The SAP Community for SAP Predictive Analytics contains a wealth of information, blogs, tutorials, videos, etc., and can be found at *https://www.sap.com/community/topic/predictive-analytics.html*.

You'll also find a forum where you can browse discussions, post new questions, or even answer open questions. The community is moderated and monitored by SAP's product group, giving you a direct channel for all your technical questions.

To ask a question, just click on **Actions** on the top right and choose **Ask a Question**. To ensure that your question shows up in the right community, set the primary tag of your question to **SAP Predictive Analytics**.

Most of following items listed in this chapter can also be opened directly from that community.

SAP also publishes a newsletter on SAP Predictive Analytics. To subscribe, just go to *https://www.sap.com/cmp/nl/predictive-analytics-newsletter/index.html*.

17.2.2   Product Documentation and Product Availability Matrix

If you search for "SAP Predictive Analytics" on *https://help.sap.com/*, you'll find a broad range of documentation, well beyond conventional help files, as shown in Figure 17.5. Be sure to have the correct product version selected on that site on the top right-hand side.

The supported environments for SAP Predictive Analytics are documented in the Product Availability Matrix (PAM). Find the latest version by searching for the product name at *http://support.sap.com/pam*.

> **Note**
>
> All product roadmaps are shared by SAP at *http://go.sap.com/solution/roadmaps.html.*

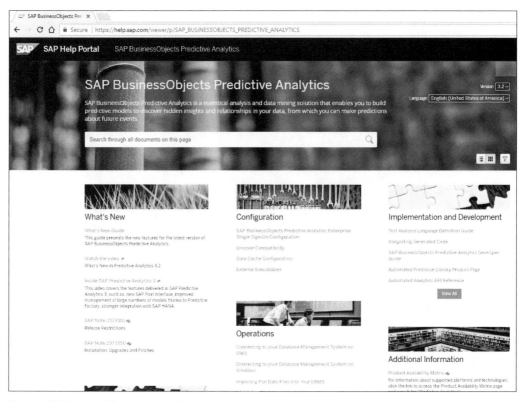

Figure 17.5 Product Documentation

17.2.3   Tutorials and Webinars

Many video tutorials from SAP about SAP Predictive Analytics are available at *http://bit.ly/2z95SRO.*

On the same page, you'll also find a link to a monthly webinar series on SAP Predictive Analytics. You can register for upcoming sessions or view recordings and slides from past webinars.

17.2.4   SAP Notes

A great deal of detailed information about SAP Predictive Analytics is documented in SAP Notes and related documents. Try the search engine at *https://support.sap.com/en/index.html*. The most relevant component for SAP Predictive Analytics is BI-RA-PA.

Some SAP Notes that we believe are particularly important and helpful include the following:

- SAP Note 2373381: SAP Predictive Analytics 3.2 Release Restrictions
- SAP Note 2373350: SAP Predictive Analytics 3.2: Installation, Upgrades, and Patches
- SAP Note 2426527: SAP Predictive Analytics License Key Not Working As Intended

17.3   Summary

By now, you're familiar with the most important best practices of creating strong predictive models with SAP Predictive Analytics. Consider coming back to this chapter once in a while, just as a reminder of these best practices. Some points might seem clear when reading them but might still slip your mind in the middle of the project.

We're almost at the end of this book, but your journey with SAP Predictive Analytics is just starting. In the following chapter, the conclusion, we'll do a brief recap of what we covered in this book and preview what might be next for SAP Predictive Analytics.

Chapter 18
Conclusion

Now that we're at the end, let's take a quick moment to see what you've learned from the book (at least we hope!), what the future of SAP Predictive Analytics could look like, and where to go from here.

18.1 Lessons Learned

In the first part of the book, you learned what predictive analysis is and how to successfully drive a predictive project; our goal was to ensure you have a broad understanding of the requirements, the benefits, and the structure of predictive projects.

You then learned, in the following sections, how to put a project into practice using the SAP Predictive Analytics suite: the SAP Predictive Analytics server and Predictive Factory components for building models, managing the lifecycle of a project, and mass producing your projects as well as the automated client components for data preparation, clustering, and Social Network Analysis.

Finally, you discovered some advanced uses of the solution for highly customized projects and learned methods for embedding your models into external applications.

All throughout the book, our goal was to show you what to do next to avoid getting lost in a workflow. Hopefully, you are now independent and confident in your own projects.

18.2 The Future of SAP Predictive Analytics

SAP Predictive Analytics is a continually evolving solution. As we mentioned, its general purpose is to ensure companies get the predictive results they need to improve their business processes. Based on where the market and customer expectations are moving (more simplicity, cloud-based services, performance, big data), we should

18

expect two sets of enhancements: making the user experience simpler and making the solution faster and less complex to deploy and administer.

On user experience, we will probably see an evolution towards a more cloud-based functionality so that the solution can be used in a software-as-a-service model to simplify or even do away with installation requirements. User interfaces will probably move more to browser-based access with no thick clients, and integration within other SAP solutions should expand. You can already use SAP Predictive Analytics functionality embedded in SAP Analytics Cloud and other solutions seamlessly; you simply benefit from this integration. SAP Predictive Analytics will continue as a standalone solution, but its technology might also be embedded as a component in other applications with their own dedicated and simplified interfaces.

Consolidating all functionalities is a great opportunity to reinforce the core benefits of the solution. According to public information, the SAP Predictive Analytics roadmap aims for the unification of all the data preparation, model creation, and model management capabilities into a single platform, with a single user interface. For expert needs, a new interface called Predictive Composer seems to be in the works.

For a detailed list of functionalities under consideration by the development team at SAP, refer to the official SAP roadmap at *http://go.sap.com/solution/roadmaps.html*.

18.3   Next Steps

Now, it's time for you to play with the solution by yourself. When you install the Automated Analytics desktop component, you'll have a great deal of sample data that you can use to run some workflows and better understand how the solution functions. If possible, start using the solution on your own data so that you get an immediate (and possibly actionable) business understanding of the results. You can first try answering easy questions, for instance, using a basic time series analysis or a simple classification exercise, and then, when you are confident, you can start using all the possible functionalities and enhance your data with the Data Manager.

Well, we are at the end of this book and wish you success in your predictive projects—now go out and have fun with SAP Predictive Analytics!

The Authors

Antoine Chabert is a product manager for SAP Predictive Analytics. He joined SAP in 2007 as a product owner for SAP BusinessObjects, where he work was dedicated to the semantic layer. In 2013, he became a product expert on SAP Lumira. Later, he moved on to an innovation project for semantic search. He changed to his current role in 2015, where he contributes to both the customer and product success of SAP Predictive Analytics. Antoine holds a master's degree in computer science engineering.

Andreas Forster is a member of SAP's Global Center of Excellence for Analytics, based in Switzerland. He joined Crystal Decisions in 2001 as product specialist and moved into presales in 2005. Initially, he supported SAP BusinessObjects and SAP HANA before concentrating exclusively on SAP Predictive Analytics. In his current role, he focuses on scaling the SAP Predictive Analytics organisation through enablement, business development, and strategic deal support. Andreas holds a master's degree in computer science, a bachelor's degree in business administration, as well as a graduate certificate in statistics.

Laurent Tessier is a predictive analytics expert at the Global Center of Excellence for SAP Predictive Analytics. His work encompasses all phases of the sales cycle, from positioning presentations and discovery workshops to scoping and project execution. Laurent also works closely with the product management team to provide improvements to SAP Predictive Analytics.

Laurent has a master's degree in fluid mechanics and a PhD in applied mathematics. Previously, he worked as a scientist at INRA (Institut National de la Recherche Agronomique) for 6 years before moving on to consulting. He was hired by KXEN in 2008 and became their manager of presales in 2011.

Pierpaolo Vezzosi is director of product management in the SAP Analytics organization. He joined BusinessObjects in 2000 as a technology alliances manager. There he worked to develop company relationships with key technological partners, and monitor innovating trends, including offshore activities in India. In 2006 he moved to product management in the Semantic Layer area to define the strategy for SAP BusinessObjects BI universes and the Information Design Tool. After two years in the SAP Predictive Analytics product management he is currently working on analytics on big data, semantics, Web Intelligence and SAP Leonardo.

Before joining BusinessObjects, Pierpaolo held several positions in the software industry as an analyst, developer, support engineer, and technical documentation editor. He holds a master's degree in aeronautics and space engineering.

Index

- Walk through installation, configuration, and usage scenarios

- Build full-scale applications for planning, OLAP analysis, and more

- Learn how to use and develop SDK extensions

Chang, Hacking, van der A

SAP BusinessObjects Design Studio

The Comprehensive Guide

Breathe some life into your analysis applications and reports with this guide to SAP BusinessObjects Design Studio! This second edition is jam-packed with the need-to-know details for report developers—from using the IDE to implementing CSS styles. Enhance your applications even further with information on advanced scripting and SDK extensions. Are you ready to take your BI to the next level?

738 pages, 2nd edition, pub. 02/2016
E-Book: $69.99 | **Print:** $79.95 | **Bundle:** $89.99

www.sap-press.com/3951

- Your one-stop reference for all things WebI

- From report creation to publication, and everything in between

- Updated for release 4.2, SAP HANA, and more

Ah-Soon, Brogden, Marks, Orthous, Sinkwitz

SAP BusinessObjects Web Intelligence

The Comprehensive Guide

Bring your data presentations into focus with this comprehensive guide to SAP BusinessObjects Web Intelligence. Updated for WebI 4.2, this book will teach you to create, design, and share your reports, while exploring the fundamentals of WebI and its extended capabilities. This fourth edition includes information on data source options for building new documents and queries, and a new HTML5-based viewing interface. Punch up your reporting and analysis!

814 pages, 4th edition, pub. 09/2017
E-Book: $69.99 | **Print:** $79.95 | **Bundle:** $89.99

www.sap-press.com/4412

- Explore the new data warehousing solution from SAP

- Learn about data modeling, reporting, analytics, and administration

- Discover how SAP BW/4HANA changes your BI landscape

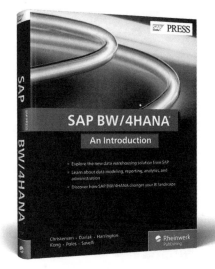

Christensen, Darlak, Harrington, Kong, Poles, Savelli

SAP BW/4HANA

An Introduction

What is SAP BW/4HANA? More importantly, what can it do for you? Between these pages, you'll explore the answers to these questions, from simplified data models and SAP BW/4HANA Analytics to automated data lifecycle management. You'll find step-by-step instructions for installation and set-up, a guide to administrative tasks to keep your SAP BW/4HANA system in tip-top shape, and the low-down on security in your new system. Explore the data warehouse of the future!

427 pages, pub. 06/2017
E-Book: $59.99 | **Print:** $69.95 | **Bundle:** $79.99

www.sap-press.com/4377

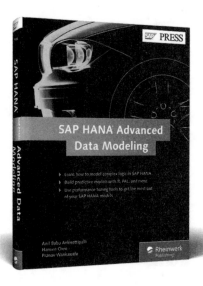

- Learn how to model complex logic in SAP HANA

- Build predictive models with R, PAL, and more

- Use performance tuning tools to get the most of out of your SAP HANA models

Ankisettipalli, Chen, Wankawala

SAP HANA Advanced Data Modeling

Move past the SAP HANA basics and into some real data model design! Discover how to build and design predictive, simulation, and optimization models straight from the experts via step-by-step instructions and screenshots. From information views to AFL models, you'll learn to scale for large datasets and performance-tune your models to perfection.

392 pages, pub. 10/2015
E-Book: $69.99 | **Print:** $79.95 | **Bundle:** $89.99

www.sap-press.com/3863

Interested in reading more?

Please visit our website for all new book
and e-book releases from SAP PRESS.

www.sap-press.com